Nick Holt has published a number of books on sport, music, film, and other aspects of popular culture. His particular passion is football.

Recent Mammoth titles

The Mammoth
Football Quiz Book
Nick Holt

ROBINSON

ROBINSON

First published in Great Britain in 2016 by Robinson

Copyright © Nick Holt, 2016

1 3 5 7 9 10 8 6 4 2

A CIP catalogue record for this book
is available from the British Library.

ISBN: 978-1-47213-763-0 (paperback)

Typeset in Whitman by Hewer Text UK Ltd, Edinburgh
Printed and bound in Great Britain by CPI Group (UK) Ltd, Croydon CR0 4YY
Papers used by Robinson are from well-managed
forests and other responsible sources

MIX
Paper from
responsible sources
FSC® C104740

Robinson
is an imprint of
Little, Brown Book Group
Carmelite House
50 Victoria Embankment
London EC4Y 0DZ

An Hachette UK Company
www.hachette.co.uk

www.littlebrown.co.uk

Contents

Introduction

There have been other football quiz books, some good; some bad. I've tried to take the good bits from the good ones and learned the lesson from the ones I've flung across the room in frustration. I ended up with a few rules, which I shall share, so you understand how I put the book together.

- Don't make a quiz book too easy. Much of your audience is pretty knowledgeable, and most people do quizzes as a group or in couples, so they can pool their knowledge. If I look at a quiz book and can get virtually all the questions on the first page, I reject it.
- Don't make a quiz book too difficult. If I look at a quiz book and I can't answer a single question, I conclude the author is more interested in showing off his own esoteric knowledge (or his ability to use search engines) and reject the book.
- Don't ask boring questions. Who was Fulham's top scorer in 1969–70 is a boring question because there is no way you would know this unless you're a staunch Fulham fan (and anyone who has been in the away end at Craven Cottage knows even their staunchest fans can be pretty indifferent in their passion). Do something different with the question. Which Fulham top scorer from 1969–70 shares his name with an American alternative country singer – is it (a) Frankie Lee (b) Tom Russell (c) Johnny Cash OR (d) Steve Earle? Even if one of the names doesn't trigger a memory, you have a one in four chance and there's at least a bit of humour and lateral expansion to the question, and a soup-con of, 'Oh I never knew there was a footballer with that name . . .' When you do a public quiz there is usually a bit of opinion and jokery from the question master, so I do try to replicate that repartee.
- Try to avoid list-style questions; they are repetitive and get dull. A few teasing lists with a bit of flavour maybe, but a whole load of them just smacks of lazy authorship and photocopying chunks of *Rothmans Football Yearbooks* (I struggle to call it Sky Sports – once a Rothmans Yearbook, always a Rothmans Yearbook; in my book anyway. And it is *my* book!).
- Avoid dating questions – either add a rider that indicates when the

question was written or phrase it in such a way that you acknowledge it isn't definitive. It is June/August 2016. Who is Manchester United's top goalscorer of all-time? Answer: Bobby Charlton. But by the time this book is published later in the year, Wayne Rooney will probably have overtaken Sir Bobby, and made the book outdated already. So you could just ask: whose all-time goalscoring record for Manchester United is Wayne Rooney likely to overtake in the 2016–17 season?

- Don't make all the questions about the last ten years. Most of the audience for a quiz book are a little older, and their best memories will often be from their formative years as a teenager when they pored over the stats on the paper and, in due course, the internet, just as the latest generation get obsessive about management sim games and the associated factoids. The 'feel' of a quiz book is, by nature, the stuff you talk about in the pub or at social gatherings – that's where quizzes tend to take place.

Which brings us to the question of being up to date. As I write this I feel foolish, because Leicester City have won the Premier League and I am pretty sure somewhere in this book I wrote that only four or five teams will ever win the Premier League – and Leicester City were not on that list! Apologies to them and congratulations for restoring faith in the power of football to amaze. Enjoy your Champions League adventure, I – in company with a gazillion other non-Leicester fans – will be cheering for you.

The European Championships are on as we speak. England have been playing well and I am praying that their collective courage will not fail them. Again, apologies for not including too many questions on this tournament – deadlines and the need to print long before publication prevented any more than the one or two that were shoehorned in. No apologies for not asking any questions about the latter stages of the Champions League; it was dull and predictable and will remain so unless some sort of financial fair play is imposed on the two big Spanish clubs.

I hope you enjoy the book. If you find a tiny error or a repeat question, please don't write in or abuse me on Facebook or on Amazon – there are a lot of questions here, the odd ricket is inevitable. And, when you come to think of it, 'the odd ricket' sounds like a description of a one-time one-cap England international who may or not feature in these pages . . .

Quiz 1: General 1 (30)

1 CONCACAF. What is it? (2)

2 What does the Bayern part of Bayern Munich mean? And how does it differ from the Bayer in Bayer Leverkusen? (2)

3 Here is the Chelsea team that won the Champions League in 2012 (4-5-1): Petr Cech; Jose Bosingwa, Gary Cahill, David Luiz, Ashley Cole; Jon Obi Mikel; Salomon Kalou, Juan Mata, Frank Lampard, Ryan Bertrand; Didier Drogba. Who was the only player to come through Chelsea's youth system and from which clubs did Chelsea buy the other ten players? (11)

4 *Offside* (2006) was a film made about a young girl's efforts to get into the crowd and watch a World Cup qualifier in which country? (1)

5 Which defender is the only player to make more than 500 appearances for Leeds United without ever playing under Don Revie? (1)

6 Which member of the Ireland 2002 World Cup squad played alongside his uncle Gary Kelly? (1)

7 Which was the last World Cup finals tournament to feature only sixteen teams? (1)

8 Who was the Ireland manager bawled out by Roy Keane at the 2002 World Cup finals, an incident that resulted in Keane leaving the squad? (1)

9 Why was South Korean international Ahn Jung-hwan sacked by Italian club Perugia in 2002? (1)

10 Which two strikers, one an overseas star who arrived via Celtic and the other an Arsenal reject, scored 52 goals between them as Nottingham Forest won promotion straight back to the Premier League in 1997–98? (2)

11 Which resort city provided the southern-most venue for the 2004 European Championships in Portugal? (1)

12 Which country's team was under the management of Egil Olsen for most of the 1990s? Which Premier League club did he join in 1999, only to be sacked just before they were relegated from the top flight? (2)

13 Which German was the first winner of the FIFA World Player of the Year award in 1991? (1)

14 Who was the agent at the centre of the controversial transfer that led to Carlos Tevez joining West Ham? Who was the other player in the deal? (2)

15 Which town had a football club that was promoted to the Football League in 1988–89, went bust in 1992, reformed and joined the Kent County Fourth Division, and have since clawed their way back up to the Conference South (they have picked up the old club name even though officially they are a new entity)? (1)

Answers on p.401

Quiz 2: Premier League 1 (40)

1 A study showed that all but one of the Premier League clubs made a loss on transfers in the five years to the end of 2000: which club made a profit and which highly rated defender's transfer to Leeds United earlier that year made them the exception? (2)

2 Which pair, already with a combined total of eighteen career red cards, were sent off in the Premier League clash between Arsenal and Chelsea in August 2001? (2)

3 Here are five terrible signings by Premier League sides in the 1995–96 season: can you name the guilty clubs – Andrea Silenzi (£1.8M, Torino,); Marco Boogers (£1M, Sparta Rotterdam); Ruel Fox (£4.2M, Newcastle United); Graham Fenton (£1.5M, Aston Villa); Tomas Brolin (£4.5M, Parma)? (5)

4 Liverpool were so anxious about their goalkeeping strength that they bought two in the summer of 2001, from Feyenoord and Coventry City: who were they, and who was relegated to no.3 and left for Real Sociedad? (3)

5 What two things do Peter Atherton, Kevin Campbell, Jason Dodd, Garry Flitcroft, Kevin Nolan, Chris Perry, Matty Taylor, Steve Watson and Alan Wright have in common, statistically? Who is first amongst equals on the list? And who is the only non-English player to fit into this category? (4)

6 Which Dutch international and Chelsea player, not exactly known for his ferocious tackling, was sent off twice in the 2005–06 Premiership season? (1)

7 Which player was sent off for the first time in his Arsenal career in a league defeat at Sunderland in 1996, but destroyed the same opposition in a rearranged FA Cup tie a few days later? (1)

8 Which two midfield players did Chelsea add before the end of the summer 2003 transfer window, for similar fees (£15M & £13M approx.): one would prove an expensive misfit, the other one of their best bits of business? (2)

9 Who had an unhappy year at West Ham United in 1997–98 so moved to Aston Villa in the summer, only to ask to move again a week later? Where did he end up the following month, having already played the first few years of his career there? (2)

10 Who was a surprising second place in the Premier League goalscoring charts for 2000–01, with nineteen league goals, including a fine hat-trick at Southampton which helped his team to go third in the table (they would finish fifth)? Which was his club? And who topped the chart with 23 goals for Chelsea? (3)

11 Why does the sequence Peacock – Ginola – Ferdinand – Shearer – Albert hold particularly fond memories of 1996 for Newcastle United fans? (2)

12 Who did Manchester City buy from Real Madrid for £32.5M in 2008, sneaking him from under Chelsea's noses on the last day of the summer transfer window? (1)

13 Which two Liverpool defenders have started every Premier League game in more than one season? (2)

14 To the end of the 2015–16 season, which six players have made more than 200 Premier League appearances for Southampton? (6)

15 Who cancelled a match against Blackburn Rovers in December 1996, claiming illness meant they had not enough players to fulfil the Premier League fixture? Who was the club's manager, and what was the consequence? (4)

Answers on p.401

Quiz 3: Champions League 1 (30)

1 Who, in 1986, became the first (and only) Romanian club to win the European Cup? Who, five years later, became the first and only team from Yugoslavia to do the same, and by what name do they prefer to be known now? What obvious similarity was there between the two Finals? Who was the Romanian international defender who played for both winning teams and became the first man to win the competition with two teams? (5)

2 Apart from Bayern Munich, which two other German sides have won the European Cup or Champions League? (2)

3 Who scored the only goal of the game in Aston Villa's 1982 European Cup triumph? Who kept goal for Villa after regular 'keeper Jimmy Rimmer was injured in the warm-up? Who were Villa's opponents, strongly fancied to lift the trophy? (3)

4 Who are the three members of the Real Madrid side that won the Champions League Final in 2000 who have subsequently played for Bolton Wanderers? (3)

5 Which Scottish side were one of the losing semi-finalists in the very first European Cup in 1956 – was it Ayr United, Heart of Midlothian, Hibernian or Raith Rovers? (1)

6 Which English team qualified for the Champions League in 2005, the first time they had qualified to play with the big boys since 1970? (1)

7 Why did AC Milan supporters sing *You'll Never Walk Alone* before their 1989 European Cup semi-final against Real Madrid? (1)

8 Who was coach of Juventus from 1977 to 1985, delivering the club's first European Cup and a host of other titles – was it (a) Giovanni Trappatoni (b) Arrigo Sacchi (c) Enzo Bearzot or (d) Ferruccio Valcareggi? (1)

9 APOEL and Anorthosis are the sole representatives of which island nation at the group stage of the Champions League, since 1992–93 (to 2015–16)? (1)

10 Who was the manager of Barcelona when they lost a stagnant European Cup Final on penalties in 1986? (1)

11 Who scored all four goals as Borussia Dortmund beat Real Madrid 4-1 in the first leg of their 2013 Champions League semi-final? What was the score in the second leg? (2)

12 How did Liverpool and Chelsea both end up in the same first phase group in the 2005–06 Champions League? (2)

13 Who were the Austrian champions who lost 5-0 away to Rangers and Monaco in the group stage of the 2000–01 Champions League, but won all their home games and advanced at the expense of both those clubs? (1)

14 Which Dutch star scored from a free kick to give Barcelona their first European Cup triumph in 1992? Who was their manager? And which Italian club did they beat in that club's only Final appearance? (3)

15 Which former Chelsea player scored a late equaliser for Paris St Germain that saved their Last 16 Champions League tie against Chelsea in 2014–15? Which of his countrymen scored a second equaliser on the night that clinched the tie on away goals? And whose 31st-minute red card had made life tricky for the French side? (3)

Answers on p.402

Quiz 4: England 1 (30)

1 Who was the first man to be sent off while playing for England? (1)

2 Which two of these players did NOT feature in the embarrassing defeat by the US at the 1950 World Cup finals: Raich Carter, Jimmy Dickinson, Tom Finney, Stanley Matthews, Stan Mortensen, Billy Wright? (2)

3 Which England player has made the most appearances in World Cup finals with 17 (up to 2014)? (1)

4 Who was the last Blackpool player to play for England? (1)

5 In 1989, who started an England World Cup qualifier against Sweden with a white shirt and finished with a red one? (1)

6 Who were the four members of Luton's League Cup winning team of 1988 who played for England at some point in their career? (4)

7 Which deceptively languid wide player made his England debut as a Newcastle United player against the Republic of Ireland in 1985? (1)

8 How many games did England lose when Gordon Banks made his 73 appearances – was it 3, 9, 15 or 22? (1)

9 England wingers John and Peter shared which surname? (1)

10 In how many of his 33 England games did Kieron Dyer play a full 90 minutes? How many goals did he score? (2)

11 Which three England players also had fathers who played for England (in each case the son has won more caps)? (3)

12 Who were the seven Manchester United players in England's team for their World Cup qualifier against Albania in 2001? (7)

13 Whose last-gasp equaliser got England out of jail and earned direct qualification for the 2002 World Cup finals tournament? (1)

14   England were tidy rather than outstanding in qualification for the 1992 European Championships; which full back scored his only international goal (22 caps across nine years) in a 1-1 draw with the Republic of Ireland? And which wide midfielder (21 caps across nine years) scored his only international goal on his debut in a 1-0 away win in Izmir, Turkey? (2)

15   Which two players, with the same first name, missed their spot-kicks as England confirmed their ineptitude in penalty shoot-outs against Italy in the quarter-final of the 2012 European Championships? (2)

Answers on p.403

Quiz 5: General 2 (30)

1 At which ground were 33 people killed before a sixth-round FA Cup tie in 1946? (1)

2 Greg Clarke is the current incumbent of which senior football position, having been appointed in 2010 – is it (a) FA Chairman, (b) Chairman of BT Sport, (c) Chairman of the Football League or (d) English Board Member for FIFA? (1)

3 Name the nine Welsh players who made the PFA top division team of the year from 1975–2013. (9)

4 What incident made a huge dent in Italy's hopes of winning a third consecutive World Cup at the 1950 tournament? (1)

5 Which veteran Derby County and Manchester City players were the only ever joint winners of the PFA Player of the Year award in 1969? (2)

6 Which member of the Mexico 1986 World Cup squad was in the middle of a seven-year spell that made him a club legend at Real Madrid? (1)

7 Which was the only overseas team managed/coached by Ron Atkinson during his thirty-year management career – was it (a) Sevilla (b) Feyenoord (c) Sporting Lisbon (d) Atlético Madrid? (1)

8 Who was the Italian player head-butted by Zinedine Zidane in the 2006 World Cup Final? Who scored Italy's goal to cancel out Zidane's penalty? (2)

9 Why was there no Association Football tournament at the 1932 Olympic Games? (1)

10 Which three Welshmen have won the Football Writers' Association Player of the Year award? And who, in 1991, was the last Scotsman to pick up the writers' award? (3)

11 Who was manager of Portugal when they hosted and reached the final of the 2004 European Championships? Which two young forwards were the only English-based members of their squad, this being pre-José? (3)

12 Moroccan defender Noureddine Naybet played more than 200 games and won La Liga with which club? Which Premier League club brought him to England in 2004? (2)

13 Who were banned from European competition after their supporters' behaviour during a tie with Ipswich Town in the 1973–74 UEFA Cup, thereby missing the chance of entering the next season's European Cup as Italian champions? (1)

14 Who was the PFA and Football Writers' Association Player of the Year for 2014–15 but had a stinker the following season? (1)

15 When they won the Football League title in 1988–89 Arsenal were still forming the defensive phalanx that served them so well in the next decade: who kept goal for every league game that season? (1)

Answers on p.403

Quiz 6: Football League 1 (30)

1 Billy Sharp scored over 50 goals in two seasons as a youngster with which club, leading them to promotion into the Championship (second tier)? What is the club's often used nickname? (2)

2 A variant of a well-known modern club, who were the first London team to join the Football League in 1893? (1)

3 England inside forward Raich Carter and striker Bobby Gurney scored 31 goals apiece as which side won the league in 1935–36? (1)

4 Which of these clubs has had most seasons in the top division of English football (to 2015–16): Cardiff City, Crystal Palace, Queens Park Rangers, Swansea City? (1)

5 Leeds United won the league title in 1968–69 with the lowest goals total (66) to date: who was their top scorer with 14? (1)

6 Who led Lincoln City to promotion out of Division Four in 1975–76 but opted for a surprising move back to another Division Four club in the summer? (1)

7 Who was the Wimbledon Chairman in their early years in the Football League? And who was the manager, best known for a long spell with another lower division club, Crewe Alexandra, who won them their first promotion to the third tier? Where did the Chairman consider relocating the club during that same 1978–79 season? Where did both Chairman and manager leave for in 1980–81? (4)

8 Whose goals propelled Oxford United into the top flight of English football for the first time in 1984–85? (1)

9 Who brought surplus-to-requirements and injury-prone thirty-year-old Paul McGrath from Manchester United in 1989 and got another 250+ league games out of him? (1)

10 Who made his debut for Manchester United in October 1956, scoring twice against Charlton? (1)

11 Who beat Oldham Athletic 13-4 in a Division 3 (North) match in 1934, thereby helping to set the record for the highest goals aggregate in an English league match? (1)

12 Which club side fielded six players during 1982 who had captained England? Who were they? (7)

13 Which two former Tottenham midfield stars appeared for Swindon Town in the League 1 play-off Final against Leicester City in 1992–93? And which Scottish international centre half moved in the opposite direction later that summer? (3)

14 What remarkable achievement did Rochdale's Tony Ford register when he played at Kidderminster in October 2000 – was it (a) his 800th league game (b) the 100th different league ground on which he had played (c) his 500th league goal (d) the 25th anniversary of his league debut? (1)

15 Freddie Eastwood's goals pushed which club into fourth place then past Lincoln City in the play-offs and into League 1 (third tier) in 2004–05? Whose tally of 22 league goals had already taken Swansea City up in third place? Which side won the division in their first year as a league club and who was their manager? (4)

Answers on p.404

Quiz 7: World Cup 1 (30)

1 Who came off the bench to score twice and turn Australia's opening match at the 2006 World Cup finals against Japan? The result (a 3-1 win) was key in securing a place in the knockout rounds. (1)

2 What is the name of the stadium in Montevideo that hosted the first World Cup Final? (1)

3 Who was the coach who masterminded Italy's wins in the 1934 and 1938 World Cups? (1)

4 Who scored four times as Hungary beat a weakened West Germany 8-3 in a first phase match at the 1954 World Cup finals tournament? (1)

5 Who scored three of England's goals to help them out of the group stage at the 1966 World Cup finals? (1)

6 Who scored ten goals for Brazil in qualifying for the 1970 World Cup finals, but had to undergo an operation for a detached retina before playing in the tournament? (1)

7 Who qualified for the 1974 World Cup finals at England's expense? Which England player was sent off in the first game between the two sides? Who described the Polish team's goalkeeper as 'a clown' during England's home match at Wembley? And who scored from the penalty spot to give England some hope after they went 1-0 down? Which of the qualified team's key players was injured before the finals tournament started and played no part? (5)

8 Who scored twice as Austria beat West Germany for the first time in forty-odd years at the 1978 World Cup finals? Which massive club did he join that summer, finishing the following season as top scorer in one of Europe's top leagues? And which Austrian club did he play for either side of this move, captaining them to the European Cup Winners' Cup Final against Everton in 1985? (3)

9   Italy's win over Brazil in the second phase at the 1982 World Cup finals tournament was a stonewall classic, maybe even the best game the World Cup has seen. Here are the line-ups, with some gaps – can you fill them in? Brazil: Waldir Peres; Leandro, Oscar, Luizinho, MISSING; Cerezo, MISSING, MISSING, Eder; Zico; MISSING (sub: Paolo Isidoro). Italy: Zoff; MISSING: Oriali, Collovati (sub: MISSING), Gentile, Cabrini; Conti, MISSING (sub: Marini), Antognoni; Rossi, MISSING. (8)

10 Which two players saw red, one for spitting, the other for retaliation (harsh) in a tetchy Last 16 game between Germany and the Netherlands at the 1990 World Cup finals? (2)

11 Who scored Ireland's goal as they took advantage of a poor Italian performance at the 1994 World Cup finals and claimed a famous 1-0 win? (1)

12 Norway came from 1-0 down to memorably beat Brazil and qualify alongside them for the knockout phase of the 1998 World Cup finals. Who was the Chelsea striker who scored their first goal and earned the penalty that gave them the win? (1)

13 Mexico in 1986, Costa Rica in 1990, United States in 1994, Nigeria in 1998 and China in 2002: who was the coach for the World Cup finals campaigns of all these sides? (1)

14 Uruguay finished fifth out of nine teams (Brazil qualified automatically as hosts) but still scraped through to the 2014 World Cup finals after beating Jordan in a play-off; which two players scored nearly three-quarters of their goals in qualifying? (2)

15 Who was voted best player at the 2014 World Cup finals, but seemed embarrassed at the award? (1)

Answers on p.405

Quiz 8: FA Cup 1 (30)

1 Which non-league side knocked top flight Coventry City – winners of the competition two years before – out of the FA Cup on 7 January 1989? And who beat those giantkillers 8-0 in the next round? (2)

2 Who came from 3-0 down to beat Premiership Southampton 4-3 in a 2001 FA Cup tie? Which former Southampton player scored a second-half hat-trick? (2)

3 In a 1971 FA Cup tie, whose two goals for Colchester helped them knock out mighty Leeds United? With which club had he once won a Football League winner's medal? (2)

4 Which club won three FA Cup Finals in the 1920s without conceding a goal? (1)

5 Who, in 1981, became the first man to score for both sides in an FA Cup final? (1)

6 Who scored West Ham's cruel injury-time winner against Preston in the 1964 FA Cup final? (1)

7 Which third division team won at Chelsea and Sunderland en route to a 1976 FA Cup semi-final? Which second division team did they play, guaranteeing a non-top-flight finalist? (2)

8 Which three London grounds other than Wembley (old and new) have hosted an FA Cup Final? (3)

9 Whose goals in the Final against Fulham secured the FA Cup for West Ham United? (1)

10 Which Scottish striking duo scored the goals as Everton won the 1984 FA Cup Final? (2)

11 Goals by Vic Halom and Billy Hughes in a semi-final win over Arsenal ensured an FA Cup Final place for which team? (1)

12 Newcastle United lost two consecutive FA Cup Finals in 1998 and 1999; however, their line up changed considerably – who were the only five players to start both games? (5)

13 Who won the FA Cup for the only time in their history in 1894, Jimmy Logan hitting the Cup Final's first hat-trick in a 4-1 win against Bolton – was it (a) Burnley (b) Bury (c) Derby County or (d) Notts County? (1)

14 Who scored Liverpool's winner in their 2-1 semi-final victory over Everton that took them to the 2011 FA Cup Final, and scored again in their 2-1 defeat by Chelsea in that Final? (1)

15 Who did Spurs beat in a Wembley FA Cup semi-final in 1991? Who opened the scoring with a 35-yard free kick? Which player scored the other two Tottenham goals? Who were the two managers? (5)

Answers on p.406

Quiz 9: General 3 (30)

1 In 1953, which England cricketing all-rounder played for non-League Walthamstow Avenue at Old Trafford in an FA Cup 4th-round tie? (1)

2 Hendon, Luton Town (*inc Fulham*), West Ham United, Southampton, Crystal Palace, Queens Park Rangers – that list charts the career of which striker who scored 12 goals in 56 games for Northern Ireland? (1)

3 Northern Ireland's striker David Healy's career kick-started when he joined Preston North End after failing to break into the first team at which Premier League club? (1)

4 What is the largest football stadium in the county of Essex? (1)

5 Which early great (29 goals in 23 games for England) captained the successful GB team at the 1908 Olympics (while with Tottenham) and again in 1912 (by then at Chelsea)? (1)

6 Which member of the Tottenham 1960–61 Double-winning squad ended up winning the most international caps – was it (a) Danny Blanchflower (b) Bill Brown (c) Cliff Jones or (d) Dave Mackay? (1)

7 Which World Cup tournament saw the number of qualifying teams increased to 32? (1)

8 Who was the last man to play a full international for England at both cricket and football: he played one match for the football team in 1951 and six Test matches in 1958 and 1959? (1)

9 Which ten Liverpool players have won the Football Writers' Association Player of the Year since 1974 (first ten answers to be taken) ? (10)

10 Wales reached the quarter-finals of qualifying for the 1976 European Championships (the round before the actual finals). Which fading side, great in the 1950s, excellent in the 1960s, but now less potent, did they beat home and away en route? And which centre forward scored in both games for Wales? And which veteran, in his fifteenth season with Wrexham and a latecomer to the international scene, scored the goal against Austria which took Wales into the knockout round? Who finally beat them over two legs before hosting the competition? (4)

11 Who was the Celtic player who captained Bulgaria at the 2004 European Championships? For which English Premier League club did he sign in 2006? (2)

12 Other than playing for Germany, what do Miroslav Klose and Lukas Podolski have in common? (2)

13 Arsenal's first game at the Emirates Stadium in 2006 was a testimonial for which long-serving overseas player? And who were Arsenal's opponents from this player's first club? (2)

14 Who won the first league title of his twenty-year career in 2003 with Manchester United at the age of thirty-eight? (1)

15 Who took Sheffield United through the Second Division in their first season back up to bring top-flight football back to Bramall Lane in 1989–90 – was it (a) Ron Atkinson (b) Neil Warnock (c) Dave Bassett or (d) Howard Kendall? (1)

Answers on p.406

Quiz 10: European Competitions 1 (30)

1 Who was manager of FC Copenhagen when they won their third successive Danish title in 2001, his third title in different countries? (1)

2 Who are the hated local rivals of FC Zurich in Switzerland? (1)

3 Who is Denmark's third most capped player and equal highest scorer with 52 goals in 112 games? With which club did he win the Champions League? With which English club did he have an unsuccessful spell as a youngster? (3)

4 Which two clubs compete in the notorious Istanbul derby? (2)

5 Which famous Russian club attracted huge crowds to a tour of Britain in 1945? (1)

6 Who did Liverpool beat 5-4 in the Final to win the 2001 UEFA Cup? Who scored the only goal from the penalty spot in a tight semi-final against Barcelona to get Liverpool to the Final? Which former Manchester United player (not their greatest signing) was in the opposition ranks? Who were the two German players in the Liverpool starting eleven? (5)

7 Which two Romanian internationals were in the Galatasaray team that beat Arsenal on penalties in the 2000 UEFA Cup Final? In what way were Galatasaray the first UEFA Cup winners to profit from failure? (3)

8 Which Italian club recruited three Swedish stars (Gunnar Gren, Nile Liedholm and Gunnar Nordahl) in 1949 in an attempt to revive the club's fortunes? (1)

9 Which three Spanish sides not based on the mainland have played in La Liga since 2000? (3)

10 Who played more than 250 games for Olympique de Marseille before a 2014 transfer to Dynamo Moscow, and had the no.28 shirt retired from the club's roster in his honour – was it (a) Franck Ribéry (b) Ludovic Giuly (c) Mathieu Valbuena or (d) André Ayew? (1)

11 Real Madrid and Barcelona have won 53 La Liga titles between them (to 2014–15) since the competition began in 1929; which other four clubs have won more than one title? (4)

12 Mateja Kezman had an unsuccessful year at Chelsea, looking a decent player but failing to find the net with any consistency. From which club did they buy him, where he had scored at nearly a goal a game in that country's top flight? (1)

13 Who was manager of AS Monaco when they won the French title in 1988? (1)

14 Which Hungarian club played a celebrated series of friendlies against Wolves in the 1950s? (1)

15 Who became Atlético Madrid's youngest-ever captain in 2003–04, when he was nineteen? And which future Spain manager was the club's all-time top scorer? (2)

Answers on p.407

Quiz 11: Premier League 2 (40)

1 A Dutchman and a Norwegian were the only continental players on the pitch when Nottingham Forest inflicted Sheffield Wednesday's worst-ever home defeat (7-1) in April 1995; who were they? Which player, with a double-barrelled name, appeared in the game for Wednesday but signed for Forest at the end of the season? (3)

2 From which club did Manchester United sign French international goalkeeper Fabien Barthez? (1)

3 Liverpool have signed three Czech internationals during the Premier League era: who were they? (3)

4 What scoreline from the previous season repeated itself in a minor Premier League classic in March 1997 between two of the top four teams? (2)

5 Who did Manchester United beat on the memorable last day of the 2011–12 season to keep up their hopes of winning the title? Who were the scorers of two late goals for Manchester City to dent United's hopes and take the title across the city? What, in hindsight, was the decisive result that handed the title to City? (2 points if you get that last one correct)(5)

6 Which disastrous signing by Everton was the object of a fan's ire when a member of the crowd ran on to the pitch and offered to swap shirts, implying he was better qualified to represent the club, was it (a) Ibrahaim Bakayoko (£4.5M) (b) James Beattie (£6M) (c) Per Kroldrup (£5M) or (d) Alex Nyarko (£4.5M)? (1)

7 Which two Leeds United players were charged with affray after an assault on an Asian student in Leeds city centre in January 2000? (2)

8 Who didn't enjoy his return to White Hart Lane in March 2000 as Tottenham beat his Southampton side 7-2? (1)

9 Who turned down the opportunity to manage Everton at the last minute in summer 1997, preferring to maintain his media career with Sky? Who took the reins instead for his third spell in charge? (2)

10 Who, in 2004–05, broke the curse of the team lying bottom of the Premier League at Christmas always being relegated? Who got hammered 6-0 by Fulham on the final day to give the resurgent strugglers a decent chance? (2)

11 Who did Tottenham Hotspur beat 6-4 in an extraordinary Premier League game in December 2007 (they were 4-3 down with fifteen minutes to go)? Who scored four for Spurs? (2)

12 In February 2011 Newcastle United came from 4-0 down at half time to draw with Arsenal in a bizarre Premier League match. Can you name the missing players from the Newcastle line-up that day? (4-2-3-1, England unless stated): Steve Harper; Danny Simpson, MISSING (Argentina), Mike Williamson, MISSING (Spain); MISSING, Cheick Tioté (Côte d'Ivoire); Jonás Gutiérrez (Argentina), MISSING, MISSING (Denmark) (sub: Nile Ranger); Leon Best (sub: Danny Guthrie). Which of the missing players scored twice from the penalty spot? Who was the Newcastle manager at the time? (7)

13 Only two Chelsea players, apart from goalkeeper Petr Cech, have started every Premier League game in a season: which two? (2)

14 To March 2016, which four Manchester City players have made more than 200 Premier League appearances? (4)

15 Which two horse racing connected Irish tycoons bought a £30M stake in Manchester United in July 2001? And what was the name of the racehorse over which they had a falling out with Alex Ferguson? (3)

Answers on p.407

Quiz 12: Scotland 1 (30)

1 Scotland lost out on a place at the 1962 World Cup finals after losing a play-off in Brussels 4-2 to Czechoslovakia; which striker, a recent Liverpool acquisition, scored both of Scotland's goals? (1)

2 The best represented side in the Scotland squad for the 1986 World Cup finals were Dundee United. Who were the five players included? (5)

3 Two players in the Scotland squad for the 1986 World Cup finals were based outside the UK, one with Sampdoria, the other with Barcelona: who were they? (2)

4 What was the significance of Hamilton Crescent, Partick in Scottish football history? (1)

5 Tony Mowbray left which SPL club in 2006–07 to manage West Bromwich Albion? (1)

6 Who remains the only Scot to have been voted European Footballer of the Year? (1)

7 What was the centre-back pairing in Alex Ferguson's successful Aberdeen side that played together for Scotland on numerous occasions, winning 142 caps between them? (2)

8 Lawrie Reilly was a one-club man and Scotland international who was top scorer in the Scottish League for three consecutive seasons from 1950–51 – which was the club? (a) Hibernian (b) Rangers (c) East Fife or (d) Motherwell? (1)

9 Which prolific striker topped the Scottish top flight's goal charts for four years out of five between 2005–06 and 2009–10? From which club did Rangers buy him during that first season? (2)

10 Which three players have made the most appearances in a Rangers shirt? (3)

11 Which non-Premiership team reached the 2015 Scottish Cup Final? Who beat them to record their first major trophy? And who also recorded their first major trophy when they beat Dundee United in the previous year's final? (3)

12 Which Irishman is the only non-Scot in the list of top ten players with most appearances for Celtic? (1)

13 Who scored the most recent (to 2015) hat-trick in a Scottish Cup Final, as Rangers defeated Hearts 5-1 in 1996? And which overseas star scored Rangers' other two? (2)

14 Which Scottish international, after his retirement from playing, managed Bristol City, Hearts, Stoke City then Bristol City again, but spent much of the last ten years working as an assistant to Harry Redknapp at various clubs? (1)

15 Which four managers of Celtic have won the Scottish League with the club in the 21st Century (to 2014–15)? (4)

Answers on p.408

Quiz 13: General 4 (30)

1 What flew over Wembley at the 1930 FA Cup Final? (1)

2 Here are ten high-profile African stars: which five of them have taken the field in a winning team in a Champions League Final, and which of those five has done so on more than one occasion? El Hadji Diouf, Didier Drogba, Michael Essien, Samuel Eto'o, Geremi, Salomon Kalou, Samuel Kuffour, Sulley Muntari, George Weah, Taribo West (6)

3 Of the thirteen players who got onto the pitch for Wimbledon in the 1988 FA Cup Final, only one, a 32-year-old substitute, was a full international, and he hadn't played for England since 1980: who was he? Which four members of the team (three starters and one sub) would later play for England? (5)

4 What is the name of Northern Ireland's main home stadium, and which Irish league club play their home games there? (2)

5 Which Englishman was the first winner of the European Footballer of the Year in 1956? (1)

6 Which namesakes won 76 caps on the wing for England after the Second World War and 14 caps in midfield for Northern Ireland, including a place in the 1982 World Cup squad? (2)

7 Which Yugoslav born full back made 167 appearances for Southampton in two spells? Who did he manage to a Scottish Cup Final success in 1994? (1)

8 Who was the last Northern Ireland international to play in a winning FA Cup team? (1)

9 Why were Steve Heighway and Brian Hall known as 'Big Bamber' and 'Little Bamber' in the Liverpool dressing room in the 1970s? (2)

10 Since it was first awarded in 1973–74, which three Republic of Ireland internationals have won the PFA Player of the Year award? (3)

11 Who was made President of UEFA in January 2007? (1)

12 Bayern Munich, AC Milan, Middlesbrough, Liverpool, Tottenham Hotspur, Borussia Mönchengladbach: this tracks the career of which versatile left-sided German? (1)

13 In 2004 James Hayter scored the fastest league hat-trick ever (in less than 3 minutes) after coming on as a substitute for which side against Wrexham? (1)

14 Whose appointment as Director of Football at Southampton in 2004 was thought a coup by Chairman, Rupert Lowe, and an act of hubris on the part of employer and employee by almost everybody else? (1)

15 Who topped the goalscoring charts for Arsenal in their title-winning seasons of 1988–89 and 1990–91? (2)

Answers on p.409

Quiz 14: Wales 1 (30)

1 Who were Wales' first international opponents in 1876, a game that ended in a 4-0 defeat? (1)

2 What prevents Wrexham and Cardiff from adding to their combined total of 45 Welsh Cup victories? (1)

3 From 1995–96 to 2002–03 which South Wales club won seven Welsh Premier League titles in eight seasons? (1)

4 Which Arsenal goalkeeper became Wales most-capped goalie in the 1950s and early 1960s? Who broke his record of 41 caps for a goalkeeper and went on to become his country's most-capped player? (2)

5 Which Welsh midfielder won the first of his 59 caps with Portsmouth in 1988 and the last with Birmingham City in 1996? (1)

6 What surname is shared by a utility player born in Germany who started his career with Plymouth Argyle and a defender who played for Cardiff City and Aston Villa in the 1970s (both won more than 50 caps for Wales) ? (1)

7 In qualification for the 1984 European Championships, Wales fought back from 4-2 down to draw a thriller against Yugoslavia in Titograd. Which left back scored his only goal in 72 caps to make the score 3-4? If Wales played in Titograd today, who would they be playing? (2)

8 Who scored his first Wales goal in a 1993 World Cup qualifier against Belgium? And who became the country's leading scorer in the same game? (2)

9 How many appearances and goals did Ryan Giggs make and score for Wales – was it 45 appearances (9 goals), 59 (18 goals), 64 (12 goals) or 78 (15 goals)? (1)

10 Wales' qualifying campaign for the 2004 European Championships had a great start with a win in Finland and a 2-1 victory at the Millennium Stadium over Italy; who scored the winner for Wales after Del Piero cancelled out Simon Davies' opener? And who scored a hat-trick in the return as Wales were beaten 4-0 in a faltering second half to the campaign? (2)

11 Who were the two Reading players in the starting line-up for Wales when they beat Belgium 1-0 in June 2015, virtually ensuring qualification for the 2016 European Championships? And which West Bromwich Albion reserve did sterling work as a replacement for the injured James Collins? Which two Chelsea players appeared in the same match for Belgium? (5)

12 Which Welsh striker's transfer from Aston Villa for £30,000 in 1950 broke the British transfer fee record? And who were the club, nicknamed the 'Bank of England Club', who added him to their array of stars? (2)

13 Wales beat England 4-1 in a Home International match in 1980. Name the five members of that team who played for Wrexham at some point in their career. (5)

14 Which two young Cardiff City players made their Wales debuts in Spring 2002 and played for their country until 2012, amassing 104 caps between them? (2)

15 Who was the talented Wrexham and Chelsea goalkeeper in the 1980s who won a miserable two caps because of the excellence and consistency of Neville Southall (bonus point for correct spelling) ? (2)

Answers on p.409

Quiz 15: World Cup 2 (30)

1 Which three European sides scored thirty goals or more in their ten qualifying games for the 2014 World Cup finals? (3)

2 What distinction did Bert Patenaude of the United States achieve in a World Cup match against Paraguay in 1930 – was he (a) the first goalkeeper to save a penalty (b) the first player to score a hat-trick (c) the first player to be sent off or (d) the first player to score an own goal? (1)

3 Which side beat Scotland 7-0 and later eliminated England at the 1954 World Cup? (1)

4 Failure to beat an average side cost England dear in the 1958 World Cup finals as they were forced into a play-off against a strong Soviet Union team and lost; who were that average side who managed a 2-2 draw? (1)

5 Who was the English referee who lost control of the group match between Italy and Chile at the 1962 World Cup finals? What later innovation did this official bring to the game? How many players were sent off in the match? By what name is the game remembered? What was the final score? (5)

6 Who were the only team England didn't beat at the 1966 World Cup? (1)

7 Which member of the Dutch team in the 1974 World Cup Final was based outside his home country? Which club was he playing for? And which member of the German squad, controversially left out of the side, was also playing in the same country? (3)

8 Who did Argentina beat 6-0 in their final second phase match of the 1978 World Cup finals, a match viewed afterwards with much suspicion, as the Argentinians were the hosts and needed a big victory and the opposition were particularly supine? (1)

9 Which Burnley striker scored both Northern Ireland's goals in their 2-2 draw with Austria, played in intense heat in the second phase of the 1982 World Cup finals? (1)

10 Who were the three Nottingham Forest players in the England 1990 World Cup squad? (3)

11 Who was the Colombian goalkeeper who played in both the 1994 and 2014 World Cup finals tournaments? What distinction did he achieve in 2014? (2)

12 Who is the only player to have played in three World Cup Finals? (1)

13 Which three French-speaking African countries did Henri Michel manage at the World Cup finals, as well as coaching France in 1986? (3)

14 Which Aston Villa player captained Sweden at the 2006 World Cup finals? Which former team-mate at the same English club scored in Sweden's group game against England? (2)

15 Which two Liverpool players were in the Argentina squad for the 2010 World Cup finals (one was the team captain)? (2)

Answers on p.410

Quiz 16: Premier League 3 (40)

1 Agustín Delgado was the first player from which country to play in the Premier League? For which club did he manage a paltry thirteen games in three years? (2)

2 How many players were bought and sold during Harry Redknapp's seven years as West Ham United manager – was it 82, 101 or 134? And how many minutes did Christian Bassila, whose loan spell cost £720,000, actually play for the club – was it 23, 86 or 144? (2)

3 Lots of Danish players have passed through the Premier League, but who are the only two to have played for Arsenal? (2)

4 What was Emmanuel Petit's second London club, and where did he spend an unhappy twelve-month spell after leaving Arsenal? (2)

5 Which Dutch player has made most appearances in the Premier League? And which other two have passed the 300 mark? (3)

6 Which Premier League player sued Gary Lineker over a newspaper article that questioned the integrity of his move to Liverpool? (1)

7 Which two overseas players, from the same country, shared five goals as Leeds United racked up their biggest Premier League away win, 6-1 at Charlton Athletic in April, 2003? Which penalty taker scored the other but later relinquished his spot-kick duties so one of the other guys could complete a hat-trick with the game already won? (3)

8 Who has led both Bolton Wanderers and West Ham United to promotion to the Premier League? (1)

9 Since Liverpool started an official Player of the Year award in 2001–02, Steven Gerrard has won the award four times – but who is the only player to win more than once (to 2015–16)? And which two English players other than Gerrard have won the award? (3)

10   With which four clubs did Robbie Savage play in the Premier League? Who, bridling at criticism from Savage in his capacity as a pundit in 2015–16, bizarrely stated Savage had never performed at the highest level? (5)

11   Who, in February 2010, became the first club to go into administration while still in the Premier League, suffering a nine point deduction and relegation at the end of the season? (1)

12   Reading and Queens Park Rangers drew 0-0 in the Premier League in April 2013: what was the consequence of this result? (1)

13   Which of these Liverpool players has never been an ever-present during a Premier League season – Robbie Fowler, Steven Gerrard, Steve McManaman, Martin Škrtel? (1)

14   Which ten Everton players have made the most Premier League appearances for the club? (10)

15   Who fell afoul of West Midlands police as they considered a prosecution for head-butting Robbie Savage in a 2003 Premier League match? Which two bitter rivals were the two players representing? (3)

Answers on p.411

Quiz 17: General 5 (30)

1 Rather symbolically, Manchester United won the 1999 Champions League on the 90th anniversary of the birth of which key figure in the club's history? (1)

2 What is the name of the stadium, still used by the city's major team, that was built for the 1938 World Cup in Marseille? (1)

3 Which European international goalkeeper played over 150 league games for Celtic in a five-year spell from 2005? Which English club brought him back to the UK in 2012 after a couple of seasons with Fiorentina? (2)

4 Which Newcastle United player was the only player at the 1950 World Cup finals not playing club football in the country he represented in the tournament? Which country did he play for? (2)

5 Gordon Cowans and Paul Rideout both left Aston Villa in 1985 to join which newly promoted Italian Serie A club – was it (a) Bologna (b) Bari (c) Palermo or (d) Cagliari? (1)

6 Name the four Dutch players who STARTED the 1973 European Cup Final and BOTH the 1974 and 1978 World Cup Finals. (4)

7 Who ambushed hot favourites Brazil in the final of the 2012 Olympic Football tournament, winning 2-1 with two goals from Oribe Peralta? Who scored Brazil's consolation, but had a poor tournament at the World Cup two years later? (2)

8 Who was the last team from outside the top division to win the FA Cup? (1)

9 Willie Maley was the first manager of which prestigious club, staying in charge for an impressive 43 years from 1897? (1)

10 Which three players have been voted PFA Player of the Year while playing for Aston Villa? (3)

11 Heard the one about the Pole, the German, the Scotsman and the Irishman? They all scored hat-tricks against Gibraltar during qualification for Euro 2016; can you name them? (4)

12 Gianluigi Buffon will end his career with the second most appearances for Juventus. Who sits above him, and is also the club's leading goalscorer? With which other Serie A club did Buffon start his career, playing more than 150 games before he signed for Juve? (2)

13 In December 2007 Roque Santa Cruz scored a hat-trick but finished on the losing side as his team lost 5-3 to Wigan Athletic – but which team? And which much-travelled striker scored a hat-trick for Wigan, making this the first instance of two players on opposite sides scoring three in a Premier League team? (2)

14 Whose fondness for changing his line-up at Chelsea earned him the nickname "Tinkerman"? (1)

15 Which two top-flight clubs were docked points in 1990 after 21 of the 22 players on the pitch were involved in an on-field brawl? Who was the one player excepted from the shenanigans? (3)

Answers on p.412

Quiz 18: Champions League 2 (30)

1 In winning a hat-trick of European Cup Finals from 1974 Bayern Munich beat the best Spain, England and France could throw at them: which three teams were the beaten finalists? (3)

2 Apart from Bobby Charlton, who was the only survivor of Munich to win a European Cup winner's medal in 1968? (1)

3 Why were English champions Chelsea unable to progress in the inaugural European Cup competition in 1956? (1)

4 Who were the two Nigerians who appeared in Ajax's Champions League Final win in 1995? (2)

5 With which club did French World Cup winner Bixente Lizarazu win the Champions League? (1)

6 Who were banned from European competition after their fans rioted at the 1975 European Cup Final? (1)

7 Who have been comfortably the most successful side in Belarus in recent years, qualifying for the group stage of the Champions League five times between 2009–10 and 2015–16 (the only Belarussian side to do so), and winning the League in their country ten consecutive times? (1)

8 Which three 'B'-teams were in Manchester United's group when they started their 1998–99 Champions League campaign? Whose two goals in the first leg of the quarter-final effectively put paid to Inter? (4)

9 To 2015–16 which five coaches have won the European Cup or Champions League with two different clubs? (5)

10 Which German side were the victims as Barcelona won a Last 16 second leg match 7-1, with Lionel Messi helping himself to five in the 2012 Champiosn League? And which other German side beat Swiss side Basel 7-0 the following week? (2)

11 Who scored the only goal of the tie as Arsenal beat Real Madrid 1-0 away and held them 0-0 at home in the Last 16 of the 2005–06 Champions League? (1)

12 AC Milan (1992–93), Paris St Germain (1994–95), Spartak Moscow (1995–96), Barcelona (2002–03), Real Madrid (2011–12, 2104–15) – what's the Champions League link? (2)

13 Belgian coach Raymond Goethals won the European Cup Winners' Cup and the Champions League with which two clubs, one from his homeland and one from France? (2)

14 Who scored seven of the goals between them as Real Madrid walloped Swedish champions Malmö in the group stages of the 2015–16 Champions League? Which British entrants did Malmö eliminate in the final qualifying round before the group stage? (3)

15 Up to and including 2014–15, no team has retained the Champions League title since the competition changed name and format in 1992–93; who were the last team to win back-to-back European Cup trophies? (1)

Answers on p.412

Quiz 19: Football League 2 (30)

1 Which two former Premier League clubs were relegated to the third tier (League One) in 2015–16? (2)

2 Which club clinched their fifth league title in seven years in the millennial year of 1900? (1)

3 Who were the twelve founding members of the Football League? (12)

4 Which of these clubs has had most seasons in the top division of English football (to 2015–16) – Burnley, Middlesbrough, Sheffield Wednesday, Stoke City? (1)

5 Who was manager of Derby County when they won promotion back to the First Division in 1968–69? (1)

6 Who was the manager of Liverpool when they won their ninth First Division title in 1975–76? (1)

7 Which two strikers scored 37 league goals each across Liverpool's title-winning seasons in 1978–79 and 1979–80? (2)

8 Tommy Tynan played more than 600 games in the lower divisions; he played over 200 at Newport County and later in his career scored well over 100 goals in two spells at which club? (1)

9 Which former England striker led Oldham Athletic into the top flight in 1990–91? For which club did he score more than 100 league goals (he left Oldham to take over as manager there)? (1)

10 Which Arsenal player and future England manager insisted on a contractual clause in the seasons just after the war allowing him to live and train in Liverpool? (1)

11 Which goalkeeper made a club record 583 League appearances for Charlton from 1934–56? (1)

12 Which of these clubs has had most seasons in the top division of English football (to 2015–16) – Aston Villa, Manchester City, Sunderland, Tottenham Hotspur? (1)

13 Who scored a 92nd-minute winner for Arsenal at Anfield in 1989 to pip Liverpool for the title? (1)

14 Which club's promotion out of the fourth tier of the English league featured appearances by future Premier League players Ashley Ward, Neil Lennon and Danny Murphy? (1)

15 Which strike duo fired Wigan Athletic into the Premier League in 2004–05, scoring 24 and 21 goals in the Championship (second tier)? And who was the club's left back, destined for an international future? (3)

Answers on p.413

Quiz 20: European Championships 1 (30)

1 Who made up for an awful international scoring record (3 in 84 games) by scoring a wonderful chip-and-charge effort topped off by a cool lob over the keeper in the 1980 European Championships against Belgium? (1)

2 Up to and including qualification for Euro 2016 Northern Ireland have played 110 qualifying games for the European Championships; how many have they won? (1 point for 5 either way) (2)

3 Ole Madsen was his country's first big post-war football star. He scored all six goals as his team edged past Luxembourg in a replay (after two draws) to qualify for the 1962 European Championships, their first big tournament. Which country? (1)

4 Which legend of Belgian football scored the winning goal as they clinched third place at the 1972 European Championships, having given eventual winners West Germany a good run for their money in the semis? (1)

5 Who scored both goals, including a late winner, as West Germany beat Belgium 2-1 in the final of the 1980 European Championships? (1)

6 Which country did England beat 8-0 at Wembley in a qualifier for the 1988 European Championships? Who scored a hat-trick? (2)

7 Who top-scored with nine goals as France qualified for the 1992 European Championships with an unblemished record, including impressive home and away victories over Spain? (1)

8 Which English referee had to leave the field and be replaced by fourth official Paul Durkin after picking up an injury during the France v Bulgaria match at the 1996 European Championships – was it (a) David Elleray (b) Dermot Gallagher (c) Andy D'Urso or (d) Mike Riley? (1)

9 Which three pairs of countries have hosted the European Championships (you need to get both parts of a pair to get a point)? (3)

10 Who scored a hat-trick as Spain put down their marker at the 2008 European Championships by beating a good Russian side 4-1? (1)

11 Which state of the former Yugoslavia surprised the Ukraine in their two-legged play-off for a place at the 2000 European Championships, earning their first crack at a major finals tournament? Who was their talented playmaker, who gave a couple of outstanding displays in the finals, especially against Yugoslavia, against whom he scored twice in a 3-3 draw? (2)

12 Which two Dutch centre backs took the first two penalties, and both missed, in the shoot-out against Italy in the semi-finals of the 2000 European Championships? (2)

13 Who destroyed Scotland 6-0 after losing the away leg of their play-off for a place at the 2004 European Championships to a James McFadden goal? Who scored a hat-trick? And who beat Wales in Cardiff, after a 0-0 draw away from home offered the promise of glory for Wales? (3)

14 Who came out of defence and scored the late goal against Turkey that gave Germany a 3-2 win which put them into the final of the 2008 European Championships? And whose goal put paid to their hopes in the final? (2)

15 Here is the Spanish line-up for the 2012 European Championship Final against Italy, with a few players missing – can you fill in the gaps? Spain (4-2-3-1): MISSING (Real Madrid); Alvaro Arbeloa (Real Madrid), MISSING (Barcelona), MISSING (Real Madrid), Jordi Alba (Barcelona); Sergio Busquets (Barcelona), MISSING (Real Madrid); MISSING (Manchester City) (sub: Pedro, Barcelona), Xavi (Barcelona), Andrés Iniesta (Barcelona) (sub, MISSING, Chelsea); MISSING (Barcelona) (sub: Fernando Torres, Chelsea) (7)

Answers on p.414

Quiz 21: General 6 (30)

1 'Lord Nelson, Lord Beaverbrook, Sir Winston Churchill, Sir Anthony Eden, Clement Attlee, Henry Cooper, Lady Diana – we have beaten them all. Maggie Thatcher, can you hear me?' This was a fabulous rant from a partisan commentator after which side beat England for the first time in qualifying for the 1982 World Cup? (1)

2 Hibernian*, Celtic**, AS Monaco, Everton, Fulham: which Scottish star's club path either side of the turning of the century is detailed here? (1)

3 One of the stadia used for the 1974 World Cup finals was the Parkstadion in Gelsenkirchen. But who played their club games there? (1)

4 What misfortune befell England's women's team players Claire Rafferty and Faye White in 2011? (1)

5 Which European side were ejected from qualification for the 1974 World Cup finals after refusing to send a team to a play-off against Chile under the rule of General Pinochet? (1)

6 Which newspaper labelled Bobby Robson a 'lightweight on the international stage' before the 1990 World Cup Finals and a national hero on his return? (1)

7 Wimbledon, Leeds United, Sheffield United, Chelsea, Wimbledon*, Queens Park Rangers – this is the club trail for which hard case in the 1980s and '90s? (1)

8 Who is the only player to have won the PFA Player of the Year award with two different clubs? (1)

9 This is the Fulham line-up against Bury (Fulham won 3-1) in the League Cup on 6 November 2002, which was the first in a game in England to feature eleven players (all internationals at some level) from eleven different countries. Here is the team (4-5-1): Maik Taylor; Steve Finnan, Pierre Wome, Andy Melville, Abdes Ouaddou; Bjarne Goldbaek, Lee Clark, John Collins, Junichi Inamoto, Andrejs Štolcers; Barry Hayles. Which eleven nations are represented here? (11)

10 Which striker from a footballing family became the game's most expensive teenager in 1970 when he moved to Arsenal for £1.25M in 1980? Who were the selling club? For which player from which club was he exchanged 63 days later? And where did he move twelve months later, at a loss of £750,000 for the selling club? (5)

11 Which country is, by some margin, the least populous to have qualified for a European Championships? (1)

12 Which club side supplied twelve players to the 1986 Soviet Union World Cup squad? Who was the coach, who, unsurprisingly, had achieved some success with the same club? (2)

13 Whose 24 goals for Liverpool in 2007–08 was a new record for an overseas player in his first season in the Premier League? (1)

14 Why were the Premier League fixtures scheduled for Sunday 31 August, 1997 all cancelled? (1)

15 Who started the 1992–93 season with a hat-trick and ended it with 42 goals in all (more than half his team's total) as Portsmouth pushed (but failed) to get into the top flight? Much was made of his former career – as what? (1)

Asterisk (*) indicates that the player in question made more than one hundred league appearances for the club. (**) indicates more than two hundred league appearances.

Answers on p.414

Quiz 22: England 2 (30)

1 England struggled in qualifying for the 1982 World Cup in a toughish group but just won through mainly by dint of beating Hungary (who topped the group) twice. Which midfield player, not known as a prolific scorer, scored twice in Budapest, one with his right foot) a real collector's item)? And which Liverpool midfield player finished England's joint top scorer in qualifying, with three goals? (2)

2 Which member of England's squad for the 1950 World Cup finals also played test cricket for England? (1)

3 John Barnes was the third black player to score for England – who was the first, and against which opponents did Barnes score his first England goal? (2)

4 Which five Charlton Athletic players were picked for England during the club's time in the Premier League? (5)

5 Who is the only player to have been capped for England while playing for Wigan Athletic? (1)

6 What role did Tord Grip play in international football? (2)

7 Who were the two players capped for England whilst playing for Wimbledon? (2)

8 How many goals did Bobby Moore score in his 108 games for England – was it none, 2, 4 or 6? (1)

9 Which England manager won most caps as a player? (1)

10 Who were England's first non-British or Irish opponents in 1908 – was it (a) Austria (b) Brazil (c) Germany or (d) Uruguay? (1)

11 For which club was Teddy Sheringham playing when he made his England debut? And what about when he won his last cap? (2)

12 Name the four England players capped while playing for Real Madrid. (4)

13 John Barnes, Luther Blissett, Robbie Earle and Raheem Sterling were all born in Jamaica: who is the odd one out? (2)

14 Who scored his first international goal in a 2-1 away win in Macedonia in September 2003 and what new record did he set in so doing? (2)

15 Who was England's manager for their unsuccessful qualifying campaign for the 2008 European Championships? What headline did the tabloids have in store for him after a defeat in the final game at a rain-soaked Wembley? (2)

Answers on p.415

Quiz 23: World Cup 3 (30)

1 Who was the only England player red-carded during their qualification campaign for the 2014 World Cup finals, receiving two yellow cards against Ukraine? (1)

2 What World Cup distinction is shared by only four European countries: France, Yugoslavia, Romania and Belgium? (1)

3 Ernst Wilimowski of Poland was the first man to score four goals in a World Cup finals match; which footballing powerhouse were Poland's opponents? And what was the game's other remarkable statistic? (2)

4 Which future England manager played in the 1958 World Cup finals tournament? (1)

5 Which goalkeeper became, in 1962, the first to appear in four World Cup finals tournaments? And which goalkeeper was the first to play in five tournaments? (2)

6 Who picked up an injury in England's last group match at the 1966 World Cup finals, and played no further part in the tournament despite being fit in time for the Final? (1)

7 Which two clubs, dominant in the 1970s, provided twelve of the West German 22-man squad for the 1974 World Cup finals? (2)

8 Which French defender, born in Guadeloupe, captained the team at the 1978 World Cup finals? With which club did he play most of his senior career? (2)

9 Who was the West Germany goalkeeper who was involved in a serious incident in the semi-finals of the 1982 World Cup that caused a French player to be sent to hospital? Who was the French player? What was the score after extra-time? (3)

10 Which key player was injured in England's first game of the 1986 World Cup finals and played no further part in the tournament? (1)

11 Which city was the southernmost Italian city used for games at the 1990 World Cup finals? And which city hosted the England games amidst fears of hooligan activity? (2)

12 Which Aston Villa player started the 1990 World Cup finals tournament as a regular substitute for England but finished as a first choice member of the team? (1)

13 Which Celtic player's unlucky own goal spoiled a good Scottish performance at the 1998 World Cup finals, as it handed Brazil a late winner after sterling defensive work from the Scots? Which overseas-based star scored a penalty for Scotland to cancel out Brazil's early lead? (2)

14 Fill in the gaps in this sequence: Fontana, MISSING, Feola, Moreira, MISSING, Schön, Menotti, MISSING, Bilardo, MISSING, Alberto Parreira, Jacquet, MISSING, MISSING, del Bosque, Low. (6)

15 Whose handball against Ireland en route to setting up France's winning goal earned his country a place in the 2010 World Cup finals and himself an irreparably damaged reputation? Who scored the controversial goal? And whose strike for Ireland put them temporarily in the box seat? (3)

Answers on p.416

Quiz 24: European Competition 2 (30)

1 Liverpool achieved a European record in 1974 when nine outfield players scored in an 11-0 victory over Stromsgodset – who were the nine scorers? (9)

2 When former Ipswich Town star Arnold Mühren won the UEFA Cup with Ajax in 1987, what did he become the first non-Italian (or even non-Juventus) player to achieve? (2)

3 Who lost 8-0 to FC Cologne in the 1995 Intertoto Cup, the club's record defeat? (1)

4 Which former Celtic and Nottingham Forest striker scored twice as Feyenoord beat Borussia Dortmund 3-2 to win the UEFA Cup in 2002? (1)

5 Who scored in every one of Manchester United's Champions League games in which he appeared in 2002–03, chalking up twelve goals in nine appearances? (1)

6 In a 1964 match between the Netherlands and Belgium, a goalkeeping substitution meant one team had eleven players from the same club on the pitch – which was the club? (1)

7 French star Franck Ribéry signed for which non-French club in 2007, going on to play more than 200 matches for them? (1)

8 Who was the Swedish president of UEFA from 1990 to January 2007? (1)

9 Which nation's Cup Winners, Sliema Wanderers, were hammered 17-0 on aggregate by Swansea in 1982? (1)

10 What does UEFA stand for? (2)

11 Who became the first Turkish side to lift a European trophy when they won the UEFA Cup on penalties in 2000? Which English side were the beaten finalists? (2)

12 Which English side won the 1971 European Cup Winners' Cup? Who beat them the following season in the semi-final? Which team did this side go on to beat in the Final in 1972, and which England international scored in both the original Final, which finished 1-1 and the replay, which was won 2-1? (4)

13 Which British side won their only European trophy when they lifted the 1972 European Cup Winners' Cup, beating Moscow Dynamo in the Final? (1)

14 With which club did Andrei Arshavin play more than 200 games, winning the Russian Premier League and the UEFA Cup before joining Arsenal? And for which club did he sign after leaving Arsenal? (2)

15 Which Manchester United player set a new record for Champions League appearance in 2002–03 and celebrated by scoring a rare goal in the match against Basel? (1)

Answers on p.416

Quiz 25: General 7 (30)

1 'And Smith must score' went the commentary in the dying seconds with the score at 2-2. He didn't. Which club missed their chance to win the FA Cup against Manchester United? (1)

2 Which four Moscow teams had representation in the Soviet squad for the 1962 World Cup finals? (4)

3 Which Second Division side signed a former European Footballer of the Year in 1982? Who was he and from which massive European club did he move? (3)

4 Who were the only two non-Merseyside teams to win the Football League in the 1980s? (2)

5 Which two former Liverpool players were sent off in their first games as player-managers of, respectively, Glasgow Rangers (1986) and Swindon Town (1994)? (2)

6 Which nineteen-year-old goalkeeper won an FA Cup winner's medal and the PFA Young Player of the Year in 1975? For which club was he playing at the time, and with which club did he revive his career in his thirties and play more than 200 games, winning promotion back to the top flight? (3)

7 Who are the only post-war team to concede six in an FA Cup Final (careful . . .)? (1)

8 Who was the Northern Ireland goalkeeping coach who was drafted into the team squad, aged 43, following a late injury to Roy Carroll in June 2015? (1)

9 With which club did Stan Seymour win FA Cup winner's medals as a player in 1924 and a manager in 1951? (1)

10 What was the Scottish midfield player Kim Little the first footballer to win in 2012–13? (1)

11 Which six sides that took part in qualification for Euro 2016 were formerly part of the state of Yugoslavia? (6)

12 If Benfica's ground was used for the final of the 2004 European Championships, which two clubs' grounds were used for the semi-finals? (2)

13 Which former Liverpool and England player took over as manager from Sam Allardyce when he left Bolton Wanderers, but lasted less than two months after a poor start to the season? (1)

14 Liverpool FC are owned by the Fenway Sports Group, who are also the owners of which celebrated baseball team – is it (a) Chicago White Sox (b) New York Yankees (c) Pittsburgh Steelers or (d) Boston Red Sox? (1)

15 Kevin Francis, a 6'7" striker, became a cult figure during a prolific spell as the spearhead of which side's attack in the early 1990s? (1)

Answers on p.417

Quiz 26: Premier League 4 (40)

1 Alexei Shevchenko and Sergei Rebrov formed a prolific partnership for the Ukraine and for Dynamo Kiev; which London club snapped up Rebrov for £11M in 2000? And who bought Shevchenko six years later, and from which club, where he made himself an international super-star? (3)

2 How many red and yellow cards did Tomas Repka accumulate in 164 league matches for West Ham (1 point if within 5)? (2)

3 Manchester United were crowned Premier League champions in 1999, 2000 and 2001, with Arsenal runners-up on each occasion: which three sides finished third in those seasons? (3)

4 What were the contrasting achievements of Bolton Wanderers, Barnsley and Crystal Palace in the 1996–97 Premier League with those of Fulham, Blackburn Rovers and Bolton Wanderers in the 2001–02 Premier League? (2)

5 Which Dutchman did Arsenal sign in summer 2001 from Rangers? And which striker was their other big outlay, at £10M, who managed six Premier League games, four as a substitute? (2)

6 Which four players have scored 15 goals in a Premier League season for Everton? (4)

7 Which two players, a Liverpool forward and Everton defender, were sent off in the April 1997 Merseyside derby, which finished 1-1, a result which, together with the suspension of their top scorer, damaged Liverpool's title hopes? (2)

8 Who is the only Nigerian with a Premier League winner's medal? (1)

9 Who was forced into hospital suffering chest pains following his West Ham United side's win over Middlesbrough in April 2003? Who took temporary charge of team affairs? (2)

10 Yohan Cabaye was brought back to the Premier League in 2015 by which manager, for whom he had previously played at Newcastle United? With which club in his homeland did Cabaye start his career, playing over 200 games before moving to Newcastle? (2)

11 In 2009–10 there were eight teams in the Premier League from within the old boundaries of Lancashire, including the two big Merseyside clubs and the two Manchester teams: who were the other four? (4)

12 At which ground did Sir Alex Ferguson finish his spectacularly successful managerial career in May 2013 with a preposterous 5-5 draw? Who was the opposition manager, leading his club to an impressive eighth position, their best Premier League finish? (2)

13 Only in one Premier League season have two teams both scored 100 or more goals: which two teams? (2)

14 With which other five clubs apart from Leicester City did Paul Konchesky record 321 Premier League appearances? (5)

15 Who was the teenager for whom Leeds United paid Charlton Athletic £2.6M at the start of the 1996–97 season? Which two Norwegians were brought in to strengthen the Manchester United squad that season? And who was the big signing at Middlesbrough, costing £7M from Italian giants, Juventus? (4)

Answers on p.417

Quiz 27: Football League 3 (30)

1   Which two clubs have won the Football League title but never played in the Premier League (to season 2015–16)? (2)

2   Which midlands town with a current league team (2015–16) once boasted two league sides called the Wanderers and the Swifts? (Clue: It isn't Bolton, Wolverhampton or Wycombe) (1)

3   Joe Mercer won the league title with two different clubs either side of the Second World War – which clubs? (2)

4   Which pair of famous sporting brothers played for Arsenal in their title-winning seasons of 1938 and 1948? (2)

5   Which two players comprised Everton's much-vaunted midfield trio alongside Alan Ball in their 1969–70 championship-winning side? The trio won 73 England caps between them – how many of these were won by Ball? (3)

6   Who ran away with the newly formed Division 1 (second tier) in 1992–93, winning their first eleven games under Kevin Keegan? Who had Keegan replaced in February 1992 with the club flirting with relegation into the third flight? (2)

7   Kenny Dalglish resigned as manager of Liverpool early in which year? And who was the long-serving club coach who stood in as manager while a replacement was found? Who was the replacement and which club had he been managing? (4)

8   Bristol Rovers vacated their old stadium in 1996. What was the old ground called and where did they go? To which ground did their hosts from 1996–98 move in 2014? (3)

9   In 1990–91 Crystal Palace achieved their highest-ever league finish of third under Steve Coppell – which England international was their Player of the Year? (1)

10 Which England striker scored in a record eleven successive Football League games for Blackpool between February and April 1951? (1)

11 Who made most league appearances for Liverpool – Jamie Carragher, Ian Callaghan or Emlyn Hughes? (1)

12 Which experienced England international full back was Alex Ferguson's first purchase for Manchester United? (1)

13 Which two Welsh internationals were ever-present in the Crystal Palace defence as they won promotion to the Premier League in 1993–94? And which England international goalkeeper also played in every league game that season? (3)

14 Which young on-loan future England striker scored eighteen goals for Bournemouth in the 2001–02 season to prove his credentials as an efficient poacher? Which was his parent club? (2)

15 Which 39-year-old scored the goal in the play-off final that took Hull City into the Premier League for the first time in 2007–08? And who was his young strike partner, on loan from Manchester United, who scored fifteen goals in the league as Hull finished third? (2)

Answers on p.418

Quiz 28: Women's Football 1 (30)

1 England star Kelly Smith has switched between spells playing in the US and three stints with which English club? (1)

2 If the Breakers played the Dash in a National Women's Soccer League game in the US, which two cities would be represented? (2)

3 Which Brazilian star won the FIFA Women's Player of the Year award five times consecutively from 2006 to 2010? (1)

4 Which team suffered relegation to the second tier of the Women's Super League in 2013 but fought back to win promotion in 2015? (1)

5 Who were the eight founder clubs in the FA Women's Super League, which started in 2011? (8)

6 Who is the only English woman to feature on FIFA's World Player of the Year lists, finishing third on the 2009 list? (1)

7 Who won the inaugural Women's Super League title in 2011? And who won 2015 edition? (2)

8 Which Scottish striker top scored in the US National Women's Soccer League in her first season in 2014 playing for Seattle Reign? And which English club did she leave to join Seattle? (2)

9 Which young Sunderland striker top scored with 12 goals in the 2015 Women's Super League? (1)

10 Which club dominated the early years of the Women's FA Cup, winning eight of the first eleven from 1971 to 1981? (1)

11 As of 1 August 2016, who are the five women with most caps for the England women's football team? (5)

12 Who are the only English winners of the major European competition for women's teams, winning the UEFA Women's Cup (as it was then titled) in 2006–07? (1)

13   Which member of the 2015 England Women's World Cup team was born and raised in the United States? (1)

14   Which famous German club's ladies team won their first league title in 2014–15? (1)

15   Which US star became the oldest player in a Women's World Cup finals match when she appeared in the 2015 final eleven days after her fortieth birthday? Which of her countrywomen also played in five finals tournaments from 1991 to 2007? (2)

Answers on p.419

Quiz 29: General 8 (30)

1 New gates were unveiled at Anfield in 1982 – what name did they bear? (1)

2 How did the FA Cup leave England in 1926–27? (1)

3 Park Ji-sung was still playing for Kyoto Purple Sanga when he appeared for South Korea in the 2002 World Cup finals. Where did he head next, before joining Manchester United? (1)

4 What nationality was Tofik Bakhramov, the linesman who gave Geoff Hurst's controversial goal in the 1966 World Cup Final? (1)

5 Which fifty-year-old made a twelve-minute cameo for Garforth Town against Tadcaster Albion in 2004? (1)

6 Which North African side qualified for the World Cup finals for the first time in 1978, and won their first group match against Mexico? (They haven't won a finals match since) (1)

7 Which four Italian clubs did Liam Brady play for? (4)

8 Which fine international sweeper played for both East Germany and Germany and was the only former East Germany player in the team that played in the Final of the 1996 European Championships? With which club did he enjoy a late bit of club success, winning the Champions League in 1997? (2)

9 Who has made the most appearances for Arsenal? And which other nine players make up the club's top ten appearance makers (clue: all won the Double while at the club except, oddly, the record holder)? (10)

10 Who was the only man to win caps for Scotland while playing for Barcelona? (1)

11 With which club was Carlton Palmer playing when he won all his eighteen caps for England? (1)

12   Which Division 1 (second tier) club brought Chinese star Fan Zhiyi to English football? And who was his compatriot, signed on loan as part of the same £500,000 deal? (2)

13   Which major European side used to play their home games at the Stadio Delle Alpi? (1)

14   Terry Brown was Chairman of which Premier League club from 1992 to 2006 before selling to an Icelandic consortium? Who bought the club in 2010 after the Icelanders encountered difficulties during the financial crisis? (2)

15   For which club did Alan Oakes and Tony Book make more than 1,000 appearances between them? (1)

Answers on p.419

Quiz 30: Northern Ireland 1 (30)

1 Billy Cush scored the crucial goal that sealed Northern Ireland's qualification for the 1958 World Cup finals: who did they beat 2-1? Against
   which team did he later score Northern Ireland's first-ever goals at a
   World Cup finals tournament? Which club, promoted to the top flight
   in 1956, did Cush join as captain in 1957? (3)

2 Which player, still active and in the Northern Ireland squad (as of June
   2016), has most caps for the country as an outfield player? (1)

3 Which former manager of the Northern Ireland national team took
   their FIFA rating from 124 to 27 between 2004 and 2007? His last
   managerial job was with Apollon Smyrni in 2013–14; in which league
   were Apollon playing? (2)

4 How many of the Northern Ireland 1982 World Cup finals squad had
   just completed a season in the English First Division – was it six, ten or
   sixteen? (1)

5 Which imposing centre half won his first cap for Northern Ireland in
   1990 as a youngster with Barnsley and the last (of 56) as a veteran with
   Leicester City in 2002? (1)

6 Which six clubs have shared the Northern Ireland League title in its
   various incarnations since 1964–65? Which team won the title that
   year, but currently play in the Premier League in the Republic of
   Ireland, the only team from the North in that league? (7)

7 Which survivor of the Munich air disaster kept goal for Northern
   Ireland at the 1958 World Cup finals? (1)

8 Billy Bingham had two spells in charge of Northern Ireland, the first,
   less auspicious stint being 1967–71: which player-manager took his
   place in 1971? Which other national team did Bingham manage? Of
   which English First Division club was he in charge from 1973–77? (3)

9 Keith Gillespie made his Northern Ireland debut in 1994 while playing for which club? And in what year did he play his last international? (1 point for a year either way) (3)

10 Which other former Northern Ireland international is currently working as Assistant Coach to Michael O'Neill with the national team (June 2016)? (1)

11 Northern Ireland won the last Home Championships in 1983–84. What, appropriately for the last competition between the four home nations, was the unusual composition of the final table? (2)

12 Dick Keith and Alf McMichael were the resolute full backs in Northern Ireland's 1958 World Cup campaign. For which English First Division club did both of them play? And how many goals did the pair score in their combined total of 63 caps? (2)

13 Which utility player made his Northern Ireland debut as a Portsmouth player during the 1958 World Cup finals and won the last of his 48 caps fifteen years later in a World Cup qualifier while on the books at Wolverhampton Wanderers, where he scored more than 100 goals in over 250 games? (1)

14 Oxford United*, Southampton*, Sheffield Wednesday (inc Ipswich Town), Ipswich Town** – this is the career path of which midfield general who played 52 times for Northern Ireland? (1)

15 One played 46 games for Northern Ireland between 1984 and 1995, scoring 12 goals, the other made his debut the following year and scored 4 times in 50 matches through to 2006 – but what name did they share? (1)

Asterisk (*) indicates that the player in question made more than one hundred league appearances for the club. (**) indicates more than two hundred league appearances.

Answers on p.420

Quiz 31: Global 1 (30)

1 Which two Montevideo sides provided eight of Uruguay's 1950 World Cup winning team, and fourteen of their squad for the tournament? (2)

2 La Bombonera on the outskirts of Buenos Aires is home to which famous club? (1)

3 This is the Argentina team that failed to show up for the 2007 Copa América Final against Brazil After sweeping through the tournament they lost the final 3-0 to a so-so Brazilian team. Can you fill in the missing players (4-3-2-1)? Roberto Abbondanzieri (Getafe); Javier Zanetti (Inter), MISSING (Valencia), Gabriel Milito (Barcelona), MISSING (Manchester United); Esteban Cambiasso (Inter) (sub: Pablo Aimar, Real Zaragoza), MISSING (Estudiantes) (sub: Lucho González, Porto), MISSING (Liverpool); MISSING (Barcelona), MISSING (West Ham United) (6)

4 Congo-Kinshasa (now the Democratic Republic of Congo) won the 1968 African Cup of Nations. Under what name did they win again in 1974, the same year they played in the World Cup finals for the only time in their history? Who was their forward, one of the African greats, who scored twice to help defeat Egypt in the semi-finals and all four goals as they beat Zambia 2-0 in a replay after a 2-2 draw? (2)

5 Who was the Argentinian forward who scored three times at the 1966 World Cup finals, finishing his international career the following year with an impressive 24 goals in 25 games? (1)

6 In 1975 the Copa América changed to its current format, with knockout rounds in the later stages. Which country, in their pomp at the time, won the competition for the second and last time? (1)

7 Only one player apiece from Mali, Togo and Senegal has won the African Player of the Year award: all have played in the Premier League – who are the three players in question? (3)

8 Which 22-year-old striker scored the injury-time goal that nudged Brazil closer to winning the 2004 Copa América on penalties against Argentina? (He flitted in and out of the national team for another few years but never quite fulfilled his enormous potential) (1)

9 If there was one player in the 2001 Copa América who was based in the English league system, 10 in 2007 and 15 in 2011, how many were there in 2015 – *not* including seven members of the Jamaica squad who were there as a guest participant? (1 point for 3 either way) (2)

10 Which great Ghanaian playmaker was in the team that won the 1982 African Cup of Nations and gave some stunning displays ten years later before picking up a yellow card in the semi-final and missing the final? Who was Ghana's main striker, bound for the Premier League three years later? And who beat Ghana in the final to collect the trophy for the first time, winning 11-10 in a marathon penalty shoot-out? (3)

11 In the context of the African Cup of Nations, what do Nigeria's Stephen Keshi and Mahmoud El-Gohary have in common? (2)

12 Rashidi Tekini scored which country's first-ever goal in a World Cup finals tournament, and represented them in three African Cup of Nations competitions? (1)

13 Which two players, one from Cameroon, one Ivorian, are the only four-time winners of the African Footballer of the Year award? (2)

14 Which South American nation won the 1924 and 1928 football Gold Medals at the Olympic Games, the only non-European country to do so until the 1990s? (1)

15 Which country entered the Asian Cup for the first time in 2007, reached the final in 2011 and won it in 2015, when they became the first hosts from outside the geographical region? And which country, who are in the geographical region, won the competition in 1964 but now compete in international competition as a member of UEFA? (2)

Answers on p.421

Quiz 32: World Cup 4 (30)

1 When Mario Zagallo won the World Cup Final as coach of Brazil, what was he the first man to achieve? Who subsequently matched that feat? (2)

2 What emphatic scoreline was shared by Argentina and Uruguay in winning their World Cup semi-final matches in 1930? Who were the losing teams? (3)

3 Which Brazilian star was the 1938 World Cup tournament's top scorer, with seven goals? (1)

4 Which two Manchester United players made England's 1954 World Cup squad but weren't around for the next tournament after losing their lives in the Munich air disaster? (2)

5 Which well-organised African team topped England's group at the 1986 World Cup finals? Which other European team needed an 88th-minute goal to beat them in the Last 16? (2)

6 Who scored twice from the penalty spot to rescue England against Cameroon in their 1990 World Cup quarter-final? (1)

7 Which South American country qualified for the World Cup finals for the first time in 2002? And which country did that leave as the only CONMEBOL side never to make a finals appearance? (2)

8 Which was the northernmost and which the southernmost of the cities used to host the 2006 World Cup in Germany? (2)

9 Here are the penalty takers for the 1990 World Cup semi-final shoot-out between England and Germany, with a few omissions. Fill in the gaps: MISSING (scored); Andreas Brehme (scored); Peter Beardsley (scored); MISSING (scored); MISSING (scored); Karl-Heinz Riedle (scored); Stuart Pearce (missed); Olaf Thon (scored); MISSING (missed). (4)

10 Which World Cup winner was bought by Newcastle United at the end of the tournament and sold after three months and four appearances? Who were the managers who bought and sold him, and which club bought him? (3)

11 France suffered a surprise defeat by Senegal in their opening game of the 2002 World Cup finals tournament (it got worse): who was the Senegalese scorer, and how many of their starting line-up played club football in France? (2)

12 Which European side scored most goals (34) in qualification for the 2010 World Cup finals and who was their top scorer with nine goals? (2)

13 The only blot on Germany's 2014 World Cup qualifying campaign was an extraordinary home match against Sweden – what was the score at half-time, and what was the final score? Which London-based player scored a hat-trick for Germany as the return game in Stockholm finished 5-3 to the Germans? (2)

14 Who scored Germany's extra-time winner against Argentina in the 2014 World Cup Final? (1)

15 Who was the oldest player, the captain and the only player with more than 100 caps in the Cameroon squad at the 2014 World Cup finals? (1)

Answers on p.421

Quiz 33: General 9 (30)

1 According to their nicknames, with what could Yeovil Town, Stockport County and Northampton Town provide you? (3)

2 How many of the 22-man Republic of Ireland squad that went to the 1990 World Cup finals were born in Ireland – was it 7, 10 or 15? (1)

3 Partick Thistle, Watford, Celtic, Nantes, Rangers, Everton, Hearts, Falkirk, Kansas City Wizards*: which Scotland striker's career path is detailed here? (1)

4 What nickname is shared by Barnet and Brentford? (1)

5 Who were the *carré magnifique* (magic square), the French midfield quartet that dominated the 1984 European Championships, three lighting the touchpaper for the fourth to produce the fireworks? (4)

6 Which of these former Arsenal players won most caps for France – Emmanuel Petit, Robert Pires, Mikael Silvestre and Sylvain Wiltord? (1)

7 Who are the two players (1970s and 1990s) who have scored for both teams in a Merseyside derby? (2)

8 Who was the only player in England's 2016 European Championship squad to win the 2016 Premier League title? (1)

9 With which Scottish team did Liverpool's consistent defender Steve Nicol start his career? How many caps did Nicol win for Scotland – was it 17, 27, 47 or 67? (2)

10 Which TV presenter married former Chelsea and England star Frank Lampard in December 2015? What are the names of Lampard's daughters by his previous partner, Elen Rivas – are they (a) Bella & Bea (b) Eva & Maria (c) Carmen & Julia or (d) Luna & Isla? (2)

11   This is the Netherlands team that brushed aside a nervous Soviet Union in the 1988 European Championship Final (4-4-1-1): MISSING; Berry van Aerle, MISSING, Ronald Koeman, Adri van Tiggelen; Gerald Vanenburg, MISSING, Jan Wouters, MISSING; MISSING, Marco van Basten – who are the missing quintet? And who was the coach? (6)

12   Why are there no official Serie A champions listed for the 2004–05 season? (2)

13   Which goalkeeper reached 167 consecutive Premier League appearances playing for Aston Villa in December 2008? And which Dutch goalkeeper kept a record eleven consecutive clean sheets on his way to a Premier League winner's medal in the same season? (2)

14   At the beginning of the 2009–10 Premier League season a minute's applause was conducted at each opening-week fixture out of respect for which recently deceased former Premier League and international manager? (1)

15   Who left Fulham aged 27 in 1984 and in the next eleven years broke the appearance record for Bournemouth – was it (a) Steve Fletcher (b) Carl Fletcher (c) Sean O'Driscoll or (d) Ted MacDougall? (1)

Asterisk (*) indicates that the player in question made more than one hundred league appearances for the club.

Answers on p.422

Quiz 34: Scotland 2 (30)

1 Norwich City (with two) had more players in Scotland's 1990 World Cup squad than Celtic, who had a measly one; who were the three players in question here? (3)

2 The key to Scotland's qualification for the 1998 World Cup finals was home wins over Austria and Sweden, their main rivals. Which two strikers, both with unfashionable clubs from north-west England, scored the winning goals in these two games? (2)

3 Scotland's showing at the 1954 World Cup was pretty dire; which two future managers of the national team made that squad? (2)

4 Who signed Mo Johnston, a Catholic, for Rangers? From which club? And which English club bought him two years later? (3)

5 Paul Sturrock, who played 20 games for Scotland, has managed several lower-league English clubs – but he remains a legend at which club, for whom he scored more than 100 goals in over 400 games as a mobile if not prolific striker? (1)

6 Which Scottish international also represented his country at squash, volleyball and golf? (1)

7 Who are Scotland's joint top scorers with 30? (2)

8 Who refused to play for Scotland again in October 2008 after a fall-out with manager Craig Burley? (1)

9 Who is the only Scottish player in the list of Rangers' ten most expensive signings – he was bought from Blackburn Rovers in 2005? And who tops the list, signed from the Premier League for £12M in 2000? (2)

10 Who won his 100th Scottish cap in 1986? Which five other players (only one still active) have reached 70 caps for Scotland (to 2015, but no one else is likely to reach this milestone until at least 2017)? (6)

11 Who have won the Scottish FA Cup ten times (more than any club outside Celtic and Rangers) but haven't done so since 1893? (1)

12 Two players in Scotland's list of top ten appearance makers share the same surname – who are they? (2)

13 Roy Aitken, Billy Bremner, Archie Gemmill, Andy Goram, Colin Hendry, Gary Naysmith – which two of these did NOT captain Scotland? (2)

14 Talented strikers Hughie Gallacher, Andy Gray, Charlie Nicholas and pre-war Hearts legend Tommy Walker all won the same number of caps for Scotland – did they win 9, 20, 33 or 42? (1)

15 Which Burley won most caps for Scotland – uncle George or nephew Craig? (1)

Answers on p.423

Answers on p.423

Quiz 35: Champions League 3 (30)

1 Who is the only player with 30 or more European Cup / Champions League goals to have scored at a goal per game? (1)

2 In 1971, which English club did Chelsea defeat in a European Cup Winners' Cup semi-final? (1)

3 A thirty-yarder from Georg Schwarzenbeck took which side to a European Cup Final replay (which they won) with Atlético Madrid in 1973–74? (1)

4 Who were the two non-English players in the team that won Liverpool the European Cup for the first time in 1977? (2)

5 Which side were England's representatives in the European Cup in 1990–91, the year the ban following the Heysel Stadium incident was lifted? (2)

6 Who scored a memorable hat-trick for Newcastle against Barcelona on his Champions League debut in September 1997? For which country was he an international player? (2)

7 Name the only European Cup winners from the behind the Iron Curtain? (1)

8 When Astana reached the group stage of the Champions League in 2015–16, they were the first club to do so from which former Soviet state? (1)

9 In 1995, which two Blackburn players fought each other in a Champions League tie against Spartak Moscow? (2)

10 In Chelsea's pulsating semi-final victory over Barcelona in the 2012 Champions League, which midfielder scored a crucial injury-time goal that gave ten-man Chelsea the edge on away goals? Who had been sent off earlier in the first half? And who scored Chelsea's late equaliser in the Final? Which two players missed penalties for Bayern Munich in the shoot-out, and who put away Chelsea's final penalty to bring them the trophy? (6)

11 The last time Rangers reached the knockout stage of the Champions League was in 2005–06. Which unfashionable Spanish side beat them on away goals after two draws? And which winger scored in both legs for Rangers? (2)

12 Which unlikely source of multiple goals took to the Champions League for Leeds United in 2000–01, scoring a winner against AC Milan, a goal that earned a draw with Barcelona and a brace in a 6-0 hammering of Besiktas? (1)

13 Apart from Wembley, which four British stadiums have hosted a European Cup Final? And which stadium has been designated as the venue for the 2017 Champions League Final? (5)

14 Whose superb hat-trick away to Olympiakos saved Arsenal's bacon and got them through their group in the 2015–16 Champions League? (1)

15 In what way was Manchester United's Champions League title in 1999 a first that would not have been possible before the name and format change of the competition? (2)

Answers on p.423

Quiz 36: Football League 4 (30)

1   Which of these clubs has had most seasons in the top division of English football (to 2015–16): Bolton Wanderers, Nottingham Forest, Sheffield United, West Ham United? (1)

2   Johnny Campbell was league top scorer on each occasion his team won the Football League in its early years; what was the team? (1)

3   Who was the Scottish winger who joined Liverpool in 1938, lost seven years of his career to the Second World War, but still managed more than 200 goals in over 500 games for the club, winning the league title in 1946–47? (1)

4   Taking the Football League First Division from 1946–47 until the last season prior to the Premier League in 1991–92, five clubs amassed a total of 2,000 top-flight points (or more). They were the ususal suspects, Manchester United, Liverpool, Arsenal, Everton and Tottenham Hotspur. Which other five clubs amassed more than 1,500 points in this period? (5)

5   When Everton won the First Division with some ease in 1969–70, who inflicted their only home defeat, a surprising 3-0 reverse? (1)

6   Alan Dicks was the manager of which club from 1967–1980, taking them back to the First Division in 1975–76 for the first time in 65 years – was it (a) Notts County (b) Bristol City (c) Norwich City (d) Brentford? (1)

7   Which three sides, never regarded as 'big' teams, finished runners-up to Liverpool when they won the Football League in consecutive years in 1982, 1983 and 1984? Who were the three managers who guided these teams into their place amongst the elite? Which three players finished as respective top scorers for the three teams in question? Which of the three was the first to drop out of the top flight? (10)

8   Who were Everton's top scorers in their two title-winning seasons in 1984–85 and 1986–87? (2)

9   Who took over from Ron Atkinson at Sheffield Wednesday and led them to third in the Football League in their first year back in the top flight after promotion? (1)

10 Which future England manager won a league title as a player with Chelsea in 1955? (1)

11 Who suffered a rare relegation in 1930, ran away with the Second Division the following year, and pipped reigning Champions Arsenal to the league title in 1931–32? (1)

12 Who took over as manager of Coventry City in 1961 and took them from the third division to the first? (1)

13 Which Liverpool player chipped Bruce Grobbelaar from forty yards to score a spectacular own goal against Manchester United in 1990? (1)

14 Who dropped into the bottom tier of the Football League in 1993–94 but were in the Premier League within a decade? (1)

15 Which striker, capped by England in 2013 aged 31, scored 29 goals for an ordinary middle-of-the-table Bristol Rovers side in League 1 (third tier) in 2008–09? With which club did he come to prominence and earn his England call-up? (2)

Answers on p.424

Quiz 37: General 10 (30)

1 After winning U-21 caps for England in his early days at Queens Park Rangers, for which country did Nigel Quashie win 14 full caps during a lengthy spell at Portsmouth? (1)

2 How many titles did Alan Shearer win with Newcastle United? (1)

3 Plumstead Common, Sportsman Ground, Manor Ground, Invicta Ground, Manor Ground, Highbury . . . what comes next? (1)

4 Who became joint owners of Queens Park Rangers in 2007? (2)

5 Which five clubs have represented Russia in the group stage of the Champions League since 1992–93 (to 2015–16)? (5)

6 Which three now-defunct stadia, two in the North-East and one in London, were used when England hosted the 1966 World Cup? (3)

7 Who was Chairman of the FA from 1934 to 1961, and for what post did he leave the FA? (2)

8 *Der Papereine* (loosely, the Paper Man), was a name given to which Austrian playmaker of the 1930s, a key member of that country's strongest team? Who was the Coach during their peak years before the Anschluss? (2)

9 Which Italian star spent a brief period as Crystal Palace player-manager in 1998? Who was his assistant? (2)

10 What unusual 'Double' did Shrewsbury Town win in 1978–79? (2)

11 Denmark won the 1992 European Championships. They didn't even qualify – what circumstances led to their inclusion? And who were the team referred to formally as the CIS representing? (4)

12 Which French club are known as Les Girondins? (1)

13   For many years Arsenal were alphabetically first in the listings of all the league clubs in publications such the *Rothmans / Sky Sports Football Yearbook*. The return of which two clubs to the league system put them in third place for a while? (When AFC Wimbledon returned to the league the *Sky Sports Yearbook* put them before Arsenal, who moved to fourth, but they left AFC Bournemouth under 'B', so I have discounted this change) (2)

14   Who became Arsenal's youngest player in a league match when he made his debut in September 2008? (1)

15   Carlisle United, Grimsby Town, Workington and Huddersfield Town were all ports of call for which manager before he got the job that defined his career? (1)

Answers on p.425

Quiz 38: League Cup 1 (30)

1 In a 1986–87 League Cup quarter-final Liverpool beat Coventry 3-1, all their goals coming from the penalty spot. Who tucked away all three spot-kicks (and no, it wasn't Ian Rush)? (1)

2 Which Ipswich Town player and captain chalked up an impressive 200th consecutive appearance for the club in the League Cup semi-final second leg against Birmingham in 2001? (1)

3 Who did Arsenal beat 7-5 after extra time in the 2012–13 League Cup, after trailing 4-1 at half time? Who scored a hat-trick, including an equaliser to make it 4-4 in the sixth minute of injury time, at the end of ninety minutes? (2)

4 Who won their first League Cup in 1964 against Stoke City with a winning goal from Howard Riley, but would have to wait thirty-three years for their next victory? (1)

5 Which second tier side, only just relegated from the Premier League, went out of the 1996–97 League Cup to Lincoln City, losing 4-1 away and 0-1 at home – Lincoln finished 19th in Division 3 (fourth tier)? (1)

6 In the penalty shoot-out between Manchester United and Sunderland that settled their 2014 League Cup semi-final, how many of the ten penalty kicks were scored? (1)

7 Who scored Manchester City's winner as they lifted the 1970 League Cup by beating West Bromwich Albion? Who had City seen off in a tight two-legged semi-final? (2)

8 Which Liverpool player professed an opinion that the referee 'should be shot' after two dubious decisions went against them in the 1978 League Cup Final against Nottingham Forest? Who was so fired up by the injustice that he picked up the only booking of a twenty-year Liverpool career? (2)

9 Which England international scored in both legs of the semi-final as Middlesbrough reached the 1998 League Cup Final at Liverpool's expense? And who did the same service for Chelsea as they denied Arsenal? (2)

10 Who scored twice against Bolton Wanderers in the quarter-finals and then again deep into extra-time in the semi-final against Arsenal to take Wigan Athletic to their first major cup final: what was the year? (1 point for 1 year either way) (2)

11 What does this sequence mean in recent League Cup context: Notts County (League 1); Watford (Championship); Burton Albion (League 2); Wigan Athletic (Premier League); Arsenal (Premier League); Aston Villa (Premier League)? (1)

12 Which three players, all internationals (England, Turkey, Northern Ireland) played in all three of Leicester City's League Cup Final appearances in 1997, 1999 and 2000? (3)

13 Which second tier side team managed by Ray Lewington joined powerhouses Liverpool, Chelsea and Manchester United in the League Cup semi-finals in 2004–05? Who scored in each leg as Liverpool won both games against their lower league opponents 1-0? Who took over from Lewington when he was sacked two months later? (3)

14 Who deprived Manchester United of an unprecedented Treble by beating them in the League Cup Final in 1994, giving the club a fourth win in the competition? Which two strikers scored the goals that won the final? (3)

15 Which Division 1 (second tier) side lost 2-1 to Liverpool in the 1995 League Cup Final? Whose performance, including scoring both goals, made the difference? Which player, who would go on to be an outstanding performer for the club, made his debut for the losers after joining on a free transfer from Tottenham Hotspur? And which member of the losing team would later sign for Liverpool? What was the losing team's consolation prize that season? (5)

Answers on p.426

Quiz 39: Premier League 5 (40)

1   Although Bruce Rioch's single season as Arsenal manager wasn't a great success, his first signing as manager was a significant one for the club – who was he? (1)

2   How many seasons did Wimbledon spend in the top flight before their relegation in 2000? (1 point for 1 either way) (2)

3   When Gerry Francis stepped down as Tottenham Hotspur manager in 1997, which former full back at the club briefly took charge of the team? Who was the overseas coach hired by Alan Sugar as Francis' replacement? Which Swiss club had he managed for the previous four years? To which other Swiss club did he return, winning four titles in the next decade and making the club competitive in Europe? (4)

4   Which East European star scored a hat-trick as Manchester United recorded their biggest ever win (5-0) in a Manchester derby in November 1994? (1)

5   Which proud record did Peter Schmeichel maintain even while playing for the blue half of Manchester in 2002–03? (1)

6   Which two players, one Central American, one Italian, scored more than ten goals as Derby County finished a more than respectable ninth in the Premier League in 1997–98? (2)

7   Who joined struggling Coventry City from Newcastle United in November of the first Premier League season, and scored ten goals in six matches, including two in a 5-1 hammering of Liverpool, in a run that went a long way towards securing the club's survival at the end of the season? Which striker, sold to Blackburn to cover for the injured Alan Shearer, did he replace? (2)

8   Who was manager of Leicester City in their first season back in the Premier League in 1996–97? For which defender, and to which club, did the club pay £1.6M, a club record, in January 1997? (2)

9 Who signed for Chelsea in the summer of 2005 for an astronomical fee that ended up costing Chelsea about £250,000 per Premier League appearance and over £5M per goal? To which club did he move three years later? (2)

10 In late October 2009 Arsenal threw away a 4-2 lead in the last few minutes of the game to draw 4-4 with Tottenham Hotspur. Here are the line-ups for a thrilling North London derby, can you fill in the missing players? Arsenal (4-4-2, French unless stated): Manuel Almunia (Spain); MISSING, William Gallas, Mikael Silvestre, MISSING; MISSING (England) (sub: Emmanuel Eboue, Côte d'Ivoire), Denilson (Brazil), Cesc Fàbregas (Spain), MISSING (sub: Alex Song, Cameroon); Emmanuel Adebayor (Togo), MISSING (Netherlands) (sub: Abou Diaby). Tottenham Hotspur (4-4-1-1, England unless stated): MISSING (Brazil); Alan Hutton (Scotland) (sub: Chris Gunter, Wales), Jonathan Woodgate, MISSING (Croatia), Benoît Assou-Ekotto (Cameroon); David Bentley, MISSING, Jermaine Jenas, Gareth Bale (Wales) (sub: Aaron Lennon); MISSING (Croatia); MISSING (Russia) (sub: Darren Bent) (10)

11 Who was (rightly) named Manager of the Year in the Premier League in 2013–14 after taking a floundering Crystal Palace team from bottom when he took over (November 2013) to eleventh at the end of the season? (1)

12 Who took charge of team affairs at Manchester United in 2013–14 after David Moyes was sacked following a disappointing season? (1)

13 Who was the American midfielder enjoying a great spell with Bolton Wanderers when his career was ended by a clumsy (but not malicious) tackle from Jonny Evans? (1)

14 Alan Pardew played for and managed both Charlton Athletic and Crystal Palace; which other four clubs has he managed? And for which other London side did he turn out late in his playing career? (5)

15 For which five clubs has England full back Glen Johnson appeared in the Premier League (to 2015–16)? (5)

Answers on p.426

Quiz 40: Republic of Ireland 1 (30)

1 Which Republic of Ireland striker ended his international career after a brawl with a Turkish player at the end of a play-off for qualification for the 2000 European Championships, which the Irish lost? (1)

2 Which member of the Republic of Ireland team at the 1990 World Cup finals was near the beginning of a career that would make him the first player to reach 100 caps for the country? (1)

3 Who is this: he won seven league titles, three FA Cup winner's medals, a Champions League and played 56 times for the Republic of Ireland? (1)

4 Republic of Ireland qualified for the 1990 and 1994 World Cup finals; which other team topped their group on both occasions? (1)

5 Which of the Home Nations won in Sofia in 1987 to deny Bulgaria and ensure the Republic of Ireland qualified for the 1988 European Championships? (1)

6 Which member of the Republic of Ireland squad at the 2012 European Championships was playing in Russia for Spartak Moscow at the time? (1)

7 Who were the three Liverpool players in the Republic of Ireland's squad for the 1988 European Championships? (3)

8 Republic of Ireland's campaign for qualification for the 2008 European Championships fell well short. Their away form was dire: they struggled to beat San Marino, needing an injury-time winner to scrape home 2-1, and they suffered an embarrassing 5-2 defeat to which unfancied side? Who was the Ireland manager who resigned at the end of the campaign? (2)

9 The Republic of Ireland's qualifying campaign for the 1982 World Cup was unsuccessful but promised good things to come. The Irish had a nightmare group with Belgium, France and the Netherlands and managed to finish third, behind France only on goal difference. This is the team, by club, that beat France 3-2 in a qualifier (5-3-2): Bolton Wanderers; Birmingham City, Manchester United, Liverpool, Arsenal, Tottenham Hotspur; Liverpool, Newcastle United, Juventus; Manchester United, Brighton & Hove Albion. Can you name the players? And which experienced striker, best known for his time with QPR, made a three-minute substitute appearance in his last international match? (12)

10 Maidstone United, Gillingham, Peterborough United, Birmingham City, Coventry City*, West Ham United, Sunderland*, Wolverhampton Wanderers, Barnet: this is the career path of which defender, who won 63 caps for the Republic of Ireland from 1996–2006? (1)

11 Which goalkeeper won the first of his 24 caps (as of June 2016) for the Republic of Ireland aged 32 in 2011? After nearly a decade of flitting between clubs, which London side gave him a regular place and were rewarded with a series of consistent performances? (2)

12 Republic of Ireland's home ground, the Aviva Stadium, was built on the site of their old ground: what was it called? (1)

13 Gerard Anthony Francis Conroy played more than 300 games on the wing for Stoke City, mainly in the 1970s, and also appeared 26 times for the Republic of Ireland; by what assumed first name was he generally known? (1)

14 Who was first choice left back for Tottenham Hotspur and the Republic of Ireland (53 caps) for most of the 1980s? (1)

15 Which player, first capped by the Republic of Ireland as a West Bromwich Albion player in 1966, later won caps while at Shamrock Rovers in his thirties, becoming, in 1978, the last League of Ireland-based player to score for the national team – was it (a) Fran O'Brien (b) Ray Treacy (c) Don Givens or (d) Brendan O'Callaghan? (1)

Answers on p.427

Quiz 41: General 11 (30)

1 Ajax**, Juventus, Fulham*, Manchester United* – whose career path through the 1990s and 2000s is this? And who replaced him at Juve? (2)

2 How tall was Diego Maradona at his peak? (1)

3 What is the Rasunda in Solna? (2)

4 Who returned as Watford Chairman in April 1997, and who were announced as the new co-tenants of Watford's ground, Vicarage Road? (2)

5 Who provided commentary on a record twenty-fourth FA Cup Final in 2003, and whose record did he eclipse? (2)

6 This is the Manchester City starting eleven from the 2014 League Cup Final victory over Sunderland (4-4-2): Pantilimon; Zabaleta, Kompany, Demichelis, Kolarov; Nasri, Touré, Fernandinho, Silva; Dzeko, Agüero. Which five of these players started the 2016 final against Liverpool? (5)

7 What record did Tony Meola break when he captained the United States against Czechoslovakia in a group game at the 1990 World Cup finals? (1)

8 Which flame-haired Welsh midfielder made more than 100 appearances for Derby County, Sheffield Wednesday and Everton as well as 54 for his country? With which European giants did he have a loan spell in 1998–99? (2)

9 Which of these sides has never won the FA Cup: Bradford City, Fulham, Sheffield United, Sheffield Wednesday? (1)

10 Which fifteen-year-old 'wonderkid' made his debut for Notts County in a League Cup match in 1998? Which Premier League club won the scramble for his signature? In which country did he sign a contract to play football in January 2016 – was it (a) Jamaica (b) Malaysia (c) Singapore (d) Gibraltar? (3)

11 Which four cities hosted all the matches at the 1988 European Championships in Sweden? (4)

12 Which famous club are known as The Old Lady? (1)

13 Who are the only two clubs beginning with the letter Y to have played in the Football League? (2)

14 Which Queens Park Rangers defender refused to shake John Terry's hand in 2012 after an incident the previous season which resulted in a suspension for Terry's use of racially motivated abusive language? (1)

15 Who attracted an average league gate of over 31,000 in the Third Division in 1970–71 – was it (a) Aston Villa (b) Manchester City (c) Wolverhampton Wanderers or (d) Queens Park Rangers? (1)

Asterisk (*) indicates that the player in question made more than one hundred league appearances for the club. (**) indicates more than two hundred league appearances.

Answers on p.427

Quiz 42: Wales 2 (30)

1   In qualification for the 1958 World Cup Wales finished second in their group, but were drawn out of a hat to play which nation, through to this stage after a walkthrough in their zone for political reasons? (1)

2   The New Saints are a Welsh club side based around Llansantffraid in Wales and which English town, just over the border about 13km away? (1)

3   Which Swansea-born inside forward was the first Wales player to reach fifty caps? (1)

4   Wales goalkeeper Wayne Hennessy was with which club when he made his international debut in 2007? (1)

5   Fill in the gaps in this list of Wales managers since 1974: Mike Smith; MISSING; David Williams (caretaker); Terry Yorath; John Toshack (one match); Mike Smith; MISSING: Mark Hughes; John Toshack; Brian Flynn (caretaker); MISSING; Chris Coleman. (3)

6   Who scored Wales' last ever goal in a Home Internationals tournament in May 1984 during a 1-1 draw with Northern Ireland? (1)

7   Who was the Arsenal wing half who captained the Wales team at the 1958 World Cup finals tournament? (1)

8   In 1977 Wales lost a crucial World Cup qualifier against Scotland. Whose handball led to the penalty that gave Scotland the lead? But whose hand actually touched the ball? Who converted the penalty? What was the final score? Where was the game played? (5)

9   Wales' campaign to qualify for the 2008 European Championships started miserably with defeat to the Czech Republic and a 5-1 home thrashing by Slovakia. What was the score in the return match against the Slovaks in Trnava the following year? (1)

10 Who was the exciting left winger who played 54 games for Wales as well as more than 250 for Burnley during the 1970s? (1)

11 Wales wing half Ron Burgess captained which team to the Football League title in 1951? (1)

12 Which Wales striker from the 1960s and 1970s had this career path: Chester City, Luton Town, Norwich City*, Southampton**, Portsmouth, Manchester United (inc Millwall), plus three US sides? (1)

13 Which nine clubs hired Craig Bellamy while he was winning his 78 caps for Wales? And for which other international team did he win five caps? (10)

14 Swansea City*, Crystal Palace*, Blackburn Rovers, Fulham* – whose club career is charted here? He won 32 Welsh caps in all before embarking on a successful managerial career. (1)

15 If James has 54 caps for Wales and Phillips has 58, what is the common first name? (1)

Asterisk (*) indicates that the player in question made more than one hundred league appearances for the club. (**) indicates more than two hundred league appearances.

Answers on p.428

Quiz 43: Premier League 6 (40)

1 As the Premier League began in 1992–93, what colour was it decreed that Premier League referees would wear instead of the traditional black? (1)

2 How many substitutes were allowed to sit on the bench in the first season of the Premier League? (1)

3 Only on three occasions (1993–94, 2009–10 & 2013–14) have two players from the same club scored more than twenty Premier League goals. The clubs were Chelsea, Liverpool & Newcastle United, in no particular order – who were the six players? (6)

4 Matt Le Tissier scored only one of Southampton's goals as they trounced Manchester United 6-3 in October 1996: which Norwegian scored a hat-trick and who was the on-loan Israel star who scored the other two? Who made their job easier by getting sent off? (3)

5 When Manchester United and Arsenal met at Old Trafford in September 2003 there was a tunnel fracas after the match that brought an FA investigation. Who was sent off during the game for Arsenal, and who missed a late penalty for United? What was the final score in the match? How many Arsenal players were banned as a result of the inquiry? (4)

6 Which elegant Dutch defender played nearly 200 league games for Southampton between 1992 and 1999 without ever being picked for the Netherlands? From which other English club did they sign him? (2)

7 Which two Premier League players have made more than 90 appearances for the Israel national team? (2)

8 Who led Watford into the Premier League in 2015 only to fail to agree terms for a new contract in the summer? With which team did he play in the Premier League? (2)

9 Who was sent off playing for Manchester United in the Premier League against Swindon Town in March 1994 and then dismissed again four days later against Arsenal? (1)

10 Who parted from his brother and joined Everton for £3.5M in 2005? (1)

11 Who were the first Premier League team to chalk up more than 100 goals in a Premier League season? And who ran way with the Championship (second tier) in the same season, having been relegated the previous year, and also scored over 100 goals? (2)

12 The biggest transfer of the January 2012 window involved the sale of which centre back to Chelsea? Who were the selling club? (2)

13 West Bromwich Albion appointed and dismissed two full-time managers within a single calendar year in 2014: who were these two ill-starred employees? (2)

14 At the Premier League twenty-year awards, which seven players were given the 500 Club award, having made more than 500 Premier League appearances? (7)

15 Who took over as Newcastle United manager in the Autumn of 2008 but had to take time off for heart bypass surgery in February the following year? Which pair of assistants, later a manager/assistant combination at Brighton (2015–16), took over temporarily? And who was brought in at the end of March to try (unsuccessfully) to stave off relegation? (4)

Answers on p.429

Quiz 44: Champions League 4 (30)

1 Which English player has made more Champions League appearances than any of his countrymen? (1)

2 Which five English players (to 2015–16) have scored in a Champions League Final in the 21st Century? (Five different clubs are involved) (5)

3 Accusations of bribery marred which Italian club's win over Derby County in the 1973 European Cup semi-final? (1)

4 Who scored a hat-trick against Fenerbahce in his first ever Champions League appearance in September 2004? (1)

5 Which two Chelsea players were dismissed in the spicy Champions League ties against Barcelona in 2004–05 and 2005–06? (2)

6 Who scored the only goal of Liverpool's two-legged Champions League win over Chelsea in 2004–05? The two bad-tempered games hatched the start of a long-running spat between the two clubs' managers, both new that season – who were they? (3)

7 When Milan thrashed Real Madrid 5-0 in the second leg of their European Cup semi-final in 1989, their scorers were two future Chelsea managers and three future managers of their respective countries – who were they? (5)

8 Who are the only European Cup or Champions League finalists from Scandinavia? (1)

9 Which are the only two clubs to have contested two European Cup or Champions League Finals and won both? (2)

10 Which England striker scored the only goal of the two-legged tie as Tottenham Hotspur put out AC Milan in the Last 16 of the 2010–11 Champions League? (1)

11 What was noteworthy about Arsenal's progress past Real Madrid, Juventus and Villareal in the knockout phase of the 2006 Champions League? (1)

12 Which central defender's goal for Leeds United, their third on the night in the first leg of their 2001 Champions League quarter-final at Elland Road, proved crucial as Leeds subsequently lost the second match 2-0? (1)

13 Who was the first English manager to lead a team out in a European Cup Final? (1)

14 From an English perspective, what was different about the 2014–15 Champions League entrants? (1)

15 In 1988 PSV Eindhoven won the European Cup without winning a game from the quarter-finals onwards. How many goals did the team score from that point in beating Bordeaux, Real Madrid and Benfica? Who was their manager, starting out what would become a hugely successful career (he had a second caretaker management spell at the same Premier League club in 2015–16)? Which member of the team was also managing in the Premier League in 2015–16? And who was their team captain, an experienced international Belgian right back in the twilight of his career? (4)

Answers on p.430

Quiz 45: General 12 (30)

1 Alcides Ghiggia, the scorer of the winning goal in the 1950 World Cup Final later claimed to be one of only three people to have silenced the Maracanã; which singer and world leader make up the triumvirate? (2)

2 Hull City, Oxford United, Manchester City, Huddersfield Town, Brighton & Hove Albion, Port Vale, Macclesfield Town – whose management career path is this, after a playing career that took in three of those clubs (his first management role was as player-manager of Hull)? (1)

3 When Manchester United won the Premier League in 2008–09 for the third consecutive season, five of their players were nominated for the PFA Player of the Year alongside Steven Gerrard from runners-up, Liverpool. Can you name the five? Which of them won the award? (6)

4 Ray Wilson, England's left back for their 1966 campaign, also featured in 1962. Which club was he with, and to where had he moved by 1966? Who was England's other full back, who would also have played in 1966 but for an injury that kept him out of the warm-up games and gave George Cohen his chance? (3)

5 What significant decision followed a dramatic cup tie where Everton equalised four times in a 4-4 draw with Liverpool in a 1991 FA Cup fifth round replay? (1)

6 Which former playing colleague followed Bruce Rioch into the manager's seat at both Middlesbrough and Bolton Wanderers? (1)

7 Which other nation played their home games in England between 1972 and 1974? (1)

8 Who did Crystal Palace sign from non-League Greenwich Borough in August 1985? How old was the player at the time? (2)

9 Who was the Real Madrid and West Germany defender (often used as a sweeper) who was the only member of the 1982 World Cup finals squad not based in Germany? (1)

10 Which nineties hard man was known as 'The Razor'? (1)

11 Who, in 1999, was sacked as manager of Port Vale after sixteen years in charge during which he took the club into the upper reaches of the second tier of the Football League? (1)

12 This is the Scotland team that thrashed the CIS at the 1992 European Championships (4-4-2): MISSING (Rangers); Stewart McKimmie (Aberdeen), MISSING (Rangers), Dave McPherson (Hearts), Tom Boyd (Celtic); MISSING (Celtic), MISSING (Leeds United), Stuart McCall (Rangers), MISSING (Manchester United) (sub: Jim McInally, Dundee United); Ally McCoist (Rangers), MISSING (Coventry City) (sub: Pat Nevin, Everton). Can you name the missing players and their coach? (7)

13 Walsall (*inc various loans*), Coventry City, Birmingham City, Blackburn Rovers, Crystal Palace – this is the club career of which redoubtable centre back and leader? (1)

14 Which England player moved to Liverpool for £16M in summer 2011, took a while to settle, but became an integral member of the team and an important part of the England set-up? (1)

15 Who played his final League game for Stoke aged 50 years and 5 days on 6 February 1964?? (1)

Answers on p.430

Quiz 46: World Cup 5 (30)

1 During qualification for the 2014 World Cup finals only two European teams lost all their group matches; which two? (2)

2 Austria and Switzerland shared 12 goals, a World Cup finals record, in their 1954 quarter-final; what was the actual score? (2)

3 Who were the goalkeeper and the captain of the Argentina World Cup Final team in 1978, and for which famous Buenos Aires club were they playing at the time? (3)

4 Italy never used a player from a non-Italian club in their squads for World Cup finals until 1998. Who was the Atlético Madrid striker who scored for Italy in each of their group games at the 1998 World Cup finals? And who was the other overseas player, with Chelsea in the Premier League? (2)

5 Who was the Aston Villa centre half who earned Turkey a draw in a qualifier for the 2002 World Cup finals with a hat-trick against Macedonia? (1)

6 Who did Australia beat 31-0 in an absurd mismatch of a qualifier for the 2006 World Cup finals? Who set a new world record with thirteen goals in the game? (2)

7 Who was the coach of the French side for their disastrous 2010 World Cup campaign? Which player was dismissed from the squad after a blazing row? And who was the team captain, who was left out of the last match after what was tantamount to a player mutiny? Who beat them and knocked them out in this last group game? (4)

8 Who were the opposing coaches in the 1982 World Cup Final between Italy and West Germany? (2)

9 Denis Lawrence was an English-based pro whose headed goal led to which Caribbean side qualifying for the 2006 World Cup finals after beating Bahrain in a play-off? (1)

10 Gary Lineker scored five goals in two games against which two sides to get England through to the quarter-finals of the 1986 World Cup finals tournament; who were the two opponents beaten 3-0? And who was his strike partner who scored England's other goal in the second of these 3-0 wins? (3)

11 Who was the 26-year-old captain of the Italy side at the 1990 World Cup finals, already playing in his third World Cup? (1)

12 Who was the oldest and most capped outfield player in England's 1990 World Cup squad? And who, at twenty-three and with 11 caps going into the tournament, was the youngest? (2)

13 Which experienced midfield player scored the goal against the Netherlands that effectively sealed Ireland's qualification for the 2002 World Cup finals – was it Roy Keane, Jason McAteer, Mark Kinsella or John Sheridan? (1)

14 Whose two goals against Japan at the 2006 World Cup finals took him past Gerd Müller's scoring record at World Cup finals tournaments? (1)

15 Who scored a hat-trick as England got payback for their failure to qualify for Euro 2008 with a 4-1 win away win in Zagreb against Croatia en route to qualification for the 2010 World Cup finals? And which two midfield players scored two apiece in the return match? (3)

Answers on p.431

Quiz 47: FA Cup 2 (30)

1 What deprived FA Cup winners Wimbledon of their only opportunity to play in Europe? (1)

2 How did Millwall's Curtis Weston outdo James Prinsep in 2004? (1)

3 Who did Arsenal beat for the fourth year in succession in the FA Cup in 2003–04? (1)

4 What was the excuse offered by Arsenal goalkeeper Dan Lewis for the fumble that let in the only goal in the 1927 FA Cup final – (a) his new jersey was too slippery (b) the referee would not permit him to change his gloves (c) the peak on his cap was too small and he was blinded by the sun or (d) he was distracted because he saw his father waving to him from the crowd? (1)

5 Which West Midlands side pulled off a memorable FA Cup win against Arsenal, comfortably the country's best side, in January, 1933? (1)

6 Which England centre halves with the same name won FA Cup winning medals with Everton and Sunderland? (1)

7 Who captained Coventry City to their only major trophy, the FA Cup, in 1987? (1)

8 How did Dennis Clarke make FA Cup Final history in the 91st minute in 1968 for West Bromwich Albion? (1)

9 Paul Gascoigne was stretchered off during the 1991 FA Cup Final after his own horrendous tackle on which Nottingham Forest player? (1)

10 Who destroyed Portsmouth 5-1 in a 2003–04 FA Cup quarter-final at Fratton Park, earning a standing ovation from the home support, so impressive was their display? (1)

11 Who scored a post-war record 44 goals in the FA Cup? (1)

12 Who, in 1983, became (and remains) the youngest player to score in an FA Cup Final? (1)

13 Whose attempt to look cool by turning up for the FA Cup Final in cream suits brought them well-deserved derision in the 1990s? (1)

14 Which ten nations were represented by Arsenal's fourteen players who played at some point during their 2005 FA Cup Final win on penalties against Manchester United? And which further six countries had at least one player in the thirteen that took the field for United? (16)

15 Who suffered a broken neck, but carried on and won an FA Cup winner's medal in 1956? (1)

Answers on p.431

Quiz 48: Football League 5 (30)

1 Who was manager of Ipswich Town when they won promotion to the First Division in 1960–61? What happened to the club the following season? And what was the consequence for the manager? (3)

2 Who moved from Underhill to The Hive in 2013–14 (NO, it's nothing to do with Tolkien . . .)? Where is The Hive? (2)

3 Which Lincolnshire side (currently in the Conference North) were members of the Football League from 1896 to 1912 – was it (a) Boston United (b) Spalding Town (c) Gainsborough Trinity or (d) Skegness Town? (1)

4 Jimmy Murray scored more than 200 goals for which successful club in the late 1950s and early 1960s, as well as making two appearances for England? (1)

5 Who came on as a substitute and scored the extra-time goal that took Cardiff into Division 1 (second tier) via the 2003 play-off final? Which former and future Premier League club did they beat in that final? (2)

6 Who finished bottom of Division Four for the third successive season in 1969–70, so could hardly complain about failing to be re-elected? Which university city gained league representation as a consequence? (2)

7 Who was the striker whose goals in a career purple patch propelled Hereford United into the Second Division in 1975–76 – was it (a) Alan Curtis (b) Bob Hatton (c) Ross Jenkins or (d) Dixie McNeil? (They came straight back down) (1)

8 When was the last time Notts County played in a higher division than Nottingham Forest – was it 1930–31, 1950–51, 1960–61 or 1990–91? (1)

9 In which year were the stadium disasters at both Valley Parade, Bradford and the Heysel Stadium in Brussels? What caused these two incidents? (3)

10 Who was divisional top scorer as Brentford won the Third Division in 1991–92? To which top flight club did he move at the end of that season? (2)

11 Which two players did Brian Clough bring in from Birmingham City to bolster his Nottingham Forest squad and help win the First Division in 1977–78? And which two members of the squad had already won a league title under Clough? Who was the player from that squad that Clough sold abroad? (5)

12 Who top scored in the Third Division in 1982–83 despite his club, Reading, getting relegated? Which club from the Second Division paid £150,000 for his services the following season? (2)

13 Lincoln City (Scarborough); Newport County (Lincoln City); Darlington (Maidstone) – what does this sequence represent? (2)

14 Who was the Chairman of Leyton Orient from 1995 to 2014 and with which sport is he more closely associated? (2)

15 Which attacking midfield player scored an impressive 27 goals as Leicester City came back up from League 1 (third tier) at the first attempt in 2008–09? (1)

Answers on p.432

Quiz 49: General 13 (30)

1 An embarrassing FA Cup defeat by which lower division side heralded the end of Graeme Souness' time as Liverpool manager, was it (a) Yeovil Town (b) Swindon Town (c) Crewe Alexandra or (d) Bristol City? (1)

2 If regularity is a factor, when can we next expect to see Italy in a World Cup Final? (2)

3 Reading, Newcastle United, West Ham United*, Portsmouth, West Ham United, FC Dallas: which goalkeeper's career path is this? And for which country did he appear, late in his career, at a World Cup finals tournament? (2)

4 What surname is shared by a Swindon Town stalwart full back and a diminutive winger who played his best football for Wrexham? (Both won more than 50 caps for Wales and they overlapped in the 1970s) (1)

5 Which former Arsenal and England star died of cancer in 2001, aged 33? (1)

6 Which other town apart from Marseille on the Côte d'Azur hosted a match at the 1938 World Cup (Sweden v Cuba) – was it Cannes, Monaco or Antibes? (1)

7 Who did Manchester City pay just under £1.5M for Steve Daley in September 1979? How many caps did Daley have at the time? Who did he join in the City midfield, a veteran with 97 caps for Poland to his name? (3)

8 Winston Reid has played with great success (when fit) for West Ham United since 2010: which country has he represented at the World Cup finals? (1)

9 To which Italian club did David Beckham move on loan in Spring 2010, in an attempt to make the cut for England's World Cup squad? (1)

10 Who was the right back, capped five times by England, who played more than 500 games for Queens Park Rangers, and committed suicide, aged thirty-four, while in a late career spell with Wimbledon? And for which club did his son, Neil, make more than 250 league appearances in recent years? (2)

11 Which former Welsh international wing half served as Matt Busby's assistant at Manchester United for most of his reign, taking temporary charge of the team when Busby was recovering after the 1958 Munich air crash, was it (a) Wilf McGuinness (b) Jimmy Murphy (c) Harry Gregg or (d) Frank O'Farrell? (1)

12 Who refused to pose for photographs in a Real Madrid shirt after signing a pre-contract agreement with the club in March 1999, out of respect for his current club, with which he still had a few months left to play? (1)

13 Can you name the six British players to have been voted European Footballer of The Year? (6)

14 Which two top-level countries had the same coach and captain at both the 2010 and 2014 World Cup finals tournaments? (In each case, name the country, the coach and the captain) (6)

15 Who played the first match of the 1986–87 season at near-neighbours Hartlepool because they were locked out of their own ground? (1)

Asterisk (*) indicates that the player in question made more than one hundred league appearances for the club.

Answers on p.433

Quiz 50: European Competitions 3 (30)

1   In which four countries did Ernst Happel win the league title as a coach? Which team did he lead to a World Cup finals tournament? (5)

2   Sevilla, Arsenal (*inc Real Madrid*), Atlético Madrid (*inc Benfica*), Sevilla – whose promising, but ultimately disappointing, career is mapped out here? (1)

3   Who signed for AC Milan for £26M in July, 1999, and was Serie A top scorer in his first season? (1)

4   Which Spanish club won La Liga for the first time in 1999–2000, the most recent first-time winners and the first since Real Sociedad in 1980–81? (1)

5   If Hansa Rostock, Skonto Riga, Bursaspor and Rosenborg played in a group in the UEFA League, which four countries would see some action? (4)

6   Which Spanish side beat Arsenal in the 1995 European Cup Winners' Cup Final, and what famous terrace chant was initiated by this game? (2)

7   Which future Premiership player and manager scored both of Sampdoria's goals in their 1990 European Cup Winners' Cup triumph over Anderlecht? (1)

8   In 1971, which Ireland defender scored against Real Madrid in a European Final? (1)

9   When Shakhtar Donetsk won the UEFA Cup in 2009, they had only three Ukrainians in their line-up: which other nation was better represented with five players in the Donetsk starting line-up? (1)

10 Italian sides dominated the UEFA Cup in the 1990s, winning seven titles out of ten – which three sides carved these seven titles up between them? (3)

11 Who was censured for spitting at Celtic fans during the UEFA Cup quarter-final first leg against Liverpool? For which Scottish club did he sign on loan in 2011? (2)

12 Which two sides would compete in a Seville derby match? (2)

13 FC 08 Homburg, 1. FC Kaiserslautern*, Werder Bremen, Bayern Munich, Lazio* – this is the career path of which World Cup legend? (1)

14 Who would Portuguese club Boavista, who won a solitary league title in 2001, play in their local derby? (1)

15 Who were the Dutch trio at the heart of the great AC Milan team of the late 1980s and early 1990s? Who was manager of that side? (4)

Asterisk (*) indicates that the player in question made more than one hundred league appearances for the club.

Answers on p.434

Quiz 51: World Cup 6 (30)

1 The opening goal of the 2014 World Cup finals was an own goal by which Brazilian defender? Who scored twice to ensure Brazil won the game (3-1, against Croatia)? (2)

2 Which two teams played out a violent quarter-final that came to be known as The Battle of Berne at the 1954 World Cup finals? What was the result of the game? Who was the English referee who sent off three players? (4)

3 Brazil didn't really hit full stride until the semi-finals at the 1958 World Cup in Sweden. Who announced himself as a major star with a hat-trick against Sweden in a 5-2 rout of the French? (1)

4 Italy coach Feruccio Valcareggi had difficulty choosing between his two best creative midfield players in the late 1960s and at the 1970 World Cup finals tournament, to the extent he often gave them half a game each. Who were the two players? (2)

5 Who was the latest in a line of gifted Hungarian forwards who scored the winner in a group match against England at the 1962 World Cup finals and followed up with a hat-trick against Bulgaria? And for which famous Budapest club, rapidly becoming the country's premier side, did he play his entire club career? (2)

6 Who was sent home from the 1994 World Cup finals after two matches after testing positive for the banned substance ephedrine? (1)

7 Who was the Napoli goalkeeper who understudied Enrico Albertosi for Italy at the 1970 World Cup finals? (1)

8 The Netherlands, twice finalists in the previous decade, failed to qualify for the 1986 finals when a late goal from Georges Grün gave which other European country a victory in a two-legged play-off? (1)

9 Which Middle Eastern country, who now play in the European zone for political reasons, won through the Asian qualifying to take their place at a World Cup finals tournament for the first time in 1970? (1)

10 Here is the Dutch XI that started the 2010 World Cup Final against Spain. Identify the missing players and name the three who DIDN'T get a yellow card: Stekelenburg; van der Wiel, MISSING, Mathijsen, van Bronckhorst; MISSING, De Jong, MISSING; Kuyt, MISSING, MISSING. (8)

11 Scotland earned highly creditable draws with Brazil and Yugoslavia in a tough group at the 1974 World Cup finals, but paid the price for winning by only two goals against which 'minnow' nation? What was the score when Yugoslavia played the same opponents? (2)

12 Which nation's squad for the 1974 World Cup finals included players from Safeway United, Marconi Fairfield, Footscray JUST and Pan-Hellenic? (1)

13 Mario Kempes was the only member of the Argentina team that won the World Cup Final in 1978 who was playing in Europe – for which Spanish club? (1)

14 Vittorio Pozzo, Feruccio Valcareggi, Enzo Bearzot, Arrigo Sacchi and Marcello Lippi all coached Italy to a World Cup Final; which one won a solitary international cap as a player? (1)

15 Who was the Italian striker, picked originally as a reserve, who came off the bench to score Italy's winner in their opening fixture against Austria in the 1990 World Cup finals? For which Serie B side did he play more 200 games before moving to Juventus? (2)

Answers on p.434

Quiz 52: England 3 (30)

1 Here are four players who all won between 60 and 70 caps for England, but which of them had the best goals per game ratio, and which the weakest – Kevin Keegan, Martin Peters, David Platt and Paul Scholes? (2)

2 David Gualtieri scored a goal inside a minute for which low-ranked side against England during qualifying for the 1994 World Cup finals? Who scored a hat-trick as England restored order and won 7-1? Which two teams qualified from England's group? Who was the England manager at the time, who would pay for this failure with his job? (5)

3 Who were England's opponents in October 1963 for a special international match to celebrate the FA's centenary? (1)

4 Danny Thomas, Cyrille Regis and Dion Dublin are the only three players to be capped for England while with which club during a 34-year spell in the top flight of English football? (1)

5 Which England striker became known as The Lion of Vienna after scoring a memorable goal in a friendly against Austria in the 1950s? (1)

6 In 1909, which Tottenham Hotspur forward became the first Englishman to score two international hat-tricks? (1)

7 Which seventeen-year-old became England's youngest ever full international in a friendly against Australia in February 2003? Who broke that record three years later in a match against Hungary? (2)

8 Which West Ham full back won his first England cap in 1973 but waited seven years for his second and final call-up? (1)

9 How many goals did Peter Beardsley score in 59 games for England – was it 9, 13, 17 or 23? (1)

10 Which promising centre forward was forced to retire through an injury sustained while winning his first England cap in 2008? With which club, known as a lower league talent factory, did he make his breakthrough before a 2005 transfer to Norwich City? (2)

11 Earl Barrett's 1991 England debut is the only post-war instance of a player being picked for England while at which club? (1)

12 In the 1980s England twice beat Turkey 8-0. Which winger scored twice in each game? (1)

13 Four of the following players were born outside England: identify them AND give the country of their birth from the second list. Players: Terry Butcher, Tony Dorigo, Nathaniel Clyne, Owen Hargreaves, Ricky Hill, John Salako, Gareth Southgate, Tony Woodcock. Countries of origin: Australia, Canada, Jamaica, Malta, Montserrat, Nigeria, Singapore, West Germany. (8)

14 Who scored twice in each game as England motored past Switzerland and Croatia in impressive style to reach the quarter-finals of the 2004 European Championships? (1)

15 Some England centre halves: Wes Brown, Jack Charlton, Martin Keown, Ledley King, Joleon Lescott, Colin Todd. Which of them won most caps? And who scored most goals? (2)

Answers on p.435

Quiz 53: General 14 (30)

1 Anders Svensson, Sweden's most capped player (Oct 2015), played most of his career in two spells with Elfsborg. But for which English club did he spend four years from 2001–2005? (1)

2 If Stephen played mainly non-League, Graham played for Chelsea and Brentford, and Dean played for and managed Brighton, who is the fourth brother? (1)

3 Roger Hunt, Ian Rush, Kenny Dalglish, Robbie Fowler and Michael Owen – the five Liverpool strikers with over 100 league goals for the club in the last fifty or so years. Which one scored the most? Which two share the least? Which two had more than one spell at the club? Which two never played outside the top flight with Liverpool or any other club? Who had the best goals per game strike rate? And who only scored once every three games? Which of the five made the most league appearances for Liverpool? (10)

4 What was odd about the selection of Peter Broadbent and Peter Brabrook for the second game of England's 1958 World Cup finals campaign? (1)

5 Which former Arsenal player returned to Highbury as manager in 1986? (1)

6 Which overseas manager did Ron Atkinson replace at Aston Villa in 1991? (1)

7 Who did Steve McMahon play for in between his spells on Merseyside with Everton and later Liverpool? (1)

8 Who was the Tottenham Hotspur Chairman who sacked Terry Venables as manager in 1993? (1)

9 In the 1998–99 season one second-tier club attracted crowds of over 40,000, while a third-tier club regularly played in front of more than 30,000 – who are the two clubs in question, both of whom were promoted at the end of the season? (2)

10 Sheffield Wednesday***, Rangers, Leeds United*, Boston United – this is the club career of which England one-cap-wonder right back? (1)

11 England's World Cup squad in 2010 contained five players from Tottenham Hotspur – name them. (5)

12 Who scored both Manchester United's goals to win the 1991 European Cup Winners' Cup? (1)

13 Who became the world's most expensive defender at £10.75M when signing for Manchester United in 1998? (1)

14 Which two Dutch managers took charge of South Korea at the 2002 and 2006 World Cup finals tournaments? (2)

15 Which property developer was the driver behind moving Wimbledon FC to Milton Keynes? (1)

Asterisk (*) indicates that the player in question made more than one hundred league appearances for the club. (**) indicates more than two hundred league appearances.

Answers on p.435

Quiz 54: Premier League 7 (40)

1 Aston Villa finished runners-up in the first Premier League in 1992–93: which two players scored more than ten goals that season? What was the consistent back four that played 39 of the 42 league games as a unit? And who replaced the injured Nigel Spink in goal for the last part of the season? (7)

2 If the notorious Tino Asprilla was the first Colombian to play in the Premier League, who was the second, who signed for Middlesbrough in 1998 and went on to play more than 100 league games for the club? (1)

3 Michael Proctor scored twice, Stephen Wright once and Kevin Phillips once as Sunderland played Charlton Athletic on 1 February 2003: what was the final score? (2)

4 Where did Leeds United, champions the previous season, finish in the first year of the Premier League in 1992–93? (1 point for 2 either way) (2)

5 Which England international joined Middlesbrough, just relegated, in summer 1997? And which signing by Arsène Wenger persuaded him his days at Highbury were over? (2)

6 Which Romania right back signed for Sheffield Wednesday in 1994 after a good World Cup in the United States? Which other Premier League club signed him a year later? (2)

7 Which two stars of Romania's 1994 World Cup campaign were signed by Tottenham later that summer? (2)

8 Who left the No.2 spot at Manchester United for the No.1 spot at Blackburn Rovers in late 1998? And who replaced him at United early the following year? (2)

9   Who was sent off twice in three days playing for Arsenal against Sunderland and Liverpool at the start of the 2000–01 season? And which two Liverpool midfield players, one Scottish, one German, were also red carded in the second fixture? (3)

10 Sunderland were relegated miserably in 2005–06: what was their final points total (1 point for 2 either way) ? How many goals did their three joint leading scorers manage? (3)

11 Joey Barton kept up his dismal disciplinary record on the last day of the 2011–12 season against Manchester City. For which team was he playing when he elbowed Carlos Tevez and was red carded before confronting Sergio Agüero, Vincent Kompany and Mario Balotelli on his way to the dressing room? (1)

12 Atlético Madrid cashed in £55M worth of talent to Manchester clubs in the summer of 2011 – who were the two players sold? (2)

13 Which three African strikers have scored a hat-trick in the Premier League for Portsmouth? (3)

14 During the 1996–97 season, which future England coach was widely announced in the press as the new manager of Blackburn Rovers for the following season, only to decide to stay in Italy after all? Which club did he manage the following season and eventually lead to the Serie A title? Which other future England manager did take the job at Blackburn and which Italian club did he leave to do so? (4)

15 In January 2011 Liverpool received £50M for an injury-prone player and immediately spent £35M of it on another injury-prone player. Which two players, and who were the other two clubs involved? (4)

Answers on p.436

Quiz 55: Women's Football 2 (30)

1   England's first ever Women's World Cup finals match was a 3-2 win over Canada. Which player, the first England women's player to reach 100 caps, scored twice in the match? (1)

2   Michelle Akers scored twice in the first Women's World Cup Final to give the United States a 2–1 win over which Scandinavian country? In which year and in which country did the competition take place? (3)

3   Which European country will host the 2019 Women's World Cup? (1)

4   Who are the only nation to have won the Women's World Cup on three occasions (to 2015)? (1)

5   Who reached the Final of the 1999 Women's World Cup but lost out on penalties to the United States after the game ended in stalemate? Who had the prurient tabloid newspapers in a lather by swinging her shirt above her head after scoring the winning penalty? (1)

6   What were Fulham Ladies FC the first club to do in April 2000? (2)

7   Leasowe Pacific from Hoylake in Liverpool won the 1989 Women's FA Cup Final: to which men's club did they later become affiliated? And with which major Rugby league club do they share a ground? (2)

8   Emma Byrne and Sari van Veenendaal are the two main goalkeepers on Arsenal's roster for 2015 and 2016: for which countries do the two keep goal? (2)

9   Which seven nations have contested a Women's World Cup Final? (7)

10 Chelsea beat Notts County 1-0 in the Women's FA Cup Final in 2015. Which two members of England's World Cup squad captained the two sides? Ji So-yun, who scored the only goal of the game, also won which individual award a few months previously? Which country does she represent at international level? (4)

11 Which two Manchester City stars were sent off within three weeks of each other after on-field clashes with Freda Ayisi of Birmingham City and Jade Bailey of Arsenal? (2)

12 Who is the only German player to have reached 200 international caps and also the only one to have scored more than 100 international goals? (1)

13 Who was the goalkeeper and team captain for Germany at the 2015 Women's World Cup? (1)

14 Hedvig Lindahl, the Chelsea goalkeeper, represented which country at the 2015 Women's World Cup? (1)

15 Who won promotion to the top division of the FA Women's Super League for the first time in 2015 and will take part in the new nine-team division in 2016? (1)

Answers on p.437

Quiz 56: Champions League 5 (30)

1 Which five players (to August 2016) have scored fifty or more goals in the Champions League? (5)

2 When Real Madrid won the first five European Cup competitions, which French club were beaten finalists twice – was it Bordeaux, Lens, Reims or Toulouse? (1)

3 After completing a hat-trick of European Cup wins in 1976, how long did Bayern Munich have to wait before lifting the trophy again – was it 3 years, 10 years, 25 years, or 37 years? (1)

4 In the 2001–02 Champions League, which Spanish side beat Manchester United home and away in the initial group phase, only to lose home and away to the English team in the quarter-final? Who beat United on away goals in the next round? And which further two Spanish sides contested the other semi-final? (4)

5 Which two England internationals have played for Real Madrid in a European Cup Final? (2)

6 Which defender scored the solitary goal in the 2006 Champions League semi-final tie that sent Arsenal into the Final at the expense of Villareal? (1)

7 Who was the Milan coach when Liverpool came back from 3-0 down to win the 2005 Champions League on penalties? (1)

8 The 1955 meeting that led to the inauguration of the European Cup was organised by which French sports paper? (1)

9 In the 2015 Champions League, who scored for Barcelona in both legs of the quarter-final, both legs of the semi-final and the Final? Which three sides, French, German and Italian, were on the receiving end? (4)

10 Which Argentinian striker enjoyed his best year in 2009–10 when he scored both goals in Internazionale's 2-0 Champions League Final win against Bayern Munich? Who were the managers of the two finalists? (3)

11 Which pair of clubs from the same league have met each other on five occasions in the Champions League? (2)

12 In 2010–11 Milan knocked Bayern Munich out of the Champions League after losing the first leg: which Macedonian international, the country's all-time leading goalscorer, scored the late goal that clinched a famous 3-2 victory in Munich – was it (a) Goran Pandev (b) Robert Vittek (c) Mario Mandžukić or (d) Darko Pančev ? (1)

13 Which club did Sven-Göran Eriksson lead to the European Cup Final in his earlier coaching days – was it (a) Malmö (b) Sampdoria (c) Benfica or (d) Sporting Lisbon? (1)

14 Which Polish side beat Celtic 4-1 and 2-0 in the preliminary stages of the 2014–15 Champions League, only to be thrown out of the competition for fielding an ineligible player? And who were the Slovenian side who put Celtic out of their misery in the next qualifying round? (2)

15 Which English team were the first to win a penalty shoot-out in the European Cup in 1970, beating Borussia Mönchengladbach after both ties finished 1-1? Who beat the victors on away goals in the next round and went on to become the only club from their Mediterranean country to reach the Final? (1)

Answers on p.438

Quiz 57: General 15 (30)

1 Argentinian international Gonzalo Higuaín is also qualified by birth to play for which country, where he was born in December 1987? (1)

2 Name six of the Football League clubs for which Steve Claridge played more than ten league games during his career. The first six answers will be taken. (6)

3 Who did Manchester City beat in the play-off final to claw their way out of Division 2 (third tier) at the first time of asking? Which Scottish international striker scored the injury-time equaliser at the end of the ninety minutes to force the match to extra time and penalties? Who was their top scorer as they shook off a sluggish start to finish third in the regular season? Who was the club's manager at the time? Who won the division with 101 points? (5)

4 In 1959–60 Huddersfield Town lost their manager to Liverpool and their best player to Manchester City: who were they? (2)

5 Which former Celtic player sandwiched his year as manager of the club between two spells as manager of Stoke City? (1)

6 Which pair of brothers faced each other in a World Cup match at the 2010 finals? (2)

7 Who dropped Boscombe from their name in 1972? (1)

8 Who was the venture capitalist in charge of Rangers when they went into liquidation in 2012? (1)

9 Who left his job at Exeter City to become manager of Southampton in January 1994? (1)

10 In a pre-Suarez biting incident, which Chelsea player was caught on camera having a nibble of Real Mallorca's Marcelino in a 1999 European Cup Winners' Cup match? (1)

11 Mohamed Diab Al-Attar, known as Ad-Diba, scored all four goals as which country won the inaugural running of which tournament? (2)

12 What do St Gallen of Switzerland in 2000–01, Hapoel Tel Aviv of Israel in 2001–02 and Viking Stavanger of Norway in 2002–03 have in common? (2)

13 Alexander Hleb was the first player (and only one of any significance) from which country to appear in the Premier League? (1)

14 Who devised the system known as push-and-run football while manager of Tottenham Hotspur from 1949–55? What achievement were that Spurs side the first to record in seasons 1949–50 and 1950–51? (2)

15 In 1977–78 which two long-serving Chelsea players both played their 700th league game? Which of the two holds the club's record for appearances? (2)

Answers on p.438

Quiz 58: Football League 6 (30)

1 In 1965–66 when Liverpool won the league their back five (including goalkeeper) played every game bar two as a unit: who were those five players? All won caps for their countries (three Englishmen and two Scots), but how many did they win between them – was it 14, 70 or 140? (5)

2 Which small Derbyshire town claims the prize as the smallest town to have ever boasted a team in the top division of English football, is it (a) Buxton, (b) Matlock, (c) Ashbourne or (d) Glossop? (1)

3 This is the Ipswich Town line-up from the 2000 play-off Final when the team won promotion to the Premier League – can you fill in the gaps (5-3-2)? MISSING; Gary Croft, MISSING, Mark Venus, John McGreal, MISSING; MISSING, MISSING, Jermaine Wright (sub: Fabian Wilnis); David Johnson (sub: Richard Naylor), MISSING (sub: Martijn Reuser) (5)

4 Who spent two years as player-manager of Millwall between 2003 and 2005? (1)

5 Which three founder members of the Football League have not yet played in the Premier League? (3)

6 Which club, currently (2015–16) in the Conference North, finished eighth in the second tier under Gary Megson in 1997–98, their best ever league placing? (1)

7 Who spearheaded Bradford City's promotion charge to the Premier League in 1998–99 with 23 goals? From which other Division 1 club was he bought in the summer? Who was the team's ever-present goalkeeper? And where did he emerge as a teenage prospect in the previous decade? (4)

8 Who top scored for Portsmouth and headed the Division 1 (second tier) list as Pompey won promotion to the Premier League in 2002–03? Who played in goal in every league game of that promotion season? (2)

9 Which West Country-born full back scored eleven times (including six penalties) as West Ham United gained promotion into the Premier League in 1992–93? What other unenviable statistic did he rack up in the same season? (2)

10 Who was the first man to win the league title with Arsenal as both player and manager? (1)

11 In August 1965, Keith Peacock became the Football League's first substitute when he came on for which side? (1)

12 Scunthorpe United*, Luton Town*, Preston North End***, Burnley*, Preston North End – this is the career path of which model pro, who played into his forties? (1)

13 Which Northern Ireland international scored an impressive 35 goals as Reading won Division 2 (third tier) in 1993–94? (1)

14 Bradford City fans were stopped from bringing confetti into the ground in 2001 as this new favourite game was: (a) costing the club £4,600 per week in extra cleaning bills; (b) the loose confetti was choking the local bird population; (c) the confetti was getting wet and blocking the club's drains; or (d) the club were receiving complaints from local residents about the confetti spoiling their gardens and littering the streets? (1)

15 Jason Scotland once top scored for a Welsh club, Swansea, in the English league; but for which country did he win 41 international caps? (1)

Asterisk (*) indicates that the player in question made more than one hundred league appearances for the club. (***) indicates more than three hundred league appearances.

Answers on p.439

Quiz 59: Northern Ireland 2 (30)

1 Why did Jackie Blanchflower, brother of captain Danny and first choice centre half for his country, not play for Northern Ireland at the 1958 World Cup finals? (1)

2 Northern Ireland came within a whisper of qualifying for the 1966 World Cup finals in England; a late equaliser by which other side in their group denied them their place – was it the Netherlands, Switzerland or Albania? (1)

3 Whose record of 36 goals for Northern Ireland is more than double his nearest rival (Sep 2015)? (1)

4 Real Mallorca signed which lower division striker in 1983 on the basis of his performances at the 1982 World Cup finals? (1)

5 Who scored Northern Ireland's goal when they beat England in qualification for the 2006 World Cup finals? (1)

6 Who won his 100th cap for Northern Ireland against Austria in September 1983? (1)

7 Which veteran defender, a regular for Northern Ireland in their magnificent Euro 2016 campaign, won his first cap whilst playing for Lincoln City after years in the NIFL Premiership, but has enjoyed his prime years in his thirties at Ipswich Town and West Bromwich Albion? (1)

8 Fans were invited to vote for their Greatest Ever Northern Ireland team in a recent (2015) poll. Here is the team, in 4-4-2, with the players represented by the club for which they played the most league games: Tottenham Hotspur; Manchester United, Newcastle United, Manchester United, Luton Town; Manchester United, Tottenham Hotspur, Rangers (but still playing at a different club), Crystal Palace; Preston North End, Manchester City. How many can you identify? (11)

9 Which of Northern Ireland's twenty most-capped players was born in England – was it (a) Jimmy Nicholl (b) Maik Taylor (c) Iain Dowie or (d) Nigel Worthington? (1)

10 Which teenager made his Northern Ireland debut against Scotland in March 2015? (1)

11 Which is the most common surname in the list of players capped by Northern Ireland, is it Campbell, Doherty, Hamilton or O'Neill? (1)

12 He was a massively talented inside forward who won the Football League title with Manchester City in 1937 and the FA Cup with Derby County in 1946. He missed most of his best international years to the Second World War but was appointed the first manager of the Northern Ireland team in 1951 – who was he? (1)

13 Allan Hunter made his Northern Ireland debut as a centre half with Blackburn Rovers in 1969, but he won most of his caps in the following decade as an integral member of which successful team? (1)

14 Which Northern Ireland international centre half, who shares his name with the main songwriter in The Undertones, played more than 300 games for Leicester City, played at the World Cup finals in 1982 and 1986, but played only thirty-four minutes for new club Norwich City when his leg was shattered in a shocking tackle with John Fashanu of Wimbledon? (1)

15 Fill in the gaps in this Northern Ireland team that clinched qualification for the 2016 European Championships with a win over Greece: Michael McGovern (Hamilton Academical); MISSING (Manchester United), Gareth McAuley (West Bromwich Albion), MISSING (Watford), Chris Brunt (West Brom); MISSING (Nottingham Forest), MISSING (Blackburn Rovers), MISSING (Southampton), Oliver Norwood (Reading), Stuart Dallas (Leeds United); MISSING (Kilmarnock) (6)

Answers on p.440

Quiz 60: World Cup 7 (30)

1 Which two players scored twice each as the Netherlands demolished holders Spain 5-1 in their opening group game at the 2014 World Cup finals? Who beat Spain in their next match and knocked them out? (3)

2 Who was the only black player in the Uruguay team that won the first World Cup Final in 1930? (1)

3 Which Rhineland club provided five of West Germany's World Cup winning team in 1954? (1)

4 After a sluggish start at the 1958 World Cup finals the Brazilian coach Vicente Feola drafted in two reserves, Edson do Nascimento and Manuel dos Santos. In true Brazilian style these players adopted 'football names' – who were they? (2)

5 Which club team had the most players (five, including the captain) in Scotland's 1974 World Cup finals squad? (1)

6 Which pair of twins played in the 1978 World Cup Final? With which club had they just won the Dutch league? (3)

7 Name the ten players who have made twenty or more appearances in World Cup finals matches. (There are five from one country and only two South Americans, stats up to and including 2014 tournament) (10)

8 Who scored a hat-trick for the Soviet Union in their classic 1986 World Cup finals encounter with Belgium, but still ended up on the losing side as Belgium won 4-3? (1)

9 Who was the pony-tailed goalkeeper for the United States in their World Cup finals campaigns of 1990 and 1994 – was it Mark Bosnich, Kasey Keller, Tony Meola or David Vanole? (1)

10 Said Al-Owairan of Saudi Arabia scored a brilliant solo winning goal in the 1994 World Cup finals to take his team to the knockout phase of the tournament: which team were on the receiving end? (1)

11 Which France-based player scored Cameroon's goal as they beat Argentina 1-0 in the opening game of the 1990 World Cup finals? (1)

12 Which skilful attacking midfield player, captain of his country, made his 100th international appearance at the 1998 World Cup finals in a 1-0 win over Saudi Arabia? (1)

13 Which former Portsmouth and Coventry City striker scored the decisive penalty in the shoot-out that led to Australia qualifying for the 2006 World Cup finals at the expense of Uruguay? (1)

14 On their first World Cup finals appearance Angola were drawn in the same group as which country, once their colonial occupiers? (1)

15 Whose goalkeeping error in England's first group game of the 2010 World Cup finals meant England had to settle for a draw against the United States? Who replaced him for the rest of the tournament? (2)

Answers on p.440

Quiz 61: General 16 (30)

1 Arnold Mühren was the first Dutch player to win the FA Cup; with which club? (1)

2 In 1969 how did Swindon Town emulate Queens Park Rangers? (2)

3 Here is the Liverpool team that won the 2001 League Cup Final against Birmingham City in a penalty shoot-out: Westerveld; Babbel, Henchoz, Hyypia, Carragher; Smicer (Barmby), Hamann, Gerrard (McAllister), Biscan (Ziege); Fowler, Heskey. Which eight nations are represented here? (8)

4 The official name of which Premier League club's ground was The Boleyn Ground (1904–2016)? By what name was it usually known? (2)

5 What was the original playing name of Sheffield Wednesday when they entered the Football League in 1892? (1)

6 Which peer of the realm and early football pioneer's record nine FA Cup Final appearances may never be beaten? (1)

7 Who ended twelve years as Everton manager in 1973 with two Football League titles and an FA Cup to his credit? (1)

8 Who was the Yugoslav goalkeeper, an early import into English football from Europe, who rapidly became a cult hero at Chelsea? (1)

9 Which two jobs was John Toshack briefly sharing from 28 January 1994? Who was unveiled as the new England coach on the same day, the game's worst kept secret at the time? And who was unsurprisingly ousted as manager of Liverpool on that day, after an FA Cup replay defeat by which non-Premier League club? (5)

10 Which club, relegated the previous year, did Watford beat in the 1999 Division 1 play-off Final to earn their first crack at the Premier League? Which team had their opponents consigned to their third successive play-off failure in the semis? (2)

11 What took place in Addis Ababa in 1976, Casablanca in 1988, Ougadougou in 1998 and Libreville in 2012? (1)

12 After the ban imposed on English clubs following the Heysel tragedy, when did Liverpool next play in the European Cup or Champions League? (1)

13 Benito Carbone was never the sort of player to hang around at one club for a long spell. With which English club did he last the longest, playing for three years from 1996–1999? (1)

14 Stan Flashman was the colourful Chairman of which London club in the 1990s? (1)

15 Who was the first £1M goalkeeper when he moved from Bristol Rovers in 1989? Who were the buying club? (2)

Answers on p.441

Quiz 62: Global 2 (30)

1 Millonarios are the premier club of which South American capital? (1)

2 Mauricio Solis was one of only two Costa Rica players at the 2006 World Cup finals with experience of playing in England, having played at Derby County alongside which of his countrymen? (1)

3 Lee Woon-jae was South Korea's captain at the 2006 World Cup. Although he never played in Europe, he was genuine world class and won 133 caps for his country. In which position? (1)

4 Who was appointed manager of the United Arab Emirates football team in July 1977? (1)

5 In which African country can you find the Craig Bellamy Foundation for Football, a massive charitable organisation founded and financed by the controversial star? (1)

6 Chile walked off while trailing Brazil 1-0 during a crucial qualifier for the 1990 World Cup finals after fans threw a firework on the pitch and the Chilean goalkeeper was carried off on a stretcher. Why was the game not awarded to Chile as would normally be the case? (2)

7 Racing Club against Peñarol would be a hotly contested local derby with a history of violent clashes, between two sides from which city? (1)

8 At which famous old ground were forty-three spectators killed after a stampede before a game between Kaiser Chiefs and Orlando Pirates? (1)

9 Which PSV Eindhoven striker scored in all three games in the final group when Brazil beat Argentina, Paraguay and Uruguay to win the 1989 Copa América? (1)

10 What did Elano, Thiago Silva, André Santos and Fred all do for Brazil at the 2011 Copa América? (2)

11   Can you name the five members of the Argentinian squad at the 2015 Copa América tournament who were based in Manchester at the time? (5)

12   Ghana won their fourth and most recent African Cup of Nations in 1982. Which North African country made it to the Final for the first (and thus far only) time, losing on penalties to Ghana? (1)

13   Seven Stars, Ajax, Celta Vigo (inc Porto), Porto, Blackburn Rovers, West Ham United, Orlando Pirates. This is the career path of which African striker, who netted 32 goals in 80 internationals between 1997 and 2012? (1)

14   Who clinched their third successive African Cup of Nations when they beat Ghana 1-0 in the Final in 2010? (1)

15   Can you name the ten member states of CONMEBOL, the South American football federation? (10)

Answers on p.442

Quiz 63: Premier League 8 (40)

1 At the end of the 1994–95 season both Blackburn Rovers and Manchester United made heavy weather of trying to win the title: who beat Blackburn in the final game of the season to leave United needing only to win, and who denied the Reds, drawing 1-1 and handing Blackburn the Premier League title? (2)

2 In 1998, which two players won the FA Cup, the Premiership and the World Cup? (2)

3 Nottingham Forest were relegated in 1998–99; which player, who would be re-employed by the club in 2015, was their top scorer with nine goals? And who was his strike partner, who refused to even play for the club for part of the season? (2)

4 Which £10.75M signing, a world record for a defender, was paraded in front of Manchester United fans before the last match of the unsuccessful 1997–98 season? From which club was he bought? (2)

5 Which five players have made over 300 appearances for Newcastle United in the Premier League era? (all appearances, not just in the Premier League) (5)

6 Which Scottish international signed for Liverpool in 2011 after a successful season with Blackpool in the Premier League? To which club did he move on after struggling to fit in at Anfield? (2)

7 Which two strikers, one who had come up from the lower leagues with the club and one who had joined that summer having been on loan at Liverpool the previous season, scored the goals as Manchester City managed their first win over their Old Trafford neighbours in November 2002? Who was the only member of the City team to have appeared on the winning side in a Manchester derby? (3)

8 Which hard-working if not exactly prolific striker was Everton's top scorer in 1998–99, 1999–2000 and 2000–01? What was the team's top finish in those seasons – was it 7th, 10th or 13th? (2)

9 Who was the 'new David Ginola' (he wasn't) signed by Newcastle United from Paris St Germain for £10M in July 2001? With which other English club did he spend half a season on loan in 2005–06 before departing for Benfica? (2)

10 Alberto Luque was signed for £9.5M from Deportivo de La Coruña by which club? Who was their manager and who sold him two years later after a paltry 21 Premier League games? (3)

11 What indignity did Aston Villa, Stoke City, Sunderland and Wigan Athletic all suffer at Stamford Bridge as Chelsea won the Premier League in 2009–10? (2)

12 Statistically, what was the significance of Chelsea's home defeat by Sunderland in April 2014? (2)

13 Which two Premier League clubs have been managed by Dutch coach Martin Jol? (2)

14 For which four clubs did Gary Speed appear in the Premier League? For which did he make the most league appearances? (5)

15 Who were promoted for the second year in succession when they finished runners-up in the Championship (second tier) in 2010–11? Who matched them the following season, also earning a second successive promotion and place among the big boys? Who were the two managers behind these success stories? (4)

Answers on p.442

Quiz 64: European Championships 2 (30)

1 Who missed the crucial penalty for England in their shoot-out at the 2004 European Championships against Portugal? (1)

2 Who scored twice to see off Bosnia and Herzegovina and ensure Republic of Ireland qualified via the play-offs for the 2016 European Championships? Who had finished ahead of them in their tough group? (3)

3 England qualified for their first European Championship finals in 1968, the first tournament with modern-style group qualification. What served as England's group? (2)

4 Who beat England 2-1 in Bratislava to deny them a place in the quarter-finals in qualifying for the 1976 European Championships? Which Manchester City player scored twice when England beat the same opposition 3-0 in the reverse fixture a few months earlier? (2)

5 Who scored the penalty for Denmark to give them victory at Wembley for the first time and ensure they, and not England, qualified for the 1984 European Championships? Which two members of the Danish squad joined major English clubs at the end of the Championships? (3)

6 The Netherlands won the 1988 European Championships, but who beat them 1-0 in the group phase? Which quick midfielder with a rasping shot scored the goal? (2)

7 Who missed the penalty that saw the Netherlands bow out of the 1992 European Championships to Denmark in a penalty shoot-out? Who scored both Denmark's goals in the game? (2)

8 At the 1996 European Championships only the reserve goalkeeper out of the Czech Republic squad was playing in England: who was he? Which member of the squad joined Manchester United the same summer? (2)

9 England's qualification campaign for the 2000 European Championships started with a bang as Alan Shearer scored in the first minute of the opening group game: who came back from that shock to beat England in that game? Whose hat-trick against Poland ensured England had a better goal difference than the Poles and therefore pipped them for second place in the group and a crack at the play-offs? (2)

10 Who came from 2-0 down in twenty minutes to beat England 3-2 in their first group match in the 2000 European Championships? And who gave away a late penalty as England failed to run down the clock against Romania in their last match? Who were the only team England beat? (3)

11 Who scored the golden goal against Italy that won the 2000 European Championships for France? (1)

12 Who did Portugal beat 1-0 with a goal from Nuno Gomes to reach the knockout phase of the 2004 European Championships after suffering an early setback with a shock defeat to Greece? (1)

13 Who scored a memorable hat-trick for Northern Ireland as they beat Spain, the eventual champions, 3-2 in a qualifier for the European Championships? (1)

14 Portugal's leaky defence meant they had to qualify for the 2012 European Championships via the play-offs; which former Yugoslav state did they beat 6-2 at home after a 0-0 draw in the first leg? And which former Soviet state did the Republic of Ireland beat to claim their place in the finals? (2)

15 The Czech Republic won their qualifying group for the 2016 European Championships, with Iceland and Turkey also qualifying in second and third. Which country finished a distant fourth, their only victories coming against Kazakhstan and Latvia? Who was dismissed after his second spell as national coach halfway through the campaign, and who took over? (3)

Answers on p.443

Quiz 65: General 17 (30)

1   Arsenal signed Matthew Upson as a teenager after he played a single game for which club? (1)

2   In 1984 Barcelona sold their star player to an Italian side for £6.9M. Who was he, and which Serie A side bought him? (2)

3   Sunderland*, Liverpool*, Newcastle United*, Galatasaray, Southampton – whose 1980s and 1990s career path is this (it included a couple of England caps) before he turned to some punditry? (1)

4   What was the name of the healer in whom Glenn Hoddle put a large degree of faith whilst he was England manager? Which player, when obliged to undergo a mandatory session with Hoddle's healer, reportedly sat in the chair and asked for a 'short back and sides, please'? (2)

5   Which former England international was killed in a car crash in Spain in 1989, aged only thirty-three? (1)

6   Which player from which club is the only player to score in all four divisions of the old Football League system AND the Premier League? (2)

7   Who had relegated the great Oliver Kahn to the substitutes bench by the time the 2006 World Cup finals came around? (1)

8   Who were the British Isles' only representatives at the 1994 World Cup finals in the USA? (1)

9   In 1994, who was allegedly smuggled out of Argentina in a pick-up truck after firing an air-gun at assembled journalists? (1)

10 Up to and including 2014, which ten countries have played in the most World Cup finals matches? (These stats count Soviet Union/Russia together, similarly Yugoslavia/Serbia and so on) (10)

11 When Ruud van Nistelrooy took his goal tally for Manchester United in European competition to 35 in 2004–05, whose record did he break? (1)

12 Chelsea paid well over £20M for Juan Cuadrado, but he played only 13 games before being loaned out to which Italian club at the start of the 2015–16 season? With which country did he impress at the 2014 World Cup finals? (1)

13 What was published in January 1990 and changed the match day experience in football for good? (1)

14 Which early great was a perennial top scorer in the Football League in the late 1890s and early 1900s, and set a redoubtable record for league goals with 317? For which club did he score most of them either side of a spell at Middlesbrough? How many goals did he score in his 23 England games – was it 16, 23 or 28? (3)

15 Which two top-flight goalkeepers were accused of match-fixing in the 1990s? (2)

Asterisk (*) indicates that the player in question made more than one hundred league appearances for the club.

Answers on p.444

Quiz 66: FA Cup 3 (30)

1 Going backwards: Tim Sherwood, Steve Bruce, Roberto Mancini, Kenny Dalglish, MISSING, Avram Grant, MISSING, Dave Jones, Alex Ferguson. Which two names are missing in this sequence? (2)

2 Whose most famous FA Cup victory knocked out Manchester City in 1980 – was it (a) Aldershot (b) Cambridge United (c) Torquay United or (d) Halifax Town? (1)

3 Who in 1986 was the last non-League side to win away against top-flight opposition in the FA Cup – was it (a) Altrincham (b) Macclesfield Town (c) Telford United or (d) Blyth Spartans? (1)

4 Which are the only two clubs since 1900 to retain the FA Cup twice? (2)

5 Who was the last player to score a hat-trick in an FA Cup Final? And which three players have scored twice in the Final in the twenty-first century (to 2015)? (4)

6 Which four clubs have reached an FA Cup Final for the first time in the twenty-first century? Who were the only winners amongst the quartet? (5)

7 Who won the FA Cup with Tottenham Hotspur in 1967 and 1991? Who were Spurs' opponents in the two matches? (3)

8 Which defender lost three FA Cup Finals as an Everton player, having joined the summer after their win in 1984, but finally won a winner's medal with Tottenham in 1991? (1)

9 Who missed a penalty in the 1991 FA Cup Final? Who was the Nottingham Forest goalkeeper who saved it? (2)

10 Who is the only player to score in four separate FA Cup Finals? (1)

11 Who, in 2005, became only the second player to be sent off in an FA Cup Final when he was given his marching orders by Rob Styles? (1)

12 Which North East non-League team took Wrexham to a fifth round FA Cup replay in 1979, and came within a poor refereeing decision of being the first team from outside the Football League to make the quarter-finals since the First World War? (1)

13 Which two sides were involved when an FA Cup fifth round tie was voluntarily replayed in 1998–99 because a goal had been scored when one side took advantage of possession conceded so an injured player could be treated? Who put the ball in the net? (3)

14 Which two cousins lost successive FA Cup Finals on penalties? (2)

15 Which full back was the first player to win three FA Cups with Manchester United? (1)

Answers on p.444

Quiz 67: Premier League 9 (40)

1 Barclays (initially Barclaycard) have sponsored the Premier League for most of the 21st Century; who were the sponsors from 1993 to 2001? (1)

2 In 1999–2000 Manchester United used three goalkeepers: who was the number one, bought from Aston Villa as a replacement for the departed Peter Schmeichel? Who was the second, who played just 37 league games in six years at Old Trafford? And who was bought from Venezia for £4.5M as extra cover and is widely regarded as Alex Ferguson's worst signing at the club? Who did United sign in summer, 2000, to fill this gap? (4)

3 On 19 October 2002, one player made his 500th appearance, another scored his 300th club goal, and a third became the Premier League's youngest scorer: which three players? Who eclipsed the last of these records before the year was out? (4)

4 Which African striker with Bruges performed well at the 1994 World Cup finals and spurred Everton to pay £3M for him later that summer? (1)

5 Which former employee all but ended Liverpool's title ambitions in 1997–98 as they lost 2-1 at Villa Park? (1)

6 Which signing, often derided as one of Alex Ferguson's worst, was the Premier League Player of the Month in September 2001, but struggled to stick with the pace and intensity of the English game thereafter? Which other club allowed United to recoup £15M of their £28M outlay? (2)

7 Which two Swedish wide players, who both appeared in the Premier League, made more than 100 appearances for Arsenal? (2)

8 Manchester United's back five (including goalkeeper) missed only six league games between them as United won the Premier League in 1993–94: who were they, and who made his debut at right back in the last game of the season with the title sewn up? (6)

9 Who paid nearly £5M for Gilles de Bilde (Ajax) and Gerald Sibon (PSV Eindhoven) in 1999 and got precious little from either? (1)

10 In the 2005–06 Premier League what did Marcus Bent's goal for his team achieve at Stamford Bridge that eleven sides before and seven after failed to do? Which team was Bent playing for? (2)

11 Who top scored in the Premier League for Fulham in 2003–04 and for Everton in 2009–10 with the same number of goals (13)? At which club did he underwhelm the top flight for four years in between? (2)

12 Which Stoke City goalkeeper scored after twelve seconds against Southampton in a Premier League fixture in November 2013? Which experienced East European international was his opposite number? (2)

13 Which two Southampton players were in the 2013–14 PFA Premier League Team of the Year but left at the end of the season? (2)

14 For which six teams has Nicolas Anelka appeared in the Premier League? (6)

15 Who walked away from the manager's job at Queens Park Rangers in February 2015 with the club facing relegation from the Premier League? Who was the coach who took over but couldn't keep the club in the top flight? And who replaced him in turn in November 2015? From which high-flying League 1 (third tier) club was he poached? (4)

Answers on p.445

Quiz 68: European Competitions 4 (30)

1 Who scored the only goal in the Final against Parma to clinch the 1994 European Cup Winners' Cup for Arsenal? (1)

2 Which player, best known for his involvement in off-field issues, appeared as a losing finalist for Ajax in the 1988 European Cup Winners' Cup Final before being transferred to Belgium's Mechelen? (1)

3 With which Croatian side did Slaven Bilić begin both his playing and his managerial career? (1)

4 Here is the Fulham side that lost the 2010 Europa League Final – can you fill in the gaps (4-4-1-1) ? MISSING (Australia); Chris Baird (Northern Ireland), MISSING (Northern Ireland), MISSING (Norway), Paul Konchesky (England); MISSING (Republic of Ireland) (sub: Erik Nevland, Norway), Dickson Etuhu (Nigeria), MISSING (England, captain) (sub: Jonathan Greening, England), MISSING (Wales); MISSING (Hungary); Bobby Zamora (England) (sub: MISSING, United States) (8)

5 Newcastle United reached the semi-finals of the UEFA Cup in 2003–04 by beating which former club of manager Bobby Robson? Which former Premier League goalkeeper played a blinder for Marseille in the 0-0 draw at St James's Park in the semi-finals to help eliminate Newcastle? And which future top class Premier League striker scored twice in the home leg to seal the deal? (3)

6 Apart from being the French national rugby stadium the Parc des Princes is home to which football club? (1)

7 Which powerful defender, who later played more than 100 Premier League games for Bolton Wanderers, scored the winner for Paris St Germain against Rapid Vienna in the 1996 European Cup Winners' Cup Final? (1)

8   Vojvodina and Željezničar once competed in the same league; which two republics of the former Yugoslavia do they now represent in European competition? (2)

9   Which Welsh side reached the quarter-finals of the 1980–81 European Cup Winners' Cup before going out 3-2 on aggregate to Carl Zeiss Jena? Which country did CZJ represent? (1)

10 Which English side hold a the record for an aggregate victory in a two-legged tie after thrashing Jeunesse Hautcharage 21-0 in the 1970s? What country were Jeunesse representing? (1)

11 Which three sides have, between them, won the Portuguese league title on all but two occasions? Which of the three has most titles, to 2015, with thirty-four? (4)

12 Which of the following sides has never played in the European Cup or Champions League – Burnley, Ipswich Town, Norwich City, Wolverhampton Wanderers? (1)

13 What was lifted on 18 April 1990? (1)

14 Which two teenagers kept goal for Atlético Madrid when they won the Europa League Final in 2010 and again in 2012? (2)

15 In summer 2004 both Germany and the Netherlands appointed a former great striker as their national coach: who were they? (2)

Answers on p.446

Quiz 69: General 18 (30)

1 Arsenal, Juventus, Sampdoria, Internazionale, Ascoli, West Ham United this is the career path of which Republic of Ireland star? What was his oft-used nickname? (2)

2 In 1988 Brighton & Hove Albion paid Conference side Barnet £115,000 for defender Nicky Bissett – what new record did this transfer establish? (1)

3 Terry McDermott was bought by Liverpool in November 1974 having played against them in the FA Cup Final earlier that year: who were the selling club, and where did McDermott go when he left Liverpool eight years later? (2)

4 What was the name of the stadium in Berne, Switzerland, that was used for the 1954 World Cup Final? Who play their club football there? (2)

5 Which former footballer was a co-host of the action game show *Gladiators* on the BBC in the 1990s? Which rugby union star replaced him for two of the eight seasons? Who was the female co-host for all eight seasons? (3)

6 Which player won the European Footballer of the Year award three times in the 1970s? And who emulated that feat the following decade? (2)

7 Who is the only German player to have been voted PFA Player of the Year? (1)

8 Who were the brothers who played for the Netherlands at the 1998 World Cup finals? Which three clubs did both brothers play for? (5)

9 In which year did FIFA make the reckless tackle from behind an automatic red card offence (1 point for two years either way) ? (2)

10 Brian Hillier, convicted of fraud in 1990, was Chairman of which football club at the time? Who was the luckless manager who led them to promotion only for his Chairman's misdeeds to let the club down? (2)

11 Which club was saved from dropping out of the Football League when their on-loan goalkeeper Jimmy Glass scored an unlikely winning goal from a corner in the last game of the 1998–99 season? Which team's twelve-year stint as a league club did they end (they haven't yet made it back)? (2)

12 Which major tennis star had a father who appeared in the World Cup finals for Belgium? (1)

13 Crystal Palace, Aston Villa, Middlesbrough, plus 57 caps for England: whose career path is this? (1)

14 In 1894–95, what method was introduced to separate teams finishing on the same number of points at the end of a league season? (1)

15 In one of the more bizarre deals of the 1990s, which club did Joey Beauchamp leave for West Ham United? How many games did he play for the Hammers, and why did he leave? (3)

Answers on p.446

Quiz 70: Football League 7 (30)

1 Who top scored for Birmingham City as they won Division Two in 1971–72? And for which other two clubs did he appear in the top flight in England? (3)

2 New Brighton Tower had a brief spell in the Football League in the 1900s; where do they come from? (1)

3 Bob Jackson was the only manager to win the league (he did it twice) with which English club – was it (a) Portsmouth (b) Burnley (c) Wolverhampton Wanderers or (d) Derby County? (1)

4 Tottenham were able to pick a reasonably settled side for their 1960–61 Double season; the only significant injury was Welsh international winger Cliff Jones missing a couple of months. Which other Welsh winger deputised, and played in the 1962 FA Cup Final? (1)

5 The 1970–71 season was a stinker for the famous old Lancashire clubs. Which two were relegated from the First Division and which other two, both founder members, suffered a drop to the Third Division for the first time? (4)

6 Which club finished in the top six of the First Division every year for ten years from 1972–73 without winning the league, except the year they won the FA Cup when they only just avoided relegation? (1)

7 What connects Queens Park Rangers in 2000–01, Leicester City in 2008–09 and Blackpool in 2010–11? (2)

8 Which London club achieved their highest ever league finish of third in 1985–86? Who was club manager at the time? And who were the two strikers who scored 46 league goals between them? (4)

9 Who won promotion to the Football League under Martin O'Neill in 1992–93? What impressive non-league 'Double' did they achieve? (2)

10 In the 1955–56 season, what were introduced at some English grounds for League and FA Cup matches? (1)

11 Which goalkeeper, who made more than 400 appearances for Sheffield Wednesday, was sent off after 13 seconds of the 2000–01 season? (1)

12 Which Leeds United left back won the first of his 32 caps in 1976, a year before his elder brother, also a Leeds player, won the last of his 12? With which club did he win the European Cup between two lengthy spells at Leeds? (2)

13 Which no-nonsense defender, sometimes used as a stand-in striker, scored both goals as Leicester City beat Derby County 2-1 in the play-off Final to reach the Premier League in 1993–94? How many red cards did he receive in his league career, a joint record? (1 point for 2 either way) (3)

14 Stern John scored a last minute goal against Millwall to send which side to the Division 1 (second tier) play-off Final? And which former part-time Halifax striker scored the late equaliser that took the Final against Norwich City to penalties? (2)

15 Blackpool won the Championship (second tier) play-off in 2009–10, beating which opponents 3-2 at Wembley with all the goals in the first half? Which veteran forward scored the decisive goal? (2)

Answers on p.447

Quiz 71: League Cup 2 (30)

1 How many goals did Wigan goalkeeper Mike Pollitt concede in the 2006 Carling Cup Final? (1)

2 On-loan centre half Marlon Broomes and striker Phil Jevons scored extra-time goals as which struggling Division 1 (second tier) side won at Anfield to knock holders, Liverpool, out of the League Cup in 2001– 02? (1)

3 Which Scotsman scored the only goal as Liverpool edged the first all-Merseyside League Cup Final in 1984 in a replay after 200 minutes of dull fare? (1)

4 Who scored three goals across the two-legged semi-final against holders Blackburn Rovers to put Manchester United into the 2003 League Cup Final? (1)

5 Which Division 2 (third tier) side reached their first major semi-final when they beat Premier League Southampton 2-1 in a replay in January 1997? Who was the former strike partner of Steve Bull at Wolves who scored the winner after future Everton player Brett Angell equalised Matt Le Tissier's opener? (2)

6 It was a clean sweep for north London as Tottenham Hotspur won the 1971 League Cup while Arsenal won both FA Cup and Football League: which England centre forward scored both of Spurs' goals in their 2-0 defeat of Aston Villa in the Final? Which teenager and future club captain played in the Spurs midfield and won his first trophy? (2)

7 Who, in 1979, became the first side to retain the League Cup title? Which former Liverpool star was captain of the Wolverhampton Wanderers team that stopped them making it a treble in the 1980 Final? (2)

8 Which two of their imports scored twice apiece as Chelsea turned Arsenal over 5-0 at Highbury in the 1998–99 League Cup? (2)

9 Which teenager scored in the all-London 2007 League Cup Final? (1)

10 Who were the three overseas players in Aston Villa's League Cup winning team in 1996? (3)

11 Who scored five times for Manchester City across the two-legged semi-final of the 2013–14 League Cup win over West Ham United (City won 9-0 on aggregate), but never really became a regular in the first choice City eleven? (1)

12 When Birmingham City played in the 2001 League Cup Final as a Division 1 (second tier) side, which central defender scored the late penalty to take the game to extra time and also scored his penalty in the shoot-out? Which future England striker, then a twenty-year-old, came off the bench at half time but missed the crucial penalty in the shoot-out? (2)

13 Which two future league title winners made up Norwich City's centre-back pairing as they won the 1985 League Cup Final against Sunderland? Who did Norwich see off in a keenly anticipated two-legged semi-final? (3)

14 Who did Tottenham Hotspur beat (5-1) for the first time in twenty-seven attempts to reach the 2002 League Cup Final, having lost the first leg of the semi-final 2-1? Which two Dutch stars were at the centre of an odd moment in the game when one was mistakenly sent off in the other's stead? (3)

15 In 1977 the League Cup Final went to a replay for the first time since it became a single-game affair; who won for the second time in three years, beating Everton 3-2 after a 0-0 draw at Wembley and a 1-1 draw in the first replay at Hillsborough? Which venue was used for the second replay? Which future manager of the club scored twice? And which Northern Ireland international was the source of an unlikely forty-yard screamer for the opener? Which future star and England player came into the side for both replays as an eighteen-year-old? (5)

Answers on p.448

Quiz 72: England 4 (30)

1 Who scored twice for Chile against England at Wembley, including one sensational volleyed finish, in a warm-up match for the 1998 World Cup finals? Which young striker was making his international debut that night? (2)

2 Which three players have been sent off during a World Cup finals match while playing for England, and who were England's opponents in each instance? (3)

3 How many goals did Peter Beardsley score in his 59 games for England? (1 point for 1 goal either way) (2)

4 Who (to 2015–16) was the last Crystal Palace player to be picked for England? (1)

5 Evelyn Lintoft was the first QPR player to be picked for England, in 1908: who was the next, sixty-three years later? (1)

6 In 1955 England routed Scotland 7-1, with four goals from which unheralded Wolverhampton Wanderers forward? (1)

7 Who scored hat-tricks in successive appearances for England in 1956 and 1957 – was it (a) Nat Lofthouse (b) Jackie Milburn (c) Stan Mortensen or (d) Tommy Taylor? (1)

8 Ignoring caretakers, who was England's least successful manager, with a win percentage of only 38.88? (1)

9 Which club has provided the most England internationals over the years (with 74 to November 2015)? (1)

10 Which of the following grounds has never hosted an England international – Craven Cottage, Upton Park, Selhurst Park, Burnden Park? (1)

11 Who has made the most appearances (46) for England's U-21 team? (1)

12 Which two Channel Islanders made their England debuts in the same match in 1994, Terry Venables' first in charge? Why do they not feel the kinship we might imagine they would? (4)

13 This is the England team that put nine past Scotland in a 1961 Home International. Fill in the missing players (3-3-4) – you must name them in the right order: Ron Springett (Sheffield Wednesday); MISSING (Blackpool), Peter Swan (Sheffield Wednesday), Mick McNeil (Middlesbrough); MISSING (West Bromwich Albion), MISSING (Fulham, captain), Ron Flowers (Wolverhampton Wanderers); Bryan Douglas (Blackburn Rovers), MISSING (Chelsea), MISSING (Tottenham Hotspur), Bobby Charlton (Manchester United). (5)

14 Whose late headed 'goal' for England against Portugal at the 2004 European Championships was ruled out for a foul on the goalkeeper? Who was the Portuguese goalkeeper, who shone in the penalty shoot-out, even scoring a confident spot-kick? (2)

15 Some England centre halves: Sol Campbell, Emlyn Hughes, Gareth Southgate, Des Walker, Dave Watson (1974–82, not the later one), Mark Wright. Who won most caps? Who never scored for England? Which two never captained England? (4)

Answers on p.448

Quiz 73: General 19 (30)

1 As Blackburn Rovers forked out £3.6M for Alan Shearer in summer 1992 (what a price for a league title!), who did Liverpool buy for £2.3M from Tottenham Hotspur? (1)

2 In 1989 Southampton signed an eighteen-year-old full back from Bath City, and bought sixteen years and more than 400 games of service: who was he? (1)

3 The Estádio José Amalfitani in Buenos Aires, one of the stadia for the 1978 World Cup finals, is home to Vélez Sársfield and which other sporting team? (1)

4 What was the name of the white police horse that helped clear the pitch before the 1923 FA Cup Final and became an enduring image of the event – was it (a) Alfie Double (b) Pickles (c) George Saviour or (d) Billie? (1)

5 Which former footballer was sacked as a pundit by Sky Sports for making a tasteless reference to the Asian tsunami disaster? (1)

6 Which Premier League side paid £9.5M for Albert Luque but got only twenty-one games out of him before moving him on to Ajax? With which colleague at the Dutch club did he have a half-time falling out that resulted in both players being substituted – was it (a) Edgar Davids (b) Patrick Kluivert (c) Jari Litmanen or (d) Luis Suárez? (2)

7 Who is the only Northern Ireland international to have played more than 300 games in the Premier League? (1)

8 Who were the first side still in existence to win the FA Cup, in 1884? (1)

9 Which two of these clubs were elected to the Scottish League system when it was expanded to forty clubs in 1994: Elgin City, Forfar Athletic, Gretna, (Inverness) Caledonian Thistle, Ross County, Stranraer? (2)

10 The Premier League Team of the Decade for the years 1992–2003 contained seven players who played principally for Manchester United (Schmeichel, Gary Neville, Irwin, Beckham, Scholes, Giggs and Cantona). Which other four players were selected – you can probably work out their positions? Who were voted domestic and overseas players of the decade? And which two players had two entries each in the list of ten goals of the decade? Whose much publicised 1996 goal won that award? (9)

11 Which two Southampton players were the only England-based players to earn a winner's medal at the 2016 European Championships? And which eighteen-year-old member of the winning Portuguese squad became the youngest player to play for them in a major tournament, weeks after securing a move to Bayern Munich as the most expensive player to move away from the Portuguese league? (3)

12 Which two ex-players signed five-year contracts to continue broadcasting football highlights on the BBC in August 1999? (2)

13 Fans of which club jeered and chanted during a one minute tribute to the late Sir Matt Busby before a Premier League match against Blackburn Rovers in January, 1994? (1)

14 After one season of the new Third Division in 1920–21, how did the Football League further expand itself? (1)

15 In 1990–91, after Tony Coton was sent off playing for Manchester City against Derby, which striker went in goal and saved the subsequent penalty? And which Welsh striker suffered the indignity of seeing his kick saved? Who had earlier scored a penalty for City? (3)

Answers on p.449

Quiz 74: Scotland 3 (30)

1 Which Celtic full back, arguably the best Scotland have had in his position, missed the 1978 World Cup finals through injury? (1)

2 Which London-born goalkeeper played nearly 200 games for Celtic around the turn of the century, and won two caps for Scotland (he went as uncapped third choice to the 1998 World Cup finals)? (1)

3 Scotland qualified for the 1950 World Cup finals tournament but didn't go – why? (2)

4 Who are the only two Scottish players with more than 300 Premier League appearances to their name? (2)

5 In 1976, which Rangers legend won his 44th and final Scottish cap five years after his previous international? (1)

6 Who was the captain of the 1967 European Cup winning Celtic team, and also holds the record for league appearances for Celtic, with 486? (1)

7 Which Rangers goalkeeper was voted Scottish Player of the Year in 1993? With which English club did he start his career (he was born in England but won 43 caps for Scotland)? (2)

8 Which Glasgow club haven't played in the area of the city from which they take their name since 1908? In which area do they play, reflected in the name of their stadium? (2)

9 Which two rival clubs won their one and only Scottish League titles in 1962 and 1983 respectively (you need to get them the right way round)? (2)

10 For which Scottish club did Steven Fletcher score two goals in a 5-1 trouncing of Kilmarnock in the 2007 Scottish League Cup Final? Which club, newly promoted to the Premier League, paid £2.75M for Fletcher in 2009? (1)

11 Who is Celtic's all-time leading goalscorer – is it (a) Henrik Larsson (b) Kenny Dalglish (c) Jimmy McGrory or (d) Bobby Lennox? (1)

12 Ayr United, Dunfermline Athletic, Motherwell, St Mirren – which of these four clubs have never won the Scottish FA Cup? (1)

13 Which full back and utility player enjoyed a late career bonus, winning his first Scotland cap in 2002 aged 31 and going on to collect 40 in total (he was still playing international football at 37)? (1)

14 Who was the Huddersfield Town winger who scored a hat-trick when Scotland demolished England 5-1 in 1928? What name was given to this talented Scottish side? (2)

15 Which ten clubs made up the first Scottish Premier League in 1998–99? (10)

Answers on p.450

Quiz 75: Champions League 6 (30)

1 Who was the first player to score a hat-trick in the modern Champions League for an English club when he scored three for Blackburn Rovers against Rosenborg in 1995 – was it Alan Shearer, Chris Sutton, Mike Newell or Jason Wilcox? (1)

2 Where did Manchester United's European Cup Final win over Benfica in 1968 take place? (1)

3 Along with suspended Roy Keane, which key Manchester United player missed the 1999 Champions League Final? (1)

4 Which European side have played in seven European Cup Finals, but lost all except the first two? (1)

5 How was the 2000 Champions League Final, won by Real Madrid, different from any of its predecessors? (1)

6 Who scored twice for AC Milan in the 2005 Champions League Final against Liverpool but finished on the losing side? And who netted twice as Milan won in 2007 in a repeat of the 2005 Final? (2)

7 Who scored Liverpool's equaliser in the 2005 Champions League Final? (1)

8 In 2007–08 there was an all-English Final of the Champions League for the first time. Who were Manchester United's opponents and which other English side got knocked out in the semi-finals? Who scored the crucial second leg extra-time goals that saw them through that tie? In United's semi-final against Barcelona, who scored the only goal of the two-legged tie at Old Trafford? Which three players missed their penalty kicks in the shoot-out that settled the Final? (8)

9 Whose late injury-time equaliser saw Barcelona edge past Chelsea on away goals at the semi-final stage of the 2008–09 Champions League? (1)

10 Which much-maligned Arsenal striker scored a hat-trick in the second leg of their 2009–10 Last 16 Champions League tie against Porto? (1)

11 Which former Arsenal striker scored a hat-trick as Lyon thrashed Werder Bremen 7-2 in the Last 16 of the 2004–05 Champions League for a 10-2 aggregate win? (1)

12 Who was the last English player to play in a Champions League Final for a continental side? (1)

13 Ernst Happel is the only Austrian coach to take a team to the European Cup Final and he did so on three occasions, winning twice: with which three clubs? (3)

14 Manchester United's best performance when they won the Champions League in 1999 was their semi-final victory over Juventus, especially coming from 2-0 down in Turin. This is their starting line-up – can you supply the missing players (4-4-2)? MISSING; MISSING, MISSING, Ronny Johnsen, Dennis Irwin; David Beckham, MISSING, Roy Keane, MISSING; MISSING, Dwight Yorke. (Clue: Ryan Giggs didn't play) (6)

15 Jeunesse Esch have qualified for the European Cup or Champions League on twenty-two occasions to 2014–15, twice reaching the Second Round; which country do they represent? (1)

Answers on p.450

Quiz 76: Premier League 10 (40)

1 Birmingham City enjoyed a good first season in the Premier League, finishing tenth in 2003–04. Here is the team that beat Portsmouth 2-0 to leave them fourth and unbeaten after six games (4-4-2, English unless stated): MISSING (Northern Ireland); Damien Johnson (Northern Ireland), MISSING (Republic of Ireland), Matthew Upson, Jamie Clapham; MISSING, Stephen Clemence, MISSING (Senegal), Stan Lazaridis (NATIONALITY?); MISSING (France), Mikael Forssell (NATIONALITY?). Can you fill in the gaps? (7)

2 In 2000–01 goals from Danny Murphy, Steven Gerrard and Robbie Fowler gave Liverpool their first double for 22 years over which perennial rivals? And in a twist on that story, which side did the double over Liverpool in the same season for the first time since their heyday thirty years previously, with Gerrard getting sent off in the Anfield fixture? (2)

3 On 22 September 2002, the regular penalty takers for Arsenal, Leeds United and Liverpool all missed their spot-kicks – who were the culprits? (3)

4 Which Belgian striker suffered a career-ending broken leg in a clash with Richard Wright soon after arriving in England in 2000? For which club had he signed? (2)

5 Which former Everton midfield player made more than 140 appearances later in his career for Aston Villa, and was an ever present in the side that finished second in the Premier League in 1992–93? (1)

6 Which Southampton player was banned for 10 games for pushing referee Alan Wiley in 2005? (1)

7 Which two teams both played their home games at Selhurst Park in 1992–93, the first Premier League season? (2)

8 Who received £5M, a British transfer fee record, for Chris Sutton in 1994? What did Sutton get at the end of his first season for his new club? (2)

9 Who was the Assistant Manager to Alex Ferguson when Manchester United won the treble in 1999? Which former United star did he replace in the job? (2)

10 Which centre half scored for Bradford City as they beat Liverpool 1-0 on the last day of the 1999–2000 season to avoid relegation from the Premier League? Whose defeat at Southampton meant that they went down instead? (2)

11 Which striker, playing for his fourth top-flight club, scored exactly half of Sunderland's 48 league goals as they finished thirteenth in the Premier League in 2009–10? And who was the club's only ever present, starting each of their 38 league games that season? (2)

12 In 2013–14, for the first time in the Premier League's history the top two scorers in the division were both from the same club: who were they? (2)

13 Which two London-based Belgian internationals were in the 2012–13 PFA Premier League Team of the Year? (2)

14 In the summer of 2004 new managers were installed at Chelsea, Liverpool and Tottenham Hotspur; who were the new incumbents? And who were the previous employers of the three new men? (6)

15 Kevin Kilbane won more than 100 caps for the Republic of Ireland and made over 324 appearances in the Premier League. For which four clubs did he appear in the top flight? (4)

Answers on p.451

Quiz 77: General 20 (30)

1 As the 1958 World Cup finals approached, England captain Billy Wright was in a relationship with Joy, a member of which pop group? (1)

2 In 1993 both FA Cup semi-finals were local derbies: who were the teams involved and where were the matches played? (5)

3 The Italian side for the 1990 World Cup finals included two Sampdoria forwards who would both go on to manage in the Premier League – who were they? (2)

4 What was the principal reason for East European dominance of the Olympic Football tournament between 1950 and 1980? (1)

5 Which former Georgian international full back, who played more than 200 games for Milan and was twice a Champions League winner with the club, is now his country's Deputy Prime Minister? (1)

6 Which Premiership footballer became the poster boy for Calvin Klein underwear in 2002? (1)

7 Who is the only Northern Ireland international to play in a European Cup Final or Champions League Final? (1)

8 Who were the first side to beat England after the 1966 World Cup win? (1)

9 Why did the FA cancel a friendly against Germany proposed for 20 April 1994? (2)

10 Which club lost three semi-finals in 1999–2000; to Tranmere Rovers in the League Cup, Aston Villa in the FA Cup and Ipswich Town in the Division 1 play-offs? (1)

11 What is the name given to the pointless jamboree invented as a revenue stream by FIFA, in which the champions of each continent play each other in a desultory fashion until someone is given a trophy which means very little to them? (1)

12 Which ten England internationals started the 2008 Champions League Final? (10)

13 For how many days was Steve Coppell manager of Manchester City in 1996 – was it 8, 22, 33 or 62? (1)

14 Which club won the Football League in 1929 and 1930 under different names? (1)

15 Which cultured Scottish international centre back was captain of Manchester United when they were relegated to the second tier of the Football League in 1973–74? With which Scottish club did he win his first international cap? (1)

Answers on p.452

Quiz 78: World Cup 8 (30)

1 Which Scotland-based striker scored a late, late penalty to give Greece a win over the Côte d'Ivoire and knock them out of the 2014 World Cup finals? (1)

2 Which major edifice was constructed to host the 1950 World Cup Final? (1)

3 Fill in the gaps in this Brazilian team that won the 1958 World Cup Final 5-2 against Sweden: Gylmar; RIGHT BACK, Bellini, Nilton Santos; Zito, CENTRAL MIDFIELD, Orlando, LEFT MIDFIELD; RIGHT WING, CENTRE FORWARD, Pelé. (5)

4 Who was England's first-choice centre half going into the 1962 World Cup finals but missed out after contracting dysentery? What, in part, was the reason this player won no further England caps? (2)

5 Sweden's centre forward scored twice in a crucial home match to ensure Sweden qualified for the 1970 World Cup finals at France's expense; who was he and with which club had he just won the European Cup? (2)

6 Who were a surprise package at the 1974 World Cup finals tournament, beating Argentina and Italy and scoring seven against Haiti in their group? Who scored a hat-trick in their game against Haiti? (2)

7 Brazil were surprisingly eliminated from the 1966 World Cup after losing two of their group games 3-1 to which two European countries? And what was the mitigating factor in their demise? (3)

8 After draws with Yugoslavia (creditable) and Honduras (disappointing) in their first two games of the 1982 World Cup finals, Northern Ireland had to win their last group game to go through. They did. Who did they beat, where was the game played, who scored the Northern Ireland goal, who was sent off for doing very little as a poor referee came under pressure, and who was the only teenager playing in the game? (5)

9 Jürgen Sparwasser scored the only goal for East Germany in a famous 1-0 win over which opponents in a group game at the 1974 World Cup finals? (1)

10 Who scored a late consolation for West Germany in the 1982 World Cup Final to make him the first European player to score in two World Cup finals? (1).

11 Which African nation qualified for the World Cup for the first time in 1982, but went out in the group stage despite not losing a match? (1)

12 Which successful Scottish club manager was in temporary charge of the Scotland team at the 1986 World Cup finals tournament following the death of Jock Stein? Which side did they have to get past in a two-legged play-off before qualifying – was it Australia, Iran, Japan or New Zealand? (1)

13 Which was the only quarter-final match at the 1986 World Cup finals not to be decided by penalties? (2)

14 Sergio Goycochea got his chance to play in a World Cup Final in 1990 after an injury to which 'keeper in Argentina's second match of the tournament put him out of action? (1)

15 Who scored England's consolation goal in their 4-1 thrashing by Germany in the Last 16 of the 2010 World Cup finals? And whose shot came down off the bar behind the line, only for the linesman and referee to fail to give the goal? (2)

Answers on p.453

Quiz 79: Republic of Ireland 2 (30)

1 Dundalk, Liverpool (Bradford City), Aston Villa**, Liverpool (Crystal Palace), Aston Villa, Coventry City, Walsall – which Irish mainstay's club career path is mapped out here? (1)

2 Which much-capped Republic of Ireland international was once substituted for his brother, Pierce (who won 7 caps) in a match against England)? (1)

3 Who made a good start to his international career with 4 goals from midfield for the Republic of Ireland in 6 matches, but hasn't played for his country since inventing the death of a grandmother to go and see his girlfriend in Cork instead of playing in an international match? (1)

4 Which Portsmouth midfield player scored Republic of Ireland's crucial equaliser in Dublin against Northern Ireland in 1993, securing qualification for the 1994 World Cup finals by the narrowest of margins, on goals scored, after they finished level on points with the third-placed team and shared an identical goal difference? Who was the third-placed team, who went into the campaign full of confidence as the reigning European champions? (2)

5 Which was the first major tournament for which the Republic of Ireland team qualified? (1)

6 Who scored the goal that gave Republic of Ireland a memorable 1-0 victory over England at the 1988 European Championships? (1)

7 Who became Republic of Ireland's first player-manager 1973? Of which English club was he also player-manager for the first couple of years of his tenure with Ireland? (2)

8 How many players with surnames beginning 'O apostrophe' have won caps for the Republic of Ireland (to November 2015)? (1 point for 3 either way) And which is the most common surname in that style amongst Irish international footballers? (2)

9 Which two Republic of Ireland internationals featured in both games of the feisty FA Cup Final between Leeds United and Chelsea in 1970? (2)

10 Which six players have passed 100 caps for Republic of Ireland (all of them played in the twenty-first century)? (6)

11 Which former captain of the Republic of Ireland won 46 caps between 1976 and 1985 while playing for a series of relatively unfashionable clubs (Leyton Orient, Luton Town, Brighton & Hove Albion, West Bromwich Albion)? (1)

12 Who received his first cap at full back for the Republic of Ireland shortly after his move to Manchester United in 1990? With which less fashionable club had he been an underrated performer for the previous four years? (2)

13 Before winning 71 caps as a centre half for the Republic of Ireland, Kevin Moran represented Dublin at which sport, winning an All-Ireland title? (1)

14 With which club did Andy Reid win his first cap for the Republic of Ireland in 2003? And where was he when he earned a recall in 2013 after a five-year absence from the national side? (2)

15 Here are twelve Republic of Ireland internationals: Keith Andrews, Gary Breen, Stephen Carr, Tony Cascarino, Kevin Doyle, Tony Galvin, Ian Harte, Ray Houghton, Kevin Sheedy, Steve Staunton, Sean St Ledger, Mickey Walsh. Which five were actually born in the Republic? (5)

Asterisks (**) indicate that the player in question made more than two hundred league appearances for the club.

Answers on p.453

Quiz 80: Football League 8 (30)

1 The 1907–08 season was the first in which the Football League was won by a team who much later went on to win the Premier League – who was the team? (1)

2 Which future England manager played right back in the Tottenham Hotspur team that won the league title in 1950–51? (1)

3 Which four West Bromwich Albion strikers have finished as the First Division top scorer in the years since the Second World War (the last occasion was in the early 1970s)? (4)

4 In Arsenal's Double-winning season of 1970–71, only three players played in every league game, the goalkeeper, the Scottish international skipper and the man who would end his Arsenal days with a new appearance record: who were they? (3)

5 Which England one-cap-wonder scored four goals for Ipswich Town as they demolished West Bromwich Albion 7-0 in November 1976? (1)

6 In their title-winning season of 1980–81 Aston Villa were fortunate enough to be able to field the same midfield quartet in every league game – who were these players, three Englishmen and a Scot? (4)

7 Who was Reading's senior pro and top scorer in both their promotion years of 1983–84 (Fourth Division to Third) and 1985–86 (Third to Second)? (1)

8 What was unique about the Double Kenny Dalglish won with Liverpool in 1986? (1)

9 For whom did England full back Mick Mills make more than 600 appearances? And where did he add another 100+ after a move, aged thirty-three? (2)

10 Who scored 28 goals as Brighton won promotion from the bottom division in 2000–01, winning Division 3 by ten points? Who was the club's manager that season? Which future Wales international top scored for Cardiff City as they followed Brighton up in second spot? (3)

11 Who scored a hat-trick for Leeds United in a 6-0 thrashing of Oldham Athletic in 1984, and later scored more than 100 league goals for his victims that day during Oldham's most successful spell? (1)

12 Whose goals shot Manchester City back to the Premier League as they won promotion for a second successive season in 1999–2000? And who was the former West Ham United playmaker who pulled the strings from midfield? (2)

13 Wendy Toms was the first woman to do what? (2)

14 Who won the Division 2 (third tier) title a year after winning Division 3 in 2001–02? And who scored more than thirty goals for the club for the second consecutive season? (2)

15 Whose 25 goals helped Leeds United out of a brief spell in League 1 (third tier) in 2009–10? Which Premier League club picked up the out of contract player in the summer but discovered he wasn't up to the top flight? (2)

Answers on p.454

Quiz 81: General 21 (30)

1 At the end of a fourth round FA Cup tie in 1980 Manchester City manager John Bond jumped down to the players' tunnel to commiserate with the losers, who had just been thrashed 6-0 by his team; why? (1)

2 In 2005, who tried to sue Gary Lineker for defamation of character after Lineker wrote an unflattering newspaper piece about him? (1)

3 The Jamaica squad for the 1998 World Cup finals reflected the Caribbean diaspora to England, with seven English-born and England-based players present. Two played for Portsmouth, two for Derby County, two for Wimbledon and one for Chelsea: name them all. (7)

4 What was the prospective name for Robert Maxwell's planned merger of Oxford United and Reading? (1)

5 Which former Premiership goalkeeper competed on the BBC show *Strictly Come Dancing* in 2006? Which other former footballer proved more adept on the dance floor in the 2011 version of the show? (2)

6 Which recent England international sports Ivanhoe as one of his middle names – is it (a) Glen Johnson (b) Paul Scholes (c) Jermaine Defoe or (d) Emile Heskey? (1)

7 Who is the only Scottish striker to have scored at three different World Cup tournaments? (1)

8 Who were the four members of the Brazilian squad at the 2014 World Cup finals who were on the books at Chelsea at the time? (4)

9 Fans of which club rioted and chanted racist slogans at their opponent's black players as their team were beaten by Derby County in the 1994 play-offs semi-final for a chance to win promotion to the Premier League? (1)

10 Which West Midlands side reached the Football League for the first time in 2000, having been denied a place six years previously because their ground was not up to scratch? Which former Liverpool star was their manager? Who earned the club a £700,000 windfall when he moved from West Bromwich Albion to Coventry City for £5M, invoking a 15 per cent sell-on clause for his original club? (3)

11 In 2006 German international Didi Hamann left Liverpool for which other Premier League club (on a pre-contract agreement), but instead signed for Manchester City a day later? (1)

12 Which characterful goalkeeper joined Liverpool from Vancouver Whitecaps in 1981? For which country did he win 33 international caps? (2)

13 Which is the least populated country to have played in a World Cup finals tournament? And which is the least populated to win a game at the finals? (2)

14 Who was the goalkeeper in the 1936–37 title-winning Manchester City side who went on to win 19 caps for England after the Second World War? What unfortunate fate befell the player after he retired? (2)

15 Which Northern Ireland inside forward, a key member of the 1958 World Cup squad, won the league title two years later with Burnley? (1)

Answers on p.454

Quiz 82: Global 3 (30)

1 Mohamed Al-Deayea played at the 1994 World Cup finals and ended his career in 2006 as the second most capped player in football history. For which country did he keep goal? (1)

2 Iván Hurtado ended a great 22-year international career in 2014, aged forty; for which South American country did he win 168 caps? (1)

3 Nacional, Groningen, Ajax*, Liverpool*, Barcelona – whose career path is this? (1)

4 Efe Sodje played his league football in the lower divisions of the English league, but he also made a dozen appearances for which strong African country around the turn of the century? (1)

5 Rory Fallon scored the goal that earned New Zealand a place in the 2010 World Cup finals, being the only goal in a two-legged play-off against Bahrain. For which club was Fallon playing – was it (a) Plymouth Argyle (b) Brisbane Roar (c) Ayr United or (d) Kashima Antlers? (1)

6 Premier League players Junior Hoilett, Tomasz Radzinski and Paul Stalteri have all played international football for which country? (1)

7 Costa Rica, Mexico, Canada, Haiti, Japan, Spain, United States: which two of these countries have never taken part in the Copa América as a guest nation? Which one of the six reached the Final of the competition in 1993 and 2001? (3)

8 Who scored Argentina's goals in their 2-1 victory over Mexico in the Final of the 1993 Copa América? (1)

9 This is the Uruguay team that won the 2011 Copa América Final 3-0 against Paraguay – can you fill in the missing players (4-4-2)? MISSING (Lazio); Maxi Pereira (Benfica), MISSING (Fenerbahce), Sebastián Coates (Nacional), Martín Cáceres (Sevilla) (sub; Diego Godín, Atlético Madrid); Álvaro González (Lazio), MISSING (Bologna) (sub: Sebastián Eguren, Sporting de Gijon), Egidio Arévalo Ríos (Botafogo), Álvaro Pereira (Porto) (sub: MISSING, Napoli); MISSING (Atlético Madrid), MISSING (Liverpool) (6)

10 Egypt have won the African Cup of Nations a record seven times; which other three countries have won three or more titles, up to and including the 2015 competition? (3)

11 Who scored Nigeria's equaliser as they came from 2-0 down to draw with Cameroon in the 2000 African Cup of Nations Final? Which Liverpool (but West Ham-bound) central defender scored the decisive penalty in the shoot-out to give Cameroon victory? (2)

12 Hossam Hassan was capped 169 times for Egypt, and Ibrahim Hassan 125 times. Are they (a) father and son (b) brothers (c) brothers-in-law or (d) twin brothers? (2)

13 Which consistent and powerful centre forward had made most appearances (nine) in the top three for the African Footballer of the Year award, but only won twice? (1)

14 Why was there only a one year gap between the African Cup of Nations in 2012 and 2013? (1)

15 Which five players have won more than 100 caps for Argentina? (to March 2016, no one else will reach this target for a couple of years – two of this 100 club are still playing, all are recent) (5)

Asterisk (*) indicates that the player in question made more than one hundred league appearances for the club.

Answers on p.455

Quiz 83: Premier League 11 (40)

1　Chelsea have employed a number of Brazilians in recent years; who was their first player from that country, and from which struggling Premier League club did they buy him in 1999? For which other two Premier League clubs did he later play after his season at Stamford Bridge? (4)

2　In 2003 Chelsea, flush with money from new owner Roman Abramovic's ample piggy-bank, paid £24M to strengthen the left side of their team; which two players did they buy, from Blackburn Rovers and Southampton? (2)

3　On 31 May 1995, after the end of the season, who was the marquee free transfer signing unveiled by Chelsea manager Glenn Hoddle? Which Italian club released the player? (2)

4　'Pizzagate'. Who refereed the stormy affair at Old Trafford that saw Manchester United end Arsenal's unbeaten run at 49 Premier League games? Who scored a penalty and avoided a red card for a crude challenge, but was handed a retrospective ban? And who scored United's second, clinching goal on his birthday? (3)

5　Which two wide players scored hat-tricks as Arsenal beat Southampton 6-1 ten days before the same two teams were due to meet in the 2003 FA Cup Final (only one of the two played in the Final)? (2)

6　Who received the eleventh red card of his career playing for Manchester United against Sunderland in August 2002? Who was on the receiving end of his elbow after making sarcastic observations about some of the claims made by the perpetrator in his autobiography? (2)

7　Who was the controversial Wimbledon owner and Chairman who scribbled graffiti on the walls of West Ham's dressing room in 1993? Which club would he later buy, claiming he would turn them into a Premier League force (he never even got them into the top flight)? (2)

8 Which two players appeared in the 2015 African Cup of Nations for Algeria and were then unexpectedly mixed up in the title race the following season? (2)

9 Who was sacked as manager of Blackburn Rovers in December 2010? Who was his assistant, disastrously appointed as the new manager by the club's owners? Who were the family presiding over the club's fortunes? (3)

10 Who, in 1999, was the first English-based player to be voted African Footballer of the Year, and which club was he with? (2)

11 Which teenager did Arsenal buy for £5M in June, 2008, and from which club? (2)

12 An Englishman, a Russian and an American are the only players to score a hat-trick for Fulham in the Premier League – who are they? (3)

13 Which experienced Dutch manager was brought in towards the end of the 2014–15 Premier League season to help Sunderland stave off relegation? Who was sacked to make way for him? (2)

14 Middlesbrough were the first English Premier League club to start importing Brazilians in a major way; can you name the five that have played for the club in the top flight? (5)

15 Mark Schwarzer has made more than 500 appearances in the Premier League – for which four clubs? (4)

Answers on p.456

Quiz 84: Champions League 7 (30)

1 Who owns five Champions League winner's medals, earned with 18 years between the first and last? (1)

2 Which French side became the country's first team to reach the European Cup Final in 1976? (1)

3 Defeat by which Italian side in the 1964–65 European Cup semi-final left Liverpool manager Bill Shankly fuming about a highly debatable refereeing display? (1)

4 Steaua Bucharest against Barcelona in the European Cup Final of 1986 was the first instance of what scoreline in the competition's Finals history? (1)

5 Which Spanish side turned around a 4-1 deficit from the first leg in Milan in a 2004 Champions League quarter-final before losing to the eventual winners in the semi-final? (1)

6 Who were Manchester United's last opponents before the Munich air disaster? (1)

7 Of the AC Milan players who won successive European Cups in 1989 and 1990, name the two that have subsequently managed in the Premiership? (2)

8 Which other English side did Manchester United beat en route to the 2009 Champions League Final against Barcelona? Who scored twice in the away leg to put the seal on a comfortable 4-1 aggregate victory? (2)

9 Who scored twice in each leg as Manchester United crushed Milan 7-2 in the Last 16 of the 2009–10 Champions League? (1)

10 A Champions League quarter-final second leg was abandoned after flares were thrown onto the pitch: which two teams from the same country were battling for a place in the semi-finals? What was the score at the time the teams were taken off? Who was the goalkeeper struck by a flare? (4)

11 Who was the captain and playmaker of the Valencia side who beat Barcelona in the semi-final of the 2000 Champions League and lost to Real Madrid in another all-Spanish encounter? For which Premier League club did he sign in 2004? (2)

12 Who scored twice as Chelsea took a 3-0 lead against Barcelona before half time in the first leg of their 2000 Champions League quarter-final? Who was the referee in the second leg who gave Barcelona an extra-time penalty that proved decisive? Which Brazilian scored the penalty? (3)

13 Which country has produced the most coaches who have led a team to a Champions League Final? (1)

14 This is the Liverpool team that won the European Cup for the club in 1977, but with a few players missing. They are all English, can you name them (4-4-2)? MISSING; MISSING, Tommy Smith, MISSING, Joey Jones; Ian Callaghan, MISSING, Terry McDermott, MISSING; MISSING, Steve Heighway (6)

15 Three English clubs have competed in the modern Champions League group stage for one solitary season – which three? (3)

Answers on p.456

Quiz 85: General 22 (30)

1 At which sport did Gary and Phil Neville's sister, Tracy, represent England? Which of the Neville brothers is Tracy's twin? (2)

2 In a 1984 league match between Chelsea and West Ham United, Chelsea's Colin Lee saw his penalty saved but he knocked in the rebound only for the referee to order the kick retaken – what happened then? (1)

3 The last seven have been: Mexico, Hungary, Morocco, Italy, Argentina, England, Italy. What? (1)

4 What was the revised capacity for Wembley after safety work following the Hillsborough disaster – was it 75,000, 82,500 or 92,500? (1)

5 Which Scotland centre forward swapped Manchester for Milan in 1981? (1)

6 Who joined Blackburn Rovers late in their promotion season of 1991–92, but left after playing only six games to be replaced by a more prolific namesake? To which Scottish side did he move, where he enjoyed a late career purple patch that brought him seven Scotland caps in his thirties? (2)

7 Who were the last father and son to be involved in an FA Cup Final? (2)

8 At the 2000 European Championships, who did the Netherlands smash 6-1 in the quarter-final? Which Barcelona player scored a hat-trick? And which player, who left the Premier League for Barça after the tournament, scored two? Which other four Barça players took part in the match? (7)

9 Dean Windass played and scored goals for a number of clubs in his long career: for which two did he score more than 75 goals? (2)

10 In 1996–97 four North West clubs within a twenty-mile radius won the four divisions of the league system; which four? (4)

11 Which two of these Asian/Oceanic countries have never qualified for a World Cup finals tournament: China, Iran, Kuwait, Malaysia, New Zealand, Samoa, United Arab Emirates? (2)

12 Which Italian club lost 18 squad members in an air crash in 1949? (1)

13 Laureano Étame-Mayer came on a substitute for Cameroon against Chile at the 1998 World Cup finals and promptly got sent off; under what name did he become familiar to Premier League fans? (1)

14 Who were the last team to play in the top flight of English Football who have subsequently fallen out of the league's top four flights? (1)

15 Before going into management with Manchester United, Matt Busby played before the war for which two clubs, making more than 200 appearances for one and over 100 for the other? (2)

Answers on p.457

Quiz 86: Football League 9 (30)

1 In 1987–88, who became the first team to drop out of the top flight under the new play-off system, whereby the team placed 18th (of 21) in the First Division, engage in a knockout tournament with the teams placed 3rd, 4th and 5th in the Second Division? Who took their, turning over a 1-0 deficit from the first leg with goals from Bernie Slaven and Trevor Senior? And why were four teams relegated and only three promoted? (3)

2 Which two clubs did the Football League and FA Cup Double in the nineteenth century? (2)

3 Post-war coach Arthur Rowe developed a style of play that became known as push-and-run; the giving of a quick pass followed by lively movement to receive a return. Which team did he lead to the league title in 1950–51 using this style? (1)

4 In 1974, which referee sent off two players in a Manchester derby, then removed both teams for twenty minutes when the miscreants refused to go? Who were the players involved? How did the referee ensure the dismissed players did not take the field again? What was the score in the game? (5)

5 Who finished runners up in the First Division for three consecutive seasons in 1970, '71 and '72? Who matched this from 1999–2001? (1)

6 Which Blackpool player was Second Division top scorer in 1976–77, but is better remembered for a spectacular goal on *Match of the Day* two years earlier that won Goal of the Season? (1)

7 Who played as a striker at Chelsea but won the league with Aston Villa in 1980–81 after converting to an attacking right back? (1)

8 In which season were 5th to 12th in the First Division of the Football League placed as follows: Norwich City, Wimbledon, Luton Town, Nottingham Forest, Watford, Coventry City, Manchester United, Southampton? Who filled the four spots above these sides? (5)

9   Where did Gary Blissett of Brentford and John Uzzell of Torquay United end up after an on-field incident in December 1991? (1)

10 Which Leicester City player caused a furore when he wore black tights and gloves during a cold snap in the mid-1970s? (1)

11 Darren and Marcus Bent, while unrelated, have played together at which two clubs? (2)

12 Who was the Scottish winger, later a popular and intelligent pundit, signed by manager John Neal in 1983 to help the club get back into the top flight? Who was the selling club – was it St Johnstone, Kilmarnock, Dumbarton or Clyde? (2)

13 In 1994–95, which combative Fulham player became the first player to rack up 61 disciplinary points in the 21 years since the system came into place? (1)

14 In 2001–02, despite Crystal Palace finishing only tenth in Division 1 (second tier), two of their strikers scored more than twenty goals: who were they? (2)

15 Who was appointed manager of Blackpool in late 2012 but resigned after a mere eleven games? Which other Lancashire club did he join, lasting only sixty-seven days after they went to all the trouble to poach him from their neighbours? (2)

Answers on p.458

Quiz 87: World Cup 9 (30)

1   Who won a World Cup winner's medal with France despite being born in Ghana? (1)

2   Which city housed a stadium used in the 1934 World Cup that was named after Italian dictator Benito Mussolini? Which club now play their home games in the same, albeit revamped and renamed, stadium? (2)

3   Which four coaches have led Germany or West Germany to victory in a World Cup Final? (4)

4   In the 1994 World Cup finals Cameroon played a game in which they had two players on the pitch who were separated by an age gap of twenty-four years; who were the players? (2)

5   Who put paid to Italy in the group stage of the 1966 World Cup finals, beating them 1-0 in the World Cup's biggest shock to date and sending them home to a greeting of rotten fruit from their dismayed supporters? (1)

6   Both second phase groups at the 1974 World Cup finals went to the last round of games to be decided; which two sides were beaten by the Netherlands and West Germany in these de facto semi-finals? (2)

7   In qualifying for the 1982 World Cup finals, which team failed, for the first and only time since the Second World War, to win their usual qualification place from one of the less powerful regions? (1)

8   Who was the only member of the 1982 England World Cup squad who was playing abroad? With which club had he just finished second in the Bundesliga behind Hamburg? (2)

9   Who scored a late equaliser for Italy against Nigeria at the 1994 World Cup finals, and then scored again in injury time to get Italy through? Which Premier League star was sent off in the game (a shocking decision) twelve minutes after coming on as a substitute? (2)

10 Who became the first man to play in two World Cup Finals in 1934 and who did he represent? (3)

11 Which young Real Madrid striker scored four times as Spain walloped a disappointing Denmark 5-1 in the Last 16 of the 1986 World Cup? (1)

12 Atlanta, Chicago, Dallas, Detroit, Orlando, Palo Alto, Washington DC – which two of these seven cities did NOT host any games during the 1994 World Cup finals in the USA? (2)

13 Which former Premier League striker was playing for Sydney in Australia when he captained his country, Trinidad and Tobago, at the 2006 World Cup finals? (1)

14 Which East European striker, who spent most of the last decade playing in England, was picked for the 2006 World Cup finals by the national coach who gave him his debut in 2004, and who also happened to be his father? (1)

15 England's opening game of the 2014 World Cup finals saw five Liverpool players selected in the starting line-up: who were they? (5)

Answers on p.458

Quiz 88: FA Cup 4 (30)

1 Who scored in the 1955 FA Cup Final for Newcastle in less than a minute? Who broke this record for the fastest goal in a Final in 1997 playing for Chelsea? Who were the two teams on the receiving end? (4)

2 Who was unfortunate enough to score six in an FA Cup match against Luton Town only to see the game abandoned due to bad weather before the end? What happened next? (1)

3 Whose 1903 FA Cup Final victory was the biggest in the tournament's history? (1)

4 Roger Osborne scored the only goal of the game in an FA Cup Final to give which side their only victory in the competition? (1)

5 What links the FA Cup Finals in these years – 1967, 1975, 1982 and 2002? (1)

6 Which player was substituted in an FA Cup Final after an ineffectual performance, only to score a dazzling winner in the replay? (1)

7 He scored the winner away at Alex Ferguson's Manchester United in the FA Cup fourth round, two goals against Sheffield Wednesday in the quarter-final, another in the semi against Leeds, and a flying header to win the Cup. Who was he, and with which team did he have his glory days? (2)

8 Who are the six overseas coaches who have won the FA Cup as Chelsea manager? (6)

9 Roy Essandoh's goal knocked Leicester City out the FA Cup in 2001 and sent which third-tier side to the semi-final? Which former FA Cup winner was their manager? (2)

10 Who were the last team to field a side of eleven English players at the start of an FA Cup Final? And which was the first side to field no English players? (2)

11   Who missed the crucial penalty as Arsenal beat Manchester United in a shoot-out at the end of the 2005 FA Cup Final? (1)

12   Who scored Wigan Athletic's late winner to settle the 2013 FA Cup Final? Who were their opponents and which of them was sent off towards the end of the match? (3)

13   Who was the first goalkeeper to captain an FA Cup-winning side? (1)

14   Who was the first Argentinian to play in an FA Cup Final? (2 points if you get this) (2)

15   Which two members of Southampton's FA Cup winning side from 1976 had scored in previous Finals for Sheffield Wednesday and Chelsea? (2)

Answers on p.459

Quiz 89: General 23 (30)

1 Before signing for Tottenham Hotspur, where he was a mainstay for almost two decades, Gary Mabbutt played more than 100 league games for which club? (1)

2 In an England football context, what happened at the El Tequendama Hotel in Bogotá, Colombia? (2)

3 The launch in 1990 of which radio channel vastly increased the BBC's sports output? (1)

4 What was unusual about the squad numbers the Argentina players used at the 1978 World Cup finals – (a) they were written in Roman numerals (b) they were spelt out in Spanish (c) the players were numbered alphabetically by surname or (d) the players were numbered in descending order of age? (1)

5 Which former World Cup referee became a regular on TV's *It's A Knockout*? (1)

6 Which Scottish club has played in two English FA Cup finals? (1)

7 Who made his debut for West Ham United against Manchester United in September 1958, and who – rather symbolically – retired at the end of the same season after more than 500 appearances in a famous gold shirt? (2)

8 Who were the last team to lose the FA Cup Final in a replay before the rule change meant penalties instead of a second match? (1)

9 Who was arrested while working as a pundit for French TV following a scuffle in the press area at the Rose Bowl during the 1994 World Cup finals ? (1)

10 In England's group at the 1996 European Championships, who held them to a rather dull 1-1 draw in the opening game? Who scored a stunning goal (England's second) to wrap up a tight game against Scotland? And who scored twice each as England produced one of their best performances to destroy the Netherlands 4-1? (4)

11 The FA Cup Finals of 1992, 1994, 1996, 1998, 2000, 2002, 2004, 2005, 2008 and 2009 were refereed by some of the most high profile officials of the last twenty years: how many can you name? (10)

12 Who took his first club coaching job when he took over at Bayern Munich in summer, 2008? (1)

13 Leicester City*, Liverpool*, Birmingham City, Wigan Athletic, Aston Villa, Newcastle Jets, Bolton Wanderers – which England international's long career is this, spent mostly in the Premier League? (1)

14 In seven seasons, starting in 1937–38 and broken by the war, the same two teams finished runners-up in the First Division without either of them winning the title: which two teams? (2)

15 Which club's PA announcer was warned by police at half-time and later sacked by the club for making inflammatory remarks about a referee during a home game against Bolton in 1995? (1)

Asterisk (*) indicates that the player in question made more than one hundred league appearances for the club.

Answers on p.460

Quiz 90: Premier League 12 (40)

1 Chelsea nearly matched Arsenal's unbeaten season the following year (2004–05): which side, who finished eighth, managed to beat them in October and force a draw at Stamford Bridge in the Spring? Which future Chelsea player scored the only goal of these two matches? And which of their title rivals managed two draws? (3)

2 In 2006 *The Sunday Times* picked its Top 10 Premiership New Boys to watch during the coming season. But which clubs signed Didier Zokora, Mark González and Denny Landzaat? (3)

3 Perhaps surprisingly none of the players with the most yellow cards in Premier League history are defenders. Which veteran (still playing 2015–16) tops the list with 109? Which feisty midfield player comes second with 100? Which two players lie joint third, one a combative centre forward, one a midfielder whose manager once suggested he might ban him from tackling! (4)

4 Which celebrity fan (and a genuine one) joined the board of Norwich City in November 1996, and is now (February 2016) the joint majority shareholder with Michael Wynn Jones? Which other celebrity also served as a Director from 2010–15 and which former MP was appointed Chairman in 2015? (3)

5 Which former playing stalwart was appointed as stand-in manager when George Graham was sacked by Arsenal for his part in the 'bung' allegations? And who took over as full-time manager at the end of the season? From which club did Arsenal poach their new boss? (3)

6 Which striker cost Liverpool £7M in the summer of 2005, having made his England debut against Colombia in May? Who were the selling club? (2)

7 Which two young Arsenal defenders were the only English-based members of the Switzerland 2006 World Cup squad? (2)

8 Who scored more Premier League goals for Manchester United – David Beckham or Eric Cantona? How about Cantona vs Andrew Cole? Or Paul Scholes vs Ruud van Nistelrooy? (3)

9 Who was the first Latvian to play in the Premier League, and for which club did he play more than 100 games in England (at time of setting this question he is manager of the national team) ? (1)

10 Chilean international Gary Medel played a single season in the Premier League with which newly promoted team, who promptly went back down? (1)

11 Which manager looked a bit lost the last time West Ham United were relegated in 2010–11? (1)

12 Who, in April 2015, became the first player to score a hat-trick in the Premier League for Crystal Palace when he netted three times against Sunderland? (1)

13 Which four clubs (to 2015–16) have spent just a single season in the Premier League? (4)

14 Name the four Iceland internationals who played for Bolton Wanderers in the Premier League (4)

15 For which five Premier League clubs has James Milner played (to 2015–16)? (5)

Answers on p.460

Quiz 91: European Competitions 5 (30)

1 Which major Italian club play their home games at the Stadio Artemio Franchi? (1)

2 If you are a fan of PAOK, in which city, the country's second largest, do you watch your team's home games? (1)

3 Up to and including 2014–15, which two sides have won the French championship ten times? (2)

4 The Bundesliga top scorer in 2014–15 was the little heralded Alexander Meier, who has two caps to his name for Germany; for which club has he scored more than 100 goals in over 300 Bundesliga matches? (1)

5 Which five English teams won the UEFA Cup or its predecessor, the Inter Cities Fairs Cup, between 1967–68 and 1972–73? (5)

6 Which of these clubs has never played in European club competition: Burnley, Blackburn Rovers, Stoke City, Sheffield United? (1)

7 It will surprise no one to learn that Bayern Munich have won the German title a lot more (twenty-five times) than any of their rivals: which other eight German sides have won four or more national championships? (8)

8 Which former Premier League 'reject' scored the extra-time goal that gave Atlético Madrid a 2-1 win over Fulham in the 2010 Europa League Final? (1)

9 Which Argentinian managed Atlético Madrid when they won the 2012 Europa League and La Liga in 2014? How many of the players who won the UEFA Cup in 2010 for the club were in the starting line-up in 2012? (2)

10 Who scored his first Liverpool goal in six years and only his third in 363 matches as Liverpool beat Lithuanian side Kaunas in preliminary qualifying for the 2005–06 Champions League? (1)

11   Which Dutch star played club football for Groningen, Ajax, PSV Eindhoven, Barcelona and Feyenoord, as well as scoring 14 goals in 78 matches for the national team? What is the name of his elder brother? Where was the brother employed at the start of the 2015–16 season? (3)

12   Which Dutch striker top scored in the 2011–12 Bundesliga as a Schalke 04 player? (1)

13   Up to and including 2014–15 Juventus have most Italian championship wins with 31 – which two clubs are next in the list with eighteen each? (1)

14   Shamrock Rovers and Bohemian FC are rivals in which city? (1)

15   In 1995, whose last-minute equaliser against Rotor Volgograd preserved Manchester United's unbeaten home European record? (1)

Answers on p.461

Quiz 92: Women's Football 3 (30)

1 Germany have won the last six UEFA Women's Championships – which four teams have they beaten in the various Finals? (4)

2 What was the less than glamorous name of the stadium in Carson, California that hosted the 2003 Women's World Cup Final – was it (a) The Walmart Stadium (b) IBM Park (c) The Home Depot Center (d) The KFC Sports Bowl? (1)

3 Which five American women's soccer players have scored more than 100 international goals? (5)

4 Who captained England at the 2015 Women's World Cup in Canada? (1)

5 Who replaced Hope Powell as manager of England's women's football team in 2013 and led the team to third place at the 2015 World Cup finals? (1)

6 What stage did England reach in the 1999 and 2003 Women's World Cup finals tournaments? (1)

7 The Women's Football Association was formed in England in which year – was it 1899, 1946, 1969 or 1990? (1)

8 Which team benefited from an extra place being allocated to the top division of the Women's Super League in 2015, earning promotion back to the top flight after being relegatd in 2013? (1)

9 This is the England Women's team that played in the Final of the 2009 European Championships against Germany – they lost 6-2 but for an hour the game was tighter than that suggests. Can you name the missing players (4-3-3)? Rachel Brown (Everton); MISSING (Boston Breakers), Anita Asante (Sky Blue FC), MISSING (Arsenal, captain), MISSING (Chelsea); Karen Carney (Chicago Red Stars), MISSING (Everton), Katie Chapman (Arsenal) (sub: Emily Westwood, Everton); MISSING (St Louis Athletica) (sub: Lianne Sanderson, Chelsea), MISSING (Boston Breakers), Jill Scott (Everton). (6)

10 If a two-legged cup tie between two top English women's teams were played at Wheatsheaf Park in Staines and Meadow Park in Borehamwood, Hertfordshire, which two teams would be playing each other? (2)

11 Who joined Croydon Ladies from the Lionesses in 1991 and led them to a league and cup Double in 1996? With which men's league club are her former club, the Lionesses, associated? (2)

12 Where does women's football operate a W-League? (1)

13 The United States have played in all five Finals of the Women's Soccer tournament at the Olympic Games: who are the only team to have beaten them to the Gold Medal (in 2000)? And who did they beat in the Finals of 2004 and 2008? (2)

14 If the Australian men's soccer team are known as the Socceroos, what is the nickname of the women's team? (1)

15 London Bees, who play in the second flight of the FA Women's Super League, are affiliated with which men's league club? (1)

Answers on p.462

Quiz 93: General 24 (30)

1 Belgian stars Lorenzo Staelens, Franky van der Elst and Jan Ceulemans all made more than 300 appearances for which top Belgian club? (1)

2 In December 1993 Howard Kendall resigned as Everton manager after the board blocked the signing of which Manchester United striker? (1)

3 The Leeds United team that turned out for the 1965 FA Cup Final against Liverpool included one of the English game's first high-profile black players, a South African-born winger at Leeds; who was he? (1)

4 What were the four big continental European clubs managed by Bobby Robson? (4)

5 Which five English players started the 2005 League Cup Final between Chelsea and Liverpool? (5)

6 Which four London clubs did Terry Venables appear for in his playing career, and which of the four has he never managed? (5)

7 Which Scottish international winger of the 1980s and '90s wrote an occasional column for the *New Musical Express*? (1)

8 Who managed the Great Britain men's and women's soccer teams at the 2012 Olympic Games? (2)

9 Who were the only team to beat Hungary during a 51-match run between 1950 and 1955? (1)

10 Gudjon Thordarson (Iceland) and Dutchman Johan Boskamp were the first two (distinctly unsuccessful) managers of which English league club? Who had two spells as the club's manager either side of Boskamp? (2)

11 Jon Stead, Filipe Morais, Andy Halliday and Mark Yeates scored the goals in what remarkable result in January 2015? (2)

12 Who, in 1995–96, was the last British manager of Turkish club Galatasaray, managing to provoke a near-riot when he planted a Galatasaray flag in the middle of Fenerbahce's pitch after a local derby? (1)

13 On what grounds did Charlton Athletic attempt to have their 4-1 Premier League defeat in January 2001 replayed – was it (a) because Chelsea fans threw fireworks at their goalkeeper (b) because the sand on the waterlogged Stamford Bridge pitch constituted an illegal artificial pitch (c) because there was no hot water in the visitors' changing room which gave the home team an unfair advantage or (d) because the car park at Stamford Bridge was iced over and the players had to walk half an hour to the ground, which constituted an unfair advantage? (1)

14 Which club, in 1954–55, won their first league title with a record low number of 52 points (for a 22-team division, two points for a win)? (1)

15 Which side secured promotion as early as March, the first team to do so since the Second World War, while running away with Division 2 (third tier) in 1997–98? Who was their manager? (2)

Answers on p.462

Quiz 94: European Championships 3 (30)

1 Who scored both goals as England won 2-0 in Glasgow in a Euro 2000 qualification play-off? Who scored Scotland's goal in their consolatory 1-0 win at Wembley in the return? (2)

2 France hosted the first European Championships in 1960, with only four teams in the finals; which Communist bloc country beat the hosts 5-4, coming from 4-2 down with fifteen minutes to go? Who beat the winners in the first Final with goals from Slava Metreveli and the forgotten but potent striker Viktor Ponedelnik? (2)

3 Which three sides have beaten the Soviet Union in a European Championships Final? (3)

4 Which Belgian-based striker scored a hat-trick as the Netherlands beat their neighbours and rivals 5-0 in the first leg of their quarter-final qualifier for the 1976 European Championships? (1)

5 Ian Stewart only managed a couple of goals for Northern Ireland but one of them was enough to beat which mighty footballing power in a European Championship qualifying match in November 1982? Who was Stewart playing for at the time – was it (a) Crusaders (b) Newcastle United (c) Preston North End or (d) Queens Park Rangers? And which young Manchester United player scored as Northern Ireland completed a remarkable double in the away fixture, albeit after their opponents had already qualified? (3)

6 England had an abject European Championships in 1988; which two players, one towards the end of his international career and the other at the beginning, scored their goals in 3-1 defeats by the Soviet Union? Who scored a sensational hat-trick against England for the Dutch? (3)

7 Who scored in the 1992 European Championship Final for Denmark but became famous for not scoring when he played in England? (1)

8 Who scored twice in injury time to win a thrilling match against Yugoslavia 4-3 at the 2000 European Championships and ensure they qualified for the knockout phase along with the losers? (1)

9 France were the only team to qualify for the 2004 European Championships with a perfect win record: who was their coach for this tournament? (1)

10 Who travelled to Turkey, a notoriously tricky place to get a result at the time, and came back from 2-0 down to draw 2-2 and secure their place at the 2004 European Championships, their first major tournament? (1)

11 Which of the fancied nations had a bit of a nightmare at the 2008 European Championships, failing to score in two of their matches and getting thrashed 4-1 by the Netherlands in the other? (1)

12 Who was sent off in the last international of a great career, Romania's defeat by Italy and exit from the 2000 European Championships? (1)

13 Who won in Zaragoza to ensure they topped their qualifying group for the 2004 European Championships and consign Spain to the play-offs? (1)

14 Germany qualified for the 2012 European Championships with a perfect 10 games, 10 wins record. Which striker scored all Germany's goals as they also won their first two group matches at the finals? And which full back scored the winner against Denmark to maintain their 100 per cent record? Whose two stunning goals brought their winning streak to an end in the semi-final? (3)

15 Here is the Welsh team that beat Belgium 1-0 in 2015, a result that set them on the way to qualification for the 2016 European Championships – can you fill in the missing players (4-5-1) ? MISSING (Crystal Palace); Jazz Richards (Fulham), MISSING (Swansea City), James Chester (West Bromwich Albion), Neil Taylor (Swansea City); Chris Gunter (Reading), MISSING (Liverpool), MISSING (Arsenal), Joe Ledley (Crystal Palace), MISSING (Reading) (sub: Andy King, Leicester City); Gareth Bale (Real Madrid) (sub: MISSING, Burnley) (6)

Answers on p.463

Quiz 95: Football League 10 (30)

1 Which five players reached 600 appearances for West Ham United? (5)

2 In 1904–05 three English cities boasted two teams in the top division: which three? (3)

3 Who made a brief return as manager of Manchester United when Wilf McGuinness was dismissed in 1971? Who was the next permanent appointment, who didn't last much longer than McGuinness? (2)

4 Which two sides, based in what is now Cumbria, failed to gain re-election to the Football League in the 1970s? (2)

5 Which nineteen-year-old top scored for Arsenal (26 goals, 19 in the league) in their Double-winning season of 1970–71? Who bought him for £180,000 in 1974 and converted him into a highly effective goal-scoring midfielder? (2)

6 In 1980–81 Bristol City were relegated from the second tier of the Football League in twenty-third place; who finished below them? (1)

7 Which club instigated a unilateral ban on away fans in 1986–87? (1)

8 Bernie Slaven scored a hat-trick in the first half and Martin Foyle added one of his own in the second as which side beat Barnet 6-0 despite playing all but ten minutes with ten men? (1)

9 Newcastle United ran away with the second tier in 1991–92 under Kevin Keegan, winning their first eleven matches. Which tough-tackling, local born midfield player was the only player to play in all 46 league matches? Which former Walsall striker was their top scorer? And which new star came into the side for the last twelve games, scoring a goal per game? (3)

10 Which Second Division London derby attracted a gate of 55,003 in December 1976? (1)

11 In 1959, which striker, better known for his later work as a manager, scored his 100th League goal in fewer games than any other player? For which club? (2)

12 Dave Clements was a left-sided player with Northern Ireland who played more than 250 games for which club in the 1960s and early 1970s as they climbed from the third tier to the First Division? (1)

13 Who finished second in Division 1 (second tier) in 1994–95 but had to go through the play-off system as the Premier League was being reduced from 22 teams to 20? Who beat them 4-3 in the play-off Final, despite going 2-0 down and conceding a penalty, which was saved by Keith Branagan? Which Premier League side were similarly unlucky, finishing fourth from bottom but suffering relegation as part of the numbers game? (3)

14 Who scored seventeen goals for Gillingham in 2001–02 but spent a few months in jail after being found guilty of handling stolen goods? Which club sacked him in 2009 when he was again jailed, this time, for sexual assault and actual bodily harm? (2)

15 In 2011–12 two teams relegated from the Premier League the previous season contested the play-off Final. One was West Ham United – who were their opponents, beaten 2-1 in the Final? (1)

Answers on p.463

Quiz 96: Scotland 4 (30)

1 Which was the only Scotland World Cup finals squad that didn't include a single Celtic player? (1)

2 Who won the most caps – Archie Gemmill, Asa Hartford, Bruce Rioch or John Wark? (1)

3 Who was captain of Rangers as they reeled off nine consecutive Scottish league titles from 1988–89 to 1996–97? With which other side had he won the title as a young player? And for which English side did he play a solitary season in between? And a weird one – in which northern European capital city was he born? (4)

4 Which two members of Alex Ferguson's title-winning Aberdeen side have subsequently been manager of the club? (2)

5 What 'first' took place for the 1904 Scottish Cup Final between Celtic and Rangers? (1)

6 Who signed Henrik Larsson twice, while manager at Feyenoord and then Celtic? (1)

7 Since the demise of Gretna, which is the most southerly Scottish League club? (1)

8 Which Scottish-born Republic of Ireland international topped the Scottish top-flight goalscoring charts in 1987–88, 1990–91 and 1994–95 with three separate clubs, Dundee, Celtic and Motherwell respectively? (1)

9 Which are the only two Scottish football grounds outside Glasgow with a capacity of over 20,000? (2)

10 Which cult hero scored in both Finals as Hearts won the Scottish Cup in 2006 and 2012? Who were on the receiving end of a 5-1 thrashing in the 2012 Final? (2)

11 Joe Baker of Hibernian was the top scorer in the Scottish First Division in 1958–59: in what way was this a first? (1)

12 Dundee United*, Derby County, Blackburn Rovers, West Ham United* (inc Southampton), Rangers, Charlton Athletic – this is the career path of which consistent and underrated defender, who won 67 caps for Scotland? (1)

13 Alan Hansen, Willie Donachie, Danny McGrain, David Weir: which of these shot-shy defenders actually managed a goal for Scotland? (1)

14 Here is a list of Scotland managers since 1971, with a few gaps: Tommy Docherty, MISSING, Ally McLeod, Jock Stein, caretaker, MISSING, Craig Brown, MISSING, caretaker, MISSING, Alex McLeish, George Burley, MISSING, caretaker, Gordon Strachan. Can you name the missing managers? (4)

15 This is the Scotland team, by club, with a few players missing, that beat England 3-2 at Wembley in 1967, England's first defeat after the 1966 World Cup (4-4-2): Ronnie Simpson (Celtic); MISSING (Celtic), MISSING (Rangers), Ronnie McKinnon (Rangers), MISSING (Chelsea); Willie Wallace (Celtic), MISSING (Leeds United), MISSING (Sunderland), Bobby Lennox (Celtic); MISSING (Sheffield Wednesday), MISSING (Manchester United). Who are the missing players? (7)

Asterisk (*) indicates that the player in question made more than one hundred league appearances for the club.

Answers on p.464

Quiz 97: General 25 (30)

1 Billy Bremner had a spell as manager of the club he distinguished as a player, Leeds United; with which near-neighbours did he also have two spells as manager, one from 1978 to 1985 and the other after his spell at Leeds? (1)

2 What was the name given to the defensive tactic adopted by Helenio Herrera's Inter side in the 1960s, whereby a back four was augmented by a deep-lying sweeper, allowing the full backs license to attack as wingers? (1)

3 Which former England and Arsenal captain wrote the 1945 book *Football Ambassador*, one of the earlier footballing autobiographies? (1)

4 In fan polls of 2005 and 2015, who was voted Nottingham Forest's greatest ever player – was it (a) Archie Gemmill (b) Trevor Francis (c) Stuart Pearce or (d) John Robertson? (1)

5 Host nation Germany were among the favourites for the 1936 Olympic football tournament. Which team surprisingly eliminated them, in what is believed to be the only game attended by German Chancellor Adolf Hitler? (1)

6 Other than having earned more than 100 caps for the Netherlands, what do Phillip Cocu and Edwin van der Sar share – is it (a) they have both been married to the same lady, (b) their wives gave birth to twins on the same day, (c) they were born on exactly the same day or (d) they were both born in the Seychelles? (1)

7 What surname has connected the Northern Ireland and Republic of Ireland teams since 2013? (1)

8 Which famous sports ground in the state of Victoria, Australia, was used as a primary venue for the 2000 Olympic Football tournament, hosting a semi-final between Cameroon and Chile? (1)

9 The Second Qualifying Round for the 2015–16 Champions League featured the following sides: Hibernians FC, SK Vardar, Lech Poznań, Lincoln Red Imps, Molde, FC Žagiris Vilnius, Dundalk, Videoton and Ludogorets Razgrad. Which ten countries are represented by this list? And which two former European Champions entered the competition at this stage? (12)

10 Who missed one of the easiest sitters in living memory on his debut for Scotland in October 2008? (1)

11 When did sponsorship of the FA Cup begin – was it 1970, 1979, 1988 or 1995? Who were the first sponsors? (2)

12 Who was unfortunate enough to be diagnosed with testicular cancer days after helping Millwall to promotion to Division 1 (second tier) by scoring 28 goals in 2000–01? Which classy English defender recovered twice from the same diagnosed problem while playing for Celtic? Which two clubs were these players, happily recovered, managing in 2015–16, one in England, one in Scotland? (4)

13 Which Belgian club lost two European Finals to Liverpool in 1976 and 1978? (1)

14 He played more than 400 league games for Burnley, and was an ever-present in their championship-winning squad of 1959–60. He returned in 1970, six years after his retirement, to manage the club, and later took charge of Sunderland and Leeds. Who was he? (1)

15 Which local MP handed a Manager of the Month award to Chris Turner of Hartlepool? (1)

Answers on p.465

Quiz 98: Champions League 8 (30)

1 Eight players featured in Real Madrid's first five European Cup wins, but only one of them, a winger, was still around for their next win in 1966 – who was he? (1)

2 Which Portuguese side were the first to break the cycle of Real Madrid victories by winning the European Cup in 1961? Which of Real's great rivals put the holders out in the very first round? (2)

3 Which famous English referee took charge of the first European Cup Final in 1956 – was it Jack Taylor, Stanley Rous or Arthur Ellis? (1)

4 Dejan Savićević and Marcel Desailly were both second-time winners of the European Cup when they played for Milan in 1994. With which two sides had they won the trophy before? (2)

5 Which former Dutch international was manager of the Barcelona side that won the 2006 Champions League Final? (1)

6 Which young goalkeeper was in goal for Olympique Marseille in the 1993 European Cup Final? (1)

7 Who was applauded from the field by the home fans after scoring a superb hat-trick for Real Madrid at Old Trafford in the 2002–03 Champions League quarter-final? Who scored twice for United after coming off the bench? (2)

8 Which English referee took charge of the 2016 Champions League Final? (1)

9 What was the all-Italian back four in the Milan side that won consecutive European Cup Finals in 1989 and 1990? (4)

10 Fortuna Sittard*, PSV Eindhoven*, Barcelona, Bayern Munich*, AC Milan, PSV Eindhoven – this list charts the career of which enforcer of recent vintage? (1)

11 Costinha's last-minute goal for which team knocked Manchester United out of the 2003–04 Champions League in the Last 16? (1)

12 Which five Dutch coaches have won the Champions League (to 2014–15)? (5)

13 Who refereed Manchester United's Champions League Final against Bayern Munich in 1999? (1)

14 Liverpool won their fourth European Cup seven years after their first in 1984. Can you fill in the missing players in their line-up, with only one player common to both the '77 and '84 sides (4-4-2)? MISSING; Phil Neal, MISSING, MISSING, Alan Kennedy; Craig Johnston (sub: Steve Nicol), MISSING, Sammy Lee, MISSING; Kenny Dalglish (sub: Michael Robinson), MISSING. (6)

15 Who are the only Serbian club to have competed in the group stages of the Champions League in the twenty-first century? (1)

Asterisk (*) indicates that the player in question made more than one hundred league appearances for the club.

Answers on p.465

Quiz 99: England 5 (30)

1 Which three England players have made international appearances while playing club football with Sampdoria in Italy? (3)

2 Who played for England at the 1990 World Cup finals despite never appearing in the top flight of English football? Which was his only club? (2)

3 Which midfield player made his England debut in a friendly against Mexico in June 1985 just two weeks shy of his twenty-ninth birthday? (1)

4 Two players won two caps for England while on the books at Fulham in the twenty-first century – who were they? (2)

5 The last players to be picked for England while at the two Sheffield clubs were in 1992 (United) and 1998 (Wednesday) – who were they? (2)

6 In 1968, who won a European Cup winner's medal and reappeared at Wembley eight days later for his England debut? (1)

7 In a 2001 friendly against Mexico, who became the first three players from the same club to score in an England international? (3)

8 Who was the last England player to score five in one game, when he bagged all England's goals against Cyprus in a European Championship qualifier in 1975? (1)

9 Which of these players has never captained England: Peter Beardsley, Terry Butcher, David Platt, Gareth Southgate? (1)

10 Who compared missing a crucial penalty to 'stepping off the edge of the world into silence'? (1)

11 Who took charge of England for one game each between Kevin Keegan's resignation and Sven-Goran Eriksson's start? (2)

12 Name the five clubs with which Peter Shilton won his 125 caps (5)

13 How did Deportivo de La Coruña defender Pedro Duscher put a damp-
ener on England's World Cup prospects in April 2002? (2)

14 Arsenal had nine players at the 2004 European Championships, but
who were the only two in the England squad? (2)

15 Here are six England strikers: Mick Channon, Peter Crouch, Jermaine
Defoe, Trevor Francis, Roger Hunt, Tony Woodcock. Who played the
most games for England, and who scored the most goals? (2)

Answers on p.466

Quiz 100: Premier League 13 (40)

1 Collins Mbesuma was snapped up by which Premier League club in summer 2005 after scoring 35 goals in South Africa for Kaizer Chiefs? How many appearances did he make – was it 33, 11, 4 or none at all? (2)

2 In a February 2002 Premier League match between Arsenal and Fulham eleven French players (six for Arsenal, five for Fulham) took part – can you name them? (11)

3 Which Bradford City Chairman admitted that signing an overseas star on £40k per week may have damaged his team's finances? Who was the star? (2)

4 Which former Newcastle United players scored on both occasions as Chelsea completed a brace of 1-0 wins against Manchester United as United won the Premier League title race in 1993–94? What subject did he later study at University? (2)

5 Which striker cost Fulham a cool £11.5M from Lyon in August 2001, which worked out at just over £1M per Premier League goal? (1)

6 Which Chelsea player, in his second spell with the club, was forced to apologise for a dreadful two-footed tackle on Leeds United's Danny Mills? And who was so incensed by the challenge that he got himself sent to the stands during the match? (2)

7 Which relegated club did Liverpool beat 6-0 away and 5-0 at home (in the last match of the season) in 2001–02? Who was the manager, who had also taken the club into the Premier League two years previously? (2)

8 Which former professional footballer (Tranmere Rovers and Crewe Alexandra) was appointed Chief Executive of the FA in 2003? To what top job had his predecessor at the FA, Adam Crozier, been appointed earlier the same year? (2)

9 Which striker moved to Tottenham Hotspur from Rosenborg in December 1996 for £2.7M, only days after the Norwegian team knocked AC Milan out of the Champions League? And which former Wimbledon defender did they bring back to London from Liverpool, hijacking a proposed move to Leeds United at the last minute? (2)

10 Which veteran French international was Roberto Mancini's first new signing for Manchester City in January 2010? (1)

11 Who is the only player (to 2015–16) to have hit a Premier League hat-trick for Birmingham City? (1)

12 Who scored 21 goals in the 2004–05 Premier League season, despite his team being relegated on the last day? How many of the total were penalties, a record for one player in a Premier League season? (1 pt for 1 either way) (3)

13 Who was the Ghanaian striker whose ferocious shooting made him a cult hero at Leeds United after he was signed in 1995? (1)

14 Who won ten straight games to clinch their eleventh title in 1997–98? Who was the unlikely scorer of a spectacular celebratory volley against Everton in the title-winning game? What distinction did the club's manager achieve? (3)

15 Former England full back Luke Young played in the Premier League for which five clubs? (5)

Answers on p.467

Quiz 101: General 26 (30)

1 Bobby Smith and Terry Dyson scored the goals in a 2-0 win over Leicester City; what little piece of history was made? (1)

2 In four World Cup tournaments all the semi-finalists came from Europe; in which years did this happen? (4)

3 The six major titles a British club player could win were the league, the FA Cup, the League Cup, the European Cup (later Champions League), the European Cup Winners' Cup and the UEFA Cup – these latter two are now combined in the Europa League. Which of the six is missing from Denis Irwin's trophy cabinet? (1)

4 When France and Italy met at the 1938 World Cup there was a clash of blue shirts and Italy were told to change; what colour did they adopt instead of their usual white replacement shirts? (1)

5 Which French fourth division side reached the 2000 French Cup Final? Which English side's supporters 'adopted' them because they shared the same yellow and red colours (and because their ground was easy-ish to get to)? Which future Premiership player scored the penalty as Nantes finally beat them in the Final? (3)

6 Which side, masters of doing just enough in the group stages of major tournaments, got through to the last eight of the 1970 World Cup despite scoring only goal in three group games? (1)

7 Who missed only one penalty for Southampton in more than 50 attempts? (1)

8 Who were the opposition when an England 'friendly' in February, 1995 was abandoned after crowd trouble? What was the venue for the match? (2)

9 Which two London clubs faced each other in an FA Cup replay in February 1995 when the worst hooligan scenes for nearly a decade disrupted the evening and a troop of police horses had to clear the pitch of rioting supporters? (2)

10 Which Swindon Town midfielder was Southampton's first £1M buy in late 1990 – was it (a) Alan McLoughlin (b) Jason McAteer (c) John Sheridan or (d) Glenn Cockerill? (1)

11 This is the Middlesbrough team that won the club's first major final, beating Bolton Wanderers 2-1 in the 2004 League Cup Final. Can you fill in the gaps (4-4-1-1, English unless stated)? MISSING (Australia); Danny Mills, MISSING, Ugo Ehiogu, MISSING (France); Juninho (Brazil), MISSING (Brazil), George Boateng (Netherlands), MISSING (Netherlands); MISSING (Spain); Joseph Désiré Job (Cameroon). Which former Bolton player came on a substitute for Job? And who was Boro manager at the time? (8)

12 Which convoluted route into European competition (1995–2008) involved applying to participate and playing an extra eight matches, starting in July? (1)

13 The transfers of Tal Ben Haim to Bolton Wanderers, Michael Essien to Chelsea, Yakubu to Middlesbrough and Amdy Faye to Portsmouth were among seventeen highlighted as 'questionable' by which report into corruption in football? (1)

14 Chelsea, relegated from the First Division in 1961–62, won promotion straight back again the following season under whose management? And who was the Second Division top scorer that season, on his way to setting a new club goalscoring record? (2)

15 Which former Derby County player was the surprising scorer of a headed equaliser for Sunderland against his old club in a Division 1 (second tier) fixture in September 2003? (1)

Answers on p.467

Quiz 102: Wales 3 (30)

1 Which English ground has hosted three Wales 'home' games? (1)

2 The New Saints were once known purely by the name of which local sponsor? (1)

3 Wales midfielder Andy King has made more than 250 appearances and scored over fifty goals for which club? (1)

4 Who took Swansea City from the fourth tier to the top flight with three promotions in four seasons from 1978–1981? Who scored the goal that secured promotion to the second flight in 1979? Where did they finish in their first season in the top flight in 1981–82 – was it 4th, 6th or 17th? Which former England striker scored a hat-trick for the Swans in the memorable 5-1 win at Leeds on the opening day of the season? And which Welsh international was Swansea's only ever-present during that season? (5)

5 Who scored the most recent hat-trick for Wales in an international game (at time of writing), a 4-0 trouncing of Scotland in a 2004 friendly? (1)

6 When Wales beat Germany in a 1991 Euro qualifier, the team line-up, 5-3-2, by club, was this: Neville Southall (Everton); MISSING (Norwich City), Mark Aizlewood (Bristol City), Andy Melville (Oxford United), MISSING (Everton), MISSING (Swindon Town); Peter Nicholas (Chelsea), Barry Horne (Southampton), MISSING (Manchester United); MISSING (Derby County), Ian Rush (Liverpool). Identify the missing players. (5)

7 In qualifying for the 2014 World Cup, which was the only side Wales beat twice in a group won comfortably by Belgium? Who scored two goals in the last ten minutes to win the first of these games? And who scored another late winner in the reverse fixture as Wales again came from one down to win 2-1? (3)

8 Ioannis Okkas scored twice as which unfancied side beat Wales 3-1 in a qualifier for the 2008 European Championships? (1)

9 Which Southampton player became Wales' youngest scorer (17 years and 35 days) in a 2006 match against Slovakia? (1)

10 During qualification for the 1992 European Championships Wales pulled off an outstanding victory over Germany (June 1991). What was the venue? Who scored the Wales goal? Who was manager of Wales at the time? (3)

11 Which Welsh striker scored nearly 100 goals at one in every two games for Cardiff before the age of twenty-three, but never quite pushed on to achieve the success anticipated at the top level? How many caps and goals did he notch for Wales – was it 33/12 or 40/9 or 59/16? (2)

12 Which Belgian-born full back earned fifteen caps for Wales in the 1980s while playing for Everton? (1)

13 How many players named Davies have played for Wales (up to August 2016) – is it 19, 25, 36 or 41? Which two won over 50 caps? (3)

14 Which Wales international striker won three Scottish Premier League titles in 2002, 2004 and 2006? (1)

15 Who was the last Wales international to win a Football League title before the start of the Premier League era? (1)

Answers on p.468

Quiz 103: Football League 11 (30)

1 Who were promoted to the Premier League, barring bizarre swings in goal difference, by the end of March in the 1996–97 season, scoring 100 goals in the process? Which strike pairing scored 43 of those goals? Which other northern side made the other automatic promotion spot, eighteen points behind? And who was their top scorer, with an impressive fifteen from midfield? (5)

2 Who, in 1936, became the last of the twelve founder members of the Football League to suffer the ignominy of relegation to the Second Division? (1)

3 Which post-war striker became the first player to score more than 200 goals for Manchester United, including two in the 1948 FA Cup Final and 30 in the 1951–52 title-winning season? For which club did his younger brother, Arthur, score more than 250 goals? (2)

4 The Wales/Scotland strike partnership of Roy Vernon and Alex Young spearheaded which club's championship-winning season in 1962–63? (1)

5 What was the centre-half pairing that helped Derby County win the First Division title in 1971–72 (they later formed a short-lived managerial partnership at Bolton)? (2)

6 Prior to Leicester City in 2015–16, who were the last team to win the First Division title for the first time (to 2014–15)? (1)

7 Which former player did Everton appoint as manager in 1981 after a few seasons of under-achievement? (1)

8 Who was First Division top scorer in his first season with Liverpool as they won the title in 1987–88? From which club, relegated from the top flight without his goals, did they buy him? For which club did he play more than 250 games at the end of his career, the last two as player-manager before he retired from playing and became simply the gaffer? (3)

9 Which English club has won four League titles but none since 1927? (1)

10 Fans chanting 'Feed The Goat' was a celebration ritual greeting another goal from which striker? (1)

11 Which club were relegated from the top flight and declared bankrupt in 1982, and who rescued them from penury? (2)

12 Who were relegated alongside Southampton and Norwich City in 1973–74? Who were the managers of the two clubs mentioned, both of whom took over during the season but were unable to save them from the drop? And who was the manager of the mystery club? Along with Middlesbrough, which two sides, who have both since dropped out of the league and returned, replaced them in the top flight? (6)

13 Whose long management career included taking Scarborough into the Football League as the first club automatically promoted from the Conference, and overseeing promotions for Notts County, Huddersfield Town, Plymouth Argyle, Sheffield United and Queens Park Rangers, guiding the last two into the Premier League? (1)

14 Which Division 1 (second tier) club opened a crisp new stadium on 23 July 2002, and who cut the formal ribbon at the opening ceremony? (2)

15 Who scored an impressive 35 league goals as Huddersfield Town won promotion to the Championship (second tier) via the play-offs in 2011–12? (1)

Answers on p.469

Quiz 104: World Cup 10 (30)

1 Who was captain of the Costa Rica team at the 2014 World Cup finals and scorer of the goal that beat Italy and took them through to the knockout stages? With which English team was he officially registered and with which Dutch club had he just finished half a season on loan? (3)

2 Who were the first African side to take part in a World Cup finals tournament, losing 4-2 to Hungary in the first round in 1934? (1)

3 This is the Hungary team that lost the World Cup Final to West Germany in 1954: fill in the gaps where only positions are given. GOALKEEPER; Buzansky, Lantos; RIGHT HALF, Lóránt, Zakariás; WINGER, INSIDE FORWARD, Tóth, Kocsis, WINGER (5)

4 Who, in 1982, broke Pelé's record from 1958 as the youngest player to appear in a World Cup finals tournament? (1)

5 Who were the losing semi-finalists at the 1962 World Cup finals? (2)

6 Amid all the acrimony of England's 1966 World Cup quarter-final against Argentina, who scored the goal that sent England through? (1)

7 Which winger-cum-striker ended up as top scorer at the 1974 World Cup finals, scoring his seventh goal in the third place play-off? (1)

8 Rabah Madjer & Lakhdar Belloumi helped which side beat Nigeria home and away to qualify for their first World cup finals tournaments? Against which team did they also score the goals that ensured a famous 2-1 win in the finals? (2)

9 Mexico qualified automatically as the hosts of the 1986 World Cup finals; which other team joined them from the North and Central American region, qualifying for the first and thus far (up to 2014) only time? (1)

10 In the penalty shoot-out between France and Brazil at the 1986 World Cup finals, both captains missed with their spot kicks – who were they? (2)

11 Scotland's campaign at the 1990 World Cup finals imploded with defeat in their first match to which first time finalists? Who was the Scotland manager whose pre-match comments suggested they took their opponents far too lightly? (2)

12 Nottingham Forest were represented by two players at the 1994 World Cup finals, both in the Norway squad – who were they? (2)

13 Which Brazilian star was given a retrospective fine after getting an opponent sent off, going down clutching his face after the ball Hakan Ünsal kicked at him struck his leg with minimal force? (1)

14 The four African qualifiers for the 2006 World Cup finals in Germany were all making their debuts in the tournament proper – who were they? (4)

15 Who beat Spain in the opening match of the reigning European Champions' 2010 World Cup finals campaign? Who was the canny German manager who masterminded this hit-and-run 1-0 win? (2)

Answers on p.469

Quiz 105: General 27 (30)

1 Bolivia battled past Uruguay to reach a final play-off for qualification for the 1978 World Cup finals; which Brazilian icon scored four times as Bolivia were battered 8-0 by Brazil? And which Peruvian legend scored twice as Peru also ran riot against Bolivia, winning 5-0? (2)

2 In his playing days Ron Atkinson was a key player in which lower division side's impressive FA Cup run in 1963–64? (1)

3 The Soviet Union had a formidable team in the 1960s: but who was the gifted attacking midfield player who was missing for most of the decade after being sent to prison on rape charges? (1)

4 When the Netherlands beat England to pip them for qualification for the World Cup in 1994, they had two sets of brothers in their side. Who were they? (4)

5 Which Frenchman was FIFA President from 1921 until 1954? (1)

6 Crystal Palace finished third in Division 1 (second tier) in 1995–96, but missed out on promotion back to the Premier League when they lost to which side in the play-offs? Which future manager of the club top scored for Palace that season? (2)

7 Which side, who won a place in the Football League in 2003, boasted a record seventeen League scalps in FA Cup ties while still a non-league team? (1)

8 Which club missed the 1999–2000 FA Cup for an ill-conceived trip to play in a pointless international tournament, The World Club Cup? (1)

9 Who comprised the Queens Park Rangers strike pairing from the 1982 FA Cup Final whose names evoked a famous music hall act? And which member of the same QPR side later managed the club? (3)

10 Who made his comeback from serious injury by playing the full ninety minutes of Lazio's 2-0 win over Reggiana in Serie A in April, 1995? (1)

11 PSV Eindhoven, Barcelona, Chelsea (*inc Middlesbrough*),
    Middlesbrough, Liverpool, Olympique de Marseille, Sunderland –
    whose peripatetic career path is this? How many caps did he win for
    the Netherlands – was it 7, 23, 57 or 90? (2)

12 Which is the only one of these clubs to have played in European compe-
    tition: Bristol City, Portsmouth, Swansea City or Tranmere Rovers?
    (1)

13 What are the names of the two sons of Michael Glazer (the American
    owner of Manchester United), both currently installed as Co-Chairman
    of the club? (2)

14 Who scored four times for Burnley as they beat Manchester United 6-1
    on Boxing Day 1963 – was it (a) Andy Lochhead (b) Ray Pointer (c)
    Derek Dougan or (d) Bryan 'Pop' Robson? And which more familiar
    name scored four as Liverpool beat Stoke by the same score on the
    same day? (2)

15 Which names are missing from this list of Burnley managers since
    1970: MISSING (1970–76), Joe Brown, Harry Potts, Brian Miller, John
    Bond, John Benson, Martin Buchan, Tommy Cavanagh, Brian Miller,
    Frank Casper, MISSING (1991–96), Adrian Heath, Chris Waddle,
    MISSING (1998–2004), Steve Cotterill, MISSING (2007–10), Brian
    Laws, MISSING (2011–12), MISSING (incumbent, 2012–16)? (6)

Answers on p.470

Quiz 106: Premier League 14 (40)

1 Coventry City were trading strikers in August 1999, selling one to Leeds United for around £5M and paying an extra million for a teenager to replace him from nearby Wolverhampton Wanderers: who were the two players involved? (2)

2 In August 1992 Liverpool lost to Nottingham Forest as Teddy Sheringham scored the game's only goal: the match was a first in which way? (2)

3 Rafa Benítez frequently moaned about not being able to spend like Manchester United. From 2004 to 2009 United spent £189M. How much did Liverpool spend? (1 point for £10M either way) (2)

4 Which city slicker was Chairman of Southampton between 1996 and 2006 and returned a couple of years later just in time to take the club into administration? Which manager did he sack while he was in court clearing his name of false and heinous allegations? (2)

5 Which Frenchman is the only player from outside the British Isles to have passed 400 appearances in the Premier League? For which four clubs has he made them? (5)

6 Which striker with a 'bad boy' reputation started the season in fine style in 1993–94, scoring a hat-trick for Coventry City in a surprising 3-0 win at Highbury against Arsenal? (1)

7 Which West Bromwich Albion midfielder captained Slovenia when they made their second World Cup finals appearance in 2010? To which other English club did he move after the tournament, helping them back into the top flight? (2)

8 Who scored an injury-time winner to win a thrilling Manchester derby 4-3 in September 2009? (1)

9 Who was the goalkeeper bought by Liverpool from Vitesse Arnhem in 1999 for a British record fee? Who was his no.2, inexplicably left on the bench for the following season? Which striker joined the same Dutch club (Vitesse) from Nottingham Forest, where he was not mourned or missed? (3)

10 In the summer of 2008 Tottenham Hotspur sold a striker to Liverpool for £19M and bought a winger from Blackburn Rovers for £17M: who were the two players involved? (2)

11 To March 2016, Mark Robins, Chris Sutton and Efan Ekoku are the only Premier League hat-trick scorers for which club? (1)

12 In Blackburn's title-winning season of 1994–95 Alan Shearer scored 34 goals; how many were penalties (1 point for 1 either way)? Who was second top scorer with 15 goals? Which late addition to the Rovers squad had already won a league title? And which two members would go on to win at least one more league title elsewhere? (5)

13 Which four players have scored twenty goals in a Premier League season for Chelsea? (4)

14 Sparta Prague and Borussia Dortmund both sold Czech international midfield players to major English Premier League clubs for something over £3M in the summer of 1996: who were the two players and who were the buying clubs? (4)

15 Left-sided midfield player Matt Taylor played more than 300 Premier League games – but for which four clubs? (4)

Answers on p.470

Quiz 107: Global 4 (30)

1 Goalkeeper Peter Rufai played club football for the Go Ahead Eagles and international football for the 'Super Eagles'; identify the nationality of the club and the nationality of Rufai. (2)

2 Stern John, a much-travelled player across the English leagues, is also the highest scorer (and second most-capped player) for which country, for whom he played in their only World Cup finals tournament? (1)

3 What is the nickname given to the New Zealand soccer team, reflective of their strip, and also with a hint of parody of the Rugby Union side? (1)

4 After the 1969 Intercontinental Cup two players from Estudiantes were jailed for a month and goalkeeper Alberto Poletti was banned for life for kicking a grounded opponent in the face and breaking his cheekbone: which country were Estudiantes representing, and who were their battered Italian opponents, who won the trophy 4-2 on aggregate? (2)

5 Who is the only player based with a Japanese club to have played in a World Cup Final (he captained the team) ? (1)

6 Why did Bhutan and Montserrat play each other on the day of the 2002 World Cup Final? (1)

7 Who beat reigning world champions Brazil to the 1959 Copa América, claiming the title of honorary world champions? (1)

8 Which two Brazilian legends scored five goals each in the 1999 Copa América, as Brazil started by routing Venezuela 7-0 and never looked back, winning all six matches without recourse to penalties? (2)

9 At the 1992 African Cup of Nations Camden-born Reuben Agboola was the only player based with an English league club; he was playing for Swansea City and had previous spells at Southampton and, notably, Sunderland in the last decade. Which country was he representing? And which Norwich City player, best known in England for his spell at Wimbledon, made the squad for the same country in the same competition two years later and was also the sole English league representative? (2)

10 Atlas, AS Monaco, Barcelona*, New York Red Bulls, Leon, Verona – this the career path of which stalwart, who earned more than 100 caps for Mexico? (1)

11 Sami Al-Jaber won more than 150 caps for which country? (1)

12 Ghana and Nigeria stepped in to co-host the 2000 African Cup of Nations when it became clear that which Southern African country was not able to stage the event in an adequate manner? (1)

13 Which two Chelsea players competed at the African Cup of Nations in 2004, just before Didier Drogba and Michael Essien signed for the club? (2)

14 Who were removed from host status of the 2015 African Cup of Nations after demanding the competition be cancelled because of the ebola outbreak in West Africa? Which central African country, co-hosts in 2012, stepped in and put on the show? (2)

15 Which nine African nations have made it to more than one World Cup finals tournament (up to and including 2014)? Which of them has appeared in the most tournaments? (10)

Asterisk (*) indicates that the player in question made more than one hundred league appearances for the club.

Answers on p.471

Quiz 108: Scotland 5 (30)

1. Who won the most caps for Scotland, Billy Bremner, Gary McAllister, Graeme Souness or Gordon Strachan? (1)

2. Steve Clarke, José Mourinho's assistant at Chelsea for much of his first spell, made well over 300 appearances for the club as a player: for which Scottish club did he play more than 200 games before signing for Chelsea? (1)

3. Which former Scotland manager was appointed manager of Aberdeen in 2010, and stayed in charge for three years until he was replaced by current incumbent (November 2015) Derek McInnes? (1)

4. What was unique about season 1951–52 in Scotland? (1)

5. With which club did legendary Scottish playmaker Alex James win four league titles? (1)

6. Billy Bremner, Richard Gough, Andy Gray, Joe Jordan, Peter Lorimer, Lou Macari, Gary McAllister, Graeme Souness; four of these players have been sent off while playing for Scotland – can you name them? (4)

7. Which English striker finished as SPL top scorer in 2012–13 with Motherwell but left to play in the Netherlands at the end of the season? For which newly promoted Dutch club did he sign – was it (a) Twente Enschede (b) AZ Alkmaar (c) NEC Nijmegen or (d) Go Ahead Eagles? (2)

8. If a Scottish Cup tie pitched the principal sides of Perth and Kirkcaldy against each other, who would be playing? (2)

9. Who, in 1979, moved from St Mirren to Liverpool, didn't get a single game, and became Scotland's most expensive player (briefly) when he moved back up north to join Celtic, finishing as the Scottish League's top scorer in his first season? (1)

10 Which four Scottish League clubs lie to the north of Aberdeen (name any three to claim the points)? (3)

11 When was the last time Celtic played Rangers in the Scottish Cup Final – was it 2008, 2002, 1999 or 1989? Which Danish winger scored twice for the winners? (2)

12 Which Scotland international defender was captain of Wigan Athletic when they won the FA Cup in 2013 but missed the Final through injury? (1)

13 Which centre back with Heart of Midlothian around the turn of the century won most caps (32) while with the club? (1)

14 Who scored his first hat-trick for Scotland on 7 November 1962 against Northern Ireland and celebrated the anniversary by scoring another against Norway, against whom he had already scored one in the June of 1963? (1)

15 This is the team that lost 3-0 to Morocco in the last World Cup finals match Scotland played, in 1998 – can you fill in the gaps (4-4-2) ? MISSING (Aberdeen); Tom Boyd (Celtic), MISSING (Blackburn Rovers), David Weir (Hearts), MISSING (Derby County); MISSING (Celtic) Craig Burley (Celtic), MISSING (Celtic), MISSING (AS Monaco); MISSING (Blackburn Rovers), MISSING (Rangers) (8)

Answers on p.472

Quiz 109: General 28 (30)

1 Both of the losing semi-finalists at the 1990 World Cup went out on penalties; who were the two disappointed teams? (2)

2 In January 1971 Colin Stein scored a late equaliser for Rangers in an Old Firm game against Celtic at Ibrox Park: what was the unforeseen consequence? (1)

3 There was the usual celebrity parade for the draw for the 1990 World Cup finals in Italy; which opera singer and which iconic Italian movie star paraded alongside the FIFA suits? (2)

4 When Wales were narrowly beaten by Russia (1-0) in a two-leg play-off for qualification to the 2004 European Championships, on what grounds did they launch an appeal to have the result of their 1-0 defeat at home overturned? (1)

5 Which future England international did Ron Atkinson buy from Vancouver Whitecaps while manager of Manchester United, but only picked him for one game in the League Cup? (1)

6 Which six British clubs have contested the UEFA Cup/Europa League Final in the twenty-first century? (6)

7 Who moved from RFC Liege to Dunkirk in August 1990, only for the transfer to fall through? (1)

8 Who were the selling and buying clubs when Trevor Francis became Britain's first million pound footballer? (2)

9 Which Chelsea player captained his country at the 1994 World Cup finals tournament? (1)

10 Huddersfield Town*; Sheffield Wednesday* (*inc. Tottenham Hotspur*); Huddersfield Town** – this details the career of which powerful centre forward who retired in 2009? (1)

11 What was remarkable and unique about the Celtic line-up for their game against Dunfermline Athletic on 8 September 2001? (1)

12 Which all-time great's clubs read Nancy* / St Étienne* / Juventus*? (1)

13 What number did Ian Wright wear for most of his Arsenal career? (1)

14 Which Wales and Southampton striker scored half his team's goals in 1966–67, finishing as First Division top scorer despite his team finishing ninteenth out of twenty-two teams? (1)

15 Can you name the eight clubs from across the four divisions of the league system in 2015–16 that were based geographically south of the M25 at its southernmost point? (8)

Asterisk (*) indicates that the player in question made more than one hundred league appearances for the club. (**) indicates more than two hundred league appearances.

Answers on p.472

Quiz 110: World Cup 11 (30)

1 Keylor Navas' performances for which country at the 2014 World Cup finals earned him a move to Real Madrid as no.2 to Iker Casillas? Who did Madrid try to buy as the new primary 'keeper in summer, 2015, only for the deal to fall through leaving Navas as the main man following the departure of Casillas? (2)

2 One of the favourites for the 1934 World Cup was 'Das Wunderteam', a nickname ascribed to which strong European side? (1)

3 Who scored twice, including the late winner, as West Germany surprised the footballing world by beating Hungary in the 1954 World Cup Final? (1)

4 Who stepped up after Pelé was injured at the 1962 World Cup semi-finals, scoring twice in both the quarter-final and semi-final? And why was he lucky to play in the Final? (2)

5 Which member of the team that won the Final was left out of England's side after their dull opening draw at the 1966 World Cup finals, and only restored to the team for the knockout stages? (1)

6 Between 1970 and 1974, the number of players in the World Cup finals squads of the sixteen qualified teams NOT playing in the country they represented in the tournament rose from: (a) 2 to 12 (b) 9 to 27 (c) 15 to 41 (1)

7 Which two teams played out a tepid game to ensure both got the result needed to qualify for the second phase of the 1982 World Cup finals at Algeria's expense? (2)

8 Who scored Argentina's third and decisive goal in the 1986 World Cup Final against West Germany after the Germans had shown typical resilience and come back from 2-0 down – was it (a) Diego Maradona (b) Jorge Valdano (c) Jorge Burruchaga or (d) Claudio Caniggia? (1)

9 Which Manchester United reserve came on as a substitute for Uruguay at the 2002 World Cup finals and scored a goal? (1)

10 What happened for the first time at a World Cup finals match when France's captain Laurent Blanc volleyed home against Paraguay in extra-time of their Last 16 game? (1)

11 Which of the Home Nations beat Italy in a qualifier play-off for a place at the 1958 World Cup finals, the only time the Italians failed to make the finals? (1)

12 At the 1998 World Cup finals there were two players in the various squads on the books of Bolton Wanderers, Per Frandsen and Mark Fish. There were also ten players who would later turn out for the club in their strong years under Sam Allardyce – try to identify them from the following list of countries. Denmark (1), England (1), France (2), Jamaica (1), Japan (1), Nigeria (1), Scotland (1), Spain (2) (10)

13 Which much-fancied side were reduced to nine men when playing the hosts, South Korea, in a group match at the 2002 World Cup finals? (1)

14 Which four players played a part in both of France's World Cup Final appearances? (4)

15 Who scored five out of Spain's first six goals in the 2010 World Cup tournament as they eased through to the semi-finals? (1)

Answers on p.473

Quiz 111: League Cup 3 (30)

1 Who scored four as Arsenal routed Liverpool 6-3 at Anfield in the Carling Cup in January 2007? (1)

2 Which teenager came on as a substitute and scored twice as Everton cruised past Wrexham in a League Cup second round tie in October 2002? (1)

3 Arsenal and Liverpool, fourth and second in the league that year, contested the 1987 League Cup Final. Which Scottish striker, who didn't always deliver as required for Arsenal, did so on this occasion and scored twice as they won 2-1? Who delivered his first major trophy as Arsenal manager? (1)

4 Which second-tier side gave Liverpool a scare in the semi-final of the League Cup in 2002–03 but succumbed to a Michael Owen goal in extra time of the second leg at Anfield? (1)

5 Which player, ostensibly a defender, scored Leicester's winner against Aston Villa in the 2000 League Cup semi-final, and went on to score both goals in their 2-1 Final victory? Who were their second-tier opponents in the Final? (2)

6 Who was in goal for Stoke City as they beat Chelsea to win their first major trophy in the 1972 League Cup Final? Who was his opposite number for Chelsea? (2)

7 How did Cardiff City get past Luton Town in the second round of the League Cup in 1986–87 without actually taking the field? (2)

8 Which Norwegian scored the only goal of a dour two-legged League Cup semi-final in 1998–99 between Tottenham Hotspur and Wimbledon? And which English veteran scored all three of Leicester's goals as they got past Sunderland at the same stage? (2)

9 Scottish striker Kevin McDonald's finest moment came when he scored two goals for a Championship (second tier) club to knock Arsenal out of the League Cup in 2008–09 – but for which club? And who joined them in the semi-finals when a Nathan Ellington goal in injury time saw off Stoke City, who had replaced them in the Premier League at the end of the previous season? (2)

10 Whose appearance in the 1997 League Cup Final was their first in a major final? And who scored the injury-time goal in a replayed Final to win the competition for their opponents, Leicester City? (2)

11 Which Rodney Marsh-inspired Third Division side beat holders West Bromwich Albion in the 1967 League Cup Final? What was different about that final to its League Cup predecessors? (2)

12 Liverpool have won the most League Cups (eight, to 2016) and played in the most finals (twelve, up to and including 2016): which three teams have contested eight finals each? (3)

13 Which African striker scored the late winner in the 2011 League Cup Final to down hot favourites Arsenal and give Birmingham City their first major trophy for forty-eight years? Who was the club's manager at the time, and which Republic of Ireland veteran captained the team? (3)

14 Which much derided goalkeeper was a clear Man of the Match as Liverpool won the 2003 League Cup Final 2-0 against Manchester United? (1)

15 Aston Villa scraped into the 1994 League Cup Final, beating which second-tier side in the semi-final? Who scored a late goal in the away leg to reduce their deficit to 3-1, and then added another late one at Villa Park to take the tie to extra time and subsequent penalties? Which prolific veteran scored in both matches for the opposition? Who did Villa beat in the Final? Which Welsh international striker scored twice to settle this game? (5)

Answers on p.474

Quiz 112: FA Cup 5 (30)

1 In 1976 Southampton pulled off one of the great FA Cup Final shocks when they beat Manchester United 1-0 at Wembley: who scored the goal and who was the Southampton manager? Which Welsh international full back captained the team? Who knocked Southampton out in a fifth round replay the following season? (4)

2 Which non-league side beat top-flight Birmingham in the FA Cup in 1986 – was it (a) Altrincham (b) Blyth Spartans (c) Sutton United or (d) Yeovil Town? (1)

3 Against which side did George Best score six Manchester United goals in an 8-2 FA Cup thrashing? (1)

4 Who scored both goals for Bolton in their 2-0 FA Cup Final victory over a Manchester United side depleted by the Munich air disaster in 1958? (1)

5 Chelsea have won the FA Cup seven times: how many times did they win it at the original Wembley Stadium? (2)

6 Which club won their only major trophy when they beat Burnley 1-0 in the FA Cup Final in 1947, having lost the previous year's Final 4-1 to Derby County? (1)

7 Everyone remembers who Manchester United beat in the Champions League Final to seal their memorable treble in 1999, but who did they beat in the FA Cup Final a few days earlier? And who came off the bench to replace the injured Roy Keane after nine minutes, scored and was voted Man of the Match? (2)

8 Who overturned a three-goal half-time deficit with only ten men against Tottenham in the FA Cup fourth round in 2004? Who had been sent off in the first half? (2)

9 Which player, a losing finalist with Manchester United thirteen years previously, scored the winning goal when Wrexham stunned Arsenal with a 2-1 win in the 1992 FA Cup? (1)

10 Which referee's debatable decision to disallow a late 'goal' denied third tier Chesterfield a place in the 1997 FA Cup Final? Who were their opponents, and which central defenders, one who played more than 500 games for the club and one who would later manage Burnley in the Premier League, scored two of the Spireites' goals? (3)

11 Who captained Arsenal in the 2014 and 2015 FA Cup Finals (two different players)? (2)

12 What did Scottish international Bobby Johnstone of Manchester City become the first to achieve in 1956? (1)

13 Which three World Cup Final winners from 1998 played in Chelsea's FA Cup Final team of 2000? (3)

14 Which three players have kept goal for Manchester United in an FA Cup Final in the twenty-first century? (3)

15 Who were the captains of the Tottenham Hotspur and Manchester City sides that contested an excellent FA Cup Final and replay in 1981? Which of them won a solitary England cap? (3)

Answers on p.474

Quiz 113: General 29 (30)

1 Brazil and Sweden drew 1-1 in their group game; which Welsh referee disallowed a Brazil 'goal' scored ten seconds into injury time from a corner, claiming the whistle went while the ball was sailing towards the goalmouth? (1)

2 In July 1993 Southampton complained to the FA about a £2.5M transfer for a player between Tottenham Hotspur and Liverpool. Their cause was that a year earlier an FA tribunal had ruled their valuation of same player to Spurs for £1.5M excessive, and reduced the fee to £750,000. Who was the player, a defender who won one cap for England? (1)

3 This is the Manchester United team that won the FA Cup Final against Liverpool in 1976: who are missing (4-4-2)? MISSING (England); Nicholl (Northern Ireland), Greenhoff (England), MISSING (Scotland), MISSING (Scotland); Coppell (England), MISSING (Northern Ireland), Macari (Scotland), MISSING (England) (sub: McCreery (Northern Ireland); J.Greenhoff (England), MISSING (England). (6)

4 Where did Mark Warburton next find employment after he was surprisingly removed from his job at Brentford at the end of the 2014–15 season? (1)

5 Which future England manager played in the Leicester City team that reached the 1949 FA Cup Final as a Second Division club? (1)

6 Which stadium, built as a velodrome to host the finale to the Tour de France and more famous for Rugby matches than soccer, was used for the 1938 World Cup semi-final between Hungary and Sweden? (1)

7 Who once kicked West Ham colleague Eyal Berkovic in a much-publicised training ground incident? (1)

8 Who were the two Celtic players in the Ireland team that reached the quarter-finals of the 1990 World Cup? (2)

9 Watford; Sunderland**; Southampton; Aston Villa; West Bromwich Albion; Birmingham City, Blackpool (*inc Crystal Palace*), Crystal Palace, Leicester City – this charts the long career, much of it in the top flight, of which prolific English striker of the modern era? (1)

10 Stuttgart Kickers, VFB Stuttgart*, Internazionale, AS Monaco, Tottenham Hotspur, Bayern Munich, Sampdoria, Tottenham Hotspur, Orange County Blue Star – which German legend's club career path is mapped out here? (1)

11 Which American defender played more than 100 games in English football before scoring his first goal and then got a second in the same match, a 4-0 League Cup quarter-final victory over Manchester United? For which club was he playing, and which recently capped England striker scored the other two goals? Which club beat them in the next round and also signed the American defender at the end of the season? (4)

12 What were George Best's international stats at the end of his career – (a) 9 goals in 39 games (b) 13 goals in 36 games (c) 16 goals in 52 games? (1)

13 What was the name of the agent implicated in the 'bung' scandal that engulfed Arsenal manager George Graham? (1)

14 Wilf Wild led Manchester City to their first league title in 1936–37: which other three managers have steered City to the title (to 2015–16)? (3)

15 Dagenham & Redbridge and Cambridge are on almost the same longitude: can you name the five clubs across the league system that played to the east of these two in 2015–16? (5)

Asterisk (*) indicates that the player in question made more than one hundred league appearances for the club. (**) indicates more than two hundred league appearances.

Answers on p.475

Quiz 114: European Competitions 6 (30)

1 Which veteran Northern Ireland striker scored the goal that took Wolverhampton Wanderers through to the 1971 UEFA Cup Final at the expense of mighty Juventus? (1)

2 Which Scottish side reached their only European Final (UEFA Cup) in 1987? Which Swedish side beat them to become the first Swedish winners of a European club trophy? (2)

3 Which three Spanish players were in the Chelsea team that won the 2013 Europa League? Which defender scored their injury-time winner? Who was the Chelsea manager at the time, winning the competition for the second time? And who were their opponents? (6)

4 Who, in 1960, were the first British club to contest a European Final, and in which competition? (2)

5 Which South American star scored Porto's goal as they won the 2011 Europa League, one of his last major contributions before injuries started to play havoc with his career? And who was his teenage countryman who came on as a substitute? Which other Portuguese side were their opponents in the Final? (3)

6 Which Bulgarian side provided Bolton Wanderers' first opposition in Europe in the 2005–06 UEFA Cup? And which top French side beat them (0-0, 2-1) in the first knockout round after they made it through the group? (2)

7 Rayo Vallecano and Getafe both play in suburbs of which city? (1)

8 Who were the last team to win Serie A for the first time, in 1990–91? (1)

9 Ferencváros and Honvéd compete in which city's fiercest derby match? (1)

10 Which non-League Welsh club defeated Italian side Atalanta in a 1987 European Cup Winners' Cup tie – was it (a) Cefn Druids (b) Rhyl Town (c) Barry Town or (d) Merthyr Tydfil? (1)

11 When Borussia Dortmund won the Bundesliga in 2003 their coach, who won the title twice in the nineties as a player with the same club, became the first man to win the title in both capacities; who was he? (1)

12 Didier Drogba played in the 2004 UEFA Cup Final for which team? Who managed the victors, Valencia, that day? (2)

13 Which Polish signing was dubbed 'Bello di Notte' (Night Beauty) by Juventus president Agnelli due to his memorable performances on big European nights? (1)

14 Which two players were involved when Arsenal tried to be clever and pass a penalty kick to a colleague in a 2005 Premier League game against Manchester City (it didn't end well)? Which Arsenal player actually scored earlier in the game with a conventional penalty? And which two Barcelona players made a better fist of the same trick in 2016? (5)

15 What is achieved by winning the Allsvenskan? (1)

Answers on p.476

Quiz 115: Premier League 15 (40)

1 Coventry City's goalkeeper and captain both played in every game of the 1996–97 Premier League campaign: who were the two players in question? And who was the club's top scorer for the third consecutive season? (3)

2 Côte d'Ivoire lost the 2012 African Cup of Nations Final on penalties to Zambia: which two Premier League stars, one with Manchester City and one with Arsenal, missed the crucial kicks? (2)

3 Which club and which manager signed a contract worth around a million pounds a year for Paulo Futre, a Portuguese international whose injury problems meant he had failed to complete a single game for Milan the previous season? (2)

4 Who was brought in to work alongside Bryan Robson and save Middlesbrough's Premier League status after a poor start to the season in 2000–01? (1)

5 Which Premier League striker scored twelve goals by mid-January for his newly promoted club in 2001–02, won an England cap and subsequently failed to score again all season? (1)

6 Which striker, in his second spell at the club, assured Tottenham's Premier League survival in the 1997–98 season, scoring four as they thrashed Wimbledon 6-2 in their penultimate game? (1)

7 Which World Cup-winning defender joined Everton for a season in 1998–99, managing to get three red cards in 27 games? (1)

8 Which former German international managed Fulham for eleven matches in 2014, winning none, a run that cemented the club's relegation after thirteen seasons in the Premier League? (1)

9 Who scored four times as Chelsea thrashed Barnsley 6-0 at the start of the 1997–98 Premier League season? And who scored a hat-trick as they won away at Tottenham 6-1 in November? And who scored a hat-trick for Manchester United as they went one better than Chelsea and beat Barnsley 7-0 in October? (3)

10 Who was the last Blackburn Rovers player to be top scorer in the Premier League? (1)

11 Which unheralded attacking player arrived at Swansea City from Rayo Vallecano, had one sensational season and then disappeared back into the unknown? (1)

12 Who paid Brescia around £9M for Savio Nsereko and got ten Premier League games (no goals) out of the Ugandan-born Germany forward? (1)

13 This is a list of Aston Villa managers since Graham Taylor left to take the England job in 1990 up to Remi Garde, dismissed at the end of the 2015–16 season, with a few gaps: Jozef Venglos, Ron Atkinson, MISSING, John Gregory, MISSING, David O'Leary, Martin O'Neill, MISSING, MISSING, Paul Lambert, MISSING, Remi Garde. Who are the five missing names, and which four men on this list achieved a win ratio of over 40 per cent of games while in charge? (9)

14 Who made his England debut at centre half against China in May, 1996, and was an ever-present for Aston Villa the following season as they finished fifth in the Premier League? (1)

15 Ryan Giggs made 632 appearances for Manchester United in the Premier League. Which other twelve players (to April 2016) have made more than 300 appearances for a single club (there are 4 full backs, 3 defenders, 3 midfield players, 2 strikers)? (12)

Answers on p.476

Quiz 116: Football League 12 (30)

1 While manager of Manchester City in January 2002, Kevin Keegan was forced to manhandle which fiery Australian international off the pitch and down the tunnel to prevent a further incident after the player received a red card? Which two players scored 48 between them in the league as City ran away with Division 1 (second tier), scoring more than 100 goals and reaching 99 points? Who was City's captain and the rock at the heart of the defence? (4)

2 Which former Arsenal and England centre forward was the manager of Chelsea when they first won the league title? And which later England forward was captain of the team and top scorer in the title-winning season? (2)

3 From 1962 to 1972 only three players finished the season as top scorer for Manchester United: who were they? (3)

4 Which club have spent the most seasons in the top tier of English football? (1)

5 Promoted to Division 1 – relegated – promoted – 18th – 19th – relegated – promoted – 14th – relegated – promoted: whose topsy-turvy decade in the 1950s is mapped out here? (1)

6 Which founder member of the Football League were forced to resign their league status halfway through the 1961–62 season? Which club, who would reach the top flight in the 1980s, replaced them the following season? (2)

7 Which Everton legend grabbed four goals as they thrashed Southampton 8-0 in November 1971? And who was his strike partner, better known as a Liverpool player later in the decade, who also scored a hat-trick? (2)

8 Who were the last team to win the First Division the year after winning promotion from the second tier? (1)

9 Who scored four goals as newly promoted Watford annihilated Sunderland 8-0 near the start of the 1982–83 Football League season? Which young Scottish striker, with his best days ahead of him, played for Sunderland and must have envied the ammunition supplied by the Watford wingers? (2)

10 Who scored a hat-trick for his dad's team in a 4-0 defeat of Queens Park Rangers in a December 1987 First Division match? (1)

11 Which club missed a penalty on the final day of the 1923–24 season to lose the League title by 0.0241 of a goal? (1)

12 Which Irish midfield player with 34 caps played more than 200 games for both Leeds United and Sheffield Wednesday (where he won most of his caps) in the 1980s and '90s? For which club did he rack up another 150+ appearances later in his career, carrying on as player-manager even when approaching his fortieth birthday? (2)

13 Which two sides won automatic promotion from Division 3 (fourth tier) in 1996–97, and would be in the Premier League within eight years? Which other three future Premier League clubs were in the bottom tier that season? (5)

14 Who was booked three minutes into his Millwall debut in September 2002 but was appointed player-manager within twelve months? (1)

15 Who top scored for Brighton as they won promotion to the Championship (second tier) in 2010–11, then did the same for Crystal Palace as they won promotion to the Premier League in 2012–13? Against which side did he suffer a serious leg injury, thus missing Palace's win in the play-off final? (2)

Answers on p.477

Quiz 117: General 30 (30)

1 Brazilian striker José Roberto Gama de Oliveira scored 39 goals in 75 games for Brazil (1985–98) and topped the La Liga goalscoring chart in 1992–93 playing for with Deportivo de La Coruña – what is his footballing name? (1)

2 In which city can the Estádio Monumental, which has hosted a World Cup Final, be found? By what name is it more commonly known? (2)

3 Who are the only losers to score three times in an FA Cup Final? (1)

4 Who was the Lazio striker who scored twice for Italy to help eliminate France at the 1938 World Cup finals and notched another brace in the Final to help overcome Hungary? (1)

5 This player was a Champions League runner up in 2002 and 2008, and at international level was also a World Cup semi-finalist (missing the Final through suspension) and a European Championship finalist without ever winning one of these major titles. Who is he, which were the two clubs for whom he appeared in the Champions League Final, and with which three clubs did he win a league title? (6)

6 Which 17-year-old made his league debut for Newcastle United in an end of season fixture against Queens Park Rangers in 1985? (1)

7 Which future England one-cap wonder was the division's top scorer as Brighton and Hove Albion won promotion to the Second Division in 1976–77? (1)

8 Who play in the Steel City derby? (2)

9 Who were the two future Manchester United stars in the Netherlands team at the 1998 World Cup? (2)

10 In July 1995 Liverpool broke the British record transfer fee to pay £8.5M for which striker? And from which club? (2)

11 In one of his better moments as Chairman of Fulham, which struggling lower division northern club did Mohamed Al Fayed gift £50,000, Fulham's share of the gate receipts from their FA Cup tie in 2002? (1)

12 Which attacking midfield player still holds the record for most appearances for the Belgian national team (96)? (1)

13 Which Argentina international moved from Paris St Germain to Manchester United in 2004? (1)

14 Leeds United have won three league titles; which two managers have led them there? (2)

15 Since automatic promotion from the Conference was introduced, seven teams (to the end of the 2014–15 season) have earned a first crack at the Football League but subsequently slipped back and are either defunct or were playing non-League football in 2015–16. One example would be Cheltenham Town (who, coincidentally, regained their League status at the end of 2015–16), whereas Halifax Town would not count, as they were in the League already when automatic promotion started. Can you name the other six clubs? (6)

Answers on p.478

Quiz 118: England 6 (30)

1 Burnley**, Manchester United, Blackburn Rovers*, Bury* – this is the club career (1956–1973) of which England winger, a member of the 1966 World Cup squad? (1)

2 What nationality was the referee who sent off David Beckham at the 1998 World Cup finals against Argentina? Who was the Argentinian midfielder who provoked Beckham into reacting? (2)

3 Ian Wright won 33 caps for England; how many did his strike partner at Crystal Palace, Mark Bright, gain? (1)

4 Only two Fulham players have won more than ten England caps while with the club: one was club legend Johnny Haynes, who was the other? (1)

5 Who, with a single cap in 2011, is the only player since Steve Bull to have played for England while at Wolverhampton Wanderers? (1)

6 In 1985, who scored twice against West Germany in his first England start – was it (a) Mark Hateley (b) Gary Lineker (c) Clive Allen or (d) Kerry Dixon? (1)

7 Which of these players won the most caps for England – Martin Keown, Terry Fenwick, Carlton Palmer or Steve McManaman? (1)

8 Which two Ipswich Town defenders made their England debuts together against Australia in 1980? (2)

9 In 1955, the England team against Scotland contained players aged 18 and 40: who was the ill-fated tyro and who the legendary veteran? (2)

10 Between 1985 and 1992 there were five hat-tricks scored for England: who scored them? (5)

11 Who was the first black player to appear for England in a full international? In which year did this happen? (1 point for 1 either way) (3)

12 Who top scored for England as they cruised through a group containing both the Republic and Northern Ireland en route to the 1980 European Championships? For which club did he play? Who scored a cracker on his debut against Bulgaria towards the end of qualifying? (3)

13 Who was on his way back to London after only being named as a stand-in for the 2002 World Cup squad, but earned a reprieve and ended up playing a crucial wide midfield role? An injury to which Liverpool midfield player gave him the opportunity? (2)

14 England won their qualifying group for the 2004 European Championships ahead of Turkey who they beat early in the campaign at which north-eastern ground? Who scored five goals apiece in England's campaign, a large proportion of their fourteen goals? (3)

15 Viv Woodward played his last international in 1911 and set a new scoring record of 29 goals which stood for 47 years: which duo played their last match for England in 1958 having scored 30 goals apiece? (2)

Asterisk (*) indicates that the player in question made more than one hundred league appearances for the club. (**) indicates more than two hundred league appearances.

Answers on p.478

Quiz 119: World Cup 12 (30)

1 Which unfancied team kept Argentina at bay for ninety minutes in a 2014 World Cup group match before Lionel Messi's injury-time goal inflicted a cruel defeat? (1)

2 Austria and Germany both qualified for the 1938 World Cup finals tournament; why did only Germany compete? (1)

3 Who would be the English equivalent of German sports commentator Herbert Zimmerman? (1)

4 Who has captained his country on the most occasions in World Cup finals matches? (1)

5 What unenviable record did Plácido Galindo of Peru achieve in the fifty-fourth minute of their 1930 World Cup finals match against Romania? (1)

6 Which Brazilian star's eleven appearances as a substitute in the 1998 and 2002 World Cup finals tournaments set a new record for the competition? (1)

7 Who was the centre half, captain and cornerstone of the Soviet side at the 1966 World Cup finals; he would go on to tot up a record 90 caps for the USSR? (1)

8 Who was the Italian defender bitten by Luis Suárez when Uruguay played Italy at the 2014 World Cup finals? (1)

9 Marco Etcheverry helped which country inflict a first defeat on Brazil in a World Cup qualifier and help send his country to the World Cup finals for the first time? (1)

10 The younger brother of former Brazil captain Sócrates started the 1994 World Cup finals as team captain but was left out of the knockout rounds after underperforming in the group games – what is his name? (1)

11 Which former Manchester United player, by now with rivals Manchester City, captained the Northern Ireland team at the 1986 World Cup finals? (1)

12 England qualified for the 1990 World Cup finals despite only finishing second in their group. Who won the group, drawing 0-0 twice with England in the process – was it Sweden, Denmark, Norway or Italy? (1)

13 This is the England team, by club, that went toe-to-toe with Argentina in the Last 16 of the 1998 World Cup finals, eventually losing on penalties after their finest performance since the first hour against West Germany in 1970 (4-4-2): Arsenal; Manchester United, Arsenal, Tottenham Hotspur, Chelsea; Manchester United, Manchester United, Liverpool, Tottenham Hotspur; Newcastle United, Liverpool. Subs: Aston Villa, Newcastle United and Arsenal. Who were the fourteen players, and who scored the England goals that gave them a 2-1 lead after fifteen minutes? (16)

14 Who scored an injury-time winner from a Niall Quinn knock-down to earn Ireland a draw against Germany at the 2002 World Cup finals? (1)

15 Who scored five goals at each of the World Cup finals tournaments of 2010 and 2014, winning the Golden Boot in 2010 and finishing as second top scorer in 2014? (1)

Answers on p.479

Quiz 120: Champions League 9 (30)

1 Who, in 2008 and 2009, won the Champions League with two different clubs? And who repeated that feat in 2009 and 2010? Barcelona was the club common to both, which were the other two winning teams? (4)

2 Which two players scored all Real Madrid's seven goals in the legendary 7-3 victory in the 1960 European Cup Final at Hampden Park? (2)

3 Eintracht Frankfurt, Real's opponents that night at Hampden Park, beat which side 12-4 on aggregate in the semi-final, thus preventing that team playing in the Final in their home city? And who were the English champions crushed 4-0 away and 5-2 at home by Barcelona? (2)

4 Which former World Cup winner managed Monaco when they reached the Champions League Final in 2004? (1)

5 Who announced themselves as a force in Europe when they beat Bill Shankly's Liverpool 5-1 in a European Cup tie in 1966–67? Which teenager was one of their scorers that night and scored both goals in the second leg, a 2-2 draw? (2)

6 Who was Milan's £13M 'wonderkid' who played in the 1993 European Cup Final, but never quite lived up to his billing, through a combination of pressure and injuries? (1)

7 What pop-star nickname was George Best given by adoring Portuguese fans after his brilliant performance against Benfica in the European Cup in 1966? (1)

8 Which South American striker scored both goals as AC Milan beat Manchester United 1-0 both home and away in the Last 16 of the 2004–05 Champions League? (1)

9 Who scored in each leg for Bayern Munich as they beat Real Madrid home and away to win their 2001 Champions League semi-final? Who did they beat on penalties in the Final? (2)

10 In 1992, which German team were ordered to replay a Champions League game against Leeds after fielding an ineligible player as a substitute? (1)

11 Which French club have made the most appearances (thirteen) in the group stage of the Champions League since the start of the new competition in 1992 to 2015–16? (1)

12 Which French side beat Bayern Munich home and away in the group stage of the 2009–10 Champions League? And who knocked them out in an all-French quarter-final? (2)

13 Who, in 2010, became the first referee to take charge of the Champions League Final and the World Cup Final in the same season? (1)

14 Ajax's revival in the 1990s under Louis Van Gaal led to a fourth European Cup / Champions League victory in 1995. This is their team from the Final against AC Milan (4-4-1-1, Dutch unless specified). Can you fill in the missing players (to help you along we've included the number of caps they won)? MISSING (130 caps); Michael Reiziger (72), MISSING (112), MISSING (73), Danny Blind (42); Finidi George (Nigeria, 62), MISSING (74), MISSING (87) (sub: MISSING, Nigeria, 87), MISSING (86); MISSING (Finland, 137) (sub: Patrick Kluivert, 79); Ronald de Boer (67) (8)

15 Who, by some distance, are the Scandinavian club with most appearances in the group stages of the Champions League, with eleven? (1)

Answers on p.480

Quiz 121: General 31 (30)

1 In which year were FA Cup ties first played on a Sunday – was it 1974, 1981, 1989 or 1995? (1)

2 *This Time (We'll Get It Right)* was the song that accompanied which England World Cup finals campaign? (1)

3 Which 21-year-old Hamburg forward made his World Cup finals debut in Sweden in 1958; he would still be in the side in Mexico twelve years later? (1)

4 Newell's Old Boys, Valladolid (*inc Sporting Lisbon*), Paris St Germain, Manchester United, Real Madrid, Olympique de Marseille, Roma, Newell's Old Boys – this is the career path of which recently retired robust and adaptable South American defender? (1)

5 Which future manager of Scotland played left wing for Blackburn Rovers when they lost the 1960 FA Cup Final to Wolverhampton Wanderers? Which high-profile former Premier League Chairman played in that game and broke his leg? (2)

6 Which Sudbury Court player was sold to Watford for a set of playing kit in 1981? (1)

7 Who played his 1,000th competitive game in a 0-0 draw with West Bromwich Albion in the English First Division in February 1983? (1)

8 Who were the two overseas-based players in the 2006 England World Cup finals squad? (2)

9 What was the name of the ground Brighton & Hove Albion were forced to sell in 1995 to pay their debts? With which other club did they share a ground with for two years? What is the name of the athletics stadium the club used from 1999 to 2011 while their new ground was planned and built? By what name, taken from the sponsors, is the Falmer Stadium, their new ground, usually known? Who were the last opponents at the original old ground and also, coincidentally, the first league

opponents at the new ground – was it (a) Blackburn Rovers (b) Doncaster Rovers (c) Wycombe Wanderers or (d) Queens Park Rangers? (5)

10 A 2002 league match between which two clubs had to be abandoned when one side went down to less than the required seven players? Which manager engineered two spurious injuries to effect this outcome after three of his side were red-carded? (3)

11 This is the Nottingham Forest that won the League cup for the third time in 1989 against Luton Town. Who is missing (4-4-2, English unless stated)? Steve Sutton; Brian Laws, MISSING, Terry Wilson (Scotland), MISSING; Tommy Gaynor (Republic of Ireland), MISSING, Garry Parker, MISSING; Lee Chapman, MISSING. Clue: the missing players won 201 caps for England between them. (5)

12 Farul Constanta; Sportul Bucharest*; Steaua Bucharest; Real Madrid; Brescia; Barcelona; Galatasaray* – which East European legend's club career is mapped out here? (1)

13 Which Brazilian was deported immediately after signing for Arsenal for £6M in 2000 when it was found his passport was a fake? (1)

14 In 2011 Carlos Tevez became the first Manchester City player for thirty-nine years to be top scorer in the top flight of English football. Who was the previous one? And which striker from across the city was joint top scorer with Tevez? (2)

15 Which former Tottenham Hotspur star was manager of the opposition when Spurs were annihilated 8-2 by Derby County in 1976? Which former colleague was in goal for Spurs? Which midfield player scored four goals for Derby? (3)

Asterisk (*) indicates that the player in question made more than one hundred league appearances for the club.

Answers on p.480

Quiz 122: Global 5 (30)

1 Cerro Porteño, Guarani, Libertad, Nacional, Olimpia, Rubio Ñu are all top-flight clubs (2016) playing in which capital city? (1)

2 How many caps did Mark Viduka and Harry Kewell manage between them for Australia – was it 227, 194, 133 or 99? (1)

3 São Paolo, AC Milan, Real Madrid, AC Milan, Orlando City (*inc São Paolo*); which 21st-century star's career path is this (he was born Ricardo Izecson dos Santos Leite)? (1)

4 Both Ajax and Bayern Munich refused to play in the Intercontinental Cup in the 1970s because of the violent attitude of which Argentinian team in their 1972 tie against Ajax? (1)

5 Which of these North / Central American countries has never played at a World Cup finals tournament – Cuba, Haiti, Honduras, Panama, Trinidad and Tobago? (1)

6 With which Japanese team did Gary Lineker finish his playing career? (1)

7 After winning the Copa América in 1949, how many years did Brazil have to wait before they again won the tournament – was it 2, 22, 30 or 40? (1)

8 Saúl Martínez scored twice as which South American country stunned holders Brazil at the 2001 Copa América? (1)

9 Which Colombian striker signed for Wigan Athletic in 2009 and spent the next six years in England, three with the Latics and three with which London club? (2)

10 Who reached the African Cup of Nations Final for the only time in their history in 1978, with the country still ruled by a former British army officer turned military dictator? Who were the tournament hosts that year, who beat them 2-0 in the Final in Accra? (2)

11 In the 2000 African Cup of Nations only four players were based with English clubs. One was Moussa Saib of Tottenham Hotspur and Algeria, the other three were South Africans with Leeds United, Manchester United and Bolton Wanderers respectively – can you name them? (3)

12 Javier Zanetti, who won a record number of caps for Argentina (143), played more than 600 matches and spent nearly fifteen years as captain of which Italian club? (1)

13 At the 2006 African Cup of Nations, Côte d'Ivoire squeezed past Cameroon 12-11 after a superb exhibition of penalty taking. Which two all-time greats were forced to step up for a second time after all eleven players on each side had taken a kick? (2)

14 Of the 368 players named in the various squads for the 2015 African Cup of Nations, how many were based with English clubs – was it 14, 22, 33 or 5? And which two nations had (jointly) the most English-based players? (2)

15 Which ten Asian countries, one now defunct, have appeared in the World Cup finals? (exclude Australia, even though they have qualified via the Asian federation)? (10)

Answers on p.481

Quiz 123: Football League 13 (30)

1 Who came back from the 1982 World Cup to score Watford's first-ever goal in the top flight of English football? (1)

2 Which club from north-west England finished second in the league in 1914–15, the last season before the First World War, were relegated in 1923, and never saw top-flight football again until gaining promotion in 1991? (1)

3 When Derby County won the First Division in 1971–72 with 58 points, which three clubs finished on 57? (3)

4 Which duo were Liverpool's top two scorers in their title-winning seasons of 1973, 1976 and 1977? (2)

5 Who was Second Division top scorer as Leicester City fought their way back into the top flight in 1982–83? (1)

6 Which player filled the left back slot and captained the 'Busby Babes', the Manchester United side who won the First Division title in 1956 and 1957? And who was the centre half in the side who was the only ever-present in both title-winning seasons? Both players were among the eight killed in the Munich air disaster. (2)

7 Which club won successive promotions in 1967 and 1968 to take their place in the First Division for the first time? Who was the manager who oversaw this rise? Which Second Division club did he lead to an FA Cup Final a few years later? (3)

8 Which club once had snooker magnate Barry Hearn as its Chairman? (1)

9 Who were the first club to use an artificial pitch, and was it in 1974, 1981 or 1989? (2)

10 Title winners Leeds United spread their 66 goals around the team in 1973–74: which four players all reached double figures? (4)

11 Which four Southampton players each finished the season as top scorer in the English First Division between 1967 and 1982? (4)

12 Who fell into the Fourth Division for the first time in their history at the end of the 1986–87 season, losing to Aldershot (sixth in the Fourth Division) in the newly devised play-off system? Which former multiple trophy winner with Liverpool was the manager at the time, who avoided the sack and brought them back up the following season? (2)

13 Who scored the dramatic late goal that took Crystal Palace into the Premier League via the play-offs at the expense of Sheffield United in 1996–97? (1)

14 In their best season since departing the Premier League, Nottingham Forest finished sixth in Division One (second tier) in 2002–03: which former Ipswich Town striker top scored with 25 goals, and which player added a further 20, including four in a slaughter of Stoke City, in his best haul before leaving for West Ham United that summer? (2)

15 Rangers (*inc Doncaster Rovers*), Motherwell, Cardiff City, Leeds United, Fulham, Aston Villa: which Scottish international striker's club career is mapped out here (still playing in 2016–17)? (1)

Answers on p.482

Answers on p.482

Quiz 124: Scotland 6 (30)

1 Which goalkeeper, who became Scotland's most-capped no.1, was an uncapped and unused squad member at the 1982 World Cup finals? With which club did he win the Scottish league and a European trophy? Who was the manager who controversially replaced him for a 1990 FA Cup Final replay after he made an error in the first game? (3)

2 Which Celtic legend was the first winner of the Scottish Footballer of the Year award in 1965? (1)

3 Who was appointed manager of Celtic on his retirement from playing in 1999 but had an unhappy few months in charge? (1)

4 Who was the first overseas (permanent) manager of Celtic, from 1991 to 1993? (1)

5 In which year did over-enthusiastic Scottish fans tear down the goalposts and remove parts of the turf at Wembley? (1)

6 Which Scottish winger was dubbed the 'Flying Flea' by the French press after a European tie against Nantes? (1)

7 From 1904–05 to 1946–47 only Celtic or Rangers won the Scottish League title: who broke the cycle in 1948–49? (1)

8 To 2014–15 Rangers and Celtic have won 100 Scottish titles between them: which three sides have won four each? (3)

9 Who was the only player to finish as top scorer in the Scottish First Division twice in the 1980s, leaving for the north west of England after the second occasion in 1987? (1)

10 Henrik Larsson was the Scottish top flight's top scorer in five seasons out of six from 1998–99: which other Celtic player was top of the tree in 1999–2000 when Larsson missed most of the season through injury? (1)

11 Who were promoted to the Scottish Premiership in 2013–14 after over-turning a 2-0 home defeat in the first leg of the play-offs against Hibernian? Who was their manager, who departed for Norwich City at the end of that promotion season? (2)

12 Which two midfield players in the St Mirren side that won the 1988 Scottish Cup Final went on to play more than 200 games for Celtic and Rangers respectively? (2)

13 Who was the Hearts goalkeeper whose £9M transfer to Sunderland broke the British transfer fee for a goalkeeper? (1)

14 Which three grounds hosted the Scottish Cup Final in the twentieth century? (3)

15 This is the Rangers side that destroyed Aberdeen in the 2000 Scottish Cup Final, by country – can you fill in the missing names (5-3-2)? MISSING (Germany); MISSING (United States), MISSING (Australia), Tony Vidmar (Australia), MISSING (Netherlands, captain), MISSING (Netherlands); MISSING (Russia), MISSING (Scotland), Jörg Albertz (Germany); Rod Wallace (England), MISSING (Scotland) (8)

Answers on p.482

Quiz 125: General 32 (20)

1 By what first name does the striker whose surname is Aiyegbeni prefer to be known? (1)

2 In World Cup terms, what connects Paolo Maldini, Diego Forlán, Xabi Alonso and Daley Blind? (1)

3 Tim started his career in midfield just as goalkeeper Steve left the same club in 1987; what was the surname and which was the club? (2)

4 Who played in his sixth FA Cup Final in 1987, sixteen years after his first? (1)

5 Who won the PFA Young Player of the Year award in 1985, and the grown-up one in 1989, after a successful return from a largely unsuccessful stint abroad? Where was the unhappy spell abroad? (2)

6 Fulham scored an impressive 90 goals on their way to winning Division One (second tier) in 2000–01. Which three players, two imports and one who worked his way up from non-League football, scored more than fifteen each? And which three players, one a goalkeeper, one a full back and one a former Newcastle midfielder, missed only five matches between them that season? (6)

7 Who, in 1977, became the first man to have lifted both the Scottish FA Cup and the FA Cup as captain? Which was the Scottish side? (2)

8 Asa Hartford and Phil Neal both had stints as Manchester City manager in the first half of season 1996–97: who were the three full-time occupants of the post in this extraordinary merry-go-round? (3)

9 Harold Shepherdson, who died in 1995, aged seventy-six, played what role in England's World Cup victory in 1966? (1)

10 Whose famous shirt fetched a record £157,750 in auction at Christie's? (2)

11 Who were the two players from outside the British Isles in the Manchester United team that beat Nottingham Forest 1-0 in the 1992 League Cup Final? Which two players in the Forest line-up would later play for United? (4)

12 From which Argentinian club did Barcelona buy Diego Maradona? Which other Spanish club did he play for? (2)

13 Which Chelsea and Australia goalkeeper was suspended for nine months in 2003 after testing positive for cocaine? (1)

14 In 1970–71 Bournemouth climbed out of Division Four, and they nearly won promotion again the following year, finishing third. Which prolific lower division striker was top scorer in both seasons, hitting the net an impressive 77 times? (1)

15 Test Matches, played in 1894, were a precursor of what modern end-of-season system? (1)

Answers on p.483

Quiz 126: Champions League 10 (30)

1 Eight players played in all three of Bayern Munich's European Cup victories in the 1970s: you can be forgiven for not remembering Roth, Kapellman or Dürnberger, but who were the other five, all seasoned internationals? (5)

2 In 1971–72, which team lost a European Cup match 7-1 to Borussia Mönchengladbach and yet won the tie after a replay was ordered because one of their players was hit on the head by a can thrown from the crowd? (1)

3 Which German star won a European Cup winner's medal with Real Madrid in 1998 – was it Thomas Hässler, Bodo Illgner, Jürgen Klinsmann or Christian Ziege? (1)

4 Which Italian side beat Celtic in the 2006–07 Champions League after they reached the knockout phase for the first time since the new format was introduced? Which Japanese international's goal earned them a 1-0 win over Manchester United in the group phase? (2)

5 Who were the opponents when Manchester United came from 2-0 behind to win 3-2 in the semi-final of the 1999 Champions League after a 1-1 draw at Old Trafford? (1)

6 Why did referee Anders Frisk announce his retirement after Chelsea's acrimonious Champions League tie with Barcelona in Spring, 2005? (1)

7 Who were the opposing managers when Bayern Munich beat Borussia Dortmund in the Final of the 2013 Champions League? (2)

8 Which famous German club, a powerhouse in the 1970s, qualified for the group stage of the 2015–16 Champions League, their first appearance in the new competition? (1)

9 Which side were Manchester City unfortunate enough to draw in the Last 16 of the Champions League in 2014 and 2015? (1)

10 In the 2008–09 Champions League Last 16 Bayern Munich beat a hapless Sporting Lisbon side 12-1 on aggregate. Who was the only player to score in both legs as eight Bayern players got on the scoresheet? (1)

11 When Arsenal won 3-2 away at Celta Vigo in the Last 16 of the 2003–04 Champions League, two Brazilians who bore the same football name scored three of the goals: what was the name? (2)

12 Who scored a hat-trick as Dynamo Kiev beat Barcelona 4-0 away in a 1997–98 Champions League group match? And who scored a hat-trick in Kiev as Juventus beat the Ukrainians 4-1 in the away leg of the quarter-final? (2)

13 Who, to 2016, are the only two coaches to have won three European Cup or Champions League trophies? (2)

14 Real Madrid have won the major European prize five times since the advent of the Champions League (to 2014–15). Which six French players have played in those winning Finals? (6)

15 Who scored five goals as Ipswich Town, the English Champions, beat Floriana 10-0 in the European Cup in 1962? And which island nation was represented by the Floriana club? (2)

Answers on p.483

Quiz 127: FA Cup 6 (30)

1 Which side won six of the first nine FA Cup Finals? (1)

2 Who scored both goals in Newcastle's 1951 FA Cup Final victory? (1)

3 Which goalkeeper saved a penalty to earn non-Leaguers Wimbledon a goalless draw at Leeds in 1975, but retired soon after the club joined the Football League? Of which club is he currently (July 2016) the President? (2)

4 Which future FA Cup Final goalscorer won and converted the penalty for York City that eliminated Arsenal in the 1985 competition? (1)

5 Who were the only club to win the FA Cup twice in the 1970s? (1)

6 In 1986–87 Welsh valleys side Ton Pentre reached the first round proper for the only time. Who did fate pair them with in that tie, which they lost 4-1? (1)

7 Who won the FA Cup in 1923, the first year the Final was played at the newly built Wembley Stadium, and who were their Second Division opponents, beaten 2-0 by goals from David Jack and Jack Smith? (2)

8 Who are the only club to have played in four FA Cup Finals and lost the lot? (1)

9 Fill in the MISSING players from the Arsenal team that beat Sheffield Wednesday in the FA Cup Final replay in 1993 (4-3-3, they are all English): Seaman; MISSING, MISSING, MISSING, Winterburn; Davis, MISSING, Jensen; Campbell, MISSING (sub: O'Leary), MISSING (6)

10 Who scored twice from the penalty spot in the 1994 FA Cup Final against Chelsea? (1)

11 Which two managers led out the teams for the 1965 FA Cup Final between Leeds United and Liverpool in 1965? (2)

12 Which non-League side (who joined the Football League soon after) beat top flight Newcastle United 2-1 in an FA Cup third round replay in 1972? Who entered FA Cup folklore by scoring the goals? Who was the young commentator on trial with the BBC who provided the memorable TV soundtrack? (4)

13 Arsenal's line-up for the 2001 FA Cup Final had five Englishmen at the back and five Frenchmen further forward: who was the eleventh team member? (1)

14 Who scored the goal that won the 2008 FA Cup for Portsmouth? (1)

15 In the 1990 FA Cup semi-final Crystal Palace were written off against Liverpool, having lost to them at Anfield in the league at the start of the season by what score? Which player, who would later manage the club, scored Palace's winner in a 4-3 extra-time thriller? Who scored in the semi and also in the first Final at Wembley, which finished 3-3? And who returned from injury to score Palace's other two goals in that draw with Manchester United? Which full back's goal finally quashed the dream in the replay? (5)

Answers on p.484

Quiz 128: Football League 14 (30)

1 What new dimension was added to the Football League in 1892? (1)

2 Which seventeen-year-old became the youngest scorer of a First Division hat-trick in 1988? For which club? (2)

3 Which of his former players took over as manager of Nottingham Forest when Brian Clough retired after Forest were relegated from the Premier League in 1992–93? Who was their first major signing, from Southend, who proved a good investment by scoring 19 league goals as Forest returned immediately to the top flight in 1993–94? (2)

4 In an unprecedented move, Port Vale were admitted to the Second Division of the Football League in mid-season in October 1919. Which club were forcibly disbanded after financial malpractices were exposed – was it (a) Leicester Fosse (b) Leeds City (c) Woolwich Arsenal or (d) Norwich Albion? (Clue: they returned to the league the following season under their current name) (1)

5 Which former player and England international was manager of Wolverhampton Wanderers during the 1950s, by some distance their most successful era? How many league titles did they win? Who was the club captain for most of the decade? (3)

6 In 1963–64 the biggest home win was a 10-1 slaughter of Ipswich Town by Fulham (the London club's record win), while the biggest away win of the season was Blackburn's 8-2 win at West Ham: what was remarkable about these results? (1)

7 Who ended their only spell (two seasons) below the top two divisions when they strolled to the Division Three title in 1971–72 – was it (a) Manchester United (b) Tottenham Hotspur (c) Aston Villa or (d) Wolverhampton Wanderers? (1)

8 Who, in December 1935, scored all seven goals, a top-flight record that still stands, as Arsenal beat Aston Villa 7-1 at Villa Park? (1)

9 Which other club from the north-west replaced Southport in the Football League when they were voted out in 1978 after a third consecutive 23rd-place finish? And which third north-west club had actually finished bottom that season and were expected by many to be the ones to give way? (2)

10 Which club were forced to share Bath City's Twerton Park stadium for a number of years? (1)

11 1996–97 was a north-west bonanza. Manchester United won the Premiership; who won the other three divisions? (3)

12 Who made his Middlesbrough debut as a substitute in the club's 2-0 defeat by Chelsea in the 1998 League Cup Final? Which Chelsea player scored against them in a major final for the second year running? (2)

13 Who was the larger-than-life character who managed Barnet when they won promotion to the league? (1)

14 In 1975–76, which defender scored all four goals in a 2-2 draw between Aston Villa and Leicester? (1)

15 Not all clubs have changed the name of their stadium to suit their sponsors. If fixtures were played one weekend at Glanford Park, Roots Hall, Brunton Park, the Keepmoat Stadium, Prenton Park, Deepdale, Meadow Lane and Craven Cottage, who would be the eight home teams? (8)

Answers on p.485

Quiz 129: General 33 (30)

1 Cambridge United* (*inc Barnet, 1 game*), Manchester United, Coventry City*, Aston Villa* (*inc Millwall, 5 games*), Leicester City, Celtic, Norwich City: whose club career path is this from the 1990s and 2000s? (1)

2 Irish side Cobh Ramblers are best known for selling which player to Nottingham Forest for £47,000? (1)

3 To 2014–15 which six clubs have made ten or more appearances in the semi-finals of the European Cup or Champions League? (6)

4 Which army regiment has won the FA Cup? (1)

5 Which German player was the first winner, in 1991, of the FIFA World Footballer of the Year award? (1)

6 Which team pipped England on goal difference to qualification for the 1978 World Cup finals, despite England winning the last game 2-0 with a fine performance at Wembley? (1)

7 Who beat West Ham United 6-0 in the first leg of a League Cup semi-final between two Second Division teams in 1990? Which three teams, who finished fourth and seventh in the top flight and top of the second flight, did they beat on their way to the Final? Who beat them in the semi-finals of the FA Cup in a replay after they had knocked out top flight opposition (Aston Villa and Everton) in that competition as well? What did they achieve the following season? Who was the club's manager during this heady period? (7)

8 Who played more than 200 league games for Banik Ostrava in Czechoslovakia in the 1980s before playing more than 300 for West Ham United in the '90s? (1)

9 Who, according to the fans of first Manchester City and later Sunderland, had disco pants? (1)

10 In February 1996 Sepp Blatter, President of FIFA, announced a suggested proposal – was it to (a) have two referees in each match, one for each half, (b) offer the World Cup to the highest bidding nation, (c) make the goals bigger, (d) award a penalty for any tackle deemed worthy of a red card, no matter where the offence took place? (1)

11 Which combined counties club, founded on a wave of protest, attracted a crowd of 2,449 for a match against Sandhurst Town in the Combined Counties League, the ninth tier of the league and non-League system? With which non-League club did they share a ground? (2)

12 Who scored the winner for Arsenal in the 1993 League Cup Final? What, memorably/unfortunately happened next? (3)

13 Who was the balding playmaker who scored with a diving header to knock Germany out of the 1994 World Cup? For which German club was he playing at the time? (2)

14 Which seaside club won their only title (Division Four) in 1972–73 (they were the last club to be voted out of the league – in 1978 – under the old re-election system)? (1)

15 John White was an ever-present at inside forward in Tottenham's 1961 Double-winning side of 1960–61; what unfortunate fate befell White three years later – was he (a) drowned on a sailing holiday in the Mediterranean, (b) killed in a skiing accident, (c) killed when he was struck by lightning or (d) struck down with a heart attack in the middle of a training session? (1)

Asterisk (*) indicates that the player in question made more than one hundred league appearances for the club.

Answers on p.485

Quiz 130: World Cup 13 (30)

1 Which Italian star of their two World Cup wins in 1934 and 1938 gives his name to the official title of the stadium known popularly as the San Siro in Milan? (1)

2 Which Blackpool striker scored a hat-trick against Spain in a vital qualifier for the 1958 World Cup finals tournament? (1)

3 Which Colombian player broke Roger Milla's record as the oldest player to feature in a World Cup finals game? (1)

4 Name the five players (to 2014) to have been sent off in a World Cup Final (5)

5 Who lifted spirits in Peru days after a massive earthquake by scoring four times in three group games to see them through to the quarter-finals of the 1970 World Cup? (1)

6 What happened for the first time in twenty years at the opening game of the 1982 World Cup finals between Belgium and Argentina? (1)

7 Which two of these African countries have never qualified for a World Cup finals tournament – Angola, Democratic Republic of Congo, Mali, Senegal, Sierra Leone, Togo, Tunisia? (2)

8 Which two men coached Argentina to success in the World Cup? (2)

9 Who was red-carded during England's 2-1 defeat by Brazil at the 2002 World Cup finals? Whose opening goal gave England hope of a famous victory? (2)

10 Who was the 6'7" centre forward who led the attack for the Czech Republic, scoring nine goals in qualification for the 2006 World Cup? Who was his strike partner, whose performances for his country belied his shaky form with Liverpool and Aston Villa either side of the 2006 tournament? (2)

11   Which Brazilian full back, now a TV pundit, was sent off and given a lengthy ban for a shocking elbow on the USA's Tab Ramos at the 1994 World Cup finals? Who was his experienced replacement, a veteran of the previous two World Cup campaigns, who won Brazil's quarter-final against the Netherlands with a stunning free kick? (2)

12   The second leg of Turkey's play-off for a place at the 2006 World Cup finals was an intimidating affair (games in Istanbul often are). This one ended with a mass brawl in the tunnel resulting in some hefty bans and fines; who were Turkey's opponents, who qualified on away goals after a 4-2 defeat? (1)

13   Roberto Baggio, Franco Baresi, Giuseppe Bergomi, Fabio Cannavaro, Alessandro Del Piero, Paolo Maldini, Alessandro Nesta, Andrea Pirlo, Christian Vieri. Ten great Italian footballers – but which two never played in a World Cup Final? And which other three never won one? (5)

14   Who missed a penalty for Ghana against Uruguay right at the end of extra time at the 2010 World Cup finals, sending the game into a penalty shoot-out which Ghana lost? Who was given a red card for handball on the line, leading to the extra time penalty? (1)

15   Counting the Americas as one continent, which three countries have won the World Cup outside their own continent? (3)

Answers on p.486

Quiz 131: England 7 (30)

1 Which South African-born player played two games for England under Don Revie as well as making more 300 appearances for Ipswich Town – was it (a) Eric Gates (b) Trevor Whymark (c) Colin Viljoen or (d) Kevin Beattie? (1)

2 Which important figure in English football history was the team's right back at the 1950 World Cup finals? He was one of four players from which club, the best represented in the squad? (2)

3 Who was England's caretaker manager during the transition from Alf Ramsey to Don Revie in 1974? (1)

4 Who were the ten Ipswich Town players capped by England during Bobby Robson's thirteen-year tenure as manager of the club? Which of them won most caps while at the club? Who is the club's only England international since? (12)

5 Between 1975 and 1982 there was a gap of seven and a half years when no player scored a hat-trick for England. Who broke the drought against Luxembourg in 1982? (1)

6 In 1998, who became England's youngest goalscorer of the twentieth century, aged 18 years 164 days? (1)

7 'In The Name of Allah, Go!' was *The Sun*'s rather unkind exhortation to England manager, Bobby Robson after a 1-1 draw against which country in 1988? (1)

8 Who was the last player to win twenty England caps while playing with Derby County? (1)

9 Which of these sides is the only one to have beaten England in a full international: Bulgaria, Finland, Switzerland, Turkey? (1)

10 Who, in 2015, became the first man to play for England while on the books at Swansea City? (1)

11 How many of Bryan Robson's 90 caps were played as captain – was it 18, 34, 49 or 65? (1)

12 Who made his England debut against West Germany at Wembley in February 1966? (1)

13 How many times did Bobby Charlton captain England during his 106 caps – was it 3, 8, 11 or 22? (1)

14 Which defender scored his first goal for England in his first competitive match, a qualifier for the 2012 European Championships in Bulgaria? For which club was he playing, becoming the first player from that club to score for England since 1959? (2)

15 Which three midfield players have scored more than 25 goals for England? (3)

Answers on p.487

Quiz 132: Northern Ireland 3 (30)

1 Northern Ireland qualified for the World Cup finals in 1958, 1982 and 1986: who was the only man involved in the team on all three occasions? (1)

2 During qualification for the 1978 World Cup Northern Ireland enjoyed a patchy campaign, losing in Iceland but gaining a creditable 2-2 draw with the Netherlands, Cruyff et al. Which Blackpool player, a recent recruit from Bury where he made his name, scored a late equaliser to frustrate the Dutch – was it (a) Trevor Anderson (b) Derek Spence (c) Billy Hamilton or (d) Tommy Jackson? (1)

3 Which much-capped Northern Ireland player had to put his career on hold briefly in 2002 when Wimbledon and Birmingham City failed to resolve a dispute over his contract? Which club employed him the following year, aged 32, and squeezed another 100+ matches out of him? (2)

4 What connects the international careers of Mal Donaghy (91 caps for Northern Ireland), David McCreery (67) and Nigel Worthington (66)? (1)

5 Who was the first Northern Ireland player to hit 50 caps? (1)

6 When Northern Ireland won the 1979–80 Home Championships, which Blackburn Rovers winger made his debut in the first match, scored an own goal in the second, and closed it by scoring the winning goal against Wales that sealed the title? Which other winger, playing for Middlesbrough at the time, cancelled out the own goal a minute later to earn Northern Ireland a rare point at Wembley? (2)

7 The current (July 2016) inspirational captain of the Northern Ireland team, Steven Davis, was brought to Southampton from which club in 2012? (1)

8 Terry Neill's playing career with Northern Ireland spanned twelve years (1961–73) and spells with which two clubs? Neill managed both clubs and his country; which other team did he also manage from 1974 to 1976? (3)

9 Northern Ireland qualified for the 1982 World Cup finals, seeing off Sweden in the process. Which full back scored the only goal what would be a 74-cap international career in the 3-1 in over Sweden? And which

hard-working lower division striker scored vital goals to win both the home matches against Portugal and Israel 1-0? Who won the group, losing only their last game when they had already qualified as group winners? (3)

10 Qualification for the 1980 European Championships saw Northern Ireland drawn in with England and the Republic of Ireland. England predictably won the group, but which Burnley striker gave the North victory over the Republic in Belfast, to earn local bragging rights after the Dublin game was drawn 0-0? (1)

11 Who were the Arsenal full backs who played together for Northern Ireland on numerous occasions in the 1970s and won 100 caps between them? Which one of the pair won 51 caps to the other's 49? (3)

12 Willoughby Hamilton, who won a solitary cap for Northern Ireland in 1885, was a talented sportsman. What was his most considerable achievement – was it (a) holding the world record for the discus throw for two years, (b) winning Wimbledon in 1890, (c) winning a swimming Gold Medal at the 1900 Olympic Games or (d) winning the boat race with Oxford University for two years in succession? (1)

13 Which Northern Ireland left back, who made his debut in 2012, shares a surname with the country's current main striker (July 2016)? Which club do the two have in common? (2)

14 This is the Northern Ireland line-up for one of their greatest nights, the 1-0 win over Spain at the 1982 World Cup (4-4-2): Pat Jennings (Arsenal); MISSING (Toronto Blizzard), MISSING (Southampton), John McClelland (Rangers), MISSING (Luton Town); MISSING (Norwich City), David McCreery (Tulsa Roughnecks), MISSING (Stoke City) (Sub: Tommy Cassidy, Burnley), MISSING (Manchester United) (Sub: Sammy Nelson, Arsenal); Gerry Armstrong (Watford), MISSING (Burnley). Fill in the missing players. (7)

15 The first top scorer in a Home International championships (mainly by dint of bagging four against Wales) was a Northern Ireland striker – was he called (a) Olphert Stanfield (b) Billy Crone (c) Manliffe Goodbody or (d) Jack Peden? (1)

Answers on p.487

Quiz 133: General 34 (30)

1 Cameroon won the 2000 Olympic Football tournament by coming from 2-0 down to level and win on penalties; which team, containing two future World Cup winners, did they beat? (1)

2 Sponsors of a cup competition for lower division sides have included Freight Rover, Sherpa Vans and Autoglass: who are the current sponsors (2006–2016)? (1)

3 Brothers André ('Trello') and Max Abegglen were pre-war stars for which European country? (1)

4 Which band played on England's Euro '96 anthem, *Three Lions*, alongside the songs' lyricists and promoters, comedians Baddiel and Skinner? (1)

5 Celtic, Arsenal*, Aberdeen, Celtic*, Clyde: whose career path is this, from 1980 onwards, and how many goals did he score in his 20 games for Scotland? (1 point for 1 either way) (3)

6 Which goalkeeper was a mainstay of both the Barcelona and Spanish national side throughout the late Eighties and Nineties – was it (a) Zubizarrelia (b) Zubizarreta (c) Goicocechea or (d) Goicoecharreta? (1)

7 Who played twice for Brazil in 2003 and made his debut for his adopted country, Italy, in 2011? (1)

8 Who, by winning the 1996 Olympic Football tournament in Atlanta, became the first African country to win a major international competition? Who scored two late goals, one a 94th-minute Golden Goal, as they eliminated Brazil 4-3 in the semi-finals? (2)

9 Gary Briggs and Malcolm Shotton were the redoubtable central defenders as which unfashionable team won the 1986 League Cup Final against Queens Park Rangers? Which division were the team in? And which two players from that Final signed for Liverpool the following year? (4)

10 What was unusual about Team Bath, who took their place in the first round of the FA Cup in November 2002 after beating Horsham? (2)

11 This is the Blackburn Rovers side that beat Tottenham Hotspur to win the League Cup in 2002 – can you fill in the gaps (4-4-2, English unless stated)? MISSING (United States); Nils Eric Johansson (Sweden), MISSING (Norway), Martin Taylor, Stig-Inge Bjornebye (Norway); MISSING (Northern Ireland) (sub: Craig Hignett), David Dunn, MISSING (Wales), MISSING (Republic of Ireland); Matt Jansen (sub: Yordi, Spain), MISSING. Which manager brought Rovers their first major cup trophy since 1928? (7)

12 What relationship is Sergio Agüero to Argentina legend Diego Maradona? (1)

13 Which club bought Peter Crouch from Portsmouth for £4.5M in 2002? (1)

14 Which two players played in every game of both of Leeds United's title winning seasons in 1968–69 and 1973–74? (2)

15 In 1973–74 which Southampton striker finished as the First Division's top scorer despite the club being relegated? What other sport did he enter on his retirement? (2)

Asterisk (*) indicates that the player in question made more than one hundred league appearances for the club.

Answers on p.488

Quiz 134: European Competitions 7 (30)

1 Which two English clubs did Celtic overcome on their way to the 2003 UEFA Cup Final? Which four decidedly non-Scottish players scored all Celtic's goals in those two ties? (6)

2 Congratulations, your team has just won the Ekstraklasa. The what? (1)

3 He started with Empoli, but Antonio Di Natale's impressive goalscoring record in Serie A has been with which unfashionable club since 2004 – was it (a) Chievo (b) Udinese (c) Cagliari or (d) Perugia ? (1)

4 Which crack European outfit remained undefeated at home for 114 matches between 1957 and 1965? (1)

5 Who scored a hat-trick in both legs for Queens Park Rangers in their first ever European tie, an 11-0 aggregate win over SK Brann of Norway in the UEFA Cup? (1)

6 In 1998 Chelsea beat Vfb Stuttgart in the Final of the European Cup Winners' Cup: who scored the Chelsea goal within a minute of coming on as a substitute? Who was the only England international in the Chelsea team? Who was manager of Chelsea at the time? And who was the Stuttgart coach, who has gone on to enjoy a much more successful time as a manager than his counterpart? (4)

7 Which two namesakes scored five of the six Juventus goals when they hammered Dortmund 6-1 on aggregate in the 1993 UEFA Cup Final? (2)

8 Who kept goal for Aberdeen in the 1983 European Cup Winners' Cup Final? (1)

9 Who became the third Ukrainian club to contest a European club competition final when they reached the Final of the Europa League in 2015? Who beat them 3-2 on the big day? (2)

10 Who briefly went second in the Premier League in October 2005 after a Pascal Chimbonda goal gave them a 1-0 win over Fulham? Which club did Chimbonda join after an excellent first season? (2)

11 Brazilian strikers Romário and Ronaldo both had spells with which Dutch club early in their career? (1)

12 Who topped the La Liga goalscoring lists four years out of five (1959–60 to 1963–64) while playing for Real Madrid in his mid-thirties? (1)

13 Which German side play at the Westfalenstadion? (1)

14 Fill in the gaps in the Norwich City side that famously beat Bayern Munich 2-1 in Munich in the 1993–94 UEFA Cup (1-3-4-2): Bryan Gunn; MISSING; Spencer Prior, MISSING (captain), Rob Newman; Ruel Fox, MISSING, Ian Crook, MISSING; Mark Robins (sub: Daryl Sutch), MISSING. (Both missing midfield players were Welsh internationals) (5)

15 In European competition, clubs from which nation are the only ones to have beaten Manchester United more than they have lost? (1)

Answers on p.489

Quiz 135: Premier League 16 (40)

1 Croatia international Boško Balaban joined which Premier League club for £6M in 2001 but never started a Premiership match? (1)

2 In commercial terms, what was the significance of Chelsea's home game against Newcastle United on Sunday 19 August, 2001? (2)

3 Some shocking signings made in the 2004–05 season. We've listed eight players with prices, selling (laughing!) club and appearances/ goals for the purchasing club: can you name the fools easily parted from their money? Josemi (Malaga, £2M, 21/0); Mateja Kezman (PSV, £5.3M, 25/4); Jelle van Damme (Ajax, £2.5M, 6/0); Djibril Cisse (Auxerre, £14M, 49/13); Mathieu Berson (Nantes, £1.6M, 11/0); Jean Alain Boumsong (Rangers, £8M, 47/10); Aleksander Rodic (Gorica, £1M, 4/0); Francis Jeffers (Arsenal, £2.6M, 20/3). (8)

4 Which club gave Glenn Hoddle his first management job after leaving the England post? (1)

5 Which ill-fated Cameroon international did West Ham United buy from Lens for more than £4M in January 1999? And what was their other signing that week, excellent value at £1.7M from Sheffield Wednesday? (2)

6 Which team recorded the Premier League's lowest ever attendance of 3,039 in 1993 for a mid-table fixture against Everton? What was the name of the ground where this unwanted record was achieved? (2)

7 Which Yorkshire club, relegated at the end of the season, were on the receiving end as Newcastle United won 8-0 in Bobby Robson's first home game in charge in September 1999? Who scored five of the goals and who was in goal for the opposition? Which former Newcastle 'keeper replaced him for the next match? (4)

8 Who scored his first goal for Arsenal in his 98th game for the club on New Year's Eve, 1994, prompting uproar and the North Bank and subsequent t-shirts declaring 'I've seen ******** score!'? (1)

9 Who was the London-born Guyanese international who played in the Premier League with Wimbledon, Newcastle United and Wolverhampton Wanderers? (His caps came as a veteran when he was no longer a force at the top level) (1)

10 Who scored a hat-trick in the final Premier League match at Highbury as Arsenal beat Wigan Athletic 4-2 in May 2006? (1)

11 Manchester City paid £19M for Brazilian forward Jo in July 2008: from which Russian club did they buy him, and how many Premier League goals did he score for City in his three seasons at the club? (2)

12 Which Irish international scored Stoke City's first Premier League hat-trick, grabbing all his team's goals in a 3-1 win over Queens Park Rangers in January 2015? (1)

13 Who was the first player to score twenty goals in a Premier League season for Manchester City? (1)

14 To date (August 2016), thirty-six players who have played in the Premier League have also played international football for Jamaica: how many of them were born on the island (1 point for 2 each way)? Which of them has the most international caps? And which three notched up more than 200 Premier League appearances? (6)

15 Aston Villa endured a nightmarish season in 2015–16. Here is a reminder of happier days, the team that inflicted a 7-1 thrashing on Wimbledon in 1995. Can you fill in the missing players (5-2-3, English unless stated)? MISSING (Australia); Gary Charles, Shaun Teale, MISSING (Republic of Ireland), MISSING (Republic of Ireland), Bryan Small; MISSING, Andy Townsend (Republic of Ireland); MISSING (scored a hat-trick), MISSING (Wales), Dwight Yorke (Trinidad and Tobago). Which full back scored Wimbledon's solitary goal and made his England debut four days later? (7)

Answers on p.490

Quiz 136: Republic of Ireland 3 (30)

1 Which Republic of Ireland full back won the first and last of his 50 caps with Shamrock Rovers but was better known at Chelsea, Crystal Palace and West Bromwich Albion? (1)

2 For which four clubs did Damien Duff play during his international career (1998–2012)? (4)

3 For which club was Mick McCarthy playing when he won his first cap for the Republic of Ireland? (1)

4 In September 2011 Republic of Ireland held a strong Russian team to a goalless draw in Moscow which earned qualification for the 2012 European Championships: who gave an utterly heroic performance at the centre of the defence, the best of his 80-cap international career? (1)

5 Republic of Ireland were pushed into second place in their group in qualification for the 1998 World Cup finals by an excellent Romania team; who did they meet in the play-offs, when goals in each leg by PSV Eindhoven's Luc Nilis proved decisive as Ireland lost 2-3 on aggregate? (1)

6 Republic of Ireland qualified for the 2002 World Cup finals after a play-off against a lucky loser from the Asian section. They won the first leg 2-0 and lost the second 1-0 in stifling heat in which Middle Eastern city? (1)

7 Quinn + Stapleton + Aldridge + Staunton = who? (2)

8 Who scored the goal that clinched a 1-0 home win for Republic of Ireland over reigning world champions Germany during qualification for the 2016 European Championships? With which club was he playing in the Premier League when he won his first cap as a twenty-year-old in 2007? (2)

9   Which rugged centre back made his Republic of Ireland debut in 1996 while a Wimbledon player and went on to make 72 appearances over the next twelve years? (1)

10 Which two Irish full backs have played in and won a European Cup / Champions League Final with Manchester United? And which Irishman played out of position at full back when United lost to Barcelona in 2009? (3)

11 Which Leeds United full back made his debut for the Republic of Ireland in 1996 while still a teenager? How many goals did he score in his 63 games for Ireland, mostly belted home from the penalty spot (1 point for 2 either way)? And with which Spanish club did he play his last games for his country – was it Valencia, Real Betis, Levante or Tenerife? (3)

12 Which three Republic of Ireland players won the FA Cup with Arsenal in 1979? (3)

13 They won 81 caps for the Republic of Ireland between them, they were father and son, and they both played for Preston North End, although son was best known for a spell at Sheffield United. Who were they? (2)

14 Michael Robinson won 24 caps for the Republic of Ireland in the 1980s – for which English club did he play in an FA Cup Final? In which other European country did he enjoy a successful career as a TV pundit on his retirement? (2)

15 As of November 2015 Stoke City had five players on their books with caps for the Republic of Ireland: one is the veteran goalkeeper Shay Given, another the outcast Stephen Ireland. Who are the other three, whose surnames all begin with the same letter? (3)

Answers on p.490

Quiz 137: General 35 (30)

1 Côte d'Ivoire/Ivory Coast were captained by Didier Drogba at the 2006 World Cup finals; which two Arsenal players were the other Premier League representatives in their squad? (2)

2 Trevor Francis was English football's first £1M player; but which (uncapped) English forward was the first £500,000 player, signed by Ron Atkinson for West Bromwich Albion from Middlesbrough only a month before? (1)

3 Who returned for a second spell as Burton Albion manager in December 2015 and immediately led the club into the second tier for the first time in their history? (1)

4 Which teenager kept goal for Leicester City when they lost the 1969 FA Cup Final? (1)

5 Which high-profile golfer has a cousin who played seventeen games for Wales? (1)

6 Who scored nine of West Bromwich Albion's sixteen goals as they won the FA Cup in 1967–68? (1)

7 Who, in 1962, became the first man to play for England at a World Cup finals tournament while with a foreign club (Inter Milan)? (1)

8 Who stood down after fifteen years as FA Chairman in 1996 – was it (a) Ted Croker (b) Keith Wiseman (c) Ken Bates or (d) Bert Millichip? (1)

9 Sheffield United reached the semi-finals of both domestic cups as a Division 1 (second tier) side in 2002–03. Their team included a seasoned former Scottish international approaching his 40th year picked up from neighbours Bradford City, a current Wales centre half and a future England centre half: who were these three players? And who was the club's manager at the time? What further disappointment awaited them that season? And what event would have afforded them some compensatory schadenfreude? (6)

10 For which club did Arsène Wenger play league football in France – was it (a) Cannes (b) Monaco (c) Nice or (d) Strasbourg? (1)

11 This is the West Ham United line-up that played in both matches and lost the 1981 League Cup Final to Liverpool in a replay (4-4-2): Phil Parkes; Ray Stewart, MISSING, Alvin Martin, MISSING; Jimmy Neighbour, Geoff Pike, MISSING, MISSING; David Cross, MISSING. Which defender (with a measly 8 in 434 League games!) was the unlikely scorer of the winning goal for Liverpool in the replay after Kenny Dalglish equalised an early West Ham goal? (6)

12 São Paolo*, Real Zaragoza, Juventude, Palmeiras, Roma*, AC Milan*: which World Cup winner's club career is sketched out here? (1)

13 Who kept Sunderland in the Premier League in 2015–16, having taken over in October 2015 with the club in a dire position? What was his reward? (2)

14 Who top scored in the English First Division in 1974–75 and did so again with his new club in 1976–77 (jointly) after a high-profile big-money move to London? Which were the two clubs involved? (3)

15 Which two strikers both scored 20 goals as Burnley won promotion back to the Premier League in 2013–14? (2)

Asterisk (*) indicates that the player in question made more than one hundred league appearances for the club.

Answers on p.491

Quiz 138: Football League 15 (30)

1 Fill in the gaps of the sponsors of the Football League: Canon, *Today* newspaper, MISSING, Endsleigh, MISSING, Coca-Cola, MISSING, SkyBet. (3)

2 Who was the manager of Huddersfield Town when they won the first and second of a hat-trick of League titles in 1924 and 1925? (1)

3 Portsmouth won the League in consecutive years in the late 1940s: who was their England wing half, who became not only the club's leading appearance maker, but held the record for most appearances for any one club until the early 1970s? How many goals did he score in those 764 games – was it 9, 99, 109 or 199? (1)

4 Who was the manager of Tottenham Hotspur when they won the Double in 1960–61? With which club did he win the Football league title as a player? (1)

5 Who have been the Football League's most southerly representatives since they joined as a founder member of the Third Division in 1920? (1)

6 Who were relegated to the Second Division for a single season in 1976–77, the only time they were out of the top flight after 1950? (1)

7 Which two West Midlands clubs finished first and second in the First Division in 1953–54, the only time the region's clubs have achieved this level of dominance? (2)

8 The Manchester United team that won the First Division title in 1964–65 had two players called Dunne, Pat and Tony, both Irish, who were first team regulars (Pat played 37 games, Tony all 42): what positions did they fill? And who replaced Pat two years later when United won the League again? (3)

9 How many First Division titles did Liverpool win in the 1970s? (1)

10 What connects the title wins of Huddersfield Town (1923–24), Portsmouth (1949–50), Arsenal (1952–53), Manchester United (1964–65), Arsenal (1988–89) and Manchester City (2011–12)? (2)

11 Which Luton Town player was PFA Young Player of the Year in 1984, and to where did his displays earn him a lucrative move? (2)

12 Which Scottish manager took Millwall into the top division of English football for the first time in 1987–88? How many seasons did they last? Who were the two strikers whose goals took them up and made them competitive? (4)

13 Albert Iremonger played more than 600 times in goal for which famous old Midlands club between 1904 and 1926 – was it (a) Nottingham Forest (b) Aston Villa (c) Notts County or (d) Derby County? (1)

14 Which England international cricketer made a handful of appearances for Scunthorpe United in the early 1980s? (1)

15 Fill in the gaps in this list of Birmingham City managers since 1970: Fred Goodwin, Willie Bell, Sir Alf Ramsey, MISSING (1978–82), MISSING (1982–86), John Bond, Gary Pendrey, Dave Mackay, Lou Macari, Terry Cooper, MISSING (1993–96), Trevor Francis, MISSING (2001–07), MISSING (2007–11), Chris Hughton, MISSING (2012–14), Gary Rowett (incumbent, to August 2016) (6)

Answers on p.492

Quiz 139: Champions League 11 (30)

1 Who was the Danish full back who played for Bayern Munich in the 1974 and 1976 European Cup Final victories, but missed the 1975 Final through illness? And which budding superstar replaced Swedish wide player Conny Torstensson for the 1976 Final after he'd featured in '74 and '75? (2)

2 Who are the only European Cup finalists from Scandinavia? (1)

3 In 1995, which side appeared in their fifth European Cup Final in seven years? Who was the only player to appear in all five? (2)

4 Which Portuguese star won successive Champions League titles with Juventus in 1996 and Borussia Dortmund in 1997 – was it (a) Jorge Costa (b) Paulo Futre (c) Paulo Sousa or (d) Rui Costa? (1)

5 One team beat eventual 1999–2000 Champions League winners Real Madrid 4-2, 4-1 and 2-1 during the course of the competition, but were still eliminated by the Spaniards. Can you explain? (2)

6 Who won a Champions League semi-final in 2003 by scoring an away goal in their own stadium? (2)

7 Which young Spanish star scored the goal for Atlético Madrid that knocked Barcelona out of the 2014 Champions League at the quarter-final stage? (1)

8 Which four English clubs have reached the semi-final stage of the European Cup or Champions League but have not won the competition (to 2015–16)? (4)

9 Arsenal had a poor start to their 2003–04 Champions League campaign, but won their last three games to top their group, including a 5-1 away win against which European giants? (1)

10 Which overseas midfield player scored a hat-trick as Liverpool beat Turkish side Besiktas 8-0 in a Champions League group match in November 2007? (1)

278 | NICK HOLT

11 Which side were the losers when Liverpool won their first European Cup in 1977, and lost to them again in the semi-final in 1978? Which Danish striker scored their goal in a 3-1 defeat in the 1977 Final? (2)

12 Which German international scored twice as Borussia Dortmund won the 1997 Champions League Final? (1)

13 Who are the two overseas coaches to have won the Champions League with a British club (to 2015–16)? (2)

14 AC Milan reached three Champions League Finals between 2003 and 2007: which six players (two overseas, four Italian, none of them forwards) started all three matches? (6)

15 What connects the European Cup / Champions League Final wins of 1958 (Real Madrid), 1968 (Manchester United), 1970 (Feyenoord), 1992 (Barcelona) & 2014 (Real Madrid)? (2)

Answers on p.493

Quiz 140: World Cup 14 (30)

1 An injury to which goalkeeper, the first in a lineage of great Spanish goalies, hampered his country's chances of overcoming Italy in a replayed second round match at the 1934 World Cup? (1)

2 Who was the Brazilian forward who scored four times in a 7-1 demolition of Sweden in the final phase of the 1950 World Cup finals? And which Uruguayan winger scored in all three of his country's final phase matches? (2)

3 What part did Karol Galba of Czechoslovakia play in the 1966 World Cup Final? (1)

4 Who scored two hat-tricks in the group stage of the 1970 World Cup? Whose hearts did he break with a late injury-time winner in the quarter-final? (2)

5 England opened their World Cup finals campaign in 1982 with a game against France. Who scored in the first minute of the game and what was the result? (2)

6 At the 1986 World Cup the only player based outside Belgium was the vastly experienced right back. He was playing for PSV Eindhoven, who he later managed when they won the Dutch league – who is he? (1)

7 Which team humiliated Argentina, beating them 5-0 in Buenos Aires in a qualifier for the 1994 World Cup finals? Who did Argentina subsequently have to beat in a two-legged play-off to reach the main tournament? (2)

8 Which non-European team did Portugal beat 5-3 in a rousing quarter-final at the 1966 World Cup, after going three down inside twenty-five minutes? Who scored four of Portugal's goals, two from the penalty spot? Where did the game take place? Who eventually knocked out Portugal in the semi-final? Who scored both goals for the victors in that semi-final? (5)

9 Who scored for Brazil as they beat England 1-0 in a terrific group stage match at the 1970 World Cup finals? And which two players were pictured exchanging shirts in what has become an emblematic image of that tournament? (3)

10 Who was a key factor in Scotland's qualification for the 1990 World Cup finals, with six goals in the first five matches, including two in the 2-0 home win against France that proved crucial? Which country, about to break into civil war, remained unbeaten and topped the group? (2)

11 Who was coach of Switzerland when they qualified for the World Cup finals in 1994, the first time they had done so since 1966? (1)

12 Which two East European sides eliminated both the 1990 finalists, Argentina and Germany, at the Last 16 and quarter-final stages of the 1994 World Cup finals? (2)

13 Which future Premier League manager gave away the penalty that handed England victory over Argentina in the 2002 World Cup finals? Who banished ugly memories by converting the spot-kick? (2)

14 Who scored a hat-trick as Germany thrashed Portugal in their opening game of the 2014 World Cup finals tournament? (1)

15 Who scored both Colombia's goals as they strolled to a Last 16 win over Uruguay at the 2014 World Cup finals? Whither was he bound after the tournament and from whence? (3)

Answers on p.493

Quiz 141: General 36 (30)

1 Cha Bum-kun, who won the UEFA Cup with Eintracht Frankfurt (1980) and Bayer Leverkusen (1988, when he scored in the Final) was voted Asian Player of the Century – for which country did he make 135 appearances, scoring 58 goals? (1)

2 Jack Greenwell, Alf Spouncer, Ralph Kirby and James Bellamy were all pre-war managers of which famous club? (1)

3 Two non-Russian teams provided five players each to the 1970 Soviet Union World Cup squad – which two clubs? (2)

4 Which celebrity Stoke City fan (a TV presenter) paid £20,000 for Stanley Matthews' FA Cup winner's medal? (1)

5 Which Irish midfield player's account of a 1973–74 season at Millwall, *Only A Game*, is acknowledged as a classic piece of football writing? Who were the subject matter of *The Unforgettable Fire*, an official biography by the same writer published in 1988? (2)

6 Which three Football League clubs have nicknames derived from species of canine? (6)

7 Who scored the winning goal in the 2008 Olympic Football Final in Beijing, as Argentina beat Nigeria 1-0 (it wasn't Messi, although he was in the team)? (1)

8 Alex Ferguson famously kicked a boot across the dressing room after a defeat in the FA Cup in 2003; who did the boot hit in the face, and which of their rivals had just beaten United? (2)

9 This is the Chelsea line-up that started against Tottenham Hotspur in the 2015 League Cup Final, their first trophy of Jose Mourinho's second spell as Chelsea manager (4-2-3-1): Petr Cech (Czech Republic); MISSING (Serbia), MISSING (England), John Terry (England), MISSING (Spain); MISSING (France), Ramires (Brazil); MISSING (Brazil), Cesc Fàbregas (Spain), MISSING (Belgium); Diego Costa (Spain). Who are the missing players? (6)

10 Which aggressive midfield player was sent off for the first time in his career playing for Wales in 2004, aged thirty? (1)

11 Which future Premier League star scored eight times in six games at the 2004 Olympic Football tournament, including the only goal in the Final, a 1-0 win for Argentina over Nigeria? (1)

12 Chemnitzer, 1. FC Kaiserslautern, Bayer Leverkusen, Bayern Munich, Chelsea, Bayer Leverkusen: which German legend's career path is this? (1)

13 Which father of a future England international striker scored twenty goals as Derby County won promotion to the Premier League in 1995–96? And who was Derby's first team coach under experienced manager Jim Smith? (2)

14 Which team, managed by Dave Sexton, finished runners up to Liverpool in 1975–76, their highest ever league finish? (1)

15 Who cavorted across the pitch in his suit after his club escaped relegation on the last day of the 1982–83 season? Who were their opponents, who themselves were relegated as a consequence? (2)

Answers on p.494

Quiz 142: Premier League 17 (40)

1 Crystal Palace were relegated on goal difference in the first Premier League season in 1992–93: which side won 4-3 at Southampton to escape the drop while Palace lost 3-0 to Arsenal? And who scored fifteen goals for Palace despite their struggles? (2)

2 In December 2000 Paolo Di Canio sportingly caught a cross and handed the ball to the referee rather than go for goal after seeing goal-keeper Paul Gerrard lying injured in the goalmouth; which two sides were in opposition? (2)

3 Stefan Matz, who you probably won't remember unless you are an Arsenal fan, was the first German player signed by the club in the Premier League (six matches in the League); who was the second? (1)

4 Which club hold the record for the biggest home win in the Premier League? And the biggest away win? (2)

5 Which Irish international was Southampton's record outlay, at £4M in 2001? Which summer 2015 signing currently holds this distinction? (2)

6 Which teenager did Manchester United buy with some of the money from the sale of Beckham and Verón? Which striker did Bolton Wanderers sign from the same club? (2)

7 Who are the seven Italian players who have made more than 100 appearances in the Premier League? And who is the only one to pass 200 (to November 2015)? (8)

8 Who scored his fortieth goal of the 1993–94 season as Newcastle United hammered Aston Villa 5-0 in the Premier League in April 1994? Who was his strike partner, who scored 21 league goals himself? (2)

9   Who was the manager of Manchester City when they were relegated out of the Premier League in 1995–96? Which overseas player was City's top scorer for the second season running, this time with only nine goals? And who was the manager's first signing at the start of the season, at around £2M from Dinamo Tbilisi? (3)

10 Who were relegated in 2005–06 with a miserable fifteen points (a record to that date), scoring fewer goals than the Premier League top scorer Thierry Henry? (1)

11 Who scored in their forty-fourth consecutive league match, against Manchester City, in September 2002? Who had held the record since 1937? (2)

12 In July 2009 Manchester City paid a combined £43M for two overseas strikers, both from other Premier League clubs (Arsenal and Blackburn Rovers) – who were the two players? (2)

13 Massimo Maccarone, Szilárd Németh & Tuncay have all been top scorer for which club in the Premier League? (1)

14 What was bizarre about referee Gerald Ashby's decision to award a penalty to Liverpool in their match against Arsenal in the Premier League in March 1997? Was the penalty scored? And what was the result (exact score not needed) of the game? (4)

15 Who is missing from this AFC Bournemouth line-up that kick started their first season in the Premier League with a thrilling 4-3 away win at West Ham United (4-4-2, English unless stated): MISSING (Poland); Simon Francis, MISSING, Charlie Daniels, Steve Cook; MISSING (Scotland) (sub: Adam Smith), Eunan O'Kane (Republic of Ireland), Andrew Surman, MISSING (Norway) (sub: Marc Pugh); MISSING (Côte d'Ivoire) (sub: Dan Gosling), MISSING (scored a hat-trick). (6)

Answers on p.495

Quiz 143: FA Cup 7 (30)

1 Wimbledon beating Liverpool in the FA Cup Final of 1988 is occasionally talked about as the 'shock of the century': what was the actual gulf in league places between the teams? (1)

2 In 1974 Newcastle fans invaded the pitch during an FA Cup tie with their team 3-1 down. Newcastle went on to win 4-3 but the FA declared the game void and ordered a replay. Who were the opposition? (1)

3 Which of the clubs still playing League football were the earliest winners of the FA Cup? (1)

4 Who scored nine goals in an 11-0 thrashing of non-league Margate by Bournemouth in November 1971? (1)

5 Which academics won the cup in 1874 and reached three more Finals in the nineteenth century? (1)

6 Which team has appeared in nine FA Cup Finals and won eight (to 2016)? (1)

7 Who scored the only goal to earn Second-Division Chesterfield an FA Cup semi-final spot in 1997, having already scored a hat-trick to eliminate the runaway Division One leaders, Bolton Wanderers, his future employers? (1)

8 This is the team that won Ipswich Town the FA Cup in 1978. Can you fill in the missing players (4-4-2)? Cooper; MISSING, Hunter, MISSING, MISSING; Osborne (sub: Lambert), Talbot, MISSING, MISSING; Geddes, MISSING (6)

9 Which side lifted the FA Cup in the last Final staged at the original Wembley Stadium, prior to redevelopment? Where was the FA Cup Final held for six years while the new stadium was built? (2)

10 Which of these club sides have reached the FA Cup Final – Oldham Athletic, Oxford United, Norwich City, Barnsley? (1)

11 Which Arsenal central defender ought to have received the first red card in an FA Cup Final when he cynically tripped West Ham's Paul Allen in the 1980 Final? And which Manchester United defender did earn that record unfairly five years later? (2)

12 Who became the youngest player in an FA Cup Final when he played for Preston in 1963–64? And with which club did he get another loser's medal in 1968, before finally claiming a winner's medal as manager in 1984? (2)

13 Which three Manchester United players started all three of their successful FA Cup Finals in the 1990s ('94, '96 & '99)? (3)

14 Who lost the FA Cup Final with Southampton in 2003 and won it with Chelsea in 2007? What was vaguely controversial about his inclusion in 2007? (2)

15 Only four players appeared in both Portsmouth's FA Cup Finals in 2008 and 2010. One was David James, who were the other three, all African players? Who were the two managers? (5)

Answers on p.495

Quiz 144: European Championships 4 (30)

1 Which former Leicester City player captained Greece when they won the 2004 European Championships? And who was the only member of the victorious squad employed in the Premier League? (2)

2 In qualifying for the 1964 European Championships, eventual winners Spain just about squeezed past a spirited Northern Ireland team. Which great Real Madrid winger scored the solitary goal in Belfast after the Irish got a worthy draw in Bilbao? (1)

3 England won their group in qualifying for the 1972 European Championships but lost a two-legged quarter-final against which side, who would later host the finals? (1)

4 Who scored a dinked penalty over a prostrate goalkeeper to clinch the 1976 European Championships for his country in a shoot-out against West Germany and earn legendary status in Czechoslovakia? Who was the outfoxed goalkeeper? (2)

5 Which two sides were on the receiving end as Michel Platini scored two hat-tricks in France's group games at the 1984 European Championships? (2)

6 Which two players scored from the penalty spot before Marco van Basten's late winner meant the Netherlands beat West Germany at the 1988 European Championships? (2)

7 Who did the Netherlands beat in a play-off to determine the last quali-fier for the 1996 European Championships? Which teenage Ajax striker scored both Dutch goals? (2)

8 Apart from England, which other side at the 1996 European Championships progressed through the quarter-final stage via a penalty shoot-out and then fell victim to the same process in the semi-final? Which defender missed the kick that saw England eliminated? (2)

9 Who scored the only goal of the game as Greece beat France in the quarter-finals and Portugal in the Final of the 2004 European Championships? Who did they beat in the semi-final with a 'silver goal' from Traianos Dellas? Who was the coach of the Greek team? What on earth is a silver goal? (5)

10 Which legendary hard man missed the penalty kick for Spain that gave England a rare win in a penalty shoot-out at the 1996 European Championships? Who was Spain's goalkeeper and captain during the tournament? (2)

11 Which unfancied Mediterranean side shocked Spain and won their opening qualifier for the 2000 European Championships 3-2? Spain pulled their collective finger out after that defeat and won every other game, scoring an astonishing 42 goals in all eight games: who top scored with eleven of them, including successive hat-tricks against Austria (four, actually) and San Marino? And which Real Madrid player scored five, despite being ostensibly a defender? (3)

12 Who came into the Czech side during qualifying for the 2000 European Championships, scored six goals in qualifying and ended up as his country's top scorer with 55 goals? (1)

13 During qualifiers for the 2012 European Championships, two sides failed to pick up a point, managing a combined goal difference of 1 for and 78 against in their twenty matches – who were these two sides? (2)

14 Greece, champions in 2004, finished bottom of their qualifying group for the 2016 tournament: which country, with a population of fewer than 50,000 bet them home and away? (1)

15 Who had the only perfect record in qualifying for the 2016 European Championships? Which surprise package nearly matched them, winning nine and drawing one in a group that included Russia and Sweden? (2)

Answers on p.496

Quiz 145: General 37 (30)

1 Costinha, Boulahrouz, Deco, van Bronckhorst: World Cup 2006. What's the significance of that quartet? (1)

2 The Copa América was launched in which decade under the name the South American Championship? (1)

3 In which city could you watch Grasshoppers play? (1)

4 Who was or is Joe Gaetjens? (2)

5 Upton Park FC were the first winners of which international football tournament in 1900? (1)

6 Which three Football League clubs have nicknames derived from species of feline? (6)

7 Who swapped Fellows Park for the Bescot Stadium in the late 1980s? (1)

8 Who lost the FA Cup Final to Manchester United as a player in 1990 and as a manager in 2016? (1)

9 In which decade did Manchester City last employ a manager for more than five years? (1)

10 Which home counties club's decision to transfer their 'home' FA Cup tie against Arsenal to Highbury in 2003 to guarantee a financial windfall led to (rather mean) rule changes by the FA? (1)

11 This is the Aston Villa side that lost the 2010 League Cup Final to Manchester United. Can you name the missing players and also the manager, who left at the end of the season (4-4-2, England unless stated)? MISSING (United States); MISSING (Spain) (sub: John Carew, Norway), Richard Dunne (Republic of Ireland), MISSING (Wales), Stephen Warnock; Ashley Young, MISSING (England), MISSING (Bulgaria), Stewart Downing; Gabriel Agbonlahor, MISSING (England) (7)

12 Which great modern defender's club list reads: Napoli, Parma**, Internazionale, Juventus, Real Madrid, Juventus, Al-Ahli? (1)

13 Which former player and member of the coaching staff filled in as temporary manager at Anfield in 2001–02 when Gerard Houllier took time off to recover from a heart scare, and won the October Manager of the Month award? (1)

14 How many First Division titles did Brian Clough win as a manager? (1)

15 With which club did Ian Holloway enjoy three spells as a player and work as a coach and manager before being dismissed in January 2001? By which of his former clubs as a player was he then appointed manager? And which two clubs (to 2015–16) has he led to the Premier League? (4)

Asterisks (**) indicate that the player in question made more than two hundred league appearances for the club.

Answers on p.497

Quiz 146: England 8 (30)

1 Who were England's back-up goalkeepers in their 1966 World Cup squad? (2)

2 England, unusually, had five players in their 1990 World Cup squad not playing in England, but four of them were with the same club, Rangers, in the midst of a decade of dominance of Scottish domestic football. Who were the four Rangers players and for which club was the other exile, Chris Waddle, playing? (5)

3 Derek Statham was a thoroughly excellent, professional and consistent left back with West Bromwich Albion in the 1980s: explain in one single word why he won only three England caps? (1)

4 Who has won the most England caps as a Manchester City player? (1)

5 Against which nation, now a region of Germany which gives its name to a liberal, artsy lifestyle, did England play their first and only international in 1908? (1)

6 In October 2001, who came on as a substitute as England prepared a set piece against Greece in a World Cup qualifier and promptly scored five seconds after running on? (1)

7 *Addicted* was the characteristically honest 1998 autobiography of which former England captain? (1)

8 To the end of 2006, the Neville brothers won 144 caps for England; how many goals have they scored for their country between them? (1)

9 Which player scored six hat-tricks for England, more than any other? (1)

10 Who became England's first manager in 1946, and in what way was he never really in control of his destiny? (2)

11 Whose international retirement did Bobby Robson precipitate when he left him out of his first England squad in 1982? (1)

12 Who were the seven Liverpool players selected in the England starting line-up against Switzerland in September 1977? Which of them was playing for just the third time, eleven years after his second cap? (8)

13 England cricketing great Denis Compton also played professional football for which London club? (1)

14 When England were beaten 1-0 by Yugoslavia in the semi-final of the 1968 European Championships three players from the World Cup winning team of two years previously were replaced by Keith Newton, Brian Labone and Norman Hunter – which three? (3)

15 Which England player of those used in 2015 was the first to be capped by his country? (1)

Answers on p.498

Quiz 147: Premier League 18 (40)

1 David White, Rick Holden and Fitzroy Simpson all made more than twenty-five league appearances in the 1992–93 Premier League season for which club? (1)

2 Which winger, who underwent a much-publicised fall from grace in 2016, scored a hat-trick for Sunderland against Fulham in January 2014? (1)

3 In October 2000 Leeds United came from 2-0 down and 3-2 down to pull off an exciting 4-3 win over Liverpool. Which summer signing from Celtic scored all four goals for Leeds? (1)

4 The highlight of Barnsley's solitary season in the Premier League was a 1-0 away win at which top four club, courtesy of an Ashley Ward goal? (1)

5 Which club were deprived of the services of striker Duncan Ferguson when he was jailed for three months in 1995 for an on-field head-butting incident in an earlier game in Scotland? (1)

6 Which Italian became Sheffield Wednesday's record signing when he moved from Inter Milan in October 1996? And which club also made a record purchase, that of Dutch defender Ulrich van Gobbel from Galatasaray? (2)

7 Which ten Arsenal players started twenty-five or more Premier League games in their 'Invincibles' season of 2003–04? (10)

8 Who are the three Croatian internationals who have played in the Premier League for Tottenham Hotspur? (3)

9 Who went top of the Premier League for the first time since the new competition started after beating Tottenham Hotspur 2-0 on 19 December 1998? (1)

10 Who played under Harry Redknapp at West Ham United, Portsmouth and Tottenham Hotspur? And who did Harry sign while manager of Southampton, Portsmouth and Tottenham? And which other of Harry's players at both Portsmouth and Tottenham also followed him to Queens Park Rangers? (3)

11 From which two European clubs did Manchester City buy Yaya Touré and Edin Džeko for a combined fee of £55M in the 2010–11 season? (2)

12 Which Welsh international scored the first Premier League hat-trick by a West Bromwich Albion player in a 4-1 win over Charlton Athletic in March 2005? (1)

13 The biggest points margin by which a club won the Premier League came in 1999–2000 when Manchester United were utterly dominant: what was their margin of safety over second placed Arsenal (1 point for 2 either way)? (2)

14 What was the South African centre-back pairing at the 1998 World Cup finals, both of whom had just completed a season in the Premier League? Which clubs? (4)

15 This is the Leicester City line up that won 3-1 against Manchester City at the Etihad Stadium in February 2016, confirming that their title-winning chances had to be taken seriously (4-4-2, English unless stated): Kasper Schmeichel (Denmark); Danny Simpson, MISSING (Jamaica), Robert Huth (Germany), MISSING (Austria); MISSING (sub: Nathan Dyer), N'Golo Kante (France), MISSING, Riyad Mahrez (Algeria) (sub; Demarai Gray); Shinji Okazaki (Japan) (sub: MISSING, Argentina), MISSING. Who was the unlikely source of two of Leicester's three goals? (7)

Answers on p.498

Quiz 148: European Competitions 8 (30)

1 Which UEFA ruling hampered the English clubs in the European Cup in the early to mid-1990s? (1)

2 Which Brazilian striker played alongside Diego Maradona at Napoli and scored in each leg when they won the 1989 UEFA Cup against Stuttgart – was it (a) Careca (b) Bebeto (c) Romário or (d) Adriano? (1)

3 At the 1994 World Cup finals Sweden had a squad that included only ten players from their domestic league: seven of these were with which club, dominant in Sweden at the time? Who was the manager who led them to five domestic league titles and the quarter-finals of the Champions League? Who was the club's goalkeeper at the time, on his way to becoming (for a time) Sweden's most-capped player? (3)

4 Which French side won Ligue 1 in seven consecutive seasons from 2001–02 to 2007–08? Which Portuguese striker (who didn't play for them) scored most goals in Ligue 1 over that seven-year period? Which young French star was the champions' leading scorer and also Ligue 1 top scorer in the last title-winning season of 2007–08? Which six sides finished runners-up in that period and which of them did so twice and also knocked the Champions off their perch by winning the title in 2008–09? (10)

5 What is remarkable about the 25 caps won by German forward Stefan Kuntz between 1993 and 1997 – is it (a) he never played in the top division of the Bundesliga (b) he was never on the losing side (c) every match he played was outside Germany or (d) he played in every position, including a ten-minute spell as an emergency goalkeeper? (2)

6 Which Scandinavian player wore the no.10 shirt at Ajax when they won three successive league titles and reached two Champions League Finals between 1993 and 1996? (1)

7   Emmanuel Olisadebe, who scored eight goals during qualification for the 2002 World Cup finals, was the first black player to play for which East European country? (1)

8   In which city could you watch a local derby between Brondby and Lyngby? (1)

9   In 1999–2000 Jörg Butt was Hamburg's top scorer with nine goals; why is this remarkable? (1)

10 Which Spanish side eliminated Leicester City on the first two occasions they played in Europe, 36 years apart (1962 and 1998)? (1)

11 Which British club side featured in the very first European Cup Winners' Cup Final in 1961? (1)

12 Which club play at the Inonu Stadium, with a view of both Europe and Asia from the upper tiers? (1)

13 Bobby Moncur, never a prolific goalscorer, scored three goals in which English team's two-legged triumph over Újpest Dózsa in the 1969 Inter-Cities Fairs Cup Final? Who was the club's manager, still their longest-serving boss with fourteen years at the helm, and still the last to win a major trophy? (2)

14 Which British club lost the Inter-Cities Fairs Cup Finals in 1960 and 1961? (1)

15 Which three continental clubs did Bobby Robson go on to manage after PSV Eindhoven? (3)

Answers on p.499

Quiz 149: General 38 (30)

1 CSKA Sofia, Bayer Leverkusen, Tottenham Hotspur, Manchester United, Fulham, AS Monaco, PAOK: which striker's career path is this, still playing in 2015–16? (1)

2 John Langenus of Belgium was the first man to do what in a World Cup Final? (1)

3 Uwe Rösler, cult hero at Manchester City and later manager at Brentford, Wigan Athletic and Leeds United, won 5 caps for which country? (1)

4 Which Chelsea defender issued a writ against Dean Saunders after a tackle by the Welsh striker resulted in an injury that effectively ended his career? (1)

5 Which Italian club paid nearly £1M for Mark Hateley in 1984, and from which English Second Division club did they buy him? (2)

6 Whose transfer to Arsenal in 1960 was a landmark deal after a court decided the club refusing to sell him was guilty of restraint of trade? Which was the club? (2)

7 Which three French players were red carded during the 1998 World Cup finals tournament? (3)

8 Who, in 2004, was the most recent former England international to receive a knighthood? (1)

9 Maidstone United, Gillingham, Peterborough United, Birmingham City, Coventry City*, West Ham United, Sunderland*, Wolverhampton Wanderers, Barnet: whose peripatetic career, that also encompassed 63 caps for the Republic of Ireland, is mapped out here? (1)

10 How come 50,913 people watched Bristol City beat Carlisle United in April 2003? (2)

11   Here is their line-up from the 2008 League Cup Final when Tottenham Hotspur surprised Chelsea, winning 2-1 after Dimitar Berbatov's penalty equalised Didier Drogba's opener. Can you name the missing players, who scored the winning goal in extra time, who was the only uncapped player in the starting eleven, and who was Tottenham manager (4-4-2)? MISSING (England); Alan Hutton (Scotland), Jonathan Woodgate (England), MISSING (England), Pascal Chimbonda (France) (sub: Tom Huddlestone, England); Aaron Lennon (England), MISSING (England), Didier Zokora (Côte d'Ivoire), MISSING (France) (sub: MISSING, Finland); MISSING (Republic of Ireland) (sub: Younes Kaboul, France), Dimitar Berbatov (Bulgaria) (9)

12   Nantes, Marseille *(inc Bordeaux)*, Juventus, Chelsea, Valencia: whose career path is this, which also took in more than 100 games for France? (1)

13   Which goalkeeper cost Arsenal £6M in 2001, a fee that ended up being £500,000 per League game? (1)

14   Ian Moores scored a hat-trick for Tottenham in a 9-0 caning of Bristol Rovers in 1977: who went one better and scored four on his debut for the club having been bought from Torquay United earlier that week? (1)

15   Which three Football League clubs (2015–16) have played in the top flight and also been temporarily relegated to non-League football? (3)

Asterisk (*) indicates that the player in question made more than one hundred league appearances for the club.

Answers on p.500

Quiz 150: World Cup 15 (30)

1 Italy's Angelo Schiavio scored a hat-trick in a first round group match at the 1934 World Cup, and then scored the winner in the Final against which other European country? For which club does he hold the record for most league goals scored? (2)

2 Who was the other (unused) Leeds United player in the 1966 World Cup squad apart from Jack Charlton? (1)

3 Who scored a hat-trick against Paraguay in France's first game of the 1958 World Cup finals tournament, and had six goals by the time the group stage finished? How many did he score overall in the tournament, a record that is unlikely to be beaten? (2)

4 Preparations for which World Cup finals tournament were hampered by a massive earthquake along the country's seaboard? (1)

5 How many times was Diego Maradona sent off during World Cup finals matches? (1)

6 During qualification for the 2006 World Cup finals England waltzed through their group along with which European side, with whom England seemed fated to be matched in qualifying groups? (1)

7 Only one team avoided defeat against Brazil at the 1958 World Cup finals tournament, and only one team did the same in 1962: which were the two teams? (2)

8 Who were the only team to beat eventual champions Argentina in the 1978 World Cup finals? (1)

9 Who missed a crucial penalty kick with the score at 1-1 as Wales lost their last game to Romania and thus narrowly failed to qualify for the 1994 World Cup finals? (1)

10 Who, playing for Cameroon against Chile in 1998, became the first man to be sent off for the second time in a World Cup finals game? Which high-profile star matched this undesirable record in 2006? (2)

11 Who was the Milan striker who returned from injury to score both goals in Romania's quarter-final defeat by Sweden at the 1994 World Cup finals – was it (a) Gheorghe Hagi (b) Ilie Dumitrescu (c) Marius Lacatus or (d) Florin Raducioiu? (1)

12 Italy's leading light in attack at the 1970 World Cup finals was Luigi "Gigi" Riva: which club had he just lead to the Italian Serie A title for the first time in their history? (1)

13 Which midfield player's two goals helped ease Brazil past a defiant Denmark (3-2) in the Laudrup brothers' last game during the 1998 World Cup finals tournament? (1)

14 Which side did England beat 3-0 in the Last 16 of the 2002 World Cup finals? (1)

15 Here are the line-ups (with a few missing) for the 2014 World Cup semi-final between Brazil and Germany. Fill in the gaps. Brazil: MISSING; Maicon, MISSING, Dante, MISSING; Fernandinho (sub: Paulinho), Luiz Gustavo: MISSING (sub: Ramires), Oscar, Bernard; MISSING (Willian). Germany: Neuer; Lahm, Boateng, MISSING (sub: Mertesacker), MISSING; Khedira (sub: Draxler), MISSING; Muller, MISSING, MISSING; Klose (sub: MISSING). And what was the final score? (12)

Answers on p.500

Quiz 151: Women's Football 4 (30)

1 Homare Sawa was the first player to win 200 caps for which country in women's soccer? (1)

2 Which American star, who racked up an extraordinary 275 international appearances, was the inaugural FIFA Women's Player of the Year in 2001 and won the award again the following year? Who was the German star who supplanted her in 2003, winning again in 2004 and 2005? (2)

3 Which team beat England 3-0 in the quarter-final of the 1995 Women's World Cup in Sweden, but lost 2-0 to Norway in the final? (1)

4 Who did Germany beat in the two Women's World Cup Finals they won in 2003 and 2007? (2)

5 Which London club lost the 2003 and 2004 Women's FA Cup Finals 3-0 to Fulham and Arsenal respectively, but won 1-0 against Everton in the 2005 Final? Which teenage star, with a long future playing for England ahead of her, scored that winning goal in 2005? (2)

6 Who scored England's winner against Norway in the Last 16 of the 2015 Women's World Cup in Canada and scored again with a header in the quarter-final win? Who did England squeeze past in that quarter-final and who eventually beat them with a late winner in the semis? Who was the unlucky scorer of the own goal that put them out? Who scored the extra-time penalty that gave England a hard-earned third place in the competition with a first-ever win over Germany's women? (5)

7 Who was the first woman to be awarded a UEFA pro-license for coaching in 2009? (1)

8 What was unusual, uniquely so for a major football tournament, about the conditions in the stadia for the 2015 Women's World Cup? And what aid for referees was used for the first time in a major football tournament? (2)

9 Which goalkeeper and captain of the Scotland women's team holds her country's appearances record with 162 (to April 2016)? And which former Arsenal stalwart was her predecessor as captain and holds the Scotland record for international goals with 166? (2)

10 Which club were best represented in the England squad for the 2015 Women's World Cup, with five players? And which US club were the only non-English club represented, as the employers of Lianne Sanderson and Jodie Taylor? Which Women's Super League club snapped up Taylor for the 2016 season after some impressive performances? (3)

11 Which country has yielded most winners of the UEFA Women's Champions League (and its predecessor, the UEFA Women's Cup)? (1)

12 Who scored the only goal of the game as the United States won the Gold Medal match (Final) of the 2008 Women's Soccer tournament at the Olympic Games in Beijing? And which team were on the receiving end as the same striker scored twice in the Final of the 2012 tournament in London? (2)

13 Until Bayern Munich and Wolfsburg got in on the act, 1. FFC Frankfurt vied for dominance of the German Women's Bundesliga with the team from which city in the east of the country – is it (a) Leipzig (b) Dresden (c) Magdeburg or (d) Potsdam? (1)

14 Which South American star is the top scorer at the Women's World Cup finals, with 15 goals? And which two other stars, one American, one German, are one goal behind on 14? (3)

15 Which two of these US cities are NOT represented by a team in the National Women's Soccer League – Atlanta, Boston, Chicago, Miami, Portland, Seattle? (2)

Answers on p.501

Quiz 152: Football League 16 (30)

1 Who won the inaugural Football League in 1888–89 and what was remarkable about their season? (3)

2 Clem Stephenson was captain of which club as they became the first side to reel off three successive league titles in the 1920s (they have never won the league since)? (1)

3 Which Football League stalwart's career is mapped out here (he retired in the mid-1980s, aged forty, and the first four clubs represent his top-level career): Newcastle United**, West Ham United*, Sunderland, West Ham United*, Sunderland, Carlisle United, Chelsea (*inc Carlisle United*), Sunderland, Carlisle United? (1)

4 In 1988–89, which side were awarded four penalties in a game against Brighton (who also got one), and how many did they successfully convert? (1)

5 Which colourful character was manager of Bournemouth from 1970–73, and who did he manage with great distinction for seven years after that, before a less successful spell at Manchester City? (2)

6 Who was the former Welsh international who led Wrexham (as player-manager) to the Third Division title in 1977–78 – was it (a) Brian Flynn (b) Arfon Griffiths (c) Joey Jones or (d) Mickey Thomas? (1)

7 Who set a Football League record of 134 goals in a season as they won the Fourth Division in 1960–61 in their very first season as a League team? Which summer signing from Norwich City helped himself to 54 of them? (2)

8 Who achieved a second successive promotion to get back into the second tier in 1988–89, having fallen into the Fourth Division for the first time in 1986? And which local rivals took their place in the third tier, having been relegated out of the Second Division for the first time? (2)

9 In 1973–74, who established a First Division record by remaining unbeaten in their first 29 matches? (1)

10 Which Ipswich Town goalkeeper from their 1970s heyday holds the record for most penalties saved in a season (eighth out of ten)? (1)

11 Of which club was Dr Jozef Venglos a curious (and disastrous) choice as manager in 1990–91? What circumstances necessitated a new appointment at the club? Who succeeded Venglos? (3)

12 Mark Stein and Andy Walker both scored 26 goals to help their respective clubs gain promotion from the third tier (Division 2) in 1992–93: which two clubs? And which striker, who would join Bolton a few years later, did even better, scoring 30 times as West Bromwich Albion joined the two other sides via the play-offs? (3)

13 Which little-and-large combination scored more than 40 goals between them as Sunderland ran away with Division 1 (second tier) in 1998–99? (2)

14 Who won the Conference in 2000–01 and Division 3 (fourth tier) two years later? In what league are they competing in the current (2015–16) season? (2)

15 In 1998, to celebrate 100 seasons of league football, the Football League produced a list of 100 League Legends: which five players on the list once played for Blackpool? (5)

Asterisk (*) indicates that the player in question made more than one hundred league appearances for the club. (**) indicates more than two hundred league appearances.

Answers on p.502

Quiz 153: General 39 (30)

1 Denmark had three English-based players in their 1986 World Cup squad, two with Manchester United and one with Liverpool: who were they? (3)

2 Juan and Mario Evaristo of Argentina were the first brothers to play in a World Cup Final in 1930; who were the first brothers to play and win one? (2)

3 Vic Watson scored 326 goals between the two World Wars, and remains the all-time leading goalscorer for which club – is it (a) West Ham United (b) Chelsea (c) Fulham or (d) Arsenal? (1)

4 Which high profile goalkeeper was accused by *The Sun* newspaper of match-fixing in November, 1994? For which club was he playing at the time? (2)

5 Which city in south-west France had a stadium built for the 1938 World Cup but has seen its Rugby Union team enjoy more success there than the local Association team? (1)

6 Which Kent-born Republic of Ireland international (70 caps) started his career with Welling United and Weymouth before earning a contract with Southampton aged twenty-two? (1)

7 Which three members of the United States World Cup finals squad from 1994 played for Derby County, Luton Town and Coventry City respectively? (3)

8 Who was captain of the Ukraine team that made their World Cup finals debut at the 2006 tournament? Which club did he join at the end of the tournament? And where did he both start and end his career? (3)

9 Who, in a nice twist, did Arsenal beat in the 1930 FA Cup Final, to secure Herbert Chapman's first trophy with the club? (1)

10 In 1994 Eric Cantona accused Swiss referee Kurt Röthlisberger of taking bribes; what happened to Röthlisberger in 1997? (2)

11 Who stopped the rot at Everton and led them to seventh place in the Premiership in 2002–03 after a few years of flirting with relegation? Which Division 1 (second tier) club did he manage prior to the Everton appointment? (2)

12 Who won the most caps for Argentina – Batistuta, Maradona or Kempes? (1)

13 Which high-profile Premier League player was given an eight-month ban in 2003 after failing to turn up for two mandatory drug tests? (1)

14 Bolton Wanderers legend Nat Lofthouse topped the First Division goal-scoring chart in 1955–56: who is the only Bolton player to have done the same since that year? (1)

15 Wolverhampton Wanderers have had a relatively restrained eleven managers in the last thirty years (1986–2016) – can you name the ones missing from this list? Graham Turner, MISSING (1994–95), Mark McGhee, Colin Lee, MISSING (2001–04), MISSING (2004–06), MISSING (2006–12), Terry Connor, MISSING (2012–13), Dean Saunders, MISSING (incumbent, 2013–2016). (Clue: three of the missing six were international managers before their time with Wolves) (6)

Answers on p.502

Quiz 154: Global 6 (30)

1 Which former Premier League striker is the only player to have scored more than thirty goals for the Paraguay national team? (1)

2 At the 1986 African Cup of Nations, which Cameroonian striker scored in every group game, got the winner in the semi-final against the Côte d'Ivoire and converted a penalty in the shoot-out as his country lost on penalties to Egypt in the Final? (1)

3 Who won the most caps for Brazil – Pelé, Romario, Ronaldo or Ronaldinho? Which of them scored the fewest goals for Brazil? (2)

4 Brothers Milton, Jerry, Wilson and Johnny all played international football – what is their surname and for which country have they all appeared? (2)

5 Siphiwe Tshabalala will in all likelihood match him, but at time of writing who is the only player to make more than 100 appearances for South Africa (he captained the team at the 2010 World Cup finals in his home country, at which time he was playing for Portsmouth)? (1)

6 Members of which competing nation at the 1990 World Cup finals were playing domestic football in their home country for Yukong Elephants, Lucky-Goldstar Hwangso, Hyundai Horangi and POSCO Atoms? Which of these four teams plays in the country's capital city? (2)

7 Which former West Bromwich Albion, Wigan Athletic and Blackburn Rovers striker played international football for Grenada? (1)

8 Who are the only team to have held the World Cup and Copa América at the same time (we need the date of the World Cup win as well)? (2)

9 Iván Córdoba spent twelve years at Internazionale and is fondly remembered in his country for scoring the winning goal in the 2001 Copa América Final to give them their first victory in the competition: which country? (1)

10 Who did Argentina thrash 6-1 in the semi-final of the 2015 Copa América, and who beat them in the Final on penalties? (2)

11 Segun Odegbami was one of the first notable players from which country, scoring twice as they won the African Cup of Nations for the first time as the host nation in 1980? (1)

12 Which country lost the majority of its national team to an air disaster in 1993 but still managed to reach the Final of the African Cup of Nations the following year before losing to Nigeria? (1)

13 Which country withdrew from the 2010 African Cup of Nations after a terrorist attack on their team bus? Which nation was hosting the tournament? (2)

14 Which nation have won the Asian Cup most often (four times)? And which two Middle Eastern countries have won three times each? (3)

15 Mexico and the United States have appeared in fifteen and ten World Cup finals tournaments respectively as the perennial North & Central American qualifiers: which other eight countries from the region have also reached a finals tournament? (8)

Answers on p.503

Quiz 155: Premier League 19 (40)

1 During the 1997–98 season, which Austrian goalkeeper covered for the injured David Seaman and kept clean sheets in all seven matches? (1)

2 In September 2008, Uruguayan Ignacio González signed on loan for which Premier League club causing a fall-out between the manager and the Director of Football? Who were the two individuals at the heart of the dispute? (3)

3 The Premier League match between Tottenham Hotspur and Wolverhampton Wanderers on 6 March 2011, was designated as a tribute to which former pro with both clubs, who had died a couple of weeks previously at the age of thirty-six? Who did Tottenham pay £8.1M for his services? With which Yorkshire club did he begin his career and also work as a coach? (3)

4 Which club were relegated with a pitiful nineteen points in 2002–03, losing their last fifteen matches? Who took over as manager and lost eleven of these fifteen? (He recovered, reached the play-offs the following season and won promotion back to the Premier League in 2004–05) (2)

5 Which Italian striker signed for Chelsea in 1998 but suffered a career-ending cruciate injury after just ten league games for the club? (1)

6 In their title-winning season of 2001–02 Arsenal used six centre backs: can you name them? (6)

7 Who are the two Greek players to have made more than 100 appearances in the Premier League? (2)

8 Who scored nineteen goals for Leeds United in 1999–2000 but suffered a serious injury in a UEFA Cup tie and never got his career back on track? (1)

9   Who were Manchester United's opponents when they turned around a 3-0 half time deficit and won 5-3 in a Premier League match in September 2001? Which world-class defender scored his only Premier League goal in the fixture? (2)

10 Attendances in 2005–06 in the Premier League were disappointing, especially at the start of the season: interest in which concurrent event was cited as part of the reason? (1)

11 Which two players at the big two Merseyside clubs, both defenders, played every minute of every Premier League game for their clubs in the 2010–11 season? (2)

12 If you followed the Baggies in the Premier League which club do you support? (1)

13 In the context of the Premier League, what do the following teams have in common – Leeds United (1992–93), Coventry City (1999–2000), Wolverhampton Wanderers (2003–04), Norwich City (2004–05), Derby County (2007–08), Hull City (2009–10)? (2)

14 When ITV first broadcast *The Premiership*, their alternative to *Match of the Day*, who was the main presenter? Who was the analyst in the laughable Tactics Truck? In the first 68-minute episode, how many minutes of action were shown – was it 49, 39 or a mere 28? How many seasons did the programme last? Which U2 track was used as the main theme tune? And what was the pairing, one female presenter and a former pro, for the Monday night fan-based follow-up? (7)

15 A highlight of Watford's first season back in the Premier League was a 3-0 beating of Liverpool in December. Who is missing from their starting line-up (4-4-2)? MISSING (Brazil); Allan Nyom (Cameroon), MISSING (Northern Ireland), Miguel Britos (Uruguay), Nathan Aké (Netherlands); Almen Abdi (Switzerland) (sub: MISSING, Switzerland), Ben Watson (England), MISSING (France), José Manuel Jurado (Spain); MISSING (Nigeria) (sub: Adlène Guedioura, Algeria), MISSING (England) (6)

Answers on p.504

Quiz 156: Champions League 12 (30)

1 In 2004–05 Manchester United beat Sparta Prague 4-1 in a Champions League group phase match: who scored all four United goals? (1)

2 Who beat Celtic in their second European Cup Final in 1970? Who scored Celtic's goal in the 2-1 defeat, his second European Cup Final goal? Which English side did the Scottish champions beat home and away in the semi-final? (3)

3 In 2003, Clarence Seedorf became the first player to win the European Cup with three different clubs; which three clubs (all from different countries)? (3)

4 Which Brazilian goalkeeper saved three penalties in the shoot-out as Milan beat their compatriots Juventus in the 2003 Champions League Final? (1)

5 Who celebrated Manchester United's winning goal in the 1999 Champions League Final with a somersault? (1)

6 Who, in 1971, became the first (and last) Greek side to reach the European Cup Final, losing to Ajax in the Final? (1)

7 Which team ended a sequence of six English European Cup victories in 1983? Who was their Austrian coach? (2)

8 Which two Dutch clubs have made more than ten appearances in the group stage of the Champions League since 1992–93 (to 2015–16)? (2)

9 Which two French players started the 2014 Champions League Final for Real Madrid against Atlético Madrid? Whose header in injury time took the game into extra time, at which point Real ran away with it? (2)

10 In 2006, Chelsea and Barcelona drew 2-2 in a Champions League group stage match – which former and which future Chelsea player scored the Barça goals? (2)

11 Which midfield player scored two hat-tricks for Liverpool in the 1980–81 European Cup, against OPS of Finland in a 10-0 thrashing and again in a 5-1 win over CSKA Sofia? (1)

12 With which club did Zinedine Zidane play his first Champions League Final? (1)

13 Which city has hosted the most European Cup or Champions League Finals? (1)

14 Barcelona have won the Champions League four times in the twenty-first century (to 2015–16) and Lionel Messi played in the three more recent victories: which seven Spanish players have matched him and which of them went one better and played in all four Finals? (8)

15 Who are the only club to have won the European Cup or Champions League more times than they have won their domestic league title? (1)

Answers on p.504

Quiz 157: General 40 (30)

1 Lennie Godber, played by Richard Beckinsale, one of the main characters in the BBC sitcom *Porridge*, was an avid fan of which football club, a fact reflected in the programme's dialogue? (1)

2 Who did Alliance Premier League side Wealdstone sell to Coventry City in Autumn 1983? (1)

3 Who was the Portsmouth striker who served fourteen days of a 21-day prison sentence after being found guilty of driving under the influence while already banned? (1)

4 Which Northern Ireland international became Oxford United's most capped player during their years in the higher divisions? (1)

5 Vladimir Romanov was the controversial Chairman of which Scottish club between 2005 and 2014, leaving the club relegated and in dire financial trouble? (1)

6 Who, in July 1992, were re-elected to FIFA after an eighteen-year absence? (1)

7 With which side did Tom Finney spend his entire club career? (1)

8 Which city, which has also hosted a Winter Olympics, was the only one on the northerly island of Hokkaido to host games at the 2002 World Cup finals? (1)

9 Which legendary sportsman, capped for England in 1901, won twenty-six Test caps at cricket as well as representing Oxford at rugby union and holding the world long-jump record? (1)

10 What nickname was given to Leatherhead striker Chris Kelly, whose goals were instrumental in their 1974–75 FA Cup run and whose outspoken claims provided the off-field entertainment? (1)

11 Which of these sides has never reached an FA Cup Final – Nottingham Forest, Ipswich Town, Leyton Orient, Middlesbrough? (1)

12 Who was the only Welshman in the Tottenham side that won the FA Cup in 1960–61 to clinch the first Double of the twentieth century? (1)

13 With which side did Roy of the Rovers enjoy a 38-year career? (1)

14 Pop star Jim Kerr teamed up with Kenny Dalglish to launch a bid for Celtic in 1998 – of which successful Scottish band was Kerr the lead singer? (1)

15 Jamie Vardy became the seventeenth Englishman to score twenty or more goals in a Premier league season – can you name the other sixteen? (16)

Answers on p.505

Quiz 158: League Cup 4 (30)

1 Which Northern Ireland winger was hailed as the next big thing when he won the League Cup Final with Luton Town, moved to Nottingham Forest, failed to live up to his billing, but later did good service and was highly regarded at Grimsby Town? (1)

2 Which teenager came off the bench and scored, becoming Arsenal's youngest goalscorer, as they beat Wolverhampton Wanderers 5-1 in a League Cup tie in November 2003? (1)

3 Who are the only club to have won the League Cup in three consecutive seasons (they actually won four on the trot)? (1)

4 Who were the first winners of the League Cup in 1961, beating Division 3 side Rotherham United in the two-legged Final? Who was their victorious manager, who would later win the same competition with a Manchester club? (2)

5 Which manager led first Norwich City and then Manchester City to League Cup Final defeats in successive years in the 1970s before striking third time lucky in 1975 with which club? (2)

6 Which Premier League team were hammered 6-1 by Division 1 (second tier) leaders Bolton Wanderers in the 1996–97 League Cup? Who bagged a hat-trick for Wanderers? (2)

7 Jermaine Easter's goal beat Premier League side Charlton Athletic and took which lower league side to the League Cup semi-finals in 2006–07? Who beat them 4-0 in the semi-final second leg after Easter's first leg goal had earned a creditable draw? Who was the lower-league club's manager that season? (3)

8 In the 1999–2000 League Cup the major players all fell by the wayside early. Which Yorkshire team pulled off a major surprise by winning 1-0 at Stamford Bridge in the second round? And which London team from Division 1 (second tier) put out holders Tottenham Hotspur 3-1 in the fourth round? (2)

9 Which Midlands club were the first beneficiaries of an automatic European qualification spot for winning the League Cup when they won the 1973–74 competition? Which long-serving club legend near the start of his career scored the only goal of the game to beat Liverpool in the quarter-final, his team's goal in both legs of the semi-final win over Norwich City, and the winner in the Final against Manchester City? Which member of the winning team went on to score the winning goal in the FA Cup Final as an Arsenal player? (3)

10 Which Danish international scored the only goal of the game in the last minute as Tottenham Hotspur won the 1999 League Cup Final? Who were their opponents, playing in their second Final in three years? (2)

11 Which full back scored one of his rare goals for Leeds United as they beat Arsenal 1-0 in the 1968 League Cup Final? (1)

12 Who did Liverpool beat 8-0 away from home on their way to the League Cup Final in 2000–01? Who netted a hat-trick in the rout and scored Liverpool's goal in the Final before they went on to win on penalties? (2)

13 Which Championship side reached the Final of the League Cup in 2011–12 only to lose on penalties to Liverpool after one of the most exciting Wembley finals of recent years finished 2-2? Which cousins both missed in the shoot-out? (3)

14 Who scored an injury-time winner to avoid extra time as Manchester United overturned a 2-1 deficit with a 3-1 win in the second leg of their League Cup semi-final in 2009–10? Who were their opponents and which former player, now a hate figure at Old Trafford, scored all three of their goals? Who scored United's winner in the Final against Aston Villa? (4)

15 Which winger inspired Third Division Swindon Town to an unlikely League Cup Final victory over Arsenal in 1969? (1)

Answers on p.506

Quiz 159: World Cup 16 (30)

---

1 Who was the Sparta Prague inside forward who was integral to the strong Czech side of the 1930s, scoring a hat-trick in the 1934 World Cup semi-final against Germany? (1)

2 Who was the Aston Villa striker, already with an FA Cup Final winning goal in 1957, who scored five goals in four games to help Northern Ireland through a tough group at the 1958 World Cup finals? (1)

3 This is the England starting line-up, by club, for the 1970 World Cup finals match against West Germany: Chelsea; Everton, Everton, West Ham United, Leeds United; Everton, Tottenham Hotspur, Manchester United, Tottenham Hotspur: Manchester City, West Ham United. Can you name the players? (11)

4 Which two semi-finalists from the 1958 World Cup failed to make the finals four years later? (2)

5 Who was the Swiss referee who took charge of the 1966 World Cup Final? (1)

6 What was the title of the pop song by the 1970 England World Cup squad that reached no.1 in the UK charts prior to the competition? (1)

7 What were the first names of the two Müllers in West Germany's 1978 World Cup squad? (2)

8 Which Dundee United player opened the scoring in Scotland's game against Brazil at the 1982 World Cup finals, only for a brilliant Brazilian team to respond with four goals? (1)

9 The Republic of Ireland qualified for their first World Cup finals in 1990. Apart from a 2-0 defeat by Spain they did so without conceding a goal, including a famous 3-0 win in Dublin over which European rivals? (1)

10 Paul Ince and David Batty were the unlucky men who missed their spot-kicks in the shoot-out against Argentina at the 1998 World Cup finals (Ince after an inspirational performance). Which three England players scored in the shoot-out, and who was the Argentinian striker who surprisingly failed with his penalty? (4)

11 The Republic of Ireland qualified for the 1994 World Cup from a tough group, finishing above which country, the reigning European champions on goals scored as they both ended with the same points and goal difference? Who was the Portsmouth midfielder who scored the crucial goal that earned a draw in Belfast and saw the Irish home? (1)

12 Who scored the crucial penalty that took Ireland past Romania in a shoot-out in the Last 16 of the 1990 World Cup? (1)

13 Who scored a stunning free kick as Paraguay earned a hard-fought 1-1 draw in Buenos Aires during qualification for the 1998 World Cup finals? (1)

14 Which African side took Germany to extra time at the 2014 World Cup finals with a stubborn defensive performance? (1)

15 Who scored in the Last 16 and quarter-final of the 2014 World Cup and was immediately hailed as Brazil's new Golden Boy following Neymar's injury? (1)

Answers on p.506

Quiz 160: Premier League 20 (40)

1 Following Wimbledon's relegation from the Premier League in 2000, the club offloaded a striker to Newcastle United and a full back to Tottenham Hotspur for a combined £12M – who were the two players involved? (2)

2 In their miraculous unbeaten season of 2003–04 which were the only two sides Arsenal failed to beat in the Premier League (one was a major rival and the other a newly promoted team)? (2)

3 There have been plenty of players from the Côte d'Ivoire (Ivory Coast) in the Premier League. The first was Ibrahima Bakayoko, who had a single (fairly unsuccessful) season with which club in 1998–99? (1)

4 Which flamboyant overseas Everton player signed for Liverpool in 2002, the most recent direct trade between the two clubs? (1)

5 Which Liverpool player was sent off after flinging a coin that struck him back into the crowd? Which Arsenal pair, an England centre half and an overseas veteran, were already off the field in this stormy encounter? (3)

6 Which three overseas players made the Premier League team of the first twenty years (both the public and the panel XI)? (3)

7 Who scored the Premier League's first hat-trick as Leeds United beat Tottenham Hotspur 5-0 in August 1992? (1)

8 Who were relegated as Everton came from 2-0 down on the last day of the 1993–94 Premier League season? Which Scottish international scored Everton's winner? Whose flaky performance in goal for Wimbledon has since been the discussion of various conspiracy theories about how 'clean' the game was? (3)

9 Who were relegated from the Premier League (having been members from the start in 1992–93) after a 4-1 reverse at Bolton Wanderers in April 2004? Which World Cup winner scored twice for Bolton, and which striker was sent off for the losers, his second dismissal in the space of three weeks? (3)

10 Three Chelsea players were nominated for the PFA Player of the Year award in 2005–06 as they won their second successive league title – which three? (3)

11 West Bromwich Albion came from 2-0 down to draw 2-2 at Old Trafford in October 2010: what was the significance of that result in the context of the 2010–11 Premier League season, and who was West Bromwich Albion manager? (2)

12 No overseas player has scored a Premier League hat-trick for West Ham United to March 2015, although four English players have. One was Tony Cottee, who won 7 England caps; who are the other three, none of whom were capped by England? (3)

13 Which team scored the most goals by a relegated team, was it Blackpool in 2010–11, West Ham United in the same season, Sheffield Wednesday in 1999–2000 or Wigan Athletic in 2012–13? (2)

14 Which five (different) overseas players won the Football Writers' Association Player of the Year award between 1995 and 1999 (only two are from the same country, France)? (5)

15 Crystal Palace's league form in the 2015–16 Premier League season stuttered after Christmas, but the highlight of their sparkling start was a 2-1 win over Chelsea at Stamford Bridge. This is their starting line-up, can you name the missing players (4-2-3-1, English unless stated)? Alex McCarthy; Joel Ward, MISSING, MISSING (Republic of Ireland), Pape Souaré (Senegal); James McArthur (Scotland), MISSING (France) (sub: MISSING, Wales); Jason Puncheon, MISSING (Mali) (sub: Lee Chung-Yong, South Korea), Wilfred Zaha (sub: MISSING, DR of Congo); Conor Wickham (6)

Answers on p.507

Quiz 161: General 41 (30)

1 England had two players with the same first name and surname in their 1986 World Cup squad? What was the name and which clubs did the pair play for? Which of the two was in the starting line-up for the tournament? Which of them scored in an FA Cup Final? (5)

2 Leyton Orient, Chelsea, Queens Park Rangers, Manchester United, Coventry City (plus two part-time stints with England U-21s): whose management career path, which started in the 1960s, is this? (1)

3 What connects Liverpool and Viña del Mar in Chile? (1)

4 Which £400,000 snip was voted PFA Player of the Year for 2015–16? (1)

5 Which Liverpool player scored a hat-trick as Spain walloped Slovakia 5-1 in the first leg of their play-off and effectively sealed their spot at the 2006 World Cup finals? (1)

6 Which triple Champions League winner with Real Madrid around the turn of the century took over as manager of Middlesbrough in 2013? (1)

7 Who was manager of Burton Albion when they took Manchester United to a replay in the FA Cup in 2005–06? (1)

8 Who, to 2015, has won the most FA Cups, Alex Ferguson or Arsène Wenger? (1)

9 Who were the five England internationals who appeared in the 1992 League Cup Final defeat to Arsenal in 1993? (5)

10 Which former Davis Cup tennis star purchased Hull City in 1997? What made him his money after his tennis career was over? (2)

11 David Beckham wore the famous no.7 shirt at Manchester United, but what number did he wear amongst the Galácticos of Real Madrid? (1)

12 This is the Bolton Wanderers team that destroyed Aston Villa 5-2 in the home leg of their League Cup semi-final in 2004: can you fill in the gaps (4-4-1-1, English unless stated)? MISSING (Finland); Nicky Hunt, MISSING (France), MISSING (Brazil), Anthony Barness (sub: Simon Charlton); Stelios Giannakopoulos (Greece) (sub: Henrik Pedersen, Denmark), MISSING, MISSING (Spain), Jay-Jay Okocha (Nigeria); Youri Djorkaeff (France) (sub: Ibrahim Ba, France); MISSING (6)

13 Which manager accused Premier League referee Alan Wiley of not being physically fit enough to officiate at the top level after a home game against Sunderland in October 2009? (1)

14 Which Football League club were known as Black Arabs FC and Eastville Rovers in their early days? (1)

15 French-born Rudy Gestede, who signed for Aston Villa at the start of the 2015–16 season, chose to play international football for which West African country? Which other Premier League player (Sunderland and West Bromwich Albion) has more than 50 caps for the same country? (2)

Answers on p.507

Quiz 162: Football League 17 (30)

1 Which big city club won their fourth and most recent top-flight title in 1926–27? And which prolific Scottish goalscorer was their team captain? (2)

2 In 1955–56 Leeds United were promoted back to the top flight after suffering relegation in the first season after the war: who was their star player and First Division top scorer in their first season back in the top division? (1)

3 Andy McEvoy was an Irish international who finished joint top scorer in the English First Division in his best season (1964–65): which club did he play for from 1956 to 1967 – was it (a) Blackpool (b) Blackburn Rovers (c) Bolton Wanderers or (d) Liverpool? (1)

4 Which former player of theirs scored a hat-trick as Newcastle United were beaten 5-3 by Arsenal in December 1976? (1)

5 Who played into his forties and racked up more than 700 league games for Bristol Rovers, Torquay United, Bristol City*, Reading, Wimbledon, Manchester City*, Wolverhampton Wanderers*, Sheffield United, Barnsley and Mansfield Town, as well as winning three caps for England while at Manchester City? (1)

6 Which goalkeeper is Sunderland's appearance record holder, with 627 in all competitions? (1)

7 Which is the only one of these sides to have dropped into the third tier of the league: Aston Villa, Chelsea, Leicester City, West Ham United (1)

8 Who was manager of Brighton & Hove Albion when they reached the top flight for the first time in 1979 – was it (a) Harry Redknapp (b) Terry Venables (c) Alan Mullery or (d) Jimmy Melia? (1)

9 In April 1936 Joe Payne scored a league record (it still stands) ten goals in a Third Division (South) 12-0 win over Bristol Rovers for which club? (1)

10 Which club enjoyed their best league win when they thrashed Blackpool 7-0 in November 2000 with Tony Cottee in charge as player-manager? What was the end of season outcome for the two clubs? (3)

11 Which father and son, both strikers, notched up almost twenty league clubs and more than 400 goals between them from 1959 to the end of the century, and which club was the only one common to both? (3)

12 Andy Legg was a left-sided Welsh international player who enjoyed a long league career from 1988 well into the next century: for which two fierce rivals did he make more than 150 appearances? (2)

13 Leon Knight, with a late penalty, and a goal from veteran Neil Shipperley earned promotion (to Division 1 and the Premier League respectively) for which two clubs in 2003–04? (2)

14 Which defender scored an unlikely hat-trick for West Ham United in an 8-1 rout of Newcastle United in April 1986, completed when he took a late penalty in place of the regular penalty-taker, Ray Stewart? What was the unusual circumstance around the hat-trick – was it (a) that all three goals were scored in the final five minutes, (b) the three goals were hit past three different goalkeepers, (c) they were the only three goals he scored for the club, or (d) it was his successive hat-trick against Newcastle? (2)

15 There were eight players on the Football League 100 Legends list, published in 1998, who turned out for Manchester City. Can you name these players (three are best known for their association with different clubs, three played for City before the Second World War, two are goal-keepers)? (8)

Asterisk (*) indicates that the player in question made more than one hundred league appearances for the club.

Answers on p.508

Quiz 163: Premier League 21 (40)

1 For which club did Peter Schmeichel depart Manchester United? And which Premier League club brought him back to England? (2)

2 Three Finnish goalkeepers spent the majority of the 2002–03 season as first choice for Premier League clubs – names and clubs, please. (6)

3 Which Coventry City striker was the first African footballer to play in the Premier League? For which country did he make 100 appearances, scoring 38 goals? (2)

4 Which local rivals won 1-0 at Old Trafford in September 2002, having already won there 2-1 the previous season as a newly promoted side? Who scored for the visitors on both occasions? (2)

5 What first did Alan Shearer achieve on his 100th appearance for Newcastle United, the first game of the 1999–2000 season, a 1-0 home defeat to Aston Villa? (1)

6 Which three players scored ten or more goals for Chelsea when they won the first of their modern titles under José Mourinho in 2004–05? And which four players started thirty or more of their Premier League matches? (7)

7 Who became the first Mexican to play in the Premier League when he signed for Bolton Wanderers in 2005? (1)

8 Who scored two hat-tricks in three days as Queens Park Rangers beat Nottingham Forest and Everton over the Easter break in 1993? (1)

9 Who attracted a capacity crowd for his farewell match at the St Mary's Stadium in 2002? (1)

10 In March 2007 the Tottenham Hotspur goalkeeper hit a long punt upfield which bounced over the head of his opposite number in the Watford goal and hit the back of the net – which two goalkeepers were involved? (2)

11 From which club did Arsenal buy the 21-year-old Robin van Persie in 2004? How many Premier League goals did the Dutchman score in eleven years in the Premier League – was it 207, 188, 144 or 101? (2)

12 The only hat-trick by a Wimbledon player in the Premier League came against Oldham Athletic in April 1994: who scored it? (1)

13 Who swapped a less than regular place at Aston Villa for centre stage at second city rivals Birmingham City in 2010, and ended up as City's top scorer with nine from midfield, despite relegation? Where did he end up in 2014 after three seasons at Sunderland? (2)

14 What connects Leeds United at home to Derby County in 1997, Wimbledon away at West Ham United in 1998, Manchester United away at Tottenham Hotspur in 2001 and Wolverhampton Wanderers at home to Leicester City in 2003? (2)

15 On the last day of the 2014–15 season Stoke City destroyed Liverpool 6-1. Who is missing from the Stoke line-up from that game? And what was the special significance of the game for Liverpool supporters? (4-3-3)? MISSING (Bosnia and Herzegovina); Geoff Cameron (USA), MISSING (England), Marc Muniesa (Spain) (sub: Marc Wilson, England), Erik Pieters (Netherlands); Steven N'Zonzi (France), MISSING (Republic of Ireland), MISSING (Scotland); Jonathan Walters (Republic of Ireland) (sub: MISSING, Nigeria), MISSING (Austria) (sub: MISSING, England), Mame Biriam Diouf (Senegal). (8)

Answers on p.509

Quiz 164: Scotland 7 (30)

1 Which Scottish goalkeeper was signed from Everton as a replacement for Pat Jennings at Arsenal but couldn't force his way past the veteran and left three years later for Crystal Palace, where he played more than 200 matches? (1)

2 Which two Scottish-based players (one Celtic, one Rangers) have won the Golden Boot for top scorer in a European league? (2)

3 Which Hearts legend's seventeen years at the club (more than 500 games and over 200 goals from 1981 to 1998) was interrupted by an unhappy spell at Newcastle United in 1988 (only twelve games and no goals)? (1)

4 Which two former Northern Ireland internationals have been manager of Celtic? (2)

5 Which league club plays its domestic fixtures at Hampden Park? (1)

6 Which Rangers goalkeeper enjoyed 1,196 unblemished minutes before conceding a goal to Hamilton Academicals? (1)

7 When was the last time Celtic finished outside the top three of the Scottish League or SPL – was it 1994–95, 1977–78, 1964–65 or 1956–57? (1)

8 Manchester United had the best representation in Scotland's 1978 World Cup squad. Who were the four United players picked? Which one never got on the pitch? (5)

9 Former striker Jimmy McGrory was manager of Celtic from 1945 to 1965; how many league titles did the club win under his management – none, one, three or ten? (1)

10 Meadowbank Thistle entered the Scottish League in 1974, playing their games in which city? To where did they relocate in 1995, changing the club name to reflect the move? (2)

11 In the 1990 Scottish Cup Final Aberdeen beat Celtic 9-8 in a penalty shoot-out that was far more exciting than the 0-0 draw which preceded it. Which Northern Ireland defender missed the vital kick for Celtic? Who was the Dutch goalkeeper who saved it? (2)

12 Billy Bremner, John Collins, Asa Hartford, Graeme Souness – who won most caps? (1)

13 Who was the manager of Dunfermline Athletic from 1960–64 before leaving for a more prestigious job in the Scottish League? (1)

14 Kenny Dalglish, Ally McCoist, Mo Johnston, Steven Fletcher – which one has scored a hat-trick for Scotland? (1)

15 Scotland beat France home and away in trying to qualify for the 2008 European Championships. Can you name the missing players and clubs? MISSING (Sunderland); MISSING (Burnley), MISSING (Rangers), Stephen McManus (CLUB?), Alan Hutton (Rangers); Lee McCulloch (Rangers), Darren Fletcher (Manchester United) (sub: Stephen Pearson, Derby County), MISSING (Rangers), Scott Brown (CLUB?), Paul Hartley (Celtic); MISSING (Everton) (sub: Garry O'Connor, Birmingham City) (8)

Answers on p.510

Quiz 165: General 42 (30)

1 Englishman George Raynor managed which European team at the 1950 World Cup finals? (1)

2 Liverpool let Jimmy Case go in 1981: which two clubs got more than 100 and 200 games respectively out of the surplus midfielder, who played at the top level until his mid-thirties? (2)

3 What connects Manchester City (1926); Leicester (1969); Brighton (1983), Middlesbrough (1997) and Portsmouth (2010) (1)

4 Which club connects the playing careers of Alex Ferguson and David Moyes – is it (a) Rangers (b) Preston North End (c) Dunfermline Athletic or (d) Houston Dynamo? (1)

5 Which Liverpool player was jailed in 1988 for driving under the influence and reckless driving? (1)

6 Which two Dutch managers took charge of South Korea at the 2002 and 2006 World Cup finals tournaments? (2)

7 Who was manager of Liverpool when they won three Cup trophies in 2001? (1)

8 Whose career in Europe, 1993–2012, is mapped out here: Ajax, Internazionale, Arsenal*, West Bromwich Albion, Portsmouth*? (1)

9 Who was alongside Kevin Keegan as the other half of the management dream team announced by Fulham owner Mohamed Al-Fayed in September 1997? (1)

10 In 2003, Italian club Perugia signed the son of which North African political figure? (2)

11 What part have Fevernova, Teamgeist, Jabulani and Brazuca played in the last four World Cups? (2)

12 Can you name the missing players from this Sheffield Wednesday line-up for the 1991 League Cup Final win over Manchester United? Who scored the game's only goal with a sublimely struck half-volley? Who was the Wednesday manager and which former England international at the end of his career was Wednesday's other (unused) substitute? What was the icing on the cake at the end of a memorable season? Here's the line-up (4-4-2, English unless stated): Chris Turner; MISSING (Sweden), Peter Shirtliff, MISSING, Phil King; MISSING (Northern Ireland), MISSING (United States) (sub: Lawrie Madden), John Sheridan (Republic of Ireland), Nigel Worthington (Northern Ireland); Paul Williams, MISSING. (9)

13 Which member of the France team that won the 1984 European Championships has managed in the Premier League? At which club? (2)

14 Which two major Liverpool stars of the 1970s first plied their trade with Scunthorpe United? (2)

15 From which clubs did Manchester City sign Kolo Touré and his younger brother, Yaya, in 2009 and 2010 respectively? (2)

Asterisk (*) indicates that the player in question made more than one hundred league appearances for the club.

Answers on p.510

Quiz 166: World Cup 17 (30)

1 Hossam Hassan's solitary goal settled a two-legged play-off and ensured which country qualified for the 1990 World Cup finals instead of Algeria? (1)

2 Who was the Peñarol no.10 inside forward and playmaker in the 1950 Uruguay team that won the World Cup? Which Italian club snapped him up after another terrific tournament in 1954? (2)

3 England opened their qualifying campaign for the 1962 World Cup with a 9-0 away win in Luxembourg; which two players scored hat-tricks? (2)

4 Who is the only Scottish player to have been sent off at the World Cup finals, getting a red card against Morocco in a 1998 group match? (1)

5 West Germany's team for the 1966 World Cup Final included two Cologne players, both called Wolfgang; what were their surnames? (2)

6 Who became the first team to score ten goals in a match at a World Cup finals tournament when they beat El Salvador 10-1 in 1982? Who scored a hat-trick in nine minutes after coming on as a second half substitute? (2)

7 Who scored his only England goal in thirty-five games in the quarter-final against West Germany at the 1970 World Cup finals? (1)

8 Which Poland star scored a stunning hat-trick to help his side beat Belgium in the second phase of the 1982 World Cup finals tournament? Which Italian side were so impressed they bought him? (2)

9 Who knocked out Australia with a late penalty in the Last 16 of the 2006 World Cup? Which Premier League defender's challenge gave away the penalty? Who kept his nerve to score it? (3)

10 After England were beaten 4-1 in the quarter-finals of the 2010 World Cup finals (with a little help from the Uruguayan officials who refused to allow a goal), who were thrashed even more comprehensively by Germany in the next round? Who was their manager, whose lack of tactical nous was horribly exposed in the tournament? (2)

11 Who were sailing through to the 1994 World Cup finals but inexplicably lost their last two home games against Israel and Bulgaria? Which Premier League legend scored the opening goal in the 2-1 defeat to Bulgaria? And which curly haired wide player scored both Bulgaria goals? Who was the manager of the hapless losers that night? At which other Premier League star did he aim his ire after that player gave the ball away in the dying moments of the game to allow a last-gasp Bulgarian attack? (5)

12 Italy were forced into a two-legged play-off in order to qualify for the 1998 World Cup finals despite finishing their group unbeaten. Who pushed them into second place in the group and who did they beat in the play-offs? (2)

13 Who was given a second yellow card and sent off for diving against South Korea in a 2002 World Cup Last 16 match? Which player, an all-time great of the game, retired after the final whistle? (2)

14 Argentina produced a masterclass in the group stages of the 2006 World Cup finals as they butchered which European side 6-0? Which teenager made his World Cup finals debut as a substitute and scored his first goal? (2)

15 Who missed all their penalties in a Last 16 match at the 2006 World Cup finals and became the first team to exit a World Cup tournament without conceding a goal in actual play? (1)

Answers on p.511

Quiz 167: European Championships 5 (30)

1 Which great Spanish goalkeeper made a fumble that handed France their first goal in the 1984 European Championship Final? (1)

2 It was a few years before the first great generation of Dutch players flowered when they attempted to qualify for the 1964 European Championships; which of their neighbours embarrassed them with a 2-1 win in the home leg to go through? (1)

3 Who scored twice to see West Germany past Belgium in the semi-finals of the 1972 European Championship and scored another brace as the Soviet Union were easily beaten in the Final? (1)

4 A 1-0 defeat to Italy scuppered England's chances of reaching the Final of the 1980 European Championships; which redoubtable midfield player, a hero of the World Cup two years later, scored the only goal? (1)

5 Which striker (who clocked up more than 500 games and 250 goals during eighteen years at Benfica) scored the goal that took Portugal past Romania and earn a semi-final against France at the 1984 European Championships, their first major tournament since the 1966 World Cup? Which full back scored twice against them in the semi-final – his only goals for France? Who was the coach who brought France their first major tournament on home soil? (3)

6 What did five Ukrianians and a Belarusian do at the 1988 European Championships? (2)

7 Who scored in every group match for Bulgaria at the 1996 European Championships, to no avail as they finished third in their group? (1)

8 Which powerful striker came on as a substitute in the 1996 European Championship Final and scored the goals that ensured Germany came back from one-down to beat the Czech Republic? Which of his fellow strikers was the captain of the German team? (2)

9   Who scored a stunning goal to give Wales the lead in their 2016 European Championship quarter-final win over Belgium? Who finally ended the Welsh challenge in the semi-final? (2)

10 Whose extra-time golden goal penalty took France into the Final of the 2000 European Championships with a 2-1 win over Portugal? Who was the Portuguese scorer, sent off for disputing the penalty award (which was correct, although the referee missed it and had to be notified by the assistant)? (2)

11 This is the Wales team that beat Italy 2-1 in a qualifier for the 2004 European Championships in 2002 (4-4-2) – can you name the missing players? MISSING (Southampton); Mark Delaney (Aston Villa), Andy Melville (Fulham), MISSING (Cardiff City), MISSING (Newcastle United); MISSING (Tottenham Hotspur), Mark Pembridge (Everton), MISSING (Leicester City), Ryan Giggs (Manchester United); Craig Bellamy (Newcastle United), (sub: Nathan Blake, Wolverhampton Wanderers), MISSING (Celtic) (6)

12 Which Liverpool player came off the bench and scored the winning goal for the Czech Republic against Germany at the 2004 European Championships, after Marek Heinz had cancelled out Michael Ballack's opener? (1)

13 The Netherlands won their only penalty shoot-out in a major tournament during the 2004 European Championships; who did they eliminate in the quarter-finals after a 0-0 draw? Which two players, an iconic striker and the captain, a Premier League centre back, missed for the opposition? (3)

14 Which player, bound for London in 2009, put in a man of the match performance as Russia surprised the Netherlands and won 3-1 in extra time in the quarter-finals of the 2008 European Championships? (1)

15 Who scored a penalty in Solna and twice in Copenhagen to ensure Sweden beat Denmark in a play-off for the 2016 European Championships? Who had already surprised the Danes by finishing second to Portugal in their group? And which team finished way down this group having being deducted three points after fans invaded the pitch and attacked opposition players? (3)

Answers on p.512

Quiz 168: Football League 18 (30)

1 Which north-east club became the thirteenth team to join the Football League when they were elected to replace Stoke City, who finished bottom of the table in the league's first two seasons? (1)

2 Everton scored 102 goals in winning the Football League in 1927–28: who scored an even more phenomenal 60 of them? (1)

3 Who was First Division top scorer in 1959, 1961, 1963, 1964, 1965 (joint) and 1969? (1)

4 Whose bizarre rise and fall throughout the 1960s read: Div 4 (6th); Div 4 (3rd, promoted); Div 3 (8th); Div 3 (1st, promoted); Div 2 (11th); Div 2 (2nd, promoted); Div 1 (21st, relegated); Div 2 (21st, relegated); Div 3 (17th); Div 3 (21st, relegated)? Which former Wales international captain oversaw the rise (and some of the fall)? (2)

5 Which midfield player with a thunderous left foot was Derby County's top scorer when they won the First Division in 1974–75? (1)

6 Who was the only player to twice top the First Division goalscoring charts in the 1980s? (1)

7 Which young manager led Crystal Palace into the top flight in 1978–79? (1)

8 In September 1989 Liverpool recorded their highest ever league victory, a 9-0 thrashing at Anfield of which newly-promoted team? Who were the respective managers of the two clubs? (3)

9 Who finally succumbed at Anfield in December 1978 after a record forty-two top-flight Football League games unbeaten? (1)

10 Which of these sides has never dropped into the fourth tier of the league: Bolton Wanderers, Derby County, Sheffield United, Wolverhampton Wanderers? (1)

11   Cumbria is made up of the old counties of Cumberland and Westmoreland and a little spur of old Lancashire. Which three teams from the region have played League football? (3)

12   Tranmere Rovers finished fourth in the second tier in 1992–93 but lost out on a crack at the Premier League in the play-offs: which two seasoned internationals (Republic of Ireland & Scotland) scored 34 goals between them for Rovers that season? (2)

13   Hull City*, Middlesbrough, Celtic, Barnsley*, Huddersfield Town, Burnley* (*inc Blackpool*): whose career path is this, across all the divisions from 1985 to 2003, taking in more than 500 league games with over 200 goals? (1)

14   Which two experienced strikers, one bought from Birmingham City, one in his second long spell at the club (more than 400 games and 100 goals in total) scored the goals that took Queens Park Rangers back into the Championship (second tier) in 2003–04? Who was the club's manager, the last one to keep his job for over two years? (3)

15   Eight clubs have finished runners up in the top flight since the Second World War without winning the title (although four of these clubs can claim pre-war titles) – can you name them? (8)

Asterisk (*) indicates that the player in question made more than one hundred league appearances for the club.

Answers on p.512

Quiz 169: General 43 (30)

1 Everyone remembers Pickles, the dog who found the World Cup trophy after it was stolen while on display before the 1966 World Cup; but where was it stolen from – (a) Central Hall, Westminster (b) FA Headquarters, Lancaster Gate (c) The Barbican (d) The Royal Academy, Piccadilly? (1)

2 Marcos Evangelista de Morais played in four World Cup finals tournaments from 1994, but under what name? (1)

3 What connects the early careers of Les Ferdinand, Stan Collymore, Kevin Phillips, Kerry Dixon and Charlie Austin? (1)

4 Which club was managed by Joe Smith from 1935 to 1958? They were promoted to the top flight in 1937, finished third in 1951 and second in 1956, and were still there when he resigned due to ill health? For which other club, from the same region, did Smith play (as captain) in two successful FA Cup-winning sides in the 1920s? (2)

5 Which long-haired striker scored the goal that won the 1971 FA Cup Final and sealed the Double for Arsenal? (1)

6 Which two footballing nations made up the GB team for the 2012 Olympic Football tournament in London? Who captained the side? Which team eliminated GB on penalties? Who scored two goals in the group games but missed a crucial penalty in the shoot-out? (5)

7 Who was paraded in front of Darlington fans in 2002 but never actually signed up? (1)

8 Whose career is this, 1977–1994: Queens Park Rangers, West Ham United, Newcastle United, Derby County, Millwall, Ipswich Town – it also included a solitary England appearance, in which he scored, but he was never picked again? (1)

9 Which England manager separated from his wife, Anne, while in tenure? (1)

10   Ruel Fox did it in a Premier League game for Norwich City in December 1993, and the next person to do it was Steed Malbranque for Fulham in an FA Cup tie in March 2004: what? (2)

11   Who were Swansea's victims when they clinched their first major English trophy by winning the 2012–13 League Cup Final 5-0? Which Englishman scored twice and was named Man of the Match? Who was the Swansea manager? Who were the only two Welsh players to feature? (5)

12   In a poll in early 2001 for the greatest Manchester United player of all time, who were the top four? (4)

13   Which pony-tailed defender became a bit of a cult hero at Queens Park Rangers and then Newcastle after his move from Hereford United in 1990? (1)

14   Who dropped down to the Third Division for the first time in their history in 1979 and two years later dropped into the bottom tier for a solitary season, the only time the club have slipped that far? Who scored 35 goals in 1981–82 to help them out of the bottom division and then scored 34 two seasons later to help them up again? (2)

15   In 1995 the Chairman of Chelsea banned the owner of their ground, Stamford Bridge, from attending matches: who were the two feuding magnates? (2)

Answers on p.513

Quiz 170: Premier League 22 (40)

1 For which five clubs did Hermann Hreidarsson turn out in the Premier League? (5)

2 In total, fifteen of the France squad at the 1998 World Cup finals came to play in England at some point: which three were already there (all in London) at the start of the tournament? (3)

3 To the end of the 2014–15 season, which four clubs have won promotion to the Premier League on four occasions? (4)

4 Which Croatian international joined Chelsea from Parma for £5.6M in summer 2000, and scored twice on his debut against West Ham United? (1)

5 Which London-born Irish international who had spells in the Premier League with Derby County, Southampton and Stoke City was notable for his prodigious long throws, used to great effect by Tony Pulis at Stoke? (1)

6 Which three Premier League clubs employed the talented but inconsistent French striker Djibril Cissé? (3)

7 Who came on loan to Everton from Real Sociedad in January 2005 and stayed another six years? (1)

8 Who signed a contract with Everton in 2003 that took his salary from around £100 per week to around £14,000 per week? (2)

9 Who were the first team to concede 100 goals in the Premier League, failing to win any of their first fifteen games as they were relegated in what proved to be their only season in the new top division? Who left the club as manager at the start of the season, and who was his assistant who stepped up but couldn't stem the tide? (3)

10 Which striker holds the record for most Premier League hat-tricks with eleven? (1)

11 Jason Roberts endeared himself even further to West Bromwich Albion fans by taking off his shirt after scoring a goal to reveal a picture of which club legend in January 2002? Why did he do it? (2)

12 Who went down in 2002–03 with 42 points, the most in a 38-game Premier League? And who stayed up with 34 two years later, the fewest points accumulated for survival? (2)

13 Which long-time owner of Manchester City put his shares up for sale in September 1993? Which former player led the consortium that took over the running of the club? In 2007 Thaksin Sinawatra took over the club – of which country was he the former Prime Minister? From which country did the money come to buy City off Sinawatra in 2008, less than eighteen months later? (4)

14 Which three managers have led Norwich City to promotion to the Premier League, in 2004, 2011 and 2015? (3)

15 Burnley's season in the Premier League in 2014–15 ended in relegation but they fought hard, never more so than in a 1-0 win over Manchester City in March, a result that severely dented any hopes City held of retaining their League title. Who is missing from their starting line-up that day (4-4-2, English unless stated): MISSING; Kieran Trippier, MISSING (Republic of Ireland), Jason Shackell, Ben Mee; MISSING (Scotland), Scott Arfield (Canada), David Jones, Ashley Barnes (Austria); MISSING (Wales) (sub: Stephen Ward, Republic of Ireland), MISSING (sub: Steven Reid) (5)

Answers on p.513

Quiz 171: Champions League 13 (30)

1 Who were the unlikely finalists in the 2004 Champions League Final, neither of them from the 'big four' nations? (2)

2 Spain have won fifteen European Cup/Champions League titles, more than any other nation, but all of those titles were won by two teams: which country has had the most different winners, with five? (1)

3 Which Spanish striker, on loan from Real Madrid at the time, scored in both legs as Monaco knocked his parent club out of the 2004 Champions League? Against which side did he repeat the feat in the semi-final as Monaco won 5-3 on aggregate? (2)

4 In the 1975–76 European Cup, who were beaten 4-1 by Derby County only to win the second leg 5-1 and go through? (1)

5 Who destroyed Johan Cruyff's Barcelona, winning 4-0 in the 1994 European Cup Final? Who was the Frenchman playing in their midfield who later converted to playing centre back with even greater distinction? Who managed the winning side? (3)

6 Who, in 1991, became the first English player to appear in a European Cup Final since the Heysel ban when he played for Marseille against Red Star Belgrade? (1)

7 Who sent Wayne Rooney off in a Champions League match in September 2005 for sarcastically applauding a decision, and who were Manchester United's opponents? (2)

8 KRC Genk and KAA Gent have both represented which country in the group stage of the Champions League? (1)

9 From the 2000–01 season to the 2014–15 season, the 120 Champions League quarter-finalists have come from twelve countries: which two nations have more than half those representatives (61 out of 120)? (2)

10 Which two Parisian stadiums have hosted a European Cup or Champions League Final? (2)

11 Which two substitutes scored the late, late goals that won Man United the 1999 Champions League? Which two players (a striker and a wide player) did they replace when they came on? Who captained United that evening in place of the suspended Roy Keane? (5)

12 Which three players, two Italian, one French, from the Juventus side that won the 1996 Champions League Final went on to play in the Premier League? (3)

13 Two European Cup Finals were held at the Neckerstadion: in which city is this ground? (1)

14 When Internazionale won the Champions League under José Mourinho in 2010 they had no Italians in their starting line-up: which two non-European countries contributed seven of their starting eleven, and which World Cup-winning defender was the only Italian to take the field when he came on as an injury-time substitute? (3)

15 In 2002–03 which English club lost their first three matches in their Champions League group but still progressed to the knock-out stages? (1)

Answers on p.514

Quiz 172: England 9 (30)

1 England tried three different wide players in their three group games in 1966, before Alf Ramsey decided to dispense with them altogether for the knockout rounds – who were the three players? And what was the nickname given to the England team as a result of this lack of specialist wide players? (4)

2 Who were the oldest and youngest members of England's World Cup-winning team from 1966? (2)

3 Who is the only player in the modern era (since the Second World War) to score a hat-trick against England in a competitive fixture? (1)

4 Since the Second World War, which four players have won 25 England caps or more while a Newcastle United player? (4)

5 Who scored 28 goals for England in 23 appearances in the late nineteenth and early twentieth centuries? (1)

6 What did Bryan Robson achieve in 1984 that no England captain had managed in seventy-five years? (1)

7 Against which side did England's Stan Mortensen make his first international appearance, in an unofficial wartime game – was it (a) a team of POW's representing Italy (b) England, he played for Wales as they were unavoidably a man down (c) a team of airmen representing the United States (d) a team of ex-pats representing Poland (1)

8 Two England strikers of the last twenty years have shared what name? (1)

9 Who holds the record for the most England goals in one calendar year, 2006? (1)

10 Who, in 1993, was the last player to score four times in a full England international? Who were the opponents, who scored first but were beaten 7-1? (2)

11 Which three goalkeepers won a single cap each for England in the 1970s and 1980s? (3)

12 Whose long-range strike deceived David Seaman as Germany beat England at Wembley at the start of the qualifying campaign for the 2002 World Cup finals? What was the immediate post-match consequence of the defeat? (1)

13 Who, in 2012, became the first man to score a hat-trick against England for twenty-four years? (1)

14 Which two sides beat England in their final two qualifying matches for the 2008 European Championships and left them in third place with a summer on the beach? Which striker, bound for Tottenham Hotspur in September after the finals tournament, scored twice in the first of these games to leave England struggling? (3)

15 Peter Shilton won 125 caps for England, comfortably the most by any goalkeeper (although Joe Hart may one day come close): who are the others (there are four, not counting Hart) with more than 50 caps? (4)

Answers on p.515

Quiz 173: General 44 (30)

1 Fill in the gaps in this sequence: Montevideo, Rome, MISSING, Rio de Janeiro, Berne, MISSING, Santiago, London, Mexico City, MISSING, Buenos Aires, Madrid, MISSING, Rome, MISSING, Paris. (5)

2 Groningen, PSV Eindhoven, Chelsea, Real Madrid, Bayern Munich* – which modern superstar's career path is this? (1)

3 Mazzola, who scored twice in Brazil's opening game at the 1958 World Cup finals, moved to AC Milan later that summer and became a nationalised Italian and one of Serie A's all-time top scorers. He reverted to his birth name in Italy – what was it? (1)

4 What connects the nicknames of Southampton, Darlington and Plymouth Argyle (give details)? (4)

5 Which club, who enjoyed a rapid rise to Scottish top-flight status and an equally abrupt decline, reached their only Scottish Cup Final in 2006, losing on penalties to Hearts? (1)

6 Which long-established Scottish club carry the nickname, the Spiders – is it (a) Berwick Rangers (b) Celtic (c) Queens Park or (d) Partick Thistle? (1)

7 Which two Italy-based strikers made up the potent German forward line at the 1990 World Cup finals? (2)

8 Who was sacked by Chelsea in 2004 and served a seven-month ban for drug use? For which Italian club did he sign after serving his ban, and for which country did he go on to win 77 caps? (3)

9 Whose goalscoring career across Europe is this: Dinamo Zagreb, Celtic, Leeds United*, Middlesbrough, Newcastle United? In which city was he born? (2)

10 Which England international was sent off for the first time in a Scottish fixture in the November 1997 Old Firm fixture? Which other Englishman, a central defender, scored a late equaliser for Celtic? (1)

11   Andrew Watson in 1881 was the first black player to represent Scotland; which midfield player was the second, in 2004? And which full back beat him to it by twenty-five years for the Republic of Ireland? (2)

12   Cobresal (inc Cobreandino), St Gallen, Sevilla, Real Madrid*, Internazionale*, Club-America, Colo Colo: this is the club career (1983–2003) of which great Chilean footballing icon? (1)

13   Which Reading forward was involved in the serious neck injury to Chelsea goalkeeper Petr Cech in 2006–07? (1)

14   Liverpool finished the 1983–84 season as champions, but which team beat them 4-0, with a hat-trick from Terry Gibson? (1)

15   In the awards for achievement over the first 20 years of Premier League football, Alex Ferguson was quite rightly named as best manager; which other four men were short-listed? (4)

Asterisk (*) indicates that the player in question made more than one hundred league appearances for the club.

Answers on p.515

Quiz 174: World Cup 18 (30)

1 Who got through a penalty shoot-out at the 2014 World Cup finals but went out in identical manner in the next round after a dull 0-0 draw with France? (1)

2 Obdulio Varela was the captain and heartbeat of which World Cup-winning team in which year? (2)

3 Omar Sívori scored four times for Italy as they beat Israel 6-0 in the second leg of a qualifying play-off for the 1962 World Cup finals; for which other country had he already won 19 caps in the previous decade before earning Italian citizenship? (1)

4 Who are the only two players to have been sent off while playing against England in a World Cup finals match? (2)

5 Who scored the poetic final goal in Brazil's demolition of Italy in the 1970 World Cup Final? (1)

6 Who was the manager of the Scotland side that fell flat in the 1978 World Cup finals? With which Scottish side, not one of the traditional big boys, did he make his name as a manager? Who beat Scotland 3-1 in their opening group game? And which Asian first-time qualifiers held the Scots to a 1-1 draw in the second? Which jaunty tune made the UK charts before the tournament in anticipation of a less inept showing? (5)

7 Andoni Goikoetxea, who anchored the Spain midfield at the 1986 World Cup finals tournament, became notorious for nearly ending the career of which superstar with a horrific tackle? For which club did Goikoetxea play? (2)

8 Which Middle Eastern country qualified for the 1990 World Cup finals, the first and only time they have done so? Which future World Cup-winning coach was in charge of their campaign? (2)

9 Who scored against Russia at the 1994 World Cup finals to make him the competition's oldest scorer? What was the final score in the match? (2)

10 Who scored the only goal England conceded in qualification for the 1998 World Cup finals, in a 1-0 win at Wembley for Italy? (1)

11 Who scored the greatest goal in World Cup history, cushioning a 50-yard pass, cutting inside a (world-class) defender and clipping the ball past the goalkeeper to knock out Argentina in the quarter-final of the 1998 tournament? (1)

12 Fill in the gaps in this Brazilian side that lifted the 2002 World Cup (5-4-1): Marcos; Cafu, Edmilson, MISSING, Roque Júnior, MISSING; Ronaldinho (sub: MISSING), Kléberson, MISSING, MISSING; Ronaldo (sub: Denilson) (5)

13 Which future Premier League star scored two brilliant goals and hit the bar as the Czech Republic shrugged off a decent American side at the 2006 World Cup finals? (1)

14 Whose final contribution to his third World Cup campaign was to tie his shoelaces while the opposition took a free kick and allow Thierry Henry to finish at the back post completely unmarked? (1)

15 Who were the defensive trio for Brazil at the 2010 World Cup finals who were all playing club football for Internazionale? (3)

Answers on p.516

Quiz 175: European Competitions 9 (30)

1 Austria Vienna, Torino, Sevilla*, Logrones, Rayo Vallecano, Cologne**, Borussia Mönchengladbach, Austria Salzburg? This is the career path of Austria's leading scorer – who is he? (1)

2 Who beat a strong touring Spartak Moscow team 4-0 in 1954, and then Honved of Budapest 3-2, and made a claim that they were the unofficial champions of Europe? (1)

3 Who beat Celtic 3-2 in the 2003 UEFA Cup Final? Who scored both Celtic goals? (2)

4 Who were the three German internationals at the core of the Inter Milan side that won the UEFA Cup in 1991? (3)

5 In 1980–81 a Dutch club won the top division for the first time; they won again in 2008–09, and another club won their debut championship the following season, 2009–10 – which two clubs (one plays in the north-west spur of the country, North Holland, and the other is the easternmost top flight club)? Who were the two successful managers in 2009 and 2010, one Dutch, one English? (4)

6 In which city do Panathanaikos and AEK play their home games? (1)

7 Who beat Middlesbrough in the 2006 UEFA Cup Final, and what was the score? (1)

8 Which Belgian striker, until July 2016 the manager of the national team, was in the Schalke 04 side that won the 1997 UEFA Cup on penalties against Inter Milan? And which England international was in the Inter Milan line-up for the second leg? (2)

9 Who was the Chairman of Olympique de Marseille at the heart of the 1993 bribery scandal that resulted in the club being banned from European competition and stripped of the French league title? (1)

10 Mario Frick was born in Switzerland and made his international debut as a teenager in 1993; he played his last game for his country in October 2015, aged forty-one, by which time he held the record for most caps and goals. For which European country did he play? (1)

11 Who was the Chilean striker who scored for Inter as they lost the 1997 UEFA Cup Final and scored again the following year as they swept Lazio aside 3-0? Which two other Inter forwards played in the World Cup Final later that summer? (3)

12 Spanish side Osasuna are actually based in which city, better known for an altogether different kind of entertainment? (1)

13   Mario Kempes improved his skills with which Spanish club between the 1974 and 1978 World Cups? (1)

14 Which territory's main club side are AC Ajaccio? In which country's league do they play? (1)

15 Which seven British clubs have won the Fairs Cup / UEFA Cup (to 2015–16)? (7)

Asterisk (*) indicates that the player in question made more than one hundred league appearances for the club. (**) indicates more than two hundred league appearances.

Answers on p.516

Quiz 176: FA Cup 8 (30)

1 Who knocked Leeds United out of the FA Cup on 13 February 1971? Which former England international scored twice for the winners? With which club did he win a League title? (3)

2 In 1980, which non-League Essex side eliminated Leicester City in the FA Cup Third Round – was it (a) Bishop's Stortford (b) Grays Athletic (c) Harlow Town or (d) Braintree Town? (1)

3 Which club won the FA Cup three times between 1951 and 1955? (1)

4 Who scored twice in the 1989 FA Cup Final but finished on the losing side? Who scored two for the opposition that day, having also bagged a brace when the same two sides met in the Final three years earlier? (2)

5 Which teams took five matches to settle their 1980 FA Cup semi-final? (2)

6 Gary Neville was sent off in an FA Cup Manchester derby in 2003–04 for head-butting which City player? What was the result of the match? (2)

7 In the 2002 Final against Chelsea, which Arsenal player became the first man to score in successive FA Cup Finals for forty years? (1)

8 Who scored for Chelsea with an outrageous back-heeled flick from a corner in an FA Cup third round replay against Norwich City in 2001–02? (1)

9 Which pair of Arsène Wenger's early imports scored the goals that earned Arsenal a 2-0 win in the 1998 FA Cup Final against Newcastle United? (2)

10 Which four Scottish players have won the FA Cup in England in the twenty-first century (to 2016)? (4)

11 Which Israeli international came on as a substitute and scored a hat-trick as Tottenham overturned a 2-0 deficit to win 6-2 against Southampton in the 1994–95 FA Cup competition? (1)

12 Who scored a classic winning goal for Manchester United in extra time of an FA Cup semi-final against Arsenal in 1999? Who had saved an injury-time penalty to ensure the game went to extra time? (2)

13 With which three clubs did Dennis Wise play in an FA Cup Final? (3)

14 Which three sides have won both domestic cups in the same season? (3)

15 Who were the first two Brazilians to appear in an FA Cup Final when they played for Middlesbrough in the 1997 defeat by Chelsea? (2)

Answers on p.517

Quiz 177: General 45 (30)

1 For which club did Scottish international striker Mo Johnston make an FA Cup Final appearance? (1)

2 Mexico had all the stadia needed for the 1970 World Cup finals; what was the principal reason for this unusual degree of preparedness in a World Cup host? (1)

3 What did England achieve in 1961–62 that it took them a further 20 years to repeat? (2)

4 Which colourful England goalkeeper of the early years of the twentieth century was 6'6" and weighed in at 22 stone? (1)

5 Which long-haired defender in the US team earned cult status and a move to Padova in Serie A following his performances at the 1994 World Cup finals? (1)

6 Which two Italian greats missed their penalties in the 1994 World Cup Final shoot-out against Brazil? Who was the Brazilian goalkeeper who faced them? (3)

7 Who was the BBC commentator as England beat West Germany to win the World Cup in in 1966? (1)

8 Whose mainly London based career is this: QPR, Arsenal, Crystal Palace, QPR, Tottenham, Bordeaux, Manchester City, Chelsea, West Ham United, Millwall, Carlisle United (three games only)? (1)

9 In December 1997, who received an honorary knighthood at Buckingham Palace while accompanying his President on a state visit – was it (a) Pelé (b) Eusébio (c) Eric Cantona or (d) Sylvester Stallone? (1)

10 Which international striker signed for Newcastle United as Alan Shearer's partner in 2004, but saved his best form for the cup competitions, scoring only six league goals as Newcastle endured a disappointing season? (1)

11   Eleven of the former constituent states of the Soviet Union took part in qualification for Euro 2016; can you name them? (11)

12   Ghana internationals André and Jordan Ayew are both sons of which African football legend? (1)

13   Which two Newcastle United players were sent off for fighting each other as the team were beaten 3-0 by Aston Villa in April 2005 (Newcastle finished with eight men as Steven Taylor was also sent off for saving a goal-bound shot with his hand)? (2)

14   Which pair of brothers were an integral part of the Manchester United team in the mid- to late- 1970s? (2)

15   Rumours of Alan Shearer moving to Old Trafford emerged in summer 1996 because (a) his wife was seen shopping at Trafford Park mall, (b) his son was seen wearing a Manchester United shirt, (c) a travel agent cheekily added his name to a Manchester United flight schedule or (d) Shearer went to the same Spanish holiday resort as the Neville brothers and Ryan Giggs? (1)

Answers on p.518

Quiz 178: Wales 4 (30)

1 Which ground has hosted the most Wales home games? (1)

2 Who, in 1996, became the first League of Wales side to get through a round of European competition? After beating Dinaburg of Latvia and Budapest Vasutas of Hungary, which Scottish side finally ended the run? (2)

3 John Charles was the only member of the 1958 Wales World Cup squad not playing in England or Wales; which club was he with? And for which Welsh club did his brother Mel play? (2)

4 Who replaced the injured Aaron Ramsey as Wales captain in 2012 and kept the job for the splendid 2016 European Championship campaign? (1)

5 Who was the centre half and captain in the Cardiff City team that won the FA Cup in 1927, the first and only time a Welsh team has accomplished this feat? (1)

6 Wales' biggest hammering in recent years was a 7-1 loss to the Netherlands in a World Cup qualifier in November 1996; which Premier League star scored a hat-trick for the Dutch? And who scored four for Turkey the following year in another awful defensive performance by the Welsh as they lost 6-4 in Istanbul? (2)

7 In qualification for the 1994 World Cup, Wales beat one side 6-0 at home and 3-0 away. This team, not a former part of any Eastern European state, were competing in World Cup qualifying for the first time – who were they? (1)

8 Which future Premier League player scored twice as Wales suffered an embarrassing 5-0 defeat away to Georgia in a qualifier for the 1996 European Championships? (1)

9 Who was the tough-tackling full back who captained Wales to a famous 2-1 win over England in 1955? (1)

10 Name the twelve clubs Dean Saunders turned out for during a near twenty-year playing career (this includes one loan spell). (12)

11 Pat Glover, who scored five times as Wales won the 1936–37 Home International Championship, was a goal machine with which east coast English club? (1)

12 What was unusual – unique among the British international teams – about the Welsh line-up against Northern Ireland in 1955? (2)

13 Gordon Davies played only 16 games for Wales, partly because his career overlapped heavily with that of Ian Rush; for which club did he play more than 400 games and score over 150 goals in two spells, making him the club's record goalscorer? (1)

14 Which Watford-born centre half, who played all his club career at Watford and later managed Watford, made 31 appearances for Wales? (1)

15 Andy Melville, David Phillips, Kevin Ratcliffe, Kit Symons – which of these defenders won most caps for Wales? (1)

Answers on p.518

Answers on p.518

Quiz 179: Football League 19 (30)

1 Newton Heath, elected to the Football League in 1892–93, were the precursors of which modern club? (1)

2 Which goalscoring winger was top scorer for Arsenal as they won the Football League in 1933 under Herbert Chapman and again in 1934? Why was the second title tinged with sadness? (2)

3 Who recovered from the Munich air crash to be top scorer in the English First Division in 1959–60? (1)

4 In 1967–68 Manchester City won 4-3 at Newcastle on the last day of the season to win the league by two points: whose 2-1 home defeat by Sunderland helped them, as the same rivals would have pipped them on goal average had they won? (1)

5 Recent signing Micky Burns scored four goals for which club in a 7-2 thrashing of Chelsea (who would be relegated) in December 1978? (1)

6 In 1980–81 the West Midlands' clubs were riding high; Aston Villa won the League, West Bromwich Albion finished fourth and Birmingham City and Wolverhampton Wanderers also enjoyed top-flight status. How many of them were in the first Premier League in 1992–93 and how many were in the Premier League when thirty years elapsed since Villa's triumph, in 2010–11? (2)

7 How did Sunderland lose the 1989–90 Play-Off Final but still get promoted? Two goals from an ex-Ipswich veteran and an Italian-English youngster earned them a 2-0 win over Newcastle to reach that Final – who were these two players? (1)

8 Legendary Scotland captain Billy McNeill won how many caps for Scotland – was it 29, 46, 60 or 89? (1)

9 Who made the most League appearances for Blackpool and is also their most-capped player? (1)

10 Which side did Jack Charlton lead to the Second Division title in 1973–74? (1)

11 Who was the First Division's top scorer when his side, Everton, won the last league title before the Second World War? Who was he playing for on the resumption of league football after the war? And which ambitious Third Division money paid £20,000 for his services in 1947? (3)

12 Which left-sided player became the most-capped player with Plymouth Argyle when he won his twenty-first cap for Northern Ireland in 2007? (1)

13 Why did Ian Bishop wear the no.12 shirt for West Ham in a league game in 1993 (squad numbers were not used for league games at that point)? (1)

14 Who lost out in the play-offs from the Championship (second tier) in 2004–05 to West Ham United, a team who finished twelve points behind them in the season proper? Who did West Ham go on to beat by a solitary goal in the play-off, their second slip at the final hurdle in five years? And who scored four of the Hammers' five goals in these three games? (3)

15 Which ten clubs within the Football League system lie north of the Birmingham / Leicester latitude but south of Sheffield? (10)

Answers on p.519

Quiz 180: Premier League 23 (40)

1 For which two clubs did former England goalkeeper (four caps) Ian Walker play in the Premier League? (2)

2 Who won two Premier League manager of the month awards as his newly promoted Reading team finished eighth in their first season in the new league? (1)

3 Tottenham Hotspur suffered two humiliating defeats in 1996–97: who beat them 6-1 in the Coca-Cola Cup in October '96, and who walloped them 7-1 in a Premier League match two months later? (2)

4 Which Czech goalkeeper was an ever-present for West Ham United in 1993–94, their first season in the Premier League? And which of his countrymen played for Newcastle United that season? From which Czech club did both players move to England? (3)

5 Which member of the Norway 1994 World Cup squad would get a Premier League winner's medal at the end of the following season? (1)

6 Which Tottenham defender scored in under ten seconds against Bradford City in 2000, the fastest goal in the Premier League to date? And who got within a second of that record, scoring for Newcastle United against Manchester City in January 2003? (2)

7 Who cost Blackburn Rovers £7.5M in the summer of 1998, but went back to his old club after a solitary season? Who was that old club, and which striker did they exchange for their old boy? (4)

8 Who started a third spell at Middlesbrough, was injured pre-season and attracted a crowd of 20,000 for his comeback in a reserve game in February before scoring on his reappearance in the Premier League? (1)

9 Who were the two wide players who fed the 'SAS' strikeforce in Blackburn's Premier League winning side of 1993–94? (2)

10 Which two of the longer serving Premier League managers left their clubs at the end of the 2005–06 and 2006–07 seasons respectively, heralding a decline in the fortunes of the two clubs? (2)

11 Blackpool's solitary season in the Premier League in 2010–11 was an enjoyable romp. They were never short of goals, scoring 55 (the same as Tottenham Hotspur, who finished fifth), but they slumped alarmingly from eighth place at New Year. Who was their top scorer with a very respectable 13? Who scored 12 from midfield, including seven penalties and where did it earn him a contract for the following season? And who was the Ghana international goalkeeper who stood in for the injured Matt Gilks for half the season? Which top club were the only team Blackpool beat both home and away that season, 2-1 on both occasions? (5)

12 In the 2013–14 Premier League season, only four outfield players started every game for their club, one was a Cardiff City central defender, the others were midfield players with Crystal Palace, Hull City and West Ham United – can you name the four? (4)

13 Alan Shearer has scored most Premier League goals, but who has scored the most for any one club? (1)

14 Which three Premier League clubs did Paolo Di Canio turn out for? And which two English clubs has he managed in his own unique style (to 2015–16)? (5)

15 Cardiff City won the first all-Wales Premier League match against Swansea City 1-0. Swansea gained revenge in the return, winning 3-0, and this is their starting line-up (4-4-2): MISSING (Netherlands): Angel Rangel (Spain), Chico (Spain), MISSING (Wales), MISSING (Wales): Nathan Dyer (England) (sub: Neil Taylor, Wales), MISSING (Netherlands) (sub: José Alberto Cañas, Spain), MISSING (England): MISSING (Côte d'Ivoire), Marvin Emnes (Netherlands) (sub: Pablo Hernández, Spain). Can you name the missing players? (5)

Answers on p.520

Quiz 181: General 46 (30)

1 Former England international Trevor Sinclair made a brief substitute appearance in an FA Cup Final for which team at the latter end of his career in 2007? (1)

2 Michael Ballack, Jens Jeremies, Toni Kroos: why would they have won less silverware in the 1970s or 1980s? (1)

3 What did Franco Baresi and Roberto Baggio do at the 1990 World Cup finals that they failed to do four years later? (1)

4 The Football League Trophy is a tournament for which only clubs in the third and fourth tiers of the League are eligible. Who are the only club to have won the trophy three times, claiming their third success in 2015 when they beat Walsall 2-0 in the Final? (1)

5 Which manager has given Aston Villa their highest percentage of wins in proportion to the number of games played since the Second World War? (1)

6 Which two members of the Spain 1994 World Cup squad have managed Barcelona in recent years? (2)

7 Who was the Deputy Chairman of Chelsea killed in a helicopter accident while flying home from a game against Bolton Wanderers in 1996? (1)

8 Whose old goalscoring record did Ian Wright break during his time at Arsenal? And who topped Wright and also broke the earlier player's league scoring record? (2)

9 Which non-League (at the time) team claimed Premier League Newcastle United were 'afraid' to play them in an FA Cup tie in January 1997 after Newcastle manager Kenny Dalglish expressed reservations about the quality of the playing surface? (1)

10 Which three Italian players appeared in League Cup Finals for Middlesbrough? (3)

11 Here is the England team against Germany for their magical 5-1 win in qualifying for the 2002 World Cup finals – fill in the gaps, please. David Seaman; Gary Neville, MISSING, Sol Campbell, MISSING; David Beckham, Steven Gerrard (sub: MISSING), MISSING (Sub: Jamie Carragher), MISSING (Sub: Steve McManaman); Michael Owen, MISSING. (6)

12 Borussia Neunkirchen, Eintracht Frankfurt, Fenerbahce, Paris St Germain, Bolton Wanderers*, Qatar SC, Hull City – he was so good they named him twice. Whose career path is mapped out here? (1)

13 Which two strikers swapped places at Birmingham and Crystal Palace in 2002, but ended up together at Palace in 2005–06? (2)

14 Who were relegated in 1984–85 with a new record low 17 points, including just three wins and no away victories – was it (a) Sunderland (b) Middlesbrough (c) Leeds United or (d) Stoke City? (1)

15 Charlton Athletic won promotion to the Premier League via the play-offs in 1997–98. Who did they beat in the Final on penalties after the game finished 4-4? Who scored a hat-trick for Charlton, and which popular local player missed his spot-kick for the losers? Who saved it? Who were the managers of the two teams? (6)

Asterisk (*) indicates that the player in question made more than one hundred league appearances for the club.

Answers on p.520

Quiz 182: Republic of Ireland 4 (30)

1 Which trio made up the Republic of Ireland's strong central defensive line at the 1990 World Cup finals tournament? (3)

2 Which Irish international was Aston Villa's most-capped player, winning 64 caps while he was with the club? (1)

3 Noel Cantwell played a few games at centre forward for the Republic of Ireland (he scored 14 goals), but what was his usual club position at West Ham United and Manchester United, a position from which he captained United in the 1963 FA Cup Final? (1)

4 Who, in 2008, became the first overseas coach of the Republic of Ireland team? And what was mildly controversial about the appointment of his successor? (2)

5 Who did Roy Keane accuse of not even being Irish before walking out of the training camp prior to the 2002 World Cup finals? (1)

6 Gillingham**, Millwall*, Aston Villa, Celtic, Chelsea, Marseille, Nancy* – which Irish striker's career is charted here? (1)

7 Including loan spells, some very brief, Robbie Keane has played for ten clubs – name them, and then name which two picked him for more than 100 games (12)

8 Which classy full back was the first of many Irishmen to win a trophy with Manchester United, captaining the side in the 1948 FA Cup Final and during their successful league campaign of 1951–52? (1)

9 Which Republic of Ireland international spearheaded Reading's promotion to the Premier League in 2005–06, and scored 13 goals in the top flight as they enjoyed an outstanding first season at the top? (1)

10 Who is the only Irish player to play on the winning side in a Champions League Final in the twenty-first century (to 2014–15)? (1)

11 How many goals did Liverpool winger Steve Heighway score in his 34 games for the Republic of Ireland? (1 point for 1 either way) (1)

12 Which Ireland international midfield player left Charlton Athletic for Aston Villa in 2002, and which other Irish star was brought in from Ipswich Town as a replacement? (2)

13 Which Tooting-born striker, who scored 9 goals in 36 games for the Republic of Ireland, also scored more than 100 goals in two spells at Crystal Palace but, oddly, struggled to find the net at all his other clubs? (1)

14 Who was the first Republic of Ireland player to reach 20 international goals? (1)

15 Who won two caps for the Republic of Ireland in the 1960s playing with St Patrick's Athletic but was far outstripped by his son (same name) who won pretty much everything out there on top of his 53 caps? (1)

Asterisk (*) indicates that the player in question made more than one hundred league appearances for the club. (**) indicates more than two hundred league appearances.

Answers on p.521

Quiz 183: Champions League 14 (30)

1 Who was the surprising source of the goal that won the 1981 European Cup Final for Liverpool? And who scored the winning penalty three years later when they won the trophy again in a shoot-out after a 1-1 draw with Roma? (2)

2 Real Madrid and Barcelona are both multiple winners of the European Cup/Champions League: which are the only other two Spanish sides to contest the Final (twice each)? (2)

3 In the 1980–81 European Cup, the English champions beat the Scottish champions 5-0 on aggregate. Which two teams were involved? (2)

4 Which much-maligned Liverpool goalkeeper made vital saves in the 2005 Champions League Final penalty shoot-out victory? (1)

5 Hibernians (of Malta, not Scotland); Sarajevo; Górnik Zabrze; Real Madrid: who came next for Manchester United? (1)

6 Whose dismissal in the 2006 Champions League Final left Arsenal playing most of the match with ten men? Which attacking French star was immediately substituted even though only 18 minutes of the game were gone, and who replaced him? (3)

7 Who scored a hat-trick in the 1962 European Cup Final, when Benfica beat Real Madrid 5-3? (1)

8 CFR Cluj, who have been the Romanian representatives in the group stage of the Champions League on three occasions are the dominant club from which part of that country? (1)

9 In November 2012 Victor Wanyama and Tony Watt made Celtic fans very happy: what were the circumstances? (2)

10 Who scored a last-minute goal for Chelsea to win a 2007 Champions League quarter-final 2-1 against Valencia, after the first leg at Stamford Bridge finished 1-1 – was it (a) Michael Ballack (b) Michael Essien (c) Arjen Robben or (d) Michael McIntyre? (1)

11 Which two Finnish players have played in a winning Champions League Final team? For which clubs? (4)

12 Who scored in both legs for Manchester City as they beat Paris St Germain 3-2 on aggregate in the 2015–16 Champions League quarter-finals? (1)

13 In which city would you find the De Kuip stadium, which has remained intact, albeit renovated, since 1937? (1)

14 Which five Liverpool players started both the 2005 and 2007 Champions League Finals (two English, one Irish, two overseas)? (5)

15 Apart from Milan, which three European cities can boast more than one club to have played in a Champions League Final (to 2015–16 season)? (3)

Answers on p.522

Quiz 184: World Cup 19 (30)

1 Whose early goal saw Argentina beat an unambitious Belgian side in their quarter-final at the 2014 World Cup? (1)

2 Roque Máspoli is regarded as one of the best goalkeepers ever to play in South America; which country did he represent in the 1950s? (1)

3 Who was the Polish-born Reims playmaker at the heart of France's excellent campaign at the 1958 World Cup finals tournament? (1)

4 Which all-time-great of the game went to the 1962 World Cup finals as a member of the Spain squad but never featured after failing to recover from an injury? (1)

5 In 1974 North and Central America, Africa and Asia/Oceania all produced first-time finalists from their qualifying competitions. Who were these three countries, one of which now has a different name? (3)

6 Who was the winger sent home from the 1978 World Cup finals when he failed a drug test as a result of taking medication that fell afoul of the regulations? (1)

7 England's second phase games at the 1982 World Cup finals against West Germany and Spain both finished with the same score – what was it? (1)

8 Denmark qualified for the World Cup finals in 1986 for the first time. Who was the veteran team captain, with 74 caps at the age of 36 (he went to become the first Dane to reach 100 caps)? (1)

9 Which CONCACAF nation were thrown out of the 1990 World Cup in the qualifying rounds for fielding over-age players during the 1988 Olympic tournament? Who took advantage and qualified for the first time since 1950, and have qualified for every finals tournament thereafter? (1)

10 Whose goal, the only one of his international career, earned England a 1-0 win over Egypt and into the knockout phase of the 1990 World Cup finals? (1)

11 This is the Scotland team, by club, that produced a heroic performance to beat the Netherlands 3-2 at the 1978 World Cup finals (it wasn't enough to put them into the next round): Partick Thistle; Aberdeen, Rangers, Manchester United, Manchester City; Nottingham Forest, Liverpool, Manchester City, Derby County: Liverpool, Manchester United. Who were the players? And who captained the side in that game? (12)

12 Who scored the only goals of his international career (two of them) in a World Cup semi-final against Croatia in 1998 to see France into the Final? (1)

13 Which of Scotland's opponents in their qualifying group for the 1998 World Cup finals failed to turn up for their home match against the Scots? (1)

14 Who scored the solitary goal of the game in both Germany's quarter-final and semi-final at the 2002 World Cup finals? (1)

15 Portugal's 2010 World Cup squad included which three Chelsea players, two of whom moved away from the club later that summer? (3)

Answers on p.522

Quiz 185: General 47 (30)

1 George Best played for three American teams, the Aztecs, the Strikers and the Earthquakes once he was past his UK sell-by date; which three cities did those teams represent? (3)

2 Why was Tommy Docherty sacked as manager of Manchester United just six weeks after leading the club to victory in the FA Cup Final, their first major trophy for nine years? (1)

3 Who won the Football Writers' Association Player of the Year for a second time in 1963, fifteen years after he first won, and making him the first (and thus far only) man to win the award with two different clubs? Which were the clubs? (3)

4 Middlesbrough, Sheffield United, Stoke City, Everton (inc Sunderland), Manchester City, Bradford City (inc Everton, Wigan Athletic), Scunthorpe United, Grimsby Town: this is the career path of which winger, an early pioneer of the somersault goal celebration? (1)

5 What did Garry Mabbutt and Richard Gough manage to do in the 1987 Cup Finals in England and Scotland? (1)

6 Which country drafted Sven-Göran Eriksson in as manager immediately prior to the World Cup in 2010? (1)

7 Which Manchester United player was taken to the 1958 World Cup finals but never used? (1)

8 Which two members of Wimbledon's 'Crazy Gang', one born in Singapore and one in Watford, played international football for Wales in the 1990s? (2)

9 Who was the Finnish international who played more than 100 games for Crystal Palace and whose entertaining newspaper column made him something of a cult hero? (1)

10 Whose playing career is listed here (it's far less impressive than his time as a manager): Queen's Park, St Johnstone, Dunfermline, Rangers, Falkirk, Ayr United? (1)

11 Which four England internationals scored as Aston Villa impressively saw off Portsmouth 4-2 away on their way to the League Cup Final in 2009–10? Three of them scored again in the extraordinary 6-4 semi-final win over Blackburn Rovers: which two further England players scored as well? (6)

12 Enzo Francescoli was a talented no.10 who had the misfortune to play at a low ebb for which country? (1)

13 Who had three spells as Tottenham's caretaker manager between 1998 and 2003? (1)

14 Which centre half, bought from local team Tranmere Rovers, scored ten goals as Everton lifted the Football League title in 1984–85? And who was bought from Norwich City and replaced him as first choice for the 1986–87 title-winning year? (2)

15 Who were the five members of Porto's 2004 Champions League Final squad (four starters and one unused substitute) who later signed for Chelsea? (5)

Answers on p.523

Quiz 186: Premier League 24 (40)

1 Freddie Shepherd and Doug Hall were forced to resign from the board of which club after making indiscreet and offensive remarks caught by a journalist while on holiday? Who briefly resumed the Chairmanship until a new team could be brought in? (2)

2 Name the nine overseas winners of the PFA Player's Player of the Year award (i.e. not from British Isles) (9)

3 Leeds United have twice won seven consecutive top-flight games, on the second occasion in the Premier League in 1999. Which two managers were in charge on the two occasions? (2)

4 West Ham United and Tottenham Hotspur striker Frédéric Kanouté won caps for France at all levels up to U-21: for which country did he elect, aged twenty-seven, to play international football? And with which Spanish club did he win the UEFA Cup twice after leaving Spurs? (2)

5 Which defender scored two late goals at Hillsborough to turn a 1-0 deficit into a 2-1 win that was crucial in Manchester United winning the title in 1992–93? (1)

6 Which overseas midfield player, the first successful import from his country, scored twice in Chelsea's 5-0 thrashing of Manchester United in October 1999? (1)

7 Which two clubs did Fabrizio Ravanelli fail to save from relegation? (2)

8 Who did John Hartson kick in the head during a West Ham training session? (1)

9 Who threw away a three-goal lead in an FA Cup replay in February 2004, against Manchester City, but bounced back to beat Portsmouth by the same scoreline on the following Saturday? Who scored in both games and finished as the club's top scorer that season? Who scored twice on the Saturday having been cup-tied for the midweek game after joining from West Ham United in the transfer window? (3)

10 Who were relegated from the Premier League with a dismal eleven points in 2007–08? What was their negative goal difference that season – was it -40, -53 or -69? And how many goals did they score in their 38 games, a total bettered by three individuals that season (1 point for 3 either way)? (4)

11 Who won a solitary England cap in 2010 on the strength of his performances for Cardiff City in the Championship (second tier)? To which newly promoted Premier League side did he move when Cardiff failed to get promoted in 2010–11? (2)

12 Who are the only two Manchester United outfield players to have started every game of a Premier League season? (2)

13 Who scored the Premier League's fastest hat-trick in under three minutes as Southampton beat Aston Villa 6-1 in May 2015? (1)

14 Which two clubs have been in the top division in England since the end of the Second World War? (2)

15 Which six players have scored twenty Premier League goals in one season for Manchester United? (6)

Answers on p.524

Quiz 187: Scotland 8 (30)

1 Scotland qualified for the 1986 World Cup finals tournament by forcing a draw with Wales in their final game; what event overshadowed the result? (1)

2 Which Scottish midfielder nearly emulated his father by playing in the 1998 World Cup finals, but remained an unused squad member? (1)

3 Who, in December 1992, became the first player to score 200 goals in the Scottish Premier Division? (1)

4 Which two overseas players were the first non-Scots to be entered into the Scottish Football Hall of Fame in 2006, two years after the listing was started? (2)

5 Australian international Craig Moore played more than 200 games in a decade for which Scottish club? (1)

6 Which Londoner won his first Scotland cap as a Wimbledon player in 1997? (1)

7 Which old Scottish club finished third in the Scottish League in 1960–61, scoring 100 goals in the process but were relegated four years later and dropped out of the league in 1967 after going into liquidation? (1)

8 Which three Rangers players appear in the Scottish Sports Hall of Fame? (3)

9 How many managers have Livingston had since Ray Stewart left in 2000 – is it 2, 6, 23 or 34? (1)

10 What connected the two teams, Motherwell and Dundee United, who contested the 1991 Scottish Cup Final? (2)

11 Which three Scotland internationals have played more than 700 games for Dundee United, many of them in the same successful team in the 1980s? Which of the three won most caps for Scotland? (4)

12 Which Rangers defender was the first player to reach 50 caps for Scotland, winning 54 in all, 48 of them as captain? What was the Churchillian name, topical at the time, given to the parsimonious Rangers defence in the early 1950s? (2)

13 Which full back made more than 200 appearances with great distinction for Hearts and then won a first Scotland cap (of 22) in 1995, aged 31, not long after moving to Celtic – was it (a) Stewart McKimmie (b) Tosh McKinlay (c) Billy McKinlay or (d) Jackie McNamara ? (1)

14 Alan Brazil, Charlie Cooke, Arthur Graham, Bobby Lennox – which of these left-sided attackers won the most caps for Scotland? (1)

15 Celtic famously beat Liverpool on their way to the 2003 UEFA Cup Final, winning 2-0 at Anfield. Can you name the missing players from their starting line-up that night (4-4-2)? Rab Douglas (Scotland); Momo Sylla (Guinea), MISSING (Sweden), MISSING (Guinea), Joos Valgaeren (Belgium); MISSING (Scotland) MISSING (Northern Ireland), MISSING (Bulgaria), MISSING (England); MISSING (Sweden), MISSING (Wales) (8)

Answers on p.524

Quiz 188: European Competitions 10 (30)

1 Which Dutch striker scored twice in each Final as Anderlecht won the European Cup Winners' Cup in 1976 and again in 1978? Who were the English opposition beaten 4-2 in the 1976 Final? (2)

2 AZ Alkmaar, Vitesse Arnhem*, PSV Eindhoven, Barcelona**, PSV Eindhoven, Al Jazira – this is the club career of which Dutch player with more than 100 caps? (1)

3 Who became the first Russian club to lift a European club trophy when they won the UEFA Cup in 2005? And who lost that Final in their home city in Portugal? (2)

4 Which Arsenal and England midfield player scored the only Premier League hat-trick of his career in a 5-0 drubbing of Newcastle United in December 2000, months after scoring the only other hat-trick of his career against Werder Bremen in a UEFA Cup tie? (1)

5 The Final of the 2012 European Championships was held in Kyiv. Which two cities hosted the semi-finals? (2)

6 Rapid Vienna (*inc First Vienna*), Werder Bremen, Bayern Munich, Werder Bremen, Rapid Vienna, LA Galaxy: this is the career path of Austria's most capped player, an attacking midfield player who retired in 2004 – who was he? (1)

7 Who refused to take a penalty against Fiorentina when playing for Juventus in 1991? (1)

8 Jesús Gil, convicted of corruption in the late 1990s, was a controversially right-wing and sack-happy President of which Spanish club, from 1987 until 2004? (1)

9 Which two French players who have been top scorer in Serie A? (2)

10 Which British club were the surprise package in the semi-finals of the Cup Winners' Cup in 1968, having only avoided relegation into the third tier of their league the previous season? (1)

11 Which English ground hosted the last-ever European Cup Winners' Cup Final in 1999? Which Italian side were the winners, beating Spanish club Mallorca 2-1? (2)

12 In 1981 two sides (one English, one Dutch) contested their only major European final when they met in the UEFA Cup Final? Who won? Who scored against the team representing his countrymen? Who played at the back for the Dutch side but later moved to Nottingham Forest? (5)

13 Which two Argentinian players, who would both play for Chelsea later in their careers, were in the Parma team that won the 1999 UEFA Cup? (2)

14 After leaving Lazio along with coach Sven-Göran Eriksson, Roberto Mancini played a handful of games in the Premier League with which club? And which Italian club gave him his first management opportunity – was it (a) Chievo (b) Fiorentina (c) Lazio or (d) AC Milan? With which two clubs has he won national league titles? And which two managers replaced him when he was eventually sacked by those two clubs? (6)

15 Argentinian striker Gabriel Batistuta spent the 1990s scoring more than 200 goals for which Italian Serie A club? (1)

Asterisk (*) indicates that the player in question made more than one hundred league appearances for the club. (**) indicates more than two hundred league appearances.

Answers on p.525

Quiz 189: General 48 (30)

1 Gianluigi Buffon's £33M transfer from Parma to Juventus is the heftiest fee paid for a goalkeeper by some distance: which two 'keepers have been the second and third most expensive, and who were the selling clubs? (4)

2 Mike England, Stephen Ireland, Jason Scotland, Don Welsh – which of these actually played for the country indicated by his surname? (1)

3 What did Robert Smyth McColl do against Wales, Ireland and England within the space of three weeks in 1899? In what capacity did he later become even more well-known? (2)

4 Which cultured left-sided midfielder is in that small band who have played for both Merseyside clubs, although he managed only three games in four years for Liverpool before leaving for a memorable decade at Everton that brought him league titles, an FA Cup winner's medal and 46 caps for Ireland? (1)

5 Which member of the 1958 Scotland World Cup squad was the subject of the book *My Father and Other Working Class Football Heroes*? (1)

6 Who took over the captaincy of Germany when Michael Ballack was injured just before the 2010 World Cup? (1)

7 Which two nations played off for a place at the 1970 World Cup finals in the middle of an existing conflict over border territories and immigration? Who won the matches and then beat Haiti to clinch a place in the finals for the first time? (2)

8 Who was the Fiorentina player sent home from the 1994 World Cup finals by the German management for a rude gesture towards sections of the German support? (1)

9 Who, in 1957 and 1961 respectively, became the first two players to win the Football Writers' Association Player of the Year award for the second time? And who, in much more recent times, is the only player to have won this award three times, in 2003, 2004 and 2006? (3)

10 Which five continental players who scored a goal at the 1988 European Championships later managed a club in the Premier League? (5)

11 Which manager led Luton Town to victory in the 1987 League Cup Final? Who were their more illustrious opponents? Why were the winners unable to compete in the following season's UEFA Cup? (4)

12 Beveren, Metalurh Donetsk, Olimpiacos, Monaco, Barcelona, Manchester City* – this is the career path of which giant of African football? (1)

13 Who is the talented brother-in-law of Arsenal's Colombian goalkeeper David Ospina? (1)

14 In 1985 Tottenham won at Anfield for the first time since 1973: which current TV pundit scored the only goal of the game? (1)

15 What was absent from the police report on the 165th Liverpool v Everton match on 15 September 2001? (2)

Asterisk (*) indicates that the player in question made more than one hundred league appearances for the club.

Answers on p.526

Quiz 190: Football League 20 (30)

1 Which town with a well-known league club originally had a different representative with the name Ironopolis appended to the name of the town? (1)

2 Which England inside forward became the first player to command a fee of over £10,000 when Herbert Chapman brought him to Arsenal in 1928? Who were the selling club? (2)

3 Which unheralded and uncapped goalkeeper won two league titles with Derby County in the 1970s? (1)

4 Which teenager was handed the captaincy of Chelsea as they struggled (unsuccessfully) against relegation in 1974–75? Which former Chelsea player and Scotland international was the club manager at the time? (2)

5 Which teenage striker scored on his debut for West Ham United against Tottenham Hotspur on New Year's Day, 1983? (1)

6 When Bristol Rovers won the Third Division title in 1989–90 who were promoted alongside them in second place? Which Rovers striker, who would later become a cult hero at West Bromwich Albion and Bolton Wanderers, was the division's top scorer? (2)

7 Who made 713 appearances for Southampton in an eighteen-year career starting in 1957? (1)

8 Who are Wiltshire's finest (actually, only) league club? (1)

9 Which club were promoted into the First Division alongside Liverpool in 1961–62, only to be relegated the following year, leaving 1962–63 as the club's only year in the top flight – was it (a) Brentford (b) Gillingham (c) Leyton Orient or (d) Southend United? (1)

10 In 1991 Port Vale received a huge windfall from the sale of two players, Robbie Earle for £775,000 and a whopping £925,000 for Darren Beckford: who were the buying clubs? (2)

11 Which England Test cricketer played 25 games in Arsenal's 1952–53 title-winning season? (1)

12 Who were relegated from the First Division in the 1960s a mere two years after winning the league title? (1)

13 From which league club did Newcastle United buy the splendidly named Lomana Lua Lua? For what, other than squandering an abundance of natural talent, is he best remembered? (2)

14 Who top scored for League 2 (fourth tier) Rochdale in 2004–05, and went on to score in every division of the Football League? (1)

15 Ignoring dull modern metropolitan boundaries and thinking in terms of traditional county lines, which eleven clubs in the 2015–16 league system were based in Yorkshire? (11)

Answers on p.526

Quiz 191: World Cup 20 (30)

1 Who is the only player to play in four World Cup semi-finals? (1)

2 Wales and Northern Ireland both had to win play-offs to get through the group phase at the 1958 World Cup finals; which two former finalists did they beat? And which two sides eliminated them in the next round? (4)

3 Who kept goal for the Soviet Union at the 1962 World Cup finals in Chile? (1)

4 Which European nation qualified for the World Cup finals for the first time in 1966 and gave an excellent account of themselves? (1)

5 West Germany's leading scorer at the 1966 World Cup with six goals (including the opening goal in the Final) was based in Italy with Bologna – who was he? (1)

6 Who was sent off towards the end of Brazil's 3-1 win over Argentina in the second phase of the 1982 World Cup finals tournament? (1)

7 José Batista was sent off in the first minute of the last match of Scotland's final group match at the 1986 World Cup finals – who were Scotland's opponents? (1)

8 Which two players, one a defender, the other a veteran sub, scored the late goals that won Italy's 2006 World Cup semi-final against Germany? (2)

9 Who scored twice as Cameroon booked a place in the quarter-finals of the 1990 World Cup tournament with a 2-1 win over Colombia? Who was the Colombian goalkeeper whose error gave away the second, decisive goal? (2)

10 Which pin-up Argentina star scored a hat-trick against Greece in his first World Cup finals match in 1994? (1)

11 Which Spanish-based star scored seven goals as Yugoslavia slaughtered Hungary 12-1 in their two-legged play-off for a place in the 1998 World Cup finals – was it Predrag Mijatović, Savo Milošević, Dejan Savićević or Allen Bokšić? (1)

12 Who was the Real Betis winger whose missed spot-kick in a quarter-final shoot-out at the 2002 World Cup finals saw Spain go out? Who proceeded to the semi-finals at their expense? (2)

13 Who kept goal for England at the 2006 World Cup finals tournament? (1)

14 Here are the line-ups for the 2006 World Cup Final – fill in the gaps. Italy: Buffon; Zambrotta, Cannavaro, MISSING, Grosso; Perrotta (sub: De Rossi), MISSING, Gattuso, Camoranesi (sub: MISSING); MISSING, MISSING (sub: Iaquinta). France: MISSING; Abidal, MISSING, Thuram, Sagnol; MISSING (sub: Trezuguet), MISSING, Vieira (Sub: Diarra), Malouda; Zidane, MISSING (sub: Wiltord) (10)

15 Mexico were poor in qualifying for the 2014 World Cup finals, finishing an unaccustomed fourth in the CONCACAF section. Which team, winners of the Oceania section, did they beat in a play-off to earn a late place at the table? (1)

Answers on p.527

Quiz 192: England 10 (30)

1 Which talented ball-playing midfielder captained England at the 1962 World Cup finals but had a fitful tournament and played the last of his 56 matches for his country? (1)

2 Which future England manager was the manager of the West Ham side that contributed three players to the 1966 England World Cup-winning side? (1)

3 Ashley, Andrew, Joe, Carlton. We're talking Coles here. How many England caps between them (1 point for 5 either way)? They scored eleven goals between them – which player scored the most and who scored none? (5)

4 The last three Norwich City players to win caps for England have all been goalkeepers – who are they? (3)

5 Against whom did England play three successive (and pointless) internationals in 1983? (1)

6 Which Everton captain won 26 England caps as a replacement for Jack Charlton soon after the 1966 World Cup win? (1)

7 What connects Jimmy Armfield, Peter Bonetti, Gerry Byrne, George Eastham, Ron Flowers, Norman Hunter and Ron Springett? (1)

8 Which former Bolton Wanderers and Aston Villa player's solitary England cap came while he was playing for Celtic in 2004? (1)

9 Who is Arsenal's most-capped player, appearing 81 times for his country while with the club? And who is the most-capped Englishman, with 77 caps while an Arsenal player? (2)

10 England managed the unenviable feat of being even less impressive at the 1992 European Championships than they were four years earlier. After drawing 0-0 with Denmark and France they were beaten 2-1 by which country, prompting which famous newspaper headline? Who scored England's only goal and who scored the winner that sent them packing? (4)

11 Which three players have played for England while on the books at Sampdoria in Serie A? (3)

12 What was the venue for England's astonishing 5-1 win over Germany during qualification for the 2002 World Cup finals? (1)

13 Which popular defender scored his first and only England goal (he only won nine caps) in a crucial European Championship qualifying win over Yugoslavia in 1986? What debilitating condition did he battle against during his career? Which much-capped central defender scored his first goal in the reverse fixture, an easy 4-1 win in Belgrade against disinterested opposition? (3)

14 Who scored the winning goal as England came from 2-1 down to beat Sweden 3-2 at the 2012 European Championships? Who captained the England side in this tournament? (2)

15 Which member of England's World Cup Final winning eleven ended up with the fewest caps? (1)

Answers on p.528

Quiz 193: General 49 (30)

1 Glenn Hysen, Sweden's captain at the 1990 World Cup finals was the only English-based player playing for a nation other than England, Scotland or Ireland; which club did he play for? (1)

2 Mohammed Ali Amar played more than 150 games for Tottenham Hotspur between 1988 and 1993: under what name was he known to commentators and fans? (1)

3 What do George Reader, William Ling, Jack Taylor and Howard Webb all have in common? (1)

4 Which current member of the Wales squad has played for clubs based in Wales, Scotland and England? (1)

5 Jimmy Floyd Hasselbaink started his Premier League career at Leeds United in 1997, and had a profitable four-year spell at Chelsea from 2000 to 2004: with which continental club did he spend a disappointing season culminating in relegation in 1999–2000? And which club gave him his first experience of club management in England in 2014? (2)

6 Which member of the 1990 Italian World Cup squad had just won successive European Cup trophies with AC Milan and would later win two more as coach of the same club – was it (a) Carlo Ancelotti (b) Fabio Capello (c) Claudio Ranieri or (d) Arrigo Sacchi? (1)

7 Which two players have been Liverpool's top scorer for seven consecutive seasons? (2)

8 Who was the first Israeli to play in the English league when he signed for Liverpool in 1979? And with which English Premier League club did his son, Tamir, play more than fifty games from 2008 to 2011? (2)

9 Why was Brazilian goalkeeper Dida given a one-match ban after a Champions League match against Celtic? (1)

10 Mark Goldberg completed the £22.5M takeover of which London club in June 1998? Who did he immediately install as the club's new manager? (2)

11 The 1992 European Championships were before the mass influx of continental players into the English leagues, but there was a trickle started: which five players, two from Sweden and one each from France, Denmark and the CIS, were based with English clubs? Which clubs? (10)

12 Which Brazilian star became, in 2003, the first player to be voted FIFA World Player of the Year three times? (1)

13 Who returned as manager of Watford ten years after he left in 1987 and led them back into the top flight in 1999, albeit for only a single season? (1)

14 The final games of the season haven't always kicked off and ended simultaneously. In 1985 Everton had already won the title when they went into their final two games demob happy against a relegation-threatened side. Who beat them 4-1 to send Norwich City down, and what was Norwich's record points total for a relegated side in a 22-team top division? (1 point for 2 either way on the second part) (3)

15 Which club celebrated 100 seasons of top-flight football in 2002–03? (1)

Answers on p.528

Quiz 194: Champions League 15 (30)

1 Liverpool, looking for a hat-trick of European Cup wins, were instead knocked out in the first round in 1978–79 – who beat them? (1)

2 Who was the only player to feature in all of Liverpool's European Cup triumphs in the 1970s and '80s? (1)

3 In which city was the Heysel Stadium, scene of the terrible disaster at the 1985 European Cup Final between Juventus and Liverpool? (1)

4 Which Scottish side fell to Roma in the semi-finals of the 1984 European Cup, thus preventing an all-British Final against Liverpool? Which defender, most of whose goals came from the penalty spot, scored Liverpool's goal in the drawn Final, and also scored from the spot in the successful shoot-out? Whose only European trophy was this as Liverpool manager? (3)

5 Who lifted the European Cup at Old Trafford as captain of Milan in 2003? What was the connection with the 1963 Final of the competition at Wembley? (2)

6 After losing 2-1 in Barcelona, Chelsea went 3-0 up in a memorable twenty minutes in the return: who scored twice for Barcelona to put them ahead on away goals? And whose late headed goal gave Chelsea the win? (2)

7 Which is the only non-Prague-based side from the Czech Republic to have reached the group stage of the Champions League since 1992–93 (to 2105–16)? (1)

8 Which Czech international pulled the strings for Juventus and scored the winning goal as they knocked Real Madrid out of the 2002–03 Champions League in the semi-final? And which Frenchman scored in both legs? (2)

9   Which two top sides did Bayern Munich brush aside in the quarter-
    final and semi-final of the 2013 Champions League, scoring eleven
    goals and conceding none in the process? Who scored in both legs of
    the semi and also scored in the Final in Bayern's 2-1 win over Borussia
    Dortmund? (3)

10 In the 2006–07 Champions League Manchester United lost the first
    leg of their quarter-final in Rome 2-1 against AS Roma: what was the
    score in the second leg? (1)

11 Which side came back from a 4-1 defeat in Milan to beat AC Milan 5-4
    on aggregate in the 2004 Champions League? (1)

12 In the semi-finals of the 2006–07 Champions League Joe Cole gave
    Chelsea a 1-0 lead to take to Anfield: which Liverpool centre back
    cancelled out this goal to take the tie to penalties? And who scored in
    both legs as AC Milan beat Manchester United 5-3 on aggregate in the
    other game? (2)

13 Which Brazilian centre half scored Bayer Leverkusen's goal in the 2002
    Champions League Final? Who scored a stunning winning goal for the
    opposition just before half time and who were the opposition? Who
    came on as a goalkeeping substitute for the winners and played the last
    half-hour? (3)

14 Which five players, four German, one overseas, took the field for
    Bayern Munich in the Champions League Finals of 2010, 2012 and
    2013? (5)

15 Which two cities had three representatives at the group stage of the
    Champions League in 2003–04 and 2010–11? (2)

Answers on p.529

Quiz 195: Premier League 25 (40)

1 French defender Sylvain Distin first played in the Premier League on loan for which club? And for which side did he appear in 2015–16, aged thirty-eight? In between these two spells, for which two clubs did he make more than 200 appearances? How many caps did he win for his country? (5)

2 Which three goalkeepers from outside the British Isles have made more than 400 appearances in the Premier League? (3)

3 Leeds United, Charlton Athletic and Newcastle United were the only teams to beat Arsenal as they won the Premier League in 2001–02: what was unusual about those three victories? (1)

4 Which diminutive former Manchester United striker top scored for Norwich City, including a hat-trick against Oldham Athletic, as they achieved a commendable third place in the 1992–93 Premier League? And who scored Norwich's other hat-trick of the season as they beat Leeds United in April to keep in contention for the title? Who was the club's manager at the time? (2)

5 Which overseas wide player was released by Newcastle in controversial circumstances in the summer of 2015 after more than 200 appearances for the club? What difficulty did he overcome during his time with the club? (2)

6 Which two French players were the first signings made by Arsène Wenger as Arsenal manager, even though technically the players were purchased before his appointment was announced? Which former Arsenal player left Manchester City for Sunderland in the same week? (3)

7 Who did Southampton beat 3-2 in an emotional farewell to their old ground The Dell in 2001? Who scored the last-ever goal at the ground? (2)

8 Who top scored for Aston Villa as they finished fourth in the Premier League in 1995–96? And which player, short for a top-flight pro at 5'4", was an ever-present at left back in that season, after signing from Blackburn Rovers? (2)

9 Who won their first home game in the top flight for fifty years 5-0 against Southampton in August 1997? Who picked up where he left off after a hat-trick in the play-off final the previous season and scored another? (2)

10 In the last ten years three Manchester United centre backs have signed or played on loan for Sunderland: which three? (3)

11 Which former Leicester City and Leeds United player returned to England after a four-year stint with Saint Étienne in France in 2015 to join newly promoted Bournemouth in the Premier League for around £7M? (1)

12 Who overtook David James's record for keeping the most Premier League clean sheets during the 2015–16 season? (1)

13 To August 2016, which three players share the Premier League record for most red cards with eight apiece (two are unsurprising, one was a good defender who lacked a bit of pace)? (3)

14 Which two former club colleagues from their playing days led Bolton Wanderers into the Premier League in 1995 and 1997? (2)

15 Pay attention now. Of the 36 players to have scored twenty goals in a Premier League season, nine of them are the sole player from that country to reach this target. For example, Dwight Yorke is the only Trinidadian – who are the other eight? (8)

Answers on p.530

Quiz 196: Northern Ireland 4 (30)

1 Which two Belfast clubs have dominated the top flight of domestic football, winning seventy-four league titles between them? (2)

2 Who is Northern Ireland's second most-capped goalkeeper after Pat Jennings? And with which two clubs was he with from 1997 to 2011, the extent of his international career? (3)

3 Which future national team manager played on the wing for Northern Ireland at the 1958 World Cup finals? With which club had he just suffered relegation from the English top division? (2)

4 Who scored in each game as Northern Ireland got a great start to their qualification for Euro 2016 by winning away in Hungary and Greece? And which Watford centre half scored the goal in their last match away to Finland that sealed their place at the top of their group? (2)

5 Which Englishman was the only non-Irish manager of Northern Ireland, from 1998–99? (1)

6 Which Northern Ireland centre half was an integral part of Watford's rise to prominence in the 1980s? (1)

7 Here is the Northern Ireland team that managed a highly creditable 1-1 draw with Germany in Bremen in 1992 (4-4-2): MISSING (Newcastle United); Gary Fleming (Barnsley), MISSING (Barnsley), MISSING (Queens Park Rangers), Nigel Worthington (Sheffield Wednesday); Kingsley Black (Nottingham Forest) (sub: Steve Morrow of Arsenal), MISSING (Oxford United), Mal Donaghy (Manchester United), MISSING (Manchester City); Kevin Wilson (Notts County), MISSING (Portsmouth). Can you name the MISSING players? And which future Northern Ireland manager came on as a late substitute? (6)

8 Centre back Chris Nicholl, who won more than 200 caps for Northern Ireland, played over 200 games for which two clubs in the top tiers of the Football League? (2)

9 Bertie Peacock, who played 32 times for Northern Ireland between 1949 and 1961 and later managed the side, played most of his club football with which club – was it (a) Linfield (b) Derby County (c) Swansea City or (d) Celtic? (1)

10 Joe Bambrick holds the record for goals scored in a single game involving a team from the British Isles when he scored six for a united Ireland side against which opposition in 1930? (1)

11 Who was the last (to 2014–15) Northern Ireland international to win the Premier League? (1)

12 Which English-born player made his debut for the Republic of Ireland in 2007 and his debut for Northern Ireland six years later? (1)

13 Which Roman Catholic Northern Ireland international gave up international football in 2002 after receiving death threats from extremists? With which three clubs – one of which he later managed – did he make more than 100 league appearances? And, after a few months off, where did he take over as manager in October 2014? (5)

14 Alan Fettis, Willie McFaul, Colin Murdock, Jim Platt: which of these never won a cap for Northern Ireland as a goalkeeper? (1)

15 Which 26-year-old Everton player and seasoned Northern Ireland international was forced to retire in 1991 after a series of knee injuries? (1)

Answers on p.530

Quiz 197: General 50 (30)

1 Dave Beasant is best remembered for his time at Wimbledon and his penalty save in the 1988 FA Cup Final; for which other two clubs did he play more than 200 league games (he was sill first choice for one at the turn of the century in his forties)? (2)

2 Name the five main regular presenters of BBC's *Match of the Day*. (5)

3 What do Joe Jordan, Eric Cantona and Alan Smith all have in common? (3)

4 Which Danish star was appointed national team manager in 2000 and only stood down in 2015 when Denmark failed to qualify for the 2016 European Championships? (1)

5 Which member of the Croatia squad at the 2014 World Cup finals was born in Rio de Janeiro? For which Premier League club did he play from 2007 to 2010? (2)

6 Which two players were sent off after a brawl during the 1974 FA Charity Shield between Liverpool and Leeds United? (2)

7 Who was the Georgian international who became a cult figure at Manchester City in the nineties? (1)

8 Why was everyone so amused by Trevor Brooking's winning goal against Arsenal in the 1980 FA Cup Final? (1)

9 Who read out a public apology after assaulting his girlfriend, TV presenter Ulrika Jonsson, in a Paris bar on the eve of the 1998 World Cup? (1)

10 Which four players started the 2000 European Championships Final for France, but hadn't featured in the starting line-up at the 1998 World Cup Final? (4)

11 The Italian clubs Chievo and Hellas both play their home games in which city? (1)

12 Which Brazilian star of the fifties and sixties was known as 'Little Bird'? (1)

13 Who set a post-war record by scoring in eight consecutive matches for Newcastle United in 1995? (1)

14 Which club, managed by Lou Macari, set a new record of 102 points while winning the Fourth Division in 1985–86? (1)

15 Which West Midlands club achieved promotion to the Premier League for the first time in 2001–02, were relegated immediately, and promoted straight back in 2003–04? Which manager oversaw all three campaigns? Which striker was brought back to the club for that first Premier League campaign but failed to score a single league goal as the club notched up only a miserly 29 goals all season? Which Welsh international midfielder was brought in from Tranmere Rovers on the same day as the club twice broke their transfer record? (4)

Answers on p.531

Quiz 198: Legends 1 (30)

These last three quizzes are a bit of self-indulgence on my part, and hopefully a bit of speculative fun for the reader. In each quiz I have selected a squad of thirty players to represent The World, The Premier League and England respectively. All you have to do is guess the members of the squad from the clues given. I know – guess. It's an ugly word, but it is integral to the best quizzes. You hear the question, you don't know the answer, but you guess, because you only know one Peruvian international footballer and – Hey Presto! – it turns out to be right. Go for it – at least twenty of the thirty players pick themselves without any argument.

The first squad is to represent The World in a hypothetical match against Mars. The squad needs balance, so there are a couple of players included who are undoubtedly less gifted than some of those omitted – but they fulfil a role. There are five Italians, the most from any country; four from Argentina and Brazil, three each from England, France and Germany (low, but maybe a reflection of their collective team ethic and less reliance on individual brilliance). The Netherlands and Spain have two representatives each, while there is one from each of Russia, Portugal and Hungary. The last member is the only pick from the other nations in the United Kingdom.

There are three goalkeepers and ten defenders: two are full backs, three are equally comfortable at full back or in the middle, while five are centre backs, and of these ten players, three were sometimes used in midfield.

Of the eight midfield players three could be used comfortably in a deep role, but none of the eight are out-and-out tacklers. Five of the eight carry a goal threat, as do all three of the wide players, only one of whom is an old-fashioned winger. Of the six forwards, three are goalscorers, the other three combined goals with play-making abilities.

Of the thirty players, ten are from the period which essentially covers the post-war period up until around 1970 (there are no selections from before the Second World War, which just makes things easier and there is little footage to go on). Six more are from the 1970s and '80s, nine are from the early modern period – the nineties and the modern era but now retired – while five are current or have retired in the last couple of seasons.

You will disagree with some selections, I'm sure, either because you have your own favourites or because you don't remember the earlier players. Nineteen of the squad have been on the winning team in a World Cup Final, while a further five have made the Final but lost. Of the other six, two have won the European Championships (as Captain), while five of those six have won the European Cup/Champions League. Only one of the squad has had the major trophies elude him.

Answers on p.532

Quiz 199: Legends 2 (30)

The second squad is to represent an all-time post-war British Isles in a hypothetical match against the Rest of the World, Continental Europe or whoever you fancy. Again we are looking for balance, so there are one or two inclusions for that purpose in lieu of possibly more talented players – although England in particular's more maverick talents have rarely shone at their brightest for their country.

There are three goalkeepers and nine defenders: there are four full backs, two left and two right, and five central defenders. Two of these are good ball-playing liberos, three are more conventional defenders – one of these five is equally competent at full back.

There are nine midfield players, three I have designated as defensive or deeper players (two old school fighters, one scandalously under-capped, and a deep lying midfield general). Of the other six there are three play-makers, two quality box-to-box players and a creative goalscorer. The five wide players offer varied options; they score goals aplenty and offer fantastic creativity and pace – they are probably the strongest element of the squad, each brilliant in his singular way. Of the four forwards, one offers much more than mere goals, the other three are all finishers.

There are seventeen English players, six Scottish and three from Wales, while Northern Ireland and the Republic of Ireland have two repre-sentatives each. Sorry, you other home nations fans, but that just about reflects the relative success of the five nations over the years. There are fourteen players from the post-war years, five from the 1970s and '80s, eight from the modern period and three contemporary players, two recently retired internationals and one current star. If this feels biased towards the earlier years, it serves us well to remember that the home nations were more of a force then, and the British clubs were a power in Europe without the assistance of overseas stars. There are too many modern players with 100+ caps who failed to deliver when it mattered.

The squad could hardly be described as serial winners – the home nations have won very little on the international stage. All but three have at least appeared in a World Cup finals tournament, and there are a smattering of European Cup / Champions League winners in there.

Answers on p.532

Quiz 200: Legends 3 (30)

The last squad is for the Premier League generation, those who think that football records started in 1992–93. This is a squad that reflects the best players to have appeared in the Premier League. I decided on one important criteria: each member of the squad must have served at least five seasons with one club in the Premier League – no room for one or two season mercenaries.

The format of the squad is three goalkeepers, nine defenders, eight midfield players, four wide players and six attackers. The defenders include one utility defender as well as four specialist full backs and four central defenders. The midfield players include three designated as defensive midfield – one 'sitter' and two tough powerhouses; the other five midfield players are all creative box-to-box players.

The wide players include one brilliant all-round attacker and two modern wide midfield players as well as one who could fill either role equally well. The forwards consist of three playmaker 'no.10' types and three goal scorers.

Ten Englishmen make the cut, but only two others from the British Isles. There are four Scandinavians and eleven from the rest of Europe, including five from one country. That leaves only three from the rest of the world, but successful imports from outside Europe are relatively recent, especially ones who hang around at a club for longer than five minutes.

Answers on p.533

Answers 1

1. Confederation of North, Central American and Caribbean Football Association; football's regional body for North America
2. Bavarian, referring to the region of Germany in which Munich lies; Leverkusen was founded in 1904 by employees of local pharmaceutical company Bayer
3. Ryan Bertrand was the only home-grown player. The rest, in order, were bought from: Rennes, Porto, Bolton Wanderers, Benfica, Arsenal, Lyn Oslo, Feyenoord, Valencia, West Ham United, (Bertrand), Marseille
4. Iran, hence the girl's difficulties as she had to dress as a boy to be allowed in
5. Gary Kelly
6. Ian Harte – he was only three years younger than 'Uncle Gary'
7. 1978 in Argentina
8. Mick McCarthy
9. He scored the winner against Italy in a controversial World Cup quarter-final
10. Pierre van Hooijdonk & Kevin Campbell
11. Faro
12. Norway, Wimbledon
13. Lothar Matthäus
14. Kia Joorabchian; Javier Mascherano
15. Maidstone (United)

Answers 2

1. West Ham United, Rio Ferdinand
2. Patrick Vieira & Dennis Wise
3. Nottingham Forest; West Ham United; Tottenham Hotspur; Blackburn Rovers; Leeds United
4. Jerzy Dudek & Chris Kirkland; Sander Westerveld
5. All made more than 300 appearances in the Premier League without winning an international cap; Nolan made 399 appearances, and Steed Malbranque made the 300 club without ever being capped by France

6 Arjen Robben

7 Dennis Bergkamp (only more recently did bans become effective immediately)

8 Juan Sebastián Verón & Claude Makélélé

9 David Unsworth; Everton

10 Marcus Stewart of Ipswich Town; Jimmy Floyd Hasselbaink

11 They were the scorers (in that order) as Newcastle beat Manchester United 5-0

12 Robinho

13 Jamie Carragher & Sami Hyypiä

14 Jason Dodd, Claus Lundekvam, Matthew Le Tissier, Francis Benali, Matt Oakley & James Beattie

15 Middlesbrough, Bryan Robson; the game was awarded to Blackburn and Middlesbrough were relegated – a win, however unlikely, would have made the difference and kept them up

Answers 3

1 Steaua Bucharest; Red Star Belgrade – Crvena Zvezda; both finished 0-0 and were settled on penalties; Miodrag Belodedici

2 Borussia Dortmund (1997) and Hamburg (1983)

3 Peter Withe; Nigel Spink; Bayern Munich

4 Nicolas Anelka; Ivan Campo; Fernando Hierro

5 Hibernian

6 Everton

7 In memory of the victims of the Hillsborough disaster, which had taken place four days earlier

8 Giovanni Trapattoni

9 Cyprus

10 Terry Venables

11 Robert Lewandowski; 2-0 to Madrid, both goals coming in the last few minutes leading to some nervous moments for the German side's fans

12 Because Liverpool had not technically qualified as one of the English entrants, they were there by grace and favour as the holders, having finished only fifth in the Premier League in 2005

13 Sturm Graz

14 Ronald Koeman; Johan Cruyff; Sampdoria

15 David Luiz; Thiago Silva; Zlatan Ibrahimovic

Answers 4

1 Alan Mullery

2 Carter and Matthews were not in the side. The FA were pilloried (rightly) for not selecting Matthews; he arrived too late for the first match against Chile but was available for the US game

3 Peter Shilton

4 Alan Ball

5 Terry Butcher (after blood from a head wound covered his entire shirt)

6 Steve Foster, Mick Harford, Ricky Hill, Brian Stein

7 Chris Waddle

8 Nine

9 Barnes

10 Two; none

11 George Eastham jnr, Nigel Clough, Frank Lampard jnr

12 Gary Neville, Wes Brown, Nicky Butt, Paul Scholes, David Beckham, Andrew Cole, Teddy Sheringham

13 David Beckham, with a superb free kick under immense pressure; he single-handedly got England through this game as his colleagues sleep-walked for 90 minutes

14 Lee Dixon; Dennis Wise

15 Ashley Cole & Ashley Young

Answers 5

1 Burnden Park, Bolton

2 He is the Chairman of the Football League

3 Leighton James (Burnley, 1); John Toshack (Liverpool, 1); Ian Rush (Liverpool, 5); Kevin Ratcliffe (Everton, 1); Mark Hughes (Manchester United, 4); Neville Southall (Everton, 4); Gary Speed (Leeds United, 1); Ryan Giggs (Manchester United, 6); Gareth Bale (Tottenham Hotspur, 3)

4 The Superga air disaster of May 1949 wiped out the entire travelling Torino side; they were Italy's best club team and provided the core of the national team

5 Dave Mackay & Tony Book

6 Hugo Sánchez

7 Atlético Madrid

8 Marco Materazzi; also Materazzi

9 The games were held in Los Angeles and they were used to try to spread the word about American Football

10 Ian Rush, Neville Southall & Gareth Bale; surprisingly not Ryan Giggs – when Giggs won the PFA award in 2008–09 the writers went for Steven Gerrard. Gordon Strachan while at Leeds United

11 Luiz Felipe ('Big Phil') Scolari; Cristiano Ronaldo (Manchester United) & Helder Postiga (Tottenham Hotspur)

12 Deportivo de La Coruña; Tottenham, but he was 34 and past his excellent best

13 Lazio

14 Eden Hazard

15 John Lukic

Answers 6

1 Scunthorpe United; The Iron

2 Woolwich Arsenal (just Arsenal is not enough)

3 Sunderland

4 QPR have 23 seasons under their belt, Palace and Cardiff 16, Swansea only 7

5 Mick Jones; 60+ goals would become about par in the next decade, the days of teams scoring well over 100 goals were a thing of the past

6 Graham Taylor: the new job was Watford, where Elton John had just taken the reins as Chairman, with promise of funding that Taylor would never have got at Lincoln

7 Ron Noades; Dario Gradi; Milton Keynes; Crystal Palace

8 John Aldridge

9 Aston Villa

10 Bobby Charlton

11 Tranmere Rovers

12 Southampton; Alan Ball, Mick Channon, Kevin Keegan, Mick Mills, Peter Shilton, Dave Watson

13 Glenn Hoddle, the player-manager and Mickey Hazard; Colin Calderwood

14 Ford had trod the turf of 100 league grounds with his trip to newly promoted Kidderminster

15 Southend United; Lee Trundle; Yeovil Town, Gary Johnson

Answers 7

1 Tim Cahill

2 Estadio Centenario. It still stands and is owned by the municipal authority

3 Vittorio Pozzo

4 Sándor Kocsis. West Germany fielded a weakened side so as not to show their full hand, anticipating (correctly) that they would beat Turkey and progress

5 Roger Hunt

6 Tostão; it didn't seem to affect him too badly, he had a splendid competition

7 Poland; Alan Ball; Brian Clough said this of Jan Tomaszewski; Allan Clarke; Wlodek Lubanski

8 Hans Krankl; Barcelona; Rapid Vienna

9 Júnior, Sócrates, Falcão, Serginho: Scirea, Bergomi, Tardelli, Graziani

10 Frank Rijkaard of the Netherlands spat at Rudi Völler, whose response was angry but barely physical – both were sent off

11 Ray Houghton

12 Tore André Flo

13 Bora Milutinovic

14 Luis Suárez and Edinson Cavani

15 Lionel Messi: although excellent in the group games he was nondescript in the knockout rounds and couldn't influence the Final as he would have liked. Neuer or Müller of Germany would have been a much more appropriate choice

Answers 8

1 Sutton United; Norwich City
2 Tranmere Rovers; Paul Rideout
3 Ray Crawford, who won the title with Ipswich Town in 1961–62
4 Bolton Wanderers (1923, 1926, 1929)
5 Tommy Hutchison
6 Ronnie Boyce
7 Crystal Palace; Southampton
8 Kennington Oval, Crystal Palace & Stamford Bridge
9 Alan Taylor – his is one of those typical 'every dog has his day' FA Cup stories; Taylor scored twice in each of the last three rounds, but his career was a journeyman one and he never hit those heights or won any more trophies
10 Graeme Sharp & Andy Gray
11 Sunderland in 1973
12 Nikos Dabizas, Temuri Ketsbaia, Rob Lee, Alan Shearer & Gary Speed
13 Notts County
14 Andy Carroll
15 Arsenal; Paul Gascoigne; Gary Lineker; Terry Venables & George Graham

Answers 9

1 Trevor Bailey
2 Iain Dowie
3 Manchester United
4 Southend's Roots Hall ground
5 Vivian Woodward
6 Jones, with 59 for Wales to Blanchflower's 56 for Northern Ireland; Brown (the goalkeeper) won 28 for Scotland, and Mackay a surprisingly meagre 22 for Scotland
7 1998
8 Arthur Milton
9 Ian Callaghan (1974), Kevin Keegan (1976), Emlyn Hughes (1977), Kenny Dalglish (1979 & '83), Terry McDermott (1980), Ian Rush (1984),

John Barnes (1988 & '90), Steve Nicol (1989), Steven Gerrard (2009), Luis Suárez (2014)

10 Hungary; John Toshack; Arfon Griffiths; Yugoslavia
11 Stilian Petrov, Aston Villa
12 Both were born in Poland
13 Dennis Bergkamp; Ajax Amsterdam
14 Laurent Blanc
15 Dave Bassett

Answers 10

1 Roy Hodgson
2 Grasshoppers
3 Jon Dahl Tomasson; AC Milan; Newcastle United
4 Fenerbahçe and Galatasaray
5 Moscow Dynamo
6 Alaves; Gary McAllister; Jordi Cruyff; Markus Babbel (who scored the first goal) and Dietmar Hamann
7 Gheorghe Popescu & Gheorghe Hagi; Galatasaray had entered the competition by failing at the group stage of the Champions League
8 AC Milan. The plan worked
9 Mallorca, Tenerife & Las Palmas
10 Mathieu Valbuena; retiring shirts has become voguish in recent years, but retiring the no.28, really? And for a player of some skill, but hardly legendary ability . . .
11 Atlético Madrid, Athletic Bilbao, Valencia & Real Sociedad
12 PSV Eindhoven
13 Arsène Wenger
14 Honved
15 Fernando Torres; Luis Aragonés

Answers 11

1 Bryan Roy & Lars Bohinen; Chris Bart-Williams
2 AS Monaco
3 Milan Baros, Patrick Berger & Vladimir Smicer

4 Liverpool 4 Newcastle United 3

5 Sunderland; Edin Džeko & Sergio Agüero; City won 6-1 at Old Trafford – had that game finished 2-1, the teams' goals for and against would have been identical and a play-off would have been necessary

6 It was Nyarko, who failed to light up the English scene, although Bakayoko and Kroldrup (one game for £5M!) were equally ineffectual; at least Beattie could point to some good seasons at Southampton

7 Lee Bowyer (cleared of affray and GBH) & Jonathan Woodgate (guilty of affray, cleared of GBH)

8 Glenn Hoddle

9 Andy Gray; Howard Kendall

10 West Bromwich Albion; Norwich City

11 Reading; Dimitar Berbatov

12 Fabricio Coloccini, Jose Enrique, Joey Barton, Kevin Nolan, Peter Lovenkrands; it was Barton who converted both penalties and Alan Pardew was the manager

13 Frank Lampard (twice) & Ashley Cole

14 Joe Hart, Richard Dunne, Vincent Kompany & Pablo Zabaleta

15 J.P. McManus & John Magnier; Rock of Gibraltar

Answers 12

1 Ian St John

2 Eamonn Bannon, Maurice Malpas, David Narey, Richard Gough, Paul Sturrock

3 Graeme Souness & Steve Archibald

4 It was the venue for the first-ever international, Scotland v England

5 Hibernian

6 Denis Law

7 Alex McLeish & Willie Miller

8 Hibernian

9 Kris Boyd; Kilmarnock

10 John Greig, Sandy Jardine & Ally McCoist

11 Falkirk, Inverness Caledonian Thistle; St Johnstone

12 Packie Bonner

13 Gordon Durie; Brian Laudrup

14 Joe Jordan

15 Martin O'Neill (x3), Gordon Strachan (x3), Neil Lennon (x3), Ronny Deila (x1)

Answers 13

1 A Graf Zeppelin

2 Drogba & Kalou won with Chelsea in 2012, Kuffour with Bayern Munich in 2001 and Muntari with Inter in 2010; Eto'o won with Barcelona in 2006 and 2009, and a third with Inter in 2010. Both Essien and Geremi have been unused subs in a Final

3 Laurie Cunningham; Dave Beasant (1 cap); John Fashanu (2), John Scales (3); Dennis Wise (21)

4 Windsor Park; Linfield

5 Stanley Matthews

6 Thomas (Tom & Tommy) Finney

7 Ivan Golac; Dundee United

8 Roy Carroll, who replaced Tim Howard for the last six minutes of the 2004 victory over Millwall – Carroll had been first choice for much of the season

9 Both had university degrees – the Bamber came from Bamber Gascoigne, the question-master on the BBC's *University Challenge*

10 Liam Brady, Paul McGrath & Roy Keane

11 Michel Platini

12 Christian Ziege

13 Bournemouth

14 Sir Clive Woodward, the World Cup winning England rugby union coach, who proceeded to demonstrate how methods don't necessarily transfer

15 Alan Smith on both occasions

Answers 14

1 Scotland

2 A UEFA decree that states only Welsh teams can qualify for Europe via the Welsh Cup, so the Welsh FA barred all teams competing in the English club network

3 Barry Town

4 Jack Kelsey; Neville Southall

5 Barry Horne

6 Phillips – David & Leighton

7 Joey Jones; Titograd is now Podgorica, the capital of Montenegro

8 Ryan Giggs; Ian Rush scored goal number 24 to take him past Trevor Ford and Ivor Allchurch

9 Giggs made 64 appearances and scored 12 times – he (or Manchester United) was notorious for missing friendlies

10 Craig Bellamy; Filippo Inzaghi

11 Chris Gunter & Hal Robson-Kanu; James Chester; Eden Hazard & Thibaut Courtois

12 Trevor Ford, Sunderland

13 Dai Davies, Joey Jones and David Giles were with the club at the time, although Giles left that summer. Brian Flynn was with Leeds but would end his career with a long swansong at the Racecourse Ground. Mickey Thomas started with Wrexham but was with Manchester United in 1980, although he would return to North Wales for a late career flurry.

14 Danny Gabbidon (46) & Robert Earnshaw (58)

15 Eddie Niedzwiecki

Answers 15

1 Germany (36), Netherlands (34), England (31) & Bosnia and Herzegovina (30)

2 The first World Cup hat-trick

3 Uruguay

4 Austria

5 Ken Aston; red and yellow cards to make the crowd more aware of a referee's decision; three, but it could have been seven or eight; The Battle of Santiago; Chile 2 Italy 0

6 Uruguay: they drew 0-0 in the opening game

7 Johan Cruyff; he was playing for Barcelona; Günter Netzer was at Real Madrid

8 Peru; no evidence emerged that the match was flawed, but Peru were

bad – maybe it was that they had nothing to play for, unlike Argentina, who would probably have been strung up by the military Junta if they had failed

9   Billy Hamilton

10 Steve Hodge, Stuart Pearce & Des Walker (Hodge had featured in 1986 but was an unused substitute this time)

11 Faryd Mondragón; he became the oldest player (43) to appear in the World Cup finals

12 Cafu, of Brazil

13 Cameroon (1994), Morocco (1998) & Côte d'Ivoire (2006)

14 Olof Mellberg; Marcus Allbäck

15 Javier Mascherano (the captain) & Maxi Rodríguez

Answers 16

1   Ecuador; Southampton – Gordon Strachan, the Southampton manager, once declared at a press conference that an out-of-date yoghurt was a bigger priority for him than dealing with Delgado

2   Harry bought and sold 134 players, and Bassila played a whole 86 minutes

3   Nicklas Bendtner & John Jensen

4   Chelsea, Barcelona

5   George Boateng; Dennis Bergkamp & Edwin van der Sar

6   Harry Kewell. Had Lineker just questioned the value of a semi-permanently crocked player he would have been on safer ground . . .

7   Harry Kewell & Mark Viduka; Ian Harte – Viduka took the second penalty

8   Sam Allardyce

9   Luis Suárez; Danny Murphy (2002–03) & Jamie Carragher (2004–05)

10 Leicester City, Birmingham City, Blackburn Rovers, Derby County; John Terry

11 Portsmouth. They were all but down even before administration – those nine points would still have left them bottom, seven points behind West Ham United in seventeenth

12 Both teams were relegated

13 Steven Gerrard

14 Tim Howard, Leon Osman, David Unsworth, Leighton Baines, Tony Hibbert, Phil Jagielka, Phil Neville, Duncan Ferguson, David Weir, Tim Cahill

15 Dion Dublin; Aston Villa against newly promoted Birmingham City

Answers 17

1 Sir Matt Busby
2 Stade Vélodrome
3 Artur Boruc; Southampton
4 George Robledo; Chile
5 Bari
6 Arie Haan, Ruud Krol, Johan Neeskens & Johnny Rep
7 Mexico; Hulk
8 West Ham United (1980)
9 Celtic
10 Andy Gray, David Platt & Paul McGrath
11 Robert Lewandowski, André Schürrle, Steven Fletcher & Robbie Keane
12 Alessandro Del Piero; Parma
13 Blackburn Rovers; Marcus Bent
14 Claudio Ranieri; after the 2015–16 season the press tend not to take the mickey out of him anymore . . .
15 Arsenal & Manchester United; David Seaman

Answers 18

1 Atlético Madrid, Leeds United & St Étienne
2 Bill Foulkes
3 The FA would not allow them to compete
4 Kanu & Finidi George
5 Bayern Munich
6 Leeds United
7 BATE Borisov
8 Barcelona, Bayern Munich & Brondby; Dwight Yorke
9 Ernst Happel (Feyenoord, Hamburg); Ottmar Hitzfeld (Bayern

Munich, Borussia Dortmund), Jupp Heynckes (Real Madrid, Bayern Munich), José Mourinho (Porto, Inter), Pep Guardiola (Barcelona, Bayern Munich)

10 Bayer Leverkusen; Bayern Munich

11 Thierry Henry

12 All had a perfect record in their first phase group

13 Anderlecht, Marseille

14 Cristiano Ronaldo scored four times in twenty minutes either side of half time, Karim Benzema also scored a hat-trick; Malmö beat Celtic 4-3 on aggregate

15 AC Milan in 1989 and 1990

Answers 19

1 Bolton Wanderers & Charlton Athletic

2 Aston Villa

3 Accrington Stanley, Aston Villa, Blackburn Rovers, Bolton Wanderers, Burnley, Derby County, Everton, Notts County, Preston North End, Stoke City, West Bromwich Albion, Wolverhampton Wanderers

4 Wednesday, with 66: the other three all have 60, although only Stoke are currently in the top division

5 Brian Clough

6 Bob Paisley

7 Kenny Dalglish & David Johnson

8 Plymouth Argyle

9 Joe Royle; Everton

10 Joe Mercer

11 Sam Bartram

12 Spurs have 81 seasons, Sunderland 85, City 87, but Aston Villa have an impressive 105

13 Michael Thomas

14 Crewe Alexandra

15 Nathan Ellington & Jason Roberts; Leighton Baines

Answers 20

1 Ray Wilkins
2 40, they have drawn 25 and lost 45
3 Denmark
4 Paul Van Himst
5 Horst Hrubesch
6 Turkey; Gary Lineker
7 Jean-Pierre Papin
8 It was Dermot Gallagher (probably the best referee the Premier League has had; Gallagher officiated with lots of common sense, and he didn't think the public were paying to watch him first and foremost)
9 Belgium & the Netherlands; Austria & Switzerland; Poland & Ukraine
10 David Villa
11 Slovenia; Zlatko Zahovič
12 Frank De Boer (a regular penalty taker) & Jaap Stam (who wasn't, and who nearly hit a low-flying plane with his effort)
13 The Netherlands, Ruud van Nistelrooy; Russia
14 Philipp Lahm; Fernando Torres
15 Iker Casillas, Gerard Piqué, Sergio Ramos, Xabi Alonso, David Silva, Juan Mata, Cesc Fàbregas (and yes, centre forward; this was the tournament Spain played with the 'false 9' as it became termed)

Answers 21

1 Norway – the man in question was Bjørn Lillelien. Norway were an improving side but it was another decade before they became a genuine force – this was just a bad day at the office for England
2 John Collins
3 Schalke 04 (they moved to a new ground in 2001)
4 They missed the penalties that saw England eliminated by France in a shoot-out at that year's World Cup tournament
5 Soviet Union
6 *The Sun* (of course it was)
7 Vinnie Jones
8 Alan Shearer, with Blackburn Rovers and Newcastle United

9 Northern Ireland; Republic of Ireland, Cameroon, Wales, Morocco; Denmark, England, Scotland, Japan, Latvia; Jamaica. For good measure Fulham brought on a Frenchman (Martin Djetou) and an Argentinian (Facundo Sava), but spoilt things by bringing on English youth player Mark Hudson

10 Clive Allen; QPR; Kenny Sansom of Crystal Palace; back to QPR

11 Iceland, who qualified for the first time in 2016, has only around 330,000 people; the next smallest would be Northern Ireland, who also qualified for the first time in 2016 and Latvia, who played in the 2004 finals – both have a population of just under 2 million

12 Dynamo Kiev; Vladimir Lobanovskyi

13 Fernando Torres

14 The death of Diana, Princess of Wales

15 Guy Whittingham; a soldier, he was in the army

Answers 22

1 Trevor Brooking – the other goal was a corker, a fierce left-footer after a lovely move that left the ball stuck in the V-section at the corner of the goal; Terry McDermott

2 Willie Watson

3 Luther Blissett; Brazil

4 Chris Powell, Paul Konchesky, Scott Parker, Luke Young & Darren Bent

5 Emile Heskey

6 He was Sven Goran Eriksson's assistant in the England set-up

7 Warren Barton & John Fashanu (Dennis Wise wasn't picked for England until after he moved to Chelsea, ditto John Scales with Liverpool)

8 Two

9 Kevin Keegan

10 Austria

11 Tottenham Hotspur; back at Tottenham

12 David Beckham, Steve McManaman, Michael Owen & Laurie Cunningham

13 Earle, who represented the country of his birth at football while all the others played for their adopted country of residence, England

14 Wayne Rooney, he became England's youngest ever scorer

15 Steve McLaren; The Wally with the Brolly

Answers 23

1 Steven Gerrard
2 They were the only sides who travelled to the first tournament in Uruguay in 1930
3 Brazil; Wilimowski finished on the losing side as Brazil won 6-5
4 Bobby Robson
5 Antonio Carbajal of Mexico; Carbajal again, in 1966
6 Jimmy Greaves
7 Bayern Munich (7) & Borussia Mönchengladbach (5)
8 Marius Tresor; Olympique Marseille
9 Harold Schumacher; Patrick Battiston; 3-3 – the German won on penalties
10 Bryan Robson
11 Palermo; Cagliari on Sardinia, so the troublemakers were easy to contain. The plan failed as the heavy-handed Italian police behaved worse than the fans
12 David Platt
13 Tom Boyd; John Collins
14 They are the coaches of the World Cup winning sides since 1950 so missing are: Herberger, Ramsey, Bearzot, Beckenbauer, Scolari, Lippi
15 Thierry Henry; William Gallas; Robbie Keane

Answers 24

1 Alec Lindsay, Phil Boersma (2), Phil Thompson (2), Steve Heighway, Peter Cormack, Emlyn Hughes, Tommy Smith, Ian Callaghan, Ray Kennedy
2 He was the first to win all three major European competitions, having won the European Cup in his first spell at Ajax and the European Cup Winners' Cup with Ipswich
3 Tottenham Hotspur
4 Pierre van Hooijdonk
5 Ruud van Nistelrooy
6 Anderlecht of Belgium
7 Bayern Munich

8   Lennart Johansson
9   Malta
10 Union of European Football Associations
11 Galatasaray; Arsenal
12 Manchester City, Chelsea; Real Madrid, Peter Osgood
13 Rangers
14 Zenit St Petersburg; he went back to St Petersburg
15 Gary Neville

Answers 25

1   Brighton & Hove Albion in 1983 – Gordon Smith was the culprit, and Brighton lost the replay 4-0
2   CSKA Moscow, Dynamo Moscow, Torpedo Moscow & Spartak Moscow. Three of the sides are still in the Russian Premier League but Torpedo Moscow have fallen on tough times and are in the regional third tier of Russian football
3   Charlton Athletic; Allan Simonsen, Barcelona
4   Aston Villa (1980) & Arsenal (1989)
5   Graeme Souness & Steve McMahon
6   Mervyn Day; West Ham United, Leeds United
7   Brighton & Hove Albion, 1983 (two in the first match and four in the replay)
8   Maik Taylor
9   Newcastle United
10 The PFA Women's Player of the Year
11 Bosnia and Herzegovina, Croatia, Macedonia, Montenegro, Serbia, Slovenia
12 Porto (Estádio de Dragão) & Sporting Club (Estádio José Alvalade)
13 Sammy Lee
14 It is the Boston Red Sox
15 Stockport County

Answers 26

1   Tottenham Hotspur; Chelsea, AC Milan
2   Forty-four

3   Chelsea, Leeds United & Liverpool

4   The 1996–97 trio were the first to get promoted and then immediately relegated, the 2001–02 trio were the first to get promoted and all survive their first season

5   Giovanni van Bronckhorst; Francis Jeffers

6   Tony Cottee, Andrei Kanchelskis, Yakubu Aiyegbeni & Romelo Lukaku

7   Robbie Fowler & David Unsworth

8   John Obi Mikel of Chelsea – he has two

9   Glenn Roeder; Trevor Brooking

10 Alan Pardew at Crystal Palace; Lille

11 Blackburn Rovers, Bolton Wanderers, Burnley & Wigan Athletic

12 West Bromwich Albion; Steve Clarke

13 Liverpool & Manchester City in 2013–14

14 Charlton Athletic, Tottenham Hotspur, West Ham United, Fulham, Liverpool

15 Lee Bowyer; Ole Gunnar Solskjaer & Ronny Johnsen; Fabrizio Ravanelli

Answers 27

1   Preston North End & Huddersfield Town

2   Burton

3   Everton (1938–39) & Arsenal (1947–48)

4   Dennis Compton, the England cricketer, and his brother, Leslie, who also played first class cricket and gained two caps for England

5   Howard Kendall & Colin Harvey; 72 (Harvey won a solitary cap, Kendall none: worse players than either have garnered 20+)

6   Newcastle United; Ossie Ardiles

7   February 1991; Ronnie Moran; Graeme Souness, Rangers

8   The original stadium was Eastville, and Rovers moved into the Memorial Ground, owned by Bristol Rugby. Bristol Rugby had financial issues and Rovers took over the Memorial Ground. As the rugby club revived they wanted a bigger ground so moved in with Bristol City at the larger Ashton Gate

9   Geoff Thomas

10 Stan Mortensen

11 Ian Callaghan (640 league appearances)

12 Viv Anderson

13 Chris Coleman & Eric Young; Nigel Martyn

14 Jermain Defoe; Tottenham Hotspur

15 Dean Windass; Fraizer Campbell

Answers 28

1 Arsenal

2 Boston (Breakers) vs Houston (Dash)

3 Marta

4 Doncaster Rovers Belles

5 Arsenal, Birmingham City, Bristol Academy, Chelsea, Doncaster Rovers Belles, Everton, Lincoln Ladies & Liverpool

6 Kelly Smith

7 Arsenal Ladies; Chelsea

8 Kim Little; Arsenal

9 Beth Mead

10 Southampton

11 Fara Williams, Rachel Yankey, Alex Scott, Casey Stoney, Gillian Coultard

12 Arsenal Ladies

13 Goalkeeper Karen Bardsley

14 Bayern Munich

15 Christie Rampone; Kristine Lilly

Answers 29

1 The Shankly Gates

2 It was won by Cardiff City

3 PSV Eindhoven

4 Azerbaijani, but we'll also allow Soviet Union, as he was a representative of that state in the competition. Russian is incorrect

5 Sócrates, the Brazilian playmaker from the 1980s

6 Tunisia

7 Juventus, Internazionale, Sampdoria, Ascoli

8 Matthias Sammer; Borussia Dortmund

9   David O'Leary; Tony Adams, George Armstrong, Lee Dixon, Nigel Winterburn, David Seaman, Pat Rice, Peter Storey, John Radford, Peter Simpson

10 Steve Archibald

11 Sheffield Wednesday: poor old Carlton, he is cited as a symptom of the inadequacy of Graham Taylor's selection policy, but for all his lack of artistry he was a great ball-winner and had awesome lung power. Taylor picked far worse – Andy Sinton anybody?

12 Crystal Palace; Sun Jihai

13 Juventus, the stadium was rebuilt on the original site and is now called simply Juventus Stadium

14 West Ham United; David Sullivan & David Gold

15 Manchester City

Answers 30

1   Italy; Czechoslovakia; Leeds United

2   Aaron Hughes

3   Lawrie Sanchez; the second tier in Greece (Greece is fine)

4   Six, although Mal Donaghy (Luton), Gerry Armstrong (Watford) and Martin O'Neill (Norwich City) had just won promotion from Division 2, and John McLelland played in the top flight in Scotland with Rangers

5   Gerry Taggart

6   Cliftonville, Coleraine, Crusaders, Glentoran, Linfield, Portadown: Derry City

7   Harry Gregg

8   Terry Neill; Greece; Everton

9   Manchester United; 2008

10 Jimmy Nicholl

11 All four teams had the same points with one win, one draw and one defeat; Northern Ireland won on goal difference

12 Newcastle United; none (goalscoring wasn't part of a full back's armoury in the 1950s)

13 Derek Dougan

14 Jim Magilton

15 James Quinn, although the earlier Quinn went by the name Jimmy

Answers 31

1 Peñarol & Nacional; they have been utterly dominant over the years in Uruguay, winning 92 out of 111 league titles between them to 2015 (Peñarol with 47 to Nacional's 45)

2 Boca Juniors

3 Roberto Ayala, Gabriel Heinze, Juan Sebastián Verón, Javier Mascherano, Lionel Messi, Carlos Tevez

4 Zaire; Pierre Mulamba

5 Luis Artime

6 Peru – they have fallen on hard times and are among the whipping boys of the continent nowadays (although they gained a terrific 1-0 win over Brazil in the 2016 Copa América)

7 Frederick Kanouté, Emmanuel Adebayor & El Hadji Diouf

8 Adriano

9 Twenty-five

10 Abedi Pele; Tony Yeboah; Côte d'Ivoire

11 They are the two men to have won the African Cup of Nations both as a player and a coach

12 Nigeria

13 Samuel Eto'o & Yaya Touré

14 Uruguay

15 Australia, Israel

Answers 32

1 The first man to win the World Cup as both player and coach; Franz Beckenbauer achieved the same double in 1990

2 6-1; Yugoslavia & United States

3 Leônidas

4 Roger Byrne & Tommy Taylor

5 Morocco; West Germany

6 Gary Lineker; he earned both penalties, one of them highly debatable

7 Ecuador; Venezuela

8 Hamburg & Munich

9 Gary Lineker, Lothar Matthäus, David Platt, Chris Waddle

10 Stephane Guivarc'h; Kenny Dalglish & Ruud Gullit; he went to Rangers for £3.5M but only managed 14 games there before moving back to Auxerre

11 Papa Bouba Diop; all of them

12 England; Wayne Rooney

13 Germany were 4-0 up at half-time, but the game ended as a 4-4 draw; André Schürrle

14 Mario Götze

15 Samuel Eto'o

Answers 33

1 Gloves (Glovers – Yeovil); Hats (Hatters – Stockport); Shoes (Cobblers – Northampton)

2 Seven. That figure is slightly misleading – a few others were of genuine Irish stock, but quite a few were drafted in by Jack Charlton on scant acquaintance with the country

3 Maurice 'Mo' Johnston

4 Bees

5 Alain Giresse, Jean Tigana, Luis Fernández & Michel Platini

6 Alarmingly, it is Wiltord, with an inexplicable 92 caps (Pires has 79, Petit 63 and Silvestre 40)

7 David Johnson & Peter Beardsley

8 Jamie Vardy

9 Ayr United; 27 – it would have been double had he played for Rangers or Celtic, lesser players won a lot more

10 Christine Bleakley is Lampard's new partner; his daughters are Luna and Isla

11 Hans van Breukelen, Frank Rijkaard, Arnold Muhren, Erwin Koeman, Ruud Gullit; Rinus Michels

12 Due to the betting scandal known as *Calciopoli*, in which many of the top sides, including title-winners Juventus, were implicated

13 Brad Friedel; Edwin van der Sar

14 Sir Bobby Robson

15 Sean O'Driscoll (Steve Fletcher later broke the record)

Answers 34

1 Bryan Gunn (reserve goalkeeper) & Robert Fleck; Paul McStay
2 John McGinlay of Bolton Wanderers scored against Sweden and Kevin Gallacher of Blackburn Rovers scored twice against Austria
3 Tommy Docherty & Willie Ormond
4 Graeme Souness; Nantes in France; Everton
5 Dundee United
6 Alan Hansen
7 Denis Law and Kenny Dalglish
8 Kris Boyd. Burley was sacked a year later and Boyd played three further games for his country – Burley was a poor manager for Scotland, then again Boyd wasn't much missed, he wasn't international quality
9 Barry Ferguson; Tore André Flo
10 Kenny Dalglish; Jim Leighton, Alex McLeish, Paul McStay, Tom Boyd, Darren Fletcher
11 Queen's Park
12 Willie Miller & Kenny Miller
13 Goram & Naysmith
14 A mere twenty apiece. Gray's total might have been more but for injuries and the management's preference for Joe Jordan; Walker & Gallacher because there were fewer games; Nicholas because his contribution often failed to match his raw talent
15 Craig, by some distance, 46 vs 11

Answers 35

1 Gerd Müller with 35 in 35
2 Manchester City
3 Bayern Munich
4 Joey Jones (Wales) & Steve Heighway (Ireland)
5 No-one; Liverpool won the league the season before but they were made to serve an extra one year's ban
6 Faustino Asprilla; Colombia. They were Asprilla's last goals for the club, he was gone by January after bouts of absenteeism and tales of carousing

7 Steaua Bucharest (1988) – by the time Red Star Belgrade / Crvena Zvezda won in 1992 the term Iron Curtain was no longer in use

8 Kazakhstan

9 Graeme Le Saux and David Batty

10 Ramires; John Terry; Didier Drogba; Ivica Olić and Bastien Schweinsteiger; Drogba again

11 Villareal; Peter Lovenkrands

12 Lee Bowyer; he added a winner against Anderlecht and a goal against Lazio in the second phase group to finish second equal in the goal charts amongst some prodigious European strikers

13 Hampden Park, Old Trafford, City of Manchester Stadium & Villa Park; Millennium Stadium, Cardiff

14 Olivier Giroud

15 They won the trophy despite not having won their domestic league title the previous season

Answers 36

1 Sheffield United have 60, West Ham 58, Forest 56 – but Bolton were in the top flight at the start of the league and rarely dropped out until the 1960s; they have 73

2 Sunderland (there was another John Campbell in the top division at the time, he was also a prolific scorer, with Aston Villa)

3 Billy Liddell

4 In order: Chelsea, Manchester City, Wolverhampton Wanderers, Aston Villa, Nottingham Forest

5 Liverpool (of course it was)

6 Bristol City

7 Ipswich Town, Watford & Southampton; Bobby Robson, Graham Taylor & Lawrie McMenemy; Alan Brazil, Luther Blissett & Steve Moran; Ipswich, in 1985–86, four years after finishing second

8 Graeme Sharp (21) and Trevor Steven (14)

9 Trevor Francis

10 Ron Greenwood

11 Everton

12 Jimmy Hill

13 Ronnie Whelan

14 Fulham

15 Rickie Lambert; Southampton

Answers 37

1 Scotland

2 None

3 The Emirates Stadium; these are the grounds used for Arsenal home games

4 Flavio Briatore & Bernie Ecclestone. They deserved each other

5 Spartak Moscow, CSKA Moscow, Zenit St Petersburg, Lokomotiv Moscow & Rubin Kazan

6 Ayresome Park, Middlesbrough; Roker Park, Sunderland; White City, London

7 Sir Stanley Rous, President of FIFA

8 Matthias Sindelar. He died just before the Second World War – the circumstances appear suspicious, especially as he was not beloved of the Nazis; Hugo Meisl

9 Attilio Lombardo; Thomas Brolin

10 Third Division title & Welsh Cup – as a border team they were permitted to enter the Welsh Cup, but could not take the allotted European Cup Winners' Cup place if they won

11 The disqualification of Yugoslavia after civil war broke out. It was a shame, they were a talented side who scored for fun – their scorers in qualifying included Serbs, Croatians, Macedonians and a Bosnian. CIS stood for 'Confederation of Independent States' and was in effect the Soviet Union in limbo before the establishment of governments and football federations in many of the former Soviet states

12 Bordeaux; the city is in an area called La Gironde, and the club's official name is Les Girondins de Bordeaux

13 Accrington Stanley & Aldershot

14 Jack Wilshere (at 16 years, 256 days)

15 Bill Shankly

Answers 38

1 Jan Molby
2 Matt Holland
3 Reading; Theo Walcott
4 Leicester City
5 Manchester City
6 Three. Pathetic
7 Glyn Pardoe; Manchester United
8 Tommy Smith; Ian Callaghan
9 Paul Merson; Mark Hughes
10 Jason Roberts; 2006
11 They were the teams beaten by League 2 (fourth tier) Bradford City en route to the 2013 League Cup Final
12 Emile Heskey, Muzy Izzet & Neil Lennon
13 Watford; Steven Gerrard; Aidy Boothroyd
14 Aston Villa; Dean Saunders & Dalian Atkinson
15 Bolton Wanderers; Steve McManaman; Gudni Bergsson; Jason McAteer; promotion to the Premier League

Answers 39

1 Dennis Bergkamp
2 Fourteen
3 Chris Hughton; Christian Gross; Grasshoppers; Basel
4 Andrei Kanchelskis
5 He was never on the losing side in a Manchester derby
6 Paolo Wanchope & Francesco Baiano
7 Micky Quinn; Kevin Gallacher
8 Martin O'Neill, Matt Elliott, from Oxford United – it proved a wise investment
9 Shaun Wright-Phillips; back to Manchester City (one of those undisclosed fee deals, but we're betting it was less than the £21M Chelsea paid). One of the great disappointments of recent years, his time at Chelsea seemed to drain the confidence and talent from the player

10 Bacary Sagna, Gaël Clichy, Theo Walcott, Samir Nasri, Robin van Persie: Heurelho Gomes, Vedran Corluka, Tom Huddlestone, Luka Modrić, Roman Pavlyuchenko

11 Tony Pulis

12 Ryan Giggs

13 Stuart Holden

14 Reading, Southampton, West Ham United & Newcastle United; Barnet

15 West Ham United, Chelsea, Portsmouth, Liverpool, Stoke City

Answers 40

1 Tony Cascarino – neither the first nor the last to succumb to intimidation in Istanbul

2 Steve Staunton

3 Denis Irwin

4 Spain

5 Scotland

6 Aiden McGeady

7 Ray Houghton, Ronnie Whelan & John Aldridge

8 Cyprus; Steve Staunton

9 Jim McDonagh; Dave Langan, Kevin Moran, Mark Lawrenson, David O'Leary, Chris Hughton; Ronnie Whelan, Mick Martin, Liam Brady; Frank Stapleton, Michael Robinson. Don Givens was the sub

10 Gary Breen

11 David Forde; Millwall

12 Lansdowne Road

13 Terry Conroy – he was in the Stoke side that won the League Cup in 1972

14 Chris Hughton

15 Ray Treacy, who scored twice as the Republic beat Turkey 4-2 at Lansdowne Road

Answers 41

1 Edwin van der Sar; Gianluigi Buffon

2 5'5" (152cm)

3 Rasunda is the stadium that hosted the 1958 World Cup Final, situated in Solna, a small town in the Metropolitan area of Stockholm

4 Elton John, Saracens RUFC

5 John Motson, Kenneth Wolstenholme

6 Vincent Kompany, Yaya Touré, Fernandinho, David Silva & Sergio Agüero

7 He became the youngest captain at the finals at the age of twenty-one

8 Mark Pembridge, Benfica

9 Fulham

10 Jermaine Pennant; Arsenal; Singapore, for Tampines Rovers

11 Stockholm, Gothenburg, Malmö & Norrköping

12 Juventus

13 Yeovil Town & York City

14 Anton Ferdinand

15 Aston Villa

Answers 42

1 Israel; after some Middle East sides refused to play Israel they were awarded their section, but FIFA deemed it inappropriate they qualify without playing a game, so had to win a two-leg play-off against a European side

2 Oswestry

3 Ivor Allchurch

4 Wolverhampton Wanderers

5 Mike England; Bobby Gould; Gary Speed

6 Mark Hughes

7 Dave Bowen

8 David Jones; Joe Jordan, the Scotland striker; Don Masson; 2-0 to Scotland; Anfield. Welsh football fans have made a huge fuss over this injustice. The fact is it was 0-0, and that would have left Wales needing to beat European Champions Czechoslovakia in Prague to qualify. If they were that desperate to beat the Scots, they should have played the game in the passionate surroundings of Wrexham's intimate Racecourse Ground and not opted for the money-spinner over the border. The better team qualified

9   Wales won 5-2

10 Leighton James

11 Tottenham Hotspur

12 Ron Davies

13 Norwich City, Coventry City, Newcastle United, Celtic, Blackburn Rovers, Liverpool, West Ham United, Manchester City, Cardiff City; Great Britain, he was in the 2012 Olympic side

14 Chris Coleman

15 Leighton

Answers 43

1   Green

2   Three, including a goalkeeper

3   Andrew Cole & Peter Beardsley (Newcastle, 1993–94); Didier Drogba & Frank Lampard (Chelsea, 2009–10); Luis Suarez & Daniel Sturridge (Liverpool, 2013–14)

4   Egil Ostenstad, Eyal Berkovic; Roy Keane

5   Patrick Vieira, Ruud van Nistelrooy; 0-0; five

6   Ken Monkou; Chelsea

7   Eyal Berkovic & Tal Ben Haim

8   Slavisa Jokanovic; Chelsea (2000–02)

9   Eric Cantona

10 Phil Neville, who left Manchester United. It signalled the end of his international career, bar a couple of meaningless caps, which was a shame, because he improved at Everton and could have done a job as a defensive midfield player when England were sadly lacking in that position

11 Chelsea in 2009–10; Newcastle United

12 Gary Cahill; Bolton Wanderers

13 Pepe Mel & Alan Irvine

14 Ryan Giggs, David James, Gary Speed, Frank Lampard, Emile Heskey, Steven Gerrard & Sol Campbell

15 Joe Kinnear; Chris Hughton & Colin Calderwood; Alan Shearer

Answers 44

1 Paul Scholes
2 Steve McManaman (Real Madrid, 2000); Steven Gerrard (Liverpool, 2005); Sol Campbell (Arsenal, 2006); Frank Lampard (Chelsea, 2008); Wayne Rooney (Manchester United, 2011)
3 Juventus
4 Wayne Rooney
5 Didier Drogba & Asier Del Horno
6 Luis Garcia; José Mourinho & Rafa Benítez
7 Carlo Ancelotti & Ruud Gullit, Frank Rijkaard & Marco van Basten (both managed the Netherlands) and Roberto Donadoni (who managed Italy)
8 Malmö (Sweden) – that stat isn't changing any time soon
9 Nottingham Forest & Porto
10 Peter Crouch
11 They didn't concede a goal
12 Rio Ferdinand (Leeds beat Deportiva de La Coruña 3-2 on aggregate to reach the last four)
13 Jimmy Armfield with Leeds United in 1975
14 Manchester United were not one of the English qualifiers
15 Two, they won both knockout rounds on away goals after 1-1 draws away and 0-0 draws at home, and won the Final on penalties after a 0-0 draw. Guus Hiddink; Ronald Koeman (manager of Southampton); Eric Gerets

Answers 45

1 Frank Sinatra & the Pope
2 Brian Horton, who played over 200 games for Port Vale and Brighton (when they were in the top flight)
3 Ryan Giggs (the winner), Cristiano Ronaldo, Rio Ferdinand, Edwin van der Sar, Nemanja Vidić
4 Huddersfield Town, then Everton; Jimmy Armfield
5 The resignation of Kenny Dalglish as Liverpool manager
6 Colin Todd
7 Northern Ireland, it was the height of 'the troubles'

8 Ian Wright – Wright was already twenty-one, he'd slipped through the net of the big clubs at youth level

9 Uli Stielike

10 Neil Ruddock

11 John Rudge

12 Andy Goram, Richard Gough, Paul McStay, Gary McAllister, Brian McClair, Kevin Gallacher, Andy Roxburgh (coach)

13 Scott Dann

14 Jordan Henderson

15 Stanley Matthews

Answers 46

1 Andorra & San Marino

2 Switzerland 7 Austria 5

3 Ubaldo Fillol & Daniel Passarella, River Plate

4 Christian Vieri; Roberto Di Matteo

5 Alpay

6 American Samoa; Archie Thompson – hitting the net thirteen times in a game is a good effort, even if the opposition was little better than Sunday morning standard

7 Raymond Domenech; Nicolas Anelka; Patrice Evra; South Africa

8 Enzo Bearzot & Jupp Derwall

9 Trinidad and Tobago

10 Poland & Paraguay; Peter Beardsley

11 Giuseppe Bergomi

12 Bryan Robson, who was injured (again) in the second match; Paul Gascoigne

13 Jason McAteer

14 Ronaldo

15 Theo Walcott; Frank Lampard & Steven Gerrard

Answers 47

1 The Heysel disaster and subsequent ban for English clubs

2 He became the youngest player to appear in an FA Cup Final

3 Chelsea

4 His new jersey was too slippery

5 Walsall

6 Dave Watson

7 Brian Kilcline

8 He was the first Cup Final substitute

9 Gary Charles

10 Arsenal

11 Ian Rush

12 Norman Whiteside

13 Liverpool

14 Germany (Lehmann), Cameroon (Lauren), Ivory Coast (K.Toure), Switzerland (Senderos), England (Cole), Spain (Fàbregas and Reyes), France (Vieira, Pires), Brazil (Gilberto, Edu), Netherlands (Bergkamp, van Persie), Sweden (Ljungberg): United also represented Northern Ireland (Carroll), Ireland (O'Shea, Keane), Scotland (Fletcher), Wales (Giggs), Portugal (Ronaldo) & South Africa (Fortune)

15 Manchester City's goalkeeper Bert Trautmann

Answers 48

1 Alf Ramsey; Ipswich won the League the following season (1961–62); Ramsey was given the England job

2 Barnet; it is actually in Harrow, the club no longer play within the Borough of Barnet

3 Gainsborough Trinity

4 Wolverhampton Wanderers; he was their top scorer in both 1958 and 1959 (they won the League both times) and moved to Manchester City in 1963, helping them win promotion back to the top flight

5 Andy Campbell; Queens Park Rangers

6 Bradford Park Avenue; Cambridge United were elevated

7 Dixie McNeil

8 1950–51: both sides were in the bottom tier until County won promotion in 1949–50 by winning the Third Division South; Forest followed them up a year later

9 1985. The Bradford fire was caused by a discarded cigarette while the Heysel disaster was down to the collapse of a wall as Juventus

supporters tried to escape a hail of missiles from the adjacent Liverpool fans

10 Dean Holdsworth; Wimbledon

11 Peter Withe & Kenny Burns; Archie Gemmill & John McGovern were both in Clough's Derby side that won the league in 1972; Tony Woodcock was sold to 1. FC Köln in 1979

12 Kerry Dixon; Chelsea – it proved money well spent

13 The first clubs to be relegated from the Football League under the automatic system (with the clubs promoted from the Conference in their place in brackets)

14 Barry Hearn, who is snooker's best known entrepreneur

15 Matty Fryatt

Answers 49

1 Bristol City

2 2018. They reached the Final in 1970, 1982, 1994 and 2006 – all gaps of twelve years

3 Shaka Hislop; Trinidad and Tobago

4 Thomas – Rod & Mickey

5 David Rocastle

6 Antibes, it was the tiny (7,000 capacity) Stade du Fort Carré

7 Wolverhampton Wanderers; zero; Kazimierz Deyna

8 New Zealand

9 Milan; the ploy failed after Beckham picked up an injury

10 Dave Clement; West Bromwich Albion

11 Jimmy Murphy

12 Steve McManaman

13 Stanley Matthews, Denis Law, Bobby Charlton, George Best, Kevin Keegan, Michael Owen

14 Spain (Vincente del Bosque & Iker Casillas) & Germany (Joachim Löw & Phillip Lahm)

15 Middlesbrough

Answers 50

1 Austria, Belgium, the Netherlands, West Germany; the Netherlands – he took them to the Final in 1978

2 José Antonio Reyes

3 Andriy Shevchenko

4 Deportivo de La Coruña

5 Germany, Latvia, Turkey & Norway

6 Real Zaragoza – Arsenal's opponents took to singing 'Nayim from the halfway line' after Nayim lobbed David Seaman from distance for Zaragoza's winner

7 Gianluca Vialli

8 John Dempsey (in the Cup Winners' Cup for Chelsea)

9 Brazil

10 Internazionale (3), Juventus (2) & Parma (2): Italian sides also made up six of the losing teams – Juve and Inter both lost a Final, as did Fiorentina, Roma, Torino and Lazio

11 The unlovable El Hadji Diouf; Rangers

12 Sevilla & Real Betis

13 Miroslav Klose

14 Porto

15 Ruud Gullit, Frank Rijkaard, Marco van Basten; Arrigo Sacchi

Answers 51

1 Marcelo; Neymar

2 Hungary & Brazil; Hungary won 4-2; Arthur Ellis

3 Pelé. It was a brilliant hat-trick and a brilliant performance by Brazil – France actually played rather well to keep the score at 5-2

4 Gianni Rivera & Sandro Mazzola: it didn't help that Rivera played for AC Milan and Mazzola for hated rivals Inter

5 Flórián Albert; Ferencváros

6 Diego Maradona

7 Dino Zoff. He didn't play, but his day would come

8 Belgium

9 Israel

10 Heitinga, Van Bommel, Sneijder, van Persie and Robben are the missing players. Stekelenburg, Sneijder and Kuyt were the only starters who stayed card-free

11 Zaire; 9-0

12 Australia

13 Valencia

14 Bearzot, in 1955

15 Salvatore (Toto) Schillaci; Messina

Answers 52

1 Platt enjoyed an excellent ratio of one goal every 2.3 games (very similar to Bobby Charlton), Keegan scored exactly 1 in 3, Peters 1 in 3.35 games, while Scholes, perhaps surprisingly, scored only 1 in every 4.7 games

2 San Marino; Ian Wright; Norway & Netherlands; Graham Taylor

3 The Rest of the World, captained by Alfredo Di Stefano and including Eusébio, Kopa, Denis Law & Lev Yashin

4 Coventry City

5 Nat Lofthouse

6 Vivian Woodward

7 Wayne Rooney; Theo Walcott

8 Frank Lampard snr

9 Nine

10 Dean Ashton; Crewe Alexandra

11 Oldham Athletic

12 John Barnes

13 Terry Butcher (Singapore); Tony Dorigo (Australia); Owen Hargreaves (Canada); John Salako (Nigeria)

14 Wayne Rooney

15 Keown won 43 caps (Brown 23, Charlton 35, King 21, Lescott 26 & Todd 27); Charlton scored 6 times

Answers 53

1 Southampton

2 Ray Wilkins

3 Roger Hunt (245); Dalglish & Owen with 118 (Fowler scored 128, Rush 229); both Rush and Fowler moved away and returned; Dalglish & Owen never downsized; Hunt again, with a goal every 1.65 games; Dalglish (he was as much a creator for Rush as a goalscorer); Ian Rush played 469 league games for the club

4 Both were winning their first cap

5 George Graham

6 Dr Jozef Venglos

7 Aston Villa

8 Alan Sugar

9 Sunderland & Manchester City

10 Mel Sterland

11 Michael Dawson, Jermaine Defoe, Aaron Lennon, Ledley King & Peter Crouch. King got injured, Lennon played in the first two games and was dropped, Crouch played six minutes, Defoe scored against Algeria and was subbed against Germany, while Dawson played no part

12 Mark Hughes

13 Jaap Stam

14 Guus Hiddink & Dick Advocaat

15 Pete Winkleman

Answers 54

1 Dean Saunders (13) & Dalian Atkinson (11); Earl Barrett, Steve Staunton, Paul McGrath & Shaun Teale – Teale missed three matches, the others played in all 42; Mark Bosnich

2 Hamilton Ricard

3 Charlton won 3-1 – Proctor's double and Wright's effort were scored in their own goal

4 Seventeenth

5 Paul Merson; Marc Overmars

6 Dan Petrescu; Chelsea

7 Gheorghe Popescu (from PSV in the Netherlands) & Ilie Dumitrescu (from Steaua Bucharest)

8 Brian Kidd; Steve McLaren

9 Patrick Vieira; Gary McAllister & Dietmar Hamann

10　Fifteen points (3 wins, 6 draws, 29 defeats, hold your heads in shame Middlesbrough, West Bromwich Albion and Fulham . . .); three each. Oddly they were never beaten by more than three goals – and that only three times. Their problems lay at the other end

11　Queens Park Rangers. Barton is now a 'respected' pundit on the BBC – go figure

12　Sergio Agüero & David De Gea

13　Yakubu Aiyegbeni, Benjani Mwaruwari & Aruna Dindane

14　Sven-Göran Eriksson; Lazio; Roy Hodgson, Inter Milan

15　Fernando Torres (sold to Chelsea) and Andy Carroll (bought from Newcastle United)

Answers 55

1　Gillian Coultard

2　Norway; China, in 1991

3　France

4　United States

5　China; Brandi Chastain – forget the football, look there's a woman in a bra!

6　Make (five of) their players professionals

7　Everton; Widnes Vikings

8　Republic of Ireland & the Netherlands

9　United States (4), Germany (3), Japan, Norway (2), Brazil, China, Sweden (1)

10　Katie Chapman (Chelsea) & Laura Bassett (Notts County); she was voted PFA Women's Player of Year; South Korea

11　Karen Bardsley & Jill Scott

12　Birgit Prinz

13　Nadine Angerer

14　Sweden

15　Reading Ladies

Answers 56

1 Cristiano Ronaldo, Lionel Messi, Raúl, Ruud van Nistelrooy, Thierry Henry
2 Reims (1956 and 1959)
3 Twenty-five years
4 Deportivo de La Coruña; Bayer Leverkusen; Real Madrid beat Barcelona
5 Laurie Cunningham & Steve McManaman
6 Kolo Touré
7 Carlo Ancelotti
8 *L'Équipe*
9 Neymar: Paris St Germain, Bayern Munich and Juventus
10 Diego Milito; José Mourinho (Inter) & Louis Van Gaal (Munich)
11 Chelsea & Liverpool
12 Goran Pandev (Vittek is Slovakian, Mandžukíc Croatian and Pančev was much earlier)
13 Benfica
14 Legia Warsaw; Maribor
15 Everton; Panathinaikos

Answers 57

1 France
2 Bournemouth, Aldershot, Cambridge United, Luton Town, Birmingham City, Leicester City, Portsmouth, Wolverhampton Wanderers, Millwall, Wycombe Wanderers, Bradford City
3 Gillingham; Paul Dickov; Shaun Goater; Joe Royle; Fulham
4 Bill Shankly & Denis Law
5 Lou Macari
6 Jérome Boateng of Germany and Kevin Prince-Boateng of Ghana
7 AFC Bournemouth, formerly Bournemouth and Boscombe Athletic – Boscombe is the region of Bournemouth where the club's ground was located
8 Craig Whyte
9 Alan Ball
10 Dennis Wise

11 Egypt, who won the first African Cup of Nations in 1957 – only three countries, Sudan (the hosts), Egypt and Ethiopia, took part

12 They all knocked Chelsea out of the UEFA Cup

13 Belarus

14 Arthur Rowe; winning the Second Division and First Division in successive seasons

15 Peter Bonetti and Ron Harris; Harris (795 appearances in all)

Answers 58

1 Tommy Lawrence was the 'keeper, Chris Lawler & Gerry Byrne were the full backs, Tommy Smith & Ron Yeats the central pairing. Lawler missed two games. They won only 14 caps (4-4-2-1-3 in the order we named them)

2 Glossop (Town); they were promoted in 1899–1900 and only stayed in Division 1 for a single season, but they did get there

3 Richard Wright, Jamie Clapham, Matt Holland, Jim Magilton, Marcus Stewart

4 Dennis Wise

5 Accrington Stanley; Notts County; Preston North End

6 Stockport County

7 Lee Mills, Port Vale; Gary Walsh, Manchester United

8 Svetoslav Todorov – he suffered a severe cruciate knee injury in the following pre-season and was never the same again; Shaka Hislop

9 Julian Dicks; he was sent off three times (accept any reference to red cards or indiscipline)

10 George Graham

11 Charlton Athletic

12 Graham Alexander

13 Jimmy Quinn

14 (c) the drains at the club were getting a little nasty . . .

15 Trinidad and Tobago

Answers 59

1 He was involved in the Munich air disaster, and although he survived he never recovered from his injuries sufficiently to play professionally again

2 Albania, it was Albania's only point in the group; Switzerland won the group by a point after beating the Netherlands ten days previously

3 David Healy; Kyle Lafferty may spoil the equation

4 Gerry Armstrong

5 David Healy. It was a great result and a great night for Northern Ireland, but they never threatened to qualify – England actually did pretty well to head a group that included two other home nations in Northern Ireland and Wales

6 Pat Jennings

7 Gareth McAuley

8 Pat Jennings; Jimmy Nicholl, Aaron Hughes, Jackie Blanchflower, Mal Donaghy; George Best, Danny Blanchflower, Steven Davis, Michael Hughes; David Healy, Peter Doherty. (Not many quibbles – Chris Nicholl for Hughes, Martin O'Neill at right midfield and Best up front instead of Healy, who deserves respect but isn't as good as most of these guys)

9 Iain Dowie was born in Hertfordshire (Jimmy Nicholl was born in Canada and Maik Taylor's father was serving in the military in Germany when he was born; all the others in the top twenty were Ulster born)

10 Paddy McNair

11 Hamilton – there have been 8

12 Peter Doherty

13 Ipswich Town

14 John O'Neill

15 Paddy McNair, Craig Cathcart, Jamie Ward, Corry Evans, Steven Davis, Josh Magennis

Answers 60

1 Robin van Persie & Arjen Robben; Chile

2 José Leandro Andrade, who died in poverty in 1957 but is now hailed as a national hero

3 1. FC Kaiserslautern

4 Pelé & Garrincha

5 Leeds United

6 René & Willy van der Kerkhof; PSV Eindhoven

7 Lothar Matthäus (25), Miroslav Klose (24), Paolo Maldini (23), Diego Maradona (21), Uwe Seeler (21), Wladyslaw Zmuda (21), Cafu (20), Philipp Lahm (20), Grzegorz Lato (20), Bastien Schweinsteiger (20)

8 Igor Belanov – catch a copy of the game or YouTube it, a real treat

9 Tony Meola

10 Belgium

11 François Oman Biyik

12 Michael Laudrup

13 John Aloisi

14 Portugal

15 Robert Green; David James

Answers 61

1 Manchester United in 1983

2 They both achieved a rare Double of promotion from the third tier and winning the League Cup

3 The Netherlands (1), Germany (3), Switzerland (1), Finland (1), England (5), Croatia (1), Czech Republic (1), Scotland (1)

4 West Ham United; Upton Park

5 The Wednesday

6 Lord Kinnaird

7 Harry Catterick

8 Petar Borota

9 Manager (strictly speaking Technical Director) of Wales, to be combined with his existing job as manager of Real Sociedad in Spain; Terry Venables; Graeme Souness, Bristol City

10 Bolton Wanderers; Ipswich Town – they finished ten points ahead of Bolton and eight points ahead of Watford; it's a cruel system

11 The Final of the African Cup of Nations

12 2001–02

13 Sheffield Wednesday

14 Barnet

15 Nigel Martyn; Crystal Palace

Answers 62

1   Bogotá

2   Paolo Wanchope

3   Goalkeeper

4   Don Revie, less than twenty-four hours after resigning as England manager

5   Sierra Leone

6   Because video evidence proved the goalkeeper, Roberto Rojas, faked his injury, inflicting wounds on himself in an attempt to get the result annulled. Chile were subsequently banned from the 1994 qualifiers

7   Montevideo (Uruguay)

8   Ellis Park, Johannesburg

9   Romário

10 They all missed their penalties in a particularly inept shoot-out against Paraguay, who only needed to score two out of three kicks to go through

11 Sergio Agüero, Martín Demichelis & Pablo Zabaleta were at City, Ángel Di María and Marcos Rojo at United

12 Libya

13 Benni McCarthy

14 Egypt

15 Argentina, Bolivia, Brazil, Chile, Colombia, Ecuador, Paraguay, Peru, Uruguay, Venezuela

Answers 63

1   Liverpool; West Ham United

2   Patrick Vieira & Emmanuel Petit

3   Dougie Freedman, who went on to manage the club (until March 2016); Pierre van Hooijdonk

4   Jaap Stam; PSV Eindhoven

5   Shay Given, Alan Shearer, Shola Ameobi, Rob Lee, Nolberto Solano

6   Charlie Adam, Stoke City

7 Shaun Goater & Nicolas Anelka; former United goalkeeper Peter Schmeichel

8 Kevin Campbell; but he only needed thirty goals across those three seasons (9-12-9) to manage that feat as Everton finished seventeenth, fourteenth and, best of the three, thirteenth

9 Laurent Robert; Portsmouth

10 Newcastle United; Graeme Souness, Sam Allardyce

11 They all conceded seven or more goals (eight in Wigan's case)

12 It was the first home match defeat for José Mourinho as Chelsea manager, after seventy-seven unbeaten games

13 Tottenham Hotspur & Fulham

14 Leeds United, Everton, Newcastle United, Bolton Wanderers: Leeds

15 Norwich City; Southampton; Paul Lambert & Nigel Adkins

Answers 64

1 Darius Vassell – it was a poor effort and his body language as he walked forward told you he was going to miss

2 Jonathan Walters; Germany & Poland

3 The Home International Championships of 1966–67 and 1967–68

4 Czechoslovakia; Colin Bell

5 Allan Simonsen; Jan Molby (Liverpool) & Jesper Olsen (Manchester United)

6 Soviet Union; Vassily Rats

7 Marco van Basten; Henrik Larsen (not the later Swedish one who played for Celtic)

8 Pavel Srníček; Karel Poborsky

9 Sweden, who went on to win the group comfortably; Paul Scholes

10 Portugal; Phil Neville; Germany, who were at even lower ebb than England

11 David Trezeguet – it was the last time the ridiculous golden goal settled a major final

12 Spain

13 David Healy

14 Bosnia and Herzegovina; Estonia

15 The Netherlands; Guus Hiddink, Danny Blind

Answers 65

1　Luton Town
2　Diego Maradona, Napoli
3　Barry Venison
4　Eileen Drewery; Ray Parlour
5　Laurie Cunningham
6　Alan Cork of Wimbledon
7　Jens Lehmann
8　Republic of Ireland
9　Diego Maradona (who else?)
10　Germany, Brazil, Italy, Argentina, England, France, Spain, Mexico, Uruguay, Netherlands
11　Denis Law
12　Juventus; Colombia
13　The Taylor Report into the Hillsborough disaster, with recommendations of all-seater stadiums
14　Steve Bloomer; Derby County; 28 (a record that stuck until the late 1950s)
15　Bruce Grobbelaar & Hans Segers

Answers 66

1　They are the losing managers in the FA Cup Final, so the two missing are Tony Pulis (Stoke City) and David Moyes (Everton)
2　Halifax Town
3　Altrincham (2-1 at Birmingham in 1986)
4　Tottenham Hotspur (1962 & 1982) and Arsenal (2003 & 2015)
5　Stan Mortensen (for Blackpool in 1953); Michael Owen (Liverpool, 2001), Ruud van Nistelrooy (Manchester United, 2004) & Steven Gerrard (Liverpool, 2006)
6　Millwall, Stoke City & Hull City all lost, Wigan Athletic won
7　Terry Venables, player in 1967 and manager in '91; Chelsea & Nottingham Forest
8　Pat Van den Hauwe
9　Gary Lineker; Mark Crossley

10 Didier Drogba

11 José Antonio Reyes

12 Blyth Spartans

13 Arsenal & Sheffield United. As Arsenal tried to return the ball to the Sheffield United goalkeeper, Kanu, who had only just come on, lost the plot and took possession, squaring the ball for Marc Overmars who, rather than kick the ball out of play, poked it into the net

14 Rio & Anton Ferdinand, for Manchester United and West Ham United in 2005 and 2006

15 Arthur Albiston (1977, 1983, 1985)

Answers 67

1 Carling

2 Mark Bosnich; Raymond van der Gouw; Massimo Taibi; Fabien Barthez

3 Ryan Giggs, Alan Shearer, Wayne Rooney; James Milner

4 Daniel Amokachi

5 Stan Collymore

6 Juan Sebastián Verón; Chelsea

7 Anders Limpar & Freddie Ljungberg

8 Peter Schmeichel, Paul Parker, Dennis Irwin, Steve Bruce & Gary Pallister; Gary Neville (Bruce and Pallister had appeared in every game in 1992–93 as well – they were a remarkably consistent and injury-free pairing)

9 Sheffield Wednesday

10 A draw – Chelsea won 18 and drew one at home on their way to the title; Charlton Athletic

11 Louis Saha; Manchester United

12 Asmir Begovic; Artur Boruc

13 Luke Shaw & Adam Lallana

14 Arsenal, Liverpool, Manchester City, Bolton Wanderers, Chelsea, West Bromwich Albion

15 Harry Redknapp; Chris Ramsey; Jimmy Floyd Hasselbaink; Burton Albion

Answers 68

1 Alan Smith
2 Jean-Marc Bosman
3 Hajduk Split
4 Mark Schwarzer, Aaron Hughes, Brede Hangeland, Damien Duff, Danny Murphy, Simon Davies, Zoltán Gera, Clint Dempsey
5 PSV Eindhoven; Fabien Barthez; Didier Drogba
6 Paris St Germain
7 Bruno N'Gotty
8 Vojvodina are from Novi Sad in Serbia, Željezničar from Sarajevo in Bosnia and Herzegovina
9 Newport County; East Germany (they are currently languishing in one of the regional fourth tiers of German football)
10 Chelsea; Luxembourg
11 Benfica, Porto & Sporting CP (Sporting Lisbon); Benfica have won 34 to Porto's 27 and Sporting's 18
12 Norwich City
13 The ban on English clubs playing in Europe
14 David De Gea in 2010, Thibaut Courtois in 2012, two days short of his twentieth birthday
15 Jürgen Klinsmann & Marco van Basten

Answers 69

1 Liam Brady; Chippy
2 Highest fee paid for a non-League player
3 Newcastle United – he went back to Newcastle
4 The Wankdorf Stadium (rebuilt as the Stade de Suisse in 2001); the home team were Young Boys, Wankdorf, now operating as BSC Young Boys
5 John Fashanu; Jeremy Guscott; Ulrika Jonsson
6 Johan Cruyff; Michel Platini
7 Jürgen Klinsmann
8 Ronald & Frank de Boer; Ajax, Barcelona and Rangers
9 1994

10 Swindon Town; Ossie Ardiles (this was as good as it got in management for Ossie). Swindon were denied their place in the top flight and relegated instead – they maintained their place in the second tier on appeal.

11 Carlisle United; Scarborough

12 Kim Clijsters: her father, Leo, made a couple of substitute appearances in 1986

13 Gareth Southgate

14 Goal average, whereby goals scored were divided by goals conceded to give an 'average'

15 Oxford United; none; he was homesick so returned (to Swindon)

Answers 70

1 Bob Latchford. He moved to Everton in 1974, where he scored well over 100 goals, and was brought to Swansea in 1981 to add some top-flight experience to a newly promoted team

2 As you guessed, it wasn't Brighton – New Brighton is on Merseyside, so accept Merseyside or Liverpool

3 Portsmouth

4 Terry Medwin

5 Blackpool & Burnley: Blackburn Rovers & Bolton Wanderers

6 Ipswich Town

7 All were relegated with Ian Holloway in charge

8 West Ham United; John Lyall; Frank McAvennie (26) & Tony Cottee (20)

9 Wycombe Wanderers. They won the Conference and the FA Trophy, the major cup competition for non-league sides

10 Floodlights

11 Kevin Pressman

12 Frank Gray (the elder brother was Eddie Gray); Nottingham Forest, in 1980

13 Steve Walsh; 13

14 Birmingham City; Geoff Horsfield

15 Cardiff City; Brett Ormerod

Answers 71

1. None, he was injured and replaced by John Filan after fourteen minutes
2. Grimsby Town
3. Graeme Souness
4. Paul Scholes
5. Stockport County; Andy Mutch
6. Martin Chivers; Steve Perryman
7. Nottingham Forest; Emlyn Hughes
8. Luca Vialli & Gus Poyet
9. Theo Walcott
10. Mark Bosnich (Australia), Savo Milošević (Serbia) & Dwight Yorke (Trinidad and Tobago)
11. Álvaro Negredo
12. Darren Purse; Andrew Johnson
13. Steve Bruce & Dave Watson; Ipswich Town – Bruce got the winner as Norwich recovered from a 1-0 defeat at Portman Road to win the home leg 2-0
14. Chelsea; Jimmy Floyd Hasselbaink was sent off, but Mario Melchiot was the true culprit
15. Aston Villa; Old Trafford; Brian Little; Chris Nicholl; Gordon Cowans

Answers 72

1. Marcelo Salas; Michael Owen
2. Ray Wilkins (v Morocco, 1986); David Beckham (v Argentina, 1998); Wayne Rooney (v Portugal, 2006)
3. Nine
4. Wilfred Zaha in 2012
5. Rodney Marsh
6. Denis Wilshaw
7. Tommy Taylor, whose career was cut short by the Munich air disaster
8. Kevin Keegan, that percentage is miles below all the others. Steve McLaren had a better win percentage than Terry Venables – who knew?
9. Tottenham Hotspur
10. Craven Cottage

11 James Milner
12 Graeme Le Saux & Matt Le Tissier; Le Tissier is from Guernsey, Le Saux from Jersey
13 Jimmy Armfield, Bobby Robson, Johnny Haynes, Jimmy Greaves (you do NOT get a point if you listed Greaves as the Tottenham player), Bobby Smith
14 Sol Campbell; Ricardo
15 Campbell won 73 caps (Hughes 62, Southgate 57, Walker 59, Watson 65 & Wright 45); Walker never scored; Walker again, and Southgate

Answers 73

1 Paul Stewart: it was the start of twenty-five years of numerous questionable signings by the Merseyside club
2 Jason Dodd
3 The Pumas, the Argentinian Rugby Union team
4 Billie
5 Rodney Marsh
6 Newcastle United; Suárez
7 Aaron Hughes
8 Blackburn Rovers
9 Ross County & Caledonian Thistle
10 Marcel Desailly, Tony Adams, Patrick Vieira and Alan Shearer; Shearer & Eric Cantona; Denis Bergkamp & Matt Le Tissier; it was won by Beckham's audacious lob against Wimbledon
11 José Fonte & Cédric Soares; Renato Sanches
12 Gary Lineker & Alan Hansen
13 Leeds United – the unacceptable face of tribalism
14 By the creation of two Third Divisions, one for clubs from the South and one catering for the North; each divisional winner replaced one of the bottom two from the Second Division and the pack was shuffled geographically to accommodate the demoted teams
15 Niall Quinn; Dean Saunders; Quinn again

Answers 74

1 Danny McGrain

2 Jonathan Gould

3 Pure bloody-mindedness. Two places were available for the top two in that season's Home International Championship, but the Scottish FA stated they wouldn't travel as losers (that is, runners-up) and were true to their word despite pleas from their players

4 Gary McAllister & Paul Telfer

5 John Greig

6 Billy McNeill

7 Andy Goram; Oldham Athletic

8 Partick Thistle; Firhill

9 Dundee in 1962 and Dundee United in 1983

10 Hibernian; Burnley

11 Jimmy McGrory, the pre-war legend who, with 502, is 201 clear of Lennox in second. Larsson is third, Dalglish tenth – he was only twenty-six when he left for Liverpool

12 Ayr United

13 Graham Alexander

14 Alex Jackson; The Wembley Wizards. Jackson was a tremendous player, worth far more than 17 caps, but there was a downer on players based outside Scotland with the SFA (it has reappeared from time to time). He died in a car crash just after the Second World War

15 Rangers, Celtic, St Johnstone, Kilmarnock, Dundee, Heart of Midlothian, Motherwell, Aberdeen, Dundee United, Dunfermline Athletic

Answers 75

1 Mike Newell

2 Wembley

3 Paul Scholes

4 Benfica

5 Their opponents were Valencia, another Spanish side – it was the first Final between two teams from the same country

6   Hernán Crespo; Filippo Inzaghi – Milan won the follow-up 2-1 but it was easier than the scoreline suggests, Liverpool's goal was a late consolation

7   Xabi Alonso

8   Chelsea, Liverpool; Didier Drogba & Frank Lampard; Paul Scholes; Cristiano Ronaldo missed for United, John Terry & Nicolas Anelka missed for Chelsea

9   Andrès Iniesta

10 Nicklas Bendtner

11 Sylvain Wiltord

12 Owen Hargreaves (Bayern Munich, 2001)

13 Feyenoord (1970), Bruges (1978), Hamburg (1983) – both Feyenoord and Hamburg won the competition for the first and only time under Happel

14 Peter Schmeichel, Gary Neville, Jaap Stam, Nicky Butt, Jesper Blomqvist, Andy Cole

15 Luxembourg

Answers 76

1   Maik Taylor, Kenny Cunningham, David Dunn, Aliou Cissé, Australia, Christophe Dugarry, Finland.

2   Manchester United; Leeds United

3   Thierry Henry, Alan Smith & Michael Owen

4   Luc Nilis; Aston Villa

5   Kevin Richardson

6   David Prutton

7   Crystal Palace & Wimbledon, who were ground-sharing after the closure of Plough Lane

8   Norwich City; a Premier League winner's medal with Blackburn Rovers

9   Steve McLaren; Brian Kidd

10 David Wetherall; Wimbledon

11 Darren Bent; also Darren Bent

12 Luis Suárez & Daniel Sturridge (Liverpool)

13 Jan Vertonghen of Tottenham & Eden Hazard of Chelsea

14 José Mourinho (Porto), Rafael Benítez (Valencia) & Jacques Santini (French national team)

15 Sunderland, Everton, Wigan Athletic, Hull City

Answers 77

1 Joy Beverley of the Beverley Sisters

2 Arsenal & Tottenham Hotspur, Sheffield United & Sheffield Wednesday; both ties were played at Wembley

3 Gianluca Vialli & Roberto Mancini

4 The countries behind the Iron Curtain insisted their major players were 'amateur' and therefore eligible for Olympic duty. In truth most of them had notional positions in the armed forces or civil service; their main duties were training and playing football!

5 Kakha Kaladze

6 Freddie Ljungberg

7 Martin O'Neill with Nottingham Forest in 1980 (he was an unused sub in 1979, as was Jonny Evans for Manchester United in 2009)

8 Scotland

9 Because of security fears – 20 April was Hitler's birthday and the police had wind of potential neo-Nazi marches and consequent counter-demonstrations

10 Bolton Wanderers

11 Confederations Cup – I promise this is the only question in the book on this utter waste of time and resources

12 Wes Brown, Rio Ferdinand, Michael Carrick, Owen Hargreaves, Paul Scholes, Wayne Rooney, John Terry, Ashley Cole, Frank Lampard, Joe Cole

13 Thirty-three

14 Sheffield Wednesday, they were still The Wednesday when they won in 1929

15 Martin Buchan; he won only 34 caps, in large part due to the incompetence of then Scotland manager Ally McLeod

Answers 78

1 Georgios Samaras
2 The Maracanã Stadium in Rio de Janeiro
3 Djalma Santos, Didi, Mário Zagallo, Garrincha, Vavá.
4 Peter Swan of Sheffield Wednesday; he was embroiled in a betting scandal that eventually saw him banned for life and given a short jail sentence; the ban was later repealed and he returned for a swan song (geddit?) in his mid-thirties
5 Ove Kindvall, Feyenoord
6 Poland; Andrej Szarmach
7 Hungary & Portugal; they were missing Pelé, who was kicked out of Hungary game by Bulgaria in the first match, came back bravely in the third only to be hacked mercilessly by Portugal – especially a shocking double tackle by Morais that would have led to a red card plus a lengthy ban nowadays
8 Spain, Valencia, Gerry Armstrong, Mal Donaghy, Norman Whiteside
9 West Germany
10 Paul Breitner, who converted a penalty when West Germany won in 1974
11 Cameroon. They drew all three matches, but scored only once; Italy also drew three, but scored two and scraped through
12 Alex Ferguson; Australia
13 Argentina 2 England 1
14 Nery Pumpido
15 Matthew Upson; Frank Lampard

Answers 79

1 Steve Staunton
2 David O'Leary
3 Stephen Ireland
4 Alan McLoughlin; Denmark
5 European Championships in 1988
6 Ray Houghton
7 Johnny Giles; West Bromwich Albion – what a busy boy

8 Thirty-seven; O'Brien (seven of them)

9 Johnny Giles (for Leeds) & John Dempsey (for Chelsea)

10 Robbie Keane, Shay Given, Kevin Kilbane, John O'Shea, Steve Staunton, Damien Duff

11 Tony Grealish

12 Denis Irwin; Oldham Athletic

13 Gaelic Football

14 Nottingham Forest; back at Forest after largely unsuccessful spells with a variety of other clubs

15 Andrews, Carr, Doyle, Harte & Staunton were all born in Ireland; Houghton was born in Scotland, Sheedy in Wales and the rest in England

Answers 80

1 Manchester United

2 Alf Ramsey

3 Ronnie Allen (1954–55); Derek Kevan (1961–62, joint); Jeff Astle (1969–70); Tony Brown (1970–71)

4 Bob Wilson, Frank McLintock, George Armstrong

5 Trevor Whymark

6 Des Bremner, Gordon Cowans, Tony Morley & Dennis Mortimer

7 Trevor Senior

8 He was the first (and only) player-manager to win the Double

9 Ipswich Town; Southampton

10 Bobby Zamora; Micky Adams; Robert Earnshaw

11 Andy Ritchie, he is still revered at Oldham

12 Shaun Goater; Ian Bishop

13 Run the line in a Football League match (Torquay v Carlisle, 1994)

14 Brighton & Hove Albion; Bobby Zamora

15 Jermaine Beckford; Everton

Answers 81

1 Because his son Kevin was playing for Norwich

2 Harry Kewell

3 Fitzroy Simpson & Paul Hall (Portsmouth); Deon Burton & Darryl Powell (Derby), Robbie Earle & Marcus Gayle (Wimbledon); Frank Sinclair (Chelsea)

4 Thames Valley Royals

5 Peter Schmeichel; Robbie Savage

6 Emile Heskey

7 Joe Jordan (in 1974, '78 and '82)

8 David Luiz, Oscar, Ramires & Willian

9 Millwall

10 Kidderminster Harriers; Jan Molby; Lee Hughes

11 Bolton Wanderers, who were awarded £400,000 compensation

12 Bruce Grobbelaar; Zimbabwe

13 Trinidad and Tobago; Northern Ireland

14 Frank Swift; he was killed in the 1958 Munich air crash while working as a journalist

15 Jimmy McIlroy

Answers 82

1 Saudi Arabia

2 Ecuador

3 Luis Suárez

4 Nigeria

5 Plymouth Argyle

6 Canada

7 Canada & Spain – both have been invited but declined; Mexico have reached the final twice

8 Gabriel Batistuta

9 Fernando Muslera, Diego Lugano, Diego Pérez, Edinson Cavani, Diego Forlán, Luis Suárez

10 Ghana (4), Cameroon (4) & Nigeria (3)

11 Jay-Jay Okocha; Rigobert Song

12 They are twins; Hossam was a forward, one of the great African players, Ibrahim a solid right back who followed his twin from club to club

13 Didier Drogba

14 CAF, the African federation, were moving the tournament away from the even-numbered years so as not to clash with World Cup years

15 Javier Zanetti, Javier Mascherano, Roberto Ayala, Diego Simeone, Lionel Messi

Answers 83

1 Emerson Thome, Sheffield Wednesday; Sunderland & Bolton Wanderers

2 Wayne Bridge & Damien Duff

3 Ruud Gullit; Sampdoria

4 Mike Riley; Ruud van Nistelrooy; Wayne Rooney. The game proved a watershed for relations between the clubs as both Wenger and Ferguson came to realise things had gone too far. The inflammatory presence of Mourinho probably drew some of the fire.

5 Robert Pires and Jermaine Pennant

6 Roy Keane; Jason McAteer, who had been dismissive of Keane's account of the bust-up in the Irish camp at the 2002 World Cup

7 Sam Hammam; Cardiff City

8 Riyad Mahrez (Leicester City) & Nabil Bentaleb (Tottenham Hotspur)

9 Sam Allardyce; Steve Kean; Venky's

10 Nwankwo Kanu, Arsenal

11 Aaron Ramsey, Cardiff City

12 Andrew Johnson, Pavel Pogrebnyak, Clint Dempsey

13 Dick Advocaat; Gus Poyet

14 The brilliant Juninho and the less scintillating Branco, Doriva, Emerson and Fábio Rochemback

15 Middlesbrough, Fulham, Chelsea, Leicester City

Answers 84

1 Paolo Maldini

2 St Etienne

3 Internazionale; that's not English bias, the game stank

4 A nil-nil draw

5 Deportivo de La Coruña

6 Red Star Belgrade

7 Ruud Gullit; Carlo Ancelotti

8 Arsenal; Cristiano Ronaldo

9 Wayne Rooney

10 AC Milan and Inter; 1-0 to Milan, who had already won the first leg 2-0; Dida

11 Gaizka Mendieta; Middlesbrough

12 Tore André Flo (he also scored Chelsea's goal in the second leg); Anders Frisk, who years later would retire after receiving death threats for sending off Didier Drogba; Rivaldo

13 Italy, by some distance (twenty-two, compared with fourteen from Spain & Germany). Italy and Spain have had a similar number of finalists but Spanish clubs are much more likely to employ foreign coaches

14 Ray Clemence, Phil Neal, Emlyn Hughes, Jimmy Case, Ray Kennedy, Kevin Keegan

15 Blackburn Rovers, Leeds United & Tottenham Hotspur

Answers 85

1 Netball; Phil

2 Exactly the same sequence: West Ham 'keeper Tom McAlister saved the penalty only for Lee to score from the rebound

3 Countries represented by the referees of the last seven World Cup Finals

4 82,500

5 Joe Jordan moved from Manchester United to AC Milan

6 Duncan Shearer; Aberdeen

7 Steve Bruce, as manager of Hull City in 2014, picked his son, Alex Bruce

8 Yugoslavia; Patrick Kluivert & Marc Overmars; Frank De Boer, Phillip Cocu, Boudewijn Zenden & Ronald de Boer (the squad also included Michael Reiziger, also at Barcelona)

9 Bradford City (two spells) & Hull City (two spells plus a loan)

10 Manchester United, Bolton Wanderers, Bury & Wigan Athletic

11 Malaysia & Samoa

12 Torino

13 Plain old Lauren of Arsenal and Portsmouth

14 Luton Town, relegated in 1992, the summer before the Premier League started
15 Manchester City and Liverpool, probably United's two greatest rivals –
    Busby won his single Scotland cap while at City

Answers 86

1 Chelsea; Middlesbrough; because the top flight was being reduced to
   20 teams to lessen player fatigue over the season
2 Preston North End & Aston Villa
3 Tottenham Hotspur; it doesn't sound so innovative now but it was a
   definite shift away from longer passes and ball-carrying wingers and
   inside forwards
4 Clive Thomas; Mike Doyle and Lou Macari; he called the police; 0-0, it
   was a dull affair after the restart
5 Leeds United; Arsenal (Leeds lost out to three different sides, Arsenal
   suffered from the dominance of Manchester United)
6 Mickey Walsh
7 Kenny Swain
8 1986–87. Everton won the title, with Liverpool, Tottenham Hotspur &
   Arsenal second, third and fourth.
9 In court: Blissett was cleared of causing grievous bodily harm after
   catching Uzzell with his elbow in an aerial challenge
10 Keith Weller
11 Ipswich Town & Charlton Athletic
12 Pat Nevin, Clyde
13 Terry Hurlock
14 Clinton Morrison & Dougie Freedman
15 Michael Appleton; Blackburn Rovers

Answers 87

1 Marcel Desailly
2 Torino (Turin); Torino moved back in 2006 after sharing the Stadio
   delle Alpi with Juventus for a number of years
3 Sepp Herberger (1954), Helmut Schön (1974), Franz Beckenbauer
   (1990) and Joachim Löw (2014)

4 Roger Milla & Rigobert Song

5 North Korea

6 Brazil & Poland

7 Mexico

8 Tony Woodcock; 1. FC Köln (Cologne)

9 Roberto Baggio; Gianfranco Zola

10 Luis Monti; he played for Argentina in 1930 but was a nationalised Italian by the 1934 finals

11 Emilio Butragueño

12 Atlanta & Detroit

13 Dwight Yorke

14 Niko Kranjčar

15 Steven Gerrard, Jordan Henderson, Glen Johnson, Raheem Sterling & Daniel Sturridge

Answers 88

1 Jackie Milburn; Roberto Di Matteo; Manchester City & Middlesbrough

2 Denis Law, playing for Manchester City; Luton won the replayed game 3-1

3 Bury, who beat Derby County 6-0

4 Ipswich Town (against Arsenal in 1976)

5 All four Finals were played between London clubs

6 Ricardo Villa

7 Keith Houchen, Coventry City

8 Ruud Gullit, Gianluca Vialli, José Mourinho, Guus Hiddink, Carlo Ancelotti, Roberto Di Matteo

9 Wycombe Wanderers; Lawrie Sanchez (Wimbledon, 1988)

10 West Ham United in 1975; surprisingly, Liverpool in 1986 – they had four Scots and three Irishmen but no English except unused substitute Steve McMahon

11 Paul Scholes

12 Ben Watson; Manchester City, Pablo Zabaleta

13 Dave Beasant (Wimbledon, 1988)

14 Lionel Scaloni, for West Ham United in 2006

15 Jim McCalliog & Peter Osgood

Answers 89

1　Bristol Rovers
2　Bobby Moore was arrested in 1970, and accused of stealing a bracelet from a store in the hotel lobby
3　Radio Five
4　The players were listed alphabetically by surname and given the appropriate number
5　Arthur Ellis
6　Queen's Park (1884 and 1885)
7　Bobby Moore, Billy Wright
8　Sheffield Wednesday, to Arsenal in 1993
9　Eric Cantona
10　Switzerland; Paul Gascoigne; Alan Shearer & Teddy Sheringham
11　Philip Don, David Elleray, Dermot Gallagher, Paul Durkin, Graham Poll, Mike Riley, Jeff Winter, Rob Styles, Mike Dean, Howard Webb
12　Jürgen Klinsmann
13　Emile Heskey
14　Wolverhampton Wanderers (1938, 1939 & 1950); Manchester United (1947, 1948, 1949, 1951). United broke the sequence by winning in 1951–52, Wolves two years later
15　Swindon Town

Answers 90

1　Manchester City; Nicolas Anelka; Arsenal
2　Tottenham, Liverpool & Wigan
3　Gareth Barry; Lee Bowyer; Kevin Davies & Paul Scholes
4　Delia Smith (Michael Wynn Jones is her husband); Stephen Fry; former Shadow Chancellor Ed Balls
5　Stewart Houston; Bruce Rioch; Bolton Wanderers
6　Peter Crouch; Southampton
7　Philippe Senderos & Johan Djourou
8　Cantona scored 64 to Beckham's 62; Cole scored 93 so easily eclipses Eric; Scholes scored 107 to RvN's 95, but RvN's strike rate was exceptional

9   Marian Pahars, Southampton

10 Cardiff City in 2013–14

11 Avram Grant

12 Yannick Bolasie

13 Barnsley, Blackpool, Cardiff City & Swindon Town

14 Gudni Bergsson, Eidur Gudjohnsen, Arnar Gunnlaugsson & Grétar Steinsson

15 Leeds United, Newcastle United, Aston Villa, Manchester City & Liverpool

Answers 91

1   Fiorentina

2   Thessalonika

3   Olympique de Marseille & Saint-Étienne. The French League has been subject to less domination by one club – although the overseas money behind PSG is changing that and making it as boring as Italy, England, Germany and Spain, where the same clubs dominate year in year out

4   Eintracht Frankfurt; Meier would have won a lot more caps in less strong German eras

5   Leeds United (twice), Newcastle United, Arsenal, Tottenham Hotspur, Liverpool

6   Sheffield United

7   1. FC Nürnberg (9); Borussia Dortmund (8); Schalke 04 (7); Hamburg (6); Vfb Stuttgart & Borussia Mönchengladbach (5); Werder Bremen & 1. FC Kaiserslautern (4)

8   Diego Forlán

9   Diego Simeone; none

10 Jamie Carragher

11 Ronald Koeman; Erwin; he was Ronald's assistant head coach at Southampton

12 Klaas-Jan Huntelaar

13 The two Milan clubs, AC Milan and Internazionale

14 Dublin, Ireland

15 Peter Schmeichel

Answers 92

1 Norway (twice), Sweden (twice), England and Italy
2 The Home Depot Center, now called (equally prosaically) The Stub Hub Center
3 Abby Wambach, Mia Hamm, Kristine Lilly, Michelle Akers & Tiffeny Milbrett
4 Steph Houghton
5 Mark Sampson
6 They didn't, they failed to qualify
7 1969
8 Doncaster Rovers Belles
9 Alex Scott, Faye White, Casey Stoney, Fara Williams, Eniola Aluko, Kelly Smith
10 Chelsea & Arsenal
11 Hope Powell; Millwall
12 Australia
13 Norway; Brazil
14 The Matildas
15 Barnet

Answers 93

1 Club Brugge KV (Bruges)
2 Dion Dublin: Kendall was right, Dublin would have been a good acquisition
3 Albert Johanneson
4 PSV Eindhoven, Sporting Lisbon, Porto & Barcelona
5 Jamie Carragher, Steven Gerrard, John Terry, Frank Lampard and Joe Cole – Glen Johnson appeared as a substitute for Cole
6 Chelsea, Tottenham Hotspur, Queens Park Rangers, Crystal Palace; he never managed Chelsea
7 Pat Nevin
8 Stuart Pearce & Hope Powell
9 West Germany. Unfortunately for the 'Magical Magyars' it was in the 1954 World Cup Final

10 Stoke City; Tony Pulis

11 Bradford City (fourth tier) came back from 2-0 down at Stamford Bridge to knock Chelsea out of the FA Cup

12 Graeme Souness

13 Charlton claimed the pitch (which was a disgrace) was so heavily sanded the game could not be classified as played on turf

14 Chelsea – they won the title despite losing ten matches

15 Notts County; Sam Allardyce

Answers 94

1 Paul Scholes; Don Hutchison

2 Yugoslavia; Soviet Union

3 Spain (1964), West Germany (1972) & the Netherlands (1988)

4 Rob Rensenbrink

5 West Germany; QPR; Norman Whiteside – it was away defeats to Austria and Turkey that scuppered the North, they were superb against West Germany

6 Bryan Robson & Tony Adams; Marco van Basten

7 John Jensen, who struggled to find the net for Arsenal

8 Spain

9 Jacques Santini

10 Latvia

11 France

12 Gheorghe Hagi

13 Greece

14 Mario Gómez; Lars Bender; Mario Balotelli (Italy)

15 Wayne Hennessy, Ashley Williams, Joe Allen, Aaron Ramsey, Hal Robson-Kanu, Sam Vokes

Answers 95

1 Billy Bonds, Frank Lampard snr, Trevor Brooking, Bobby Moore and Alvin Martin

2 Nottingham (Forest & Notts County), Liverpool (Liverpool & Everton), Sheffield (United & The Wednesday)

3 Matt Busby; Frank O'Farrell

4 Workington (Town) & Barrow

5 Ray Kennedy; Liverpool

6 Bristol Rovers

7 Luton Town: it was a controversial decision that led to them being thrown out of the League Cup

8 Port Vale

9 Lee Clark; David Kelly; Andrew Cole

10 Chelsea v Fulham – the visitors had Moore, Best and Marsh in their team

11 Brian Clough; Middlesbrough

12 Coventry City

13 Reading; Bolton Wanderers; Crystal Palace

14 Marlon King; Wigan Athletic

15 Blackpool

Answers 96

1 1978: Danny McGrain would have played had he not been injured, but Celtic were at a low ebb

2 Hartford, with 50 (Gemmill 43, Wark 29, Rioch only 24)

3 Richard Gough; Dundee United; Tottenham Hotspur; Stockholm

4 Willie Miller & Mark McGhee

5 It was the first Scottish Cup Final to be held at Hampden Park.

6 Wim Jansen

7 Stranraer in Dumfries and Galloway; it is slightly South of Annan in the same county, home of Annan Athletic

8 Tommy Coyne

9 Pittodrie (Aberdeen) & Easter Road (Hibernian)

10 Rudi Skacel; Hibernian

11 Baker was English, born in Liverpool to Scottish parents but capped by England in 1959

12 Christian Dailly

13 Weir scored once in his 69 games, the others played 26, 35 and 62 times without scoring – McGrain is surpassed by Alex Mcleish who failed to find the net in 77 internationals. Fernando Hierro they ain't

14 Willie Ormond, Andy Roxburgh, Berti Vogts, Craig Levein
15 Tommy Gemmell, John Greig, Eddie McCreadie, Billy Bremner, Jim Baxter, Jim McCalliog, Denis Law

Answers 97

1 Doncaster Rovers
2 Catenaccio
3 Eddie Hapgood
4 John Robertson (he edged Stuart Pearce into second place on both occasions)
5 Norway
6 Cocu and Van der Sar share the same birth date – 29 October 1970
7 O'Neill. Martin was appointed manager of the Republic in 2013, his namesake Michael had already been in charge of the North's team since 2011
8 Melbourne Cricket Ground (usually referred to simply as the MCG)
9 Malta, Macedonia (they are from Skopje), Poland, Gibraltar, Norway, Lithuania, Republic of Ireland, Hungary and Bulgaria. Celtic and Steaua Bucharest were both in the same round (both won but were eliminated in the third round of qualifying)
10 Chris Iwelumo
11 1995; Littlewood's
12 Neil Harris; Alan Stubbs; Harris was back at Millwall, Stubbs was managing Hibernian
13 FC Brugge (Bruges)
14 Jimmy Adamson
15 Peter Mandelson

Answers 98

1 Francisco Gento
2 Benfica; Barcelona
3 Arthur Ellis
4 Red Star Belgrade (Crvena Zvezda) & Olympique Marseille
5 Frank Rijkaard

6 Fabien Barthez

7 Ronaldo; David Beckham – his intervention gave United a 4-3 win on the night but Real won the first leg 3-1 and so went through

8 Mark Clattenburg

9 Tassotti, Maldini, Baresi and Costacurta

10 Mark van Bommel

11 Porto

12 Rinus Michels (Ajax, 1971), Guus Hiddink (PSV, 1988), Johan Cruyff (Barcelona, 1992), Louis van Gaal (Ajax, 1995) & Frank Rijkaard (Barcelona, 2006)

13 Pierluigi Collina

14 Bruce Grobbelaar, Mark Lawrenson, Alan Hansen, Graeme Souness, Ronnie Whelan, Ian Rush

15 Partizan Belgrade

Answers 99

1 Trevor Francis, David Platt & Des Walker

2 Steve Bull, Wolverhampton Wanderers

3 Peter Reid

4 Zat Knight & Bobby Zamora

5 Brian Deane & Andy Hinchcliffe

6 Alex Stepney

7 Paul Scholes, David Beckham, Teddy Sheringham

8 Malcolm Macdonald

9 Gareth Southgate

10 Chris Waddle

11 Howard Wilkinson, Peter Taylor

12 Leicester City, Stoke City, Nottingham Forest, Southampton, Derby County

13 He broke the infamous metatarsal bone of David Beckham during a Champions League match

14 Ashley Cole & Sol Campbell

15 Defoe won most caps (55, more opportunities in modern game), Crouch scored most goals (22 in 42 matches, a better strike rate than Rooney, Shearer, Owen or Defoe, his main contemporaries)

Answers 100

1 Portsmouth; the Zambian international turned up late and overweight after struggling to get a work permit – his caps for Zambia didn't cut much mustard as their FIFA ranking was so low. He made four appearances for Pompey, all as a substitute

2 Vieira, Wiltord, Henry, Pires and subs Grimandi and Aliadière for Arsenal; Goma, Malbranque, Legwinski, Marlet and sub Saha for Fulham.

3 Geoffrey Richmond; Benito Carbone

4 Gavin Peacock; theology (at Cambridge) – Peacock later gave up his work as a TV pundit and moved with his family to Canada to further his studies with a view to becoming a Minister. Not your average footballer

5 Steve Marlet

6 Graeme Le Saux; David O'Leary

7 Ipswich Town; George Burley

8 Mark Palios; CEO of the Royal Mail

9 Steffen Iversen; John Scales

10 Patrick Vieira

11 Mikael Forssell

12 Andy Johnson, and he scored a scarcely credible eleven penalties, most of them won himself – either refs had a soft spot or his pace was too much for defenders (or he was good at . . .)

13 Tony Yeboah

14 Arsenal; Tony Adams; Arsène Wenger became the first overseas coach to win the league title in England

15 Tottenham Hotspur, Charlton Athletic, Middlesbrough, Aston Villa, Queens Park Rangers

Answers 101

1 Tottenham won the first Double of the twentieth century – it was the 1961 FA Cup Final

2 1934, 1966, 1982 and 2006

3 The UEFA Cup

4 Black; allegedly the order came down from Mussolini's office that the team must wear the colour emblematic of fascism

5 Calais; Watford; Antoine Sibierski

6 Italy, they beat Sweden 1-0 and drew 0-0 with Uruguay and Israel

7 Matt Le Tissier

8 Ireland; Dublin

9 Chelsea & Millwall

10 Alan McLoughlin

11 Mark Schwarzer, Gareth Southgate, Franck Queudrue, Doriva, Boudewijn Zenden, Gaizka Mendieta; Michael Ricketts; Steve McLaren

12 Intertoto Cup

13 The Stevens Report. The report was requested after an inflammatory BBC investigation was broadcast, but no defamation charges were made against the BBC

14 Tommy Docherty; Bobby Tambling

15 Goalkeeper Mart Poom

Answers 102

1 Anfield, Liverpool

2 Total Network Solutions FC

3 Leicester City

4 John Toshack; Toshack himself; sixth; Bob Latchford; Robbie James

5 Robert Earnshaw

6 David Phillips, Kevin Ratcliffe, Paul Bodin, Mark Hughes, Dean Saunders

7 Scotland; Gareth Bale; Hal Robson-Kanu

8 Cyprus

9 Gareth Bale

10 Cardiff Arms Park, the rugby ground; Ian Rush; Terry Yorath

11 Robert Earnshaw, and he scored 16 goals in 59 games

12 Pat Van den Hauwe

13 Forty-one; modern wide player Simon Davies and Dai Davies, goalkeeper in the late 1970s and early '80s, supplanted by Neville Southall

14 John Hartson with Celtic

15 Gary Speed with Leeds United in 1992–93

Answers 103

1 Bolton Wanderers; John McGinlay & Nathan Blake; Barnsley, Neil Redfearn

2 Aston Villa

3 Jack Rowley; Leicester City

4 Everton

5 Roy McFarland & Colin Todd

6 Nottingham Forest (1977–78)

7 Howard Kendall

8 John Aldridge; Oxford United; Tranmere Rovers

9 Newcastle United

10 Shaun Goater

11 Wolverhampton Wanderers, Jack Hayward

12 Manchester United; Lawrie McMenemy & John Bond; Tommy Docherty; Luton Town & Carlisle United (the following season Carlisle and Luton went straight back down while United and Norwich came back up)

13 Neil Warnock

14 Leicester City (it was the Walkers Stadium, crisp was a clue); old boy Gary Lineker did the honours

15 Jordan Rhodes

Answers 104

1 Bryan Ruiz; Fulham, PSV Eindhoven

2 Egypt

3 Grosics; Bozsik; Czibor, Hidegkuti, Puskás.

4 Norman Whiteside of Northern Ireland

5 Chile (despite the best efforts of the appalling officials) were beaten by Brazil and Yugoslavia were beaten by a less talented but more resolute Czechoslovakia

6 Geoff Hurst

7 Grzegorz Lato

8 Algeria. Both players are legends in North African football – Madjer could make a decent claim to be the region's finest-ever player; West Germany

9   Canada

10 Michel Platini & Sócrates

11 Costa Rica; Andy Roxburgh

12 Lars Bohinen & Alf-Inge Haaland

13 Rivaldo

14 Angola, Ghana, Côte d'Ivoire, Togo

15 Switzerland; Ottmar Hitzfeld

Answers 105

1   Zico; Téofilo Cubillas

2   Oxford United

3   Eduard Streltsov; to this day it is unclear whether the charges were
    fabricated (Streltsov was viewed with deep suspicion by the authorities
    – he was a party animal and, allegedly, a womaniser) or genuine (he was
    a party animal . . .)

4   Ronald and Erwin Koeman; Frank and Ronald de Boer

5   Jules Rimet

6   Leicester City; Dougie Freedman

7   Yeovil Town; the giant killing stopped once Yeovil entered the Football
    League

8   Manchester United

9   Mick Flanagan & Clive Allen; John Gregory

10 Paul Gascoigne

11 Boudewijn Zenden; 57

12 Swansea City

13 Joel & Avram

14 It was Andy Lochhead, who would have bagged a few caps for Scotland
    if his career hadn't paralleled that of Denis Law; Roger Hunt

15 Jimmy Adamson, Jimmy Mullen, Stan Ternent, Owen Coyle, Eddie
    Howe, Sean Dyche

Answers 106

1   Darren Huckerby & Robbie Keane

2   It was the first Premier League match televised on BSkyB

3 £251M, with a net spend of £117M to United's £28M

4 The ever-charming Rupert Lowe; David Jones, wrongly and disgracefully accused of abusing boys in his care and left out to dry by Lowe

5 Sylvain Distin; Newcastle United, Manchester City, Portsmouth, Everton

6 Mick Quinn

7 Robert Koren; Hull City

8 Michael Owen

9 Sander Westerveld; Brad Friedel; Pierre van Hooijdonk

10 Robbie Keane & David Bentley. Neither were a great success; Keane moved back to White Hart Lane for £5M less the following year and Bentley just slid from view, retiring at 30 after various half-hearted loan spells

11 Norwich City

12 Shearer scored ten penalties; Chris Sutton; David Batty (Leeds, 1991–92); Henning Berg at Manchester United & Chris Sutton with Celtic

13 Jimmy Floyd Hasselbaink, Didier Drogba, Frank Lampard & Diego Costa

14 Manchester United bought Karel Poborsky and Liverpool bought Patrik Berger

15 Portsmouth, Bolton Wanderers, West Ham United, Burnley

Answers 107

1 Go Ahead Eagles are based in Deventer in the Netherlands, the Super Eagles are Nigeria

2 Trinidad and Tobago

3 All Whites

4 Estudiantes are an Argentinian side who play in La Plata, and they were playing Milan, having beaten Manchester United the previous year in another brutal encounter

5 Dunga, in 1998, he was with Jubilo Iwata

6 They were officially the two worst sides in FIFA's rankings (202 & 203)

7 Argentina

8 Ronaldo & Rivaldo

9 Nigeria; Efan Ekoku

10 Rafael Márquez

11 Saudi Arabia

12 Zimbabwe

13 Geremi & Celestine Babayaro

14 Morocco; Equatorial Guinea

15 Cameroon (the most with 7), Nigeria (5), Algeria, Morocco, Tunisia (4), Côte d'Ivoire, Ghana, South Africa (3), Egypt (2)

Answers 108

1 McAllister. Despite periods in the wilderness, he had a long career and won 57 caps; Souness and Bremner both won 54, Strachan 50

2 St Mirren

3 Craig Brown

4 It was the first season that neither Celtic nor Rangers won a trophy

5 Arsenal

6 Gough, Gray, Jordan & Lorimer all took the long walk of shame

7 Michael Higdon; Nijmegen – little good it did them, they went straight back down, although Higdon scored a respectable 14 goals

8 St Johnstone against Raith Rovers

9 Frank McGarvey

10 Ross County, Inverness & Caledonian Thistle, Peterhead, Elgin City

11 2002; Rangers won 3-2 and Peter Lovenkrands scored twice

12 Gary Caldwell

13 Steven Pressley

14 Denis Law

15 Jim Leighton, Colin Hendry, Christian Dailly, Jackie McNamara, Paul Lambert, John Collins, Kevin Gallacher, Gordon Durie

Answers 109

1 England & Italy

2 The goal, equalising a late Celtic goal, sparked off a crush that ended up with 66 people dead

3 Luciano Pavarotti & Sophia Loren

4 One of the Russian players (Yegor Titov) later tested positive for a banned substance; the appeal was denied

5 Peter Beardsley

6 Liverpool & Chelsea won, Celtic, Middlesbrough, Rangers & Fulham all lost

7 Jean-Marc Bosman – it was the move that initiated his court case

8 Birmingham City to Nottingham Forest

9 Dmitri Kharine (Russia)

10 Andy Booth

11 It contained no Scottish players

12 Michel Platini

13 Number 8

14 Ron Davies

15 Plymouth Argyle, Exeter City, Yeovil Town, AFC Bournemouth, Southampton, Portsmouth, Crawley Town, Brighton & Hove Albion

Answers 110

1 Costa Rica; David De Gea

2 Austria

3 Helmut Rahn

4 Garrincha; he was sent off in the semi but reprieved on appeal – he wouldn't have got away with it now, the incident was a clear red card

5 Alan Ball

6 It rose from nine to twenty-seven (of the nine in 1970, five were Swedish)

7 West Germany & Austria

8 Jorge Burruchaga

9 Diego Forlán. He never settled at United, one of the few that got away under Alex Ferguson

10 The game ended: FIFA were using the 'Golden Goal' – essentially first goal wins if the game is in extra time

11 Northern Ireland

12 Stig Tofting, Les Ferdinand, Vincent Candela & Youri Djorkaeff, Ricardo Gardner, Hidetoshi Nakata, Jay-Jay Okocha, Colin Hendry, Ivan Campo & Fernando Hierro

13 Portugal. They cried foul but, unlike Spain and Italy later in the competition, they had no cause – both red cards were deserved and Couto should have followed for manhandling the referee

14 Fabien Barthez, Lilian Thuram & Zinedine Zidane started in both 1998 and 2006, while Patrick Vieira came on as a sub in 1998 and started in 2006

15 David Villa

Answers 111

1 Julio Baptista

2 Wayne Rooney

3 Charlie Nicholas; George Graham

4 Sheffield United

5 Matt Elliott; Tranmere Rovers

6 Gordon Banks; Peter Bonetti

7 Luton Town had a ban on away fans, but the Football League had not endorsed the ban and exercised their right to throw Luton out of the competition

8 Steffan Iversen; Tony Cottee

9 Burnley; Derby County

10 Middlesbrough; Steve Claridge

11 Queens Park Rangers; it was a one-off game played at Wembley rather than home and away over two legs

12 Aston Villa, Manchester United & Tottenham Hotspur

13 Obafemi Martins; Alex McLeish, Stephen Carr

14 Jerzy Dudek

15 Tranmere Rovers; Dalian Atkinson; John Aldridge; Manchester United; Dean Saunders

Answers 112

1 Bobby Stokes, Lawrie McMenemy; Peter Rodrigues; Manchester United

2 Altrincham

3 Northampton Town

4 Nat Lofthouse

5 Twice, in 1997 and 2000 (in 1970 the Final went to a replay and Chelsea won at Old Trafford)

6 Charlton Athletic

7 Newcastle United; Teddy Sheringham

8 Manchester City; Joey Barton

9 Mickey Thomas

10 David Elleray; Elleray failed to justify his decision in a bizarre and atten-tion-seeking post-match interview – had the 'goal' stood it would have left Middlesbrough 3-1 down with ten men and less than twenty minutes to go. Sean Dyche converted a penalty after Kevin Davies was fouled, and Jamie Hewitt scored a late equaliser after Chesterfield went 3-2 down

11 Mikel Arteta & Per Mertesacker

12 He was the first to score in successive FA Cup Finals

13 Didier Deschamps, Marcel Desailly & Franck Leboeuf

14 Roy Carroll, Tim Howard & Edwin van der Sar

15 Steve Perryman & Paul Power – both were good, consistent players who were unlucky not to win more international recognition, but it was Perryman who won a cap

Answers 113

1 Clive Thomas; it was a typical piece of attention seeking from Thomas. For once FIFA made a good call and didn't give him another game

2 Neil Ruddock

3 Alex Stepney, Martin Buchan, Arthur Albiston, Sammy McIlroy, Gordon Hill, Stuart Pearson

4 Rangers

5 Don Revie

6 Parc des Princes

7 John Hartson

8 Goalkeeper Packie Bonner & right back Chris Morris

9 Kevin Phillips

10 Jürgen Klinsmann

11 Jonathon Spector; West Ham United, Carlton Cole; Birmingham City

12   Best scored nine times in 39 games for Northern Ireland; like another
     Manchester United legend, Ryan Giggs, he was often unavailable and
     enjoyed far greater success in club football

13   Rune Hauge

14   Joe Mercer (1967–68), Roberto Mancini (2011–12), Manuel Pellegrini
     (2013–14)

15   Norwich City, Ipswich Town, Colchester United, Southend United &
     Gillingham

Answers 114

1   Derek Dougan

2   Dundee United; IFK Gothenburg

3   César Azpilicueta, Juan Mata & Fernando Torres; Branislav Ivanović,
    Rafa Benítez, Benfica

4   Birmingham City in the Inter-Cities Fairs Cup in 1960

5   Radamel Falcao; James Rodríguez; Braga

6   Lokomotiv Plovdiv; Olympique de Marseille

7   Madrid

8   Sampdoria

9   Budapest

10 Merthyr Tydfil

11 Matthias Sammer

12 Olympique de Marseille; Rafael Benítez

13 Zbigniew Boniek

14 Thierry Henry & Robert Pires; Pires scored in a 1-0 win; Luis Suárez &
    Lionel Messi. Maybe that's the difference between two outstanding
    players and two unbelievable ones

15 Winning the Swedish top division

Answers 115

1   Steve Ogrizovic & Gary McAllister; Dion Dublin

2   Kolo Touré & Gervinho

3   West Ham United, Harry Redknapp

4   Terry Venables

5 Michael Ricketts

6 Jürgen Klinsmann – he finished as Spurs' top scorer despite playing only 15 games

7 Marco Materazzi

8 Felix Magath

9 Gianluca Vialli; Tore André Flo; Andrew Cole

10 Chris Sutton (jointly with two others) in 1997–98

11 Michu

12 West Ham United

13 Brian Little, Graham Taylor again, Gérard Houllier, Alex McLeish and Tim Sherwood. Atkinson, Gregory, O'Neill and Little all had over 40 per cent win rates.

14 Ugo Ehiogu

15 Jamie Carragher, Steven Gerrard, Paul Scholes, John Terry, Gary Neville, Jason Dodd, Gary Kelly, Sami Hyypia, Denis Bergkamp, Leon Osman, Lee Dixon, Gabriel Agbonlahor

Answers 116

1 Danny Tiatto; Shaun Goater & Darren Huckerby; Richard Dunne

2 Ted Drake; Roy Bentley

3 Denis Law (5 times), George Best (4), David Herd (2)

4 Everton; they were founder members of the league and have only been relegated twice, spending four seasons in the second tier

5 Sheffield Wednesday

6 Accrington Stanley; Oxford United

7 Joe Royle; David Johnson (Johnson moved to Ipswich at the end of the season and on to Liverpool in 1976)

8 Nottingham Forest (1977–78)

9 Luther Blissett; Ally McCoist

10 Nigel Clough

11 Cardiff City

12 John Sheridan; Oldham Athletic

13 Fulham & Wigan Athletic; Cardiff City, Hull City & Swansea City

14 Dennis Wise

15 Glenn Murray; his former club Brighton

Answers 117

1 Bebeto
2 Buenos Aires, Argentina; the River Plate stadium, after the famous club who play their home games there
3 Bolton Wanderers (1953)
4 Silvio Piola. He remains Lazio's top scorer in Serie A
5 Michael Ballack; Bayer Leverkusen & Chelsea; 1. FC Kaiserslautern, Bayern Munich (3) & Chelsea
6 Paul Gascoigne
7 Peter Ward
8 Sheffield United & Sheffield Wednesday
9 Jaap Stam, who joined later in the summer – he had come and gone by the time the other one, Edwin van der Sar, moved to Old Trafford in 2005
10 Stan Collymore; Nottingham Forest
11 York City
12 Jan Ceulemans (the closest current player, at the end of the 2016 European Championships, is Jan Vertonghen with 81)
13 Gabriel Heinze
14 Don Revie in 1969 & 1974, Howard Wilkinson in 1992
15 Scarborough, Maidstone United, Kidderminster Harriers, Macclesfield Town, Rushden & Diamonds, Boston United

Answers 118

1 John Connelly
2 He was from Denmark (Kim Milton Nielsen), and he got it wrong; Diego Simeone
3 None. Bright was unlucky, worse players have several
4 World Cup winner George Cohen
5 Matty Jarvis
6 Kerry Dixon
7 Keown, with 43
8 Terry Butcher and Russell Osman
9 Duncan Edwards and Stanley Matthews

10 Gary Lineker scored all of them – the five points are yours if you answer Gary Lineker only, otherwise it's just one point!

11 Viv Anderson; in 1978

12 Kevin Keegan; Hamburg; Glenn Hoddle

13 Trevor Sinclair; Danny Murphy

14 Stadium of Light, Sunderland; Michael Owen and David Beckham

15 Tom Finney & Nat Lofthouse

Answers 119

1 Iran

2 Because Austria had been absorbed into Germany in March 1938, only months before the tournament began

3 Kenneth Wolstenholme: Zimmerman's commentary when West Germany scored their third goal in the 1954 World Cup Final is as legendary as Wolstenholme's 'They think it's all over . . .' from 1966. 'Tor! Tor! Tor! Tor für Deutschland . . .' (etc, etc!)

4 Diego Maradona (16)

5 He was the first player to be sent off in the finals

6 Denílson

7 Albert Shesternev

8 Giorgio Chiellini

9 Bolivia

10 Raí

11 Sammy McIlroy

12 Sweden

13 David Seaman; Gary Neville, Tony Adams, Sol Campbell, Graeme Le Saux; David Beckham, Paul Scholes, Paul Ince, Darren Anderton; Alan Shearer, Michael Owen. Subs: Gareth Southgate, David Batty & Paul Merson. Shearer scored from the penalty spot and Owen scored a sensational solo goal

14 Robbie Keane

15 Thomas Müller

Answers 120

1 Gerard Piqué; Samuel Eto'o; Piqué won with Manchester United and Barça, while Eto'o repeated the feat with Barça and Internazionale
2 Alfredo di Stéfano & Ferenc Puskás
3 Glasgow Rangers; Wolverhampton Wanderers – Barca lost to Real in the semis
4 Didier Deschamps
5 Ajax; Johan Cruyff
6 Gianluigi Lentini
7 El Beatle
8 Hernán Crespo
9 Giovane Elber; Valencia – the game finished 1-1 but even those goals were from the penalty spot
10 Vfb Stuttgart
11 Lyon
12 Bordeaux; Lyon
13 Howard Webb
14 Edwin van der Sar, Frank de Boer, Frank Rijkaard, Edgar Davids, Clarence Seedorf, Nwankwo Kanu, Marc Overmars, Jari Litmanen. That was some array of talent . . .
15 Rosenborg, from Trondheim in Norway – Gothenburg are next with four

Answers 121

1 1974
2 1982. They didn't
3 Uwe Seeler
4 Gabriel Heinze
5 Ally MacLeod; Dave Whelan
6 John Barnes
7 Pat Jennings
8 David Beckham & Owen Hargreaves
9 Goldstone Ground; Gillingham; Withdean; The Amex; Doncaster Rovers

10 Sheffield United and West Bromwich Albion; Neil Warnock (surprise, surprise), the Sheffield United manager. Justice was eventually done as West Brom were sensibly awarded the three points

11 Des Walker, Stuart Pearce, Neil Webb, Steve Hodge, Nigel Clough

12 Gheorghe Hagi

13 Edu

14 Francis Lee; Dimitar Berbatov

15 Dave Mackay; Pat Jennings; Bruce Rioch

Answers 122

1 Ascunción in Paraguay

2 99. Viduka won 43 in 13 years, Kewell 56 in 16 years – both were regularly unavailable because they played in Europe (and Kewell was injury-prone), otherwise the 227 figure would have been more likely

3 Kaká

4 Independiente

5 Panama have never qualified, the others have all played in one finals tournament

6 Grampus 8 (from Nagoya)

7 Forty years, they won in 1989, and never in between despite being three-time winners of the World Cup in that time

8 Honduras

9 Hugo Rodallega, Fulham

10 Uganda; Ghana

11 Lucas Radebe, Quinton Fortune & Mark Fish

12 Inter Milan

13 Didier Drogba, who scored, and Samuel Eto'o, who didn't. Cruelly, after scoring the only goal in the semi-final, Drogba missed his spot-kick in the shoot-out against Egypt in the Final

14 22; Senegal & Côte d'Ivoire with four each

15 South Korea (9), Japan (5), Saudi Arabia, Iran (4), North Korea (2), Dutch East Indies, China, Kuwait, Iraq & United Arab Emirates (1)

Answers 123

1 Gerry Armstrong
2 Oldham Athletic
3 Leeds United, Liverpool & Manchester City
4 Kevin Keegan & John Toshack
5 Gary Lineker
6 Roger Byrne; Mark Jones
7 Queens Park Rangers; Alec Stock (Stock suffered from asthma, and was absent for much of the following season before being unceremoniously dismissed); Fulham, in 1975
8 Leyton Orient
9 Queens Park Rangers, 1981
10 Mick Jones (14), Allan Clarke (13), Peter Lorimer (12), Billy Bremner (10)
11 Ron Davies (1967), Mick Channon (1974), Phil Boyer (1980), Kevin Keegan (1982)
12 Bolton Wanderers; Phil Neal
13 David Hopkin
14 David Johnson & Marlon Harewood
15 Ross McCormack

Answers 124

1 Jim Leighton; Aberdeen; Alex Ferguson
2 Billy McNeill
3 John Barnes
4 Liam Brady
5 1977 – over-enthusiastic is being kind
6 Jimmy Johnstone
7 Hibernian
8 Aberdeen, Heart of Midlothian, Hibernian
9 Brian McClair
10 Mark Viduka
11 Hamilton Academicals; Alex Neil
12 Paul Lambert & Ian Ferguson

13   Craig Gordon
14   Hampden Park, Celtic Park, Ibrox
15   Stefan Klos, Claudio Reyna, Craig Moore, Artur Numan, Giovanni van Bronckhorst, Andrei Kanchelskis, Barry Ferguson, Billy Dodds

Answers 125

1   Yakubu
2   All their fathers also played in the World Cup finals
3   Sherwood, Watford
4   Ray Clemence
5   Mark Hughes; Barcelona
6   Louis Saha (27), Luís Boa Morte (18) & Barry Hayles (18); Maik Taylor, Steve Finnan & Lee Clark
7   Martin Buchan; Aberdeen
8   Alan Ball, sacked soon after the start of the season, Steve Coppell, who resigned, citing stress, after 33 days, and Frank Clark, who stabilised the club and kept them in Division 1 (second tier)
9   He was the trainer (physio)
10   Pelé's no.10 Brazil shirt
11   Peter Schmeichel & Andrei Kanchelskis; Roy Keane & Teddy Sheringham
12   Boca Juniors; Sevilla
13   Mark Bosnich
14   Ted MacDougall
15   Play-offs. In the Test Matches the bottom teams in the First Division played the top teams in the Second Division to see who was most deserving of a place at the top table

Answers 126

1   Sepp Maier, Georg Schwarzenbeck, Franz Beckenbauer, Uli Hoeness & Gerd Müller
2   Internazionale; they appealed and won a replay after Roberto Boninsegna was hit and had to be replaced
3   Bodo Illgner

4   AC Milan; Shinsuke Nakamura

5   Juventus

6   Because a mindless selection of Chelsea supporters issued death threats against him in various online forums after he'd sent off Didier Drogba

7   Jupp Heynckes (Munich) & Jürgen Klopp (Dortmund)

8   Borussia Mönchengladbach

9   Barcelona: unlucky, yes, but City should have done better in the group stage and won their mini-league

10 Miroslav Klose

11 Edu

12 Andrei Shevchenko; Filippo Inzaghi

13 Bob Paisley & Carlo Ancelotti

14 Christian Karembeu, Zinedine Zidane, Nicolas Anelka, Claude Makélélé, Raphael Varane & Karim Benzema

15 Ray Crawford; Malta

Answers 127

1   The Wanderers

2   Jackie Milburn

3   Dickie Guy; AFC Wimbledon

4   Keith Houchen

5   Arsenal (in 1971 & 1979)

6   Cardiff City

7   Bolton Wanderers, West Ham United

8   Leicester City

9   Lee Dixon, Tony Adams, Andy Linighan, Paul Merson, Ian Wright, Alan Smith

10 Eric Cantona

11 Don Revie & Bill Shankly

12 Hereford United; Ronnie Radford & Ricky George; John Motson

13 Freddie Ljungberg

14 Nwankwo Kanu

15 Nine-nil; Alan Pardew; Gary O'Reilly; Ian Wright; Lee Martin

Answers 128

1   A Second Division
2   Alan Shearer; Southampton
3   Frank Clark; Stan Collymore
4   Leeds City; newly formed Leeds United were admitted direct to the Second Division at the expense of second bottom club Lincoln City, who were demoted to the newly formed Third Division
5   Stan Cullis; three; Billy Wright
6   They came on the same day, a famous selection of Boxing Day fixtures in which ten matches yielded 66 goals
7   Aston Villa
8   Ted Drake
9   Wigan Athletic; Rochdale, who have managed to hang on to league status despite long spells in the bottom tier while supposedly bigger clubs have fallen out
10 Bristol Rovers
11 Bolton Wanderers, Bury & Wigan Athletic
12 Paul Gascoigne; Roberto Di Matteo
13 Barry Fry
14 Chris Nicholl
15 Scunthorpe United, Southend United, Carlisle United, Doncaster Rovers, Tranmere Rovers, Preston North End, Notts County, Fulham

Answers 129

1   Dion Dublin
2   Roy Keane
3   Real Madrid, Bayern Munich, Barcelona, AC Milan, Manchester United, Juventus
4   The Royal Engineers, they beat Old Etonians in 1875
5   Lothar Matthäus
6   Italy – England needed to win by four
7   Oldham Athletic; Arsenal, Southampton & Leeds United; Manchester United; promotion to the top flight for the first time in nearly seventy years; Joe Royle

8 Luděk Miklǒsko

9 Niall Quinn

10 It was (c), although the others are plausible

11 AFC Wimbledon; they play at Kingsmeadow, also the home ground of Kingstonian FC

12 Steve Morrow; Tony Adams picked him up during the post-match celebrations and dropped him on his shoulder – he missed the rest of the season, including the FA Cup Final

13 Yordan Letchkov; Hamburg

14 Southport

15 He was struck by lightning while sheltering under a tree in a storm during a round of golf

Answers 130

1 Giuseppe Meazza; he played for both of the big Milanese clubs who share the stadium, so his name was deemed appropriate (and he was a genuinely great player)

2 Jackie Mudie; both Mudie and Scotland failed to shine in the finals and he was never picked again

3 Faryd Mondragon (43 years and 3 days)

4 Pedro Monzón & Gustavo Dezotti (Argentina, 1990); Marcel Desailly (France, 1990); Zinedine Zidane (France, 2006); John Heitinga (Netherlands, 2010)

5 Téofilo Cubillas

6 Someone scored a goal – Erwin Vandenbergh of Belgium, who won 1-0. The previous four tournaments had all endured tortuous 0-0 draws in their opening fixtures

7 Mali & Sierra Leone (DRC qualified as Zaire in 1974)

8 César Luis Menotti (1978) & Carlos Bilardo (1986)

9 Ronaldinho; Michael Owen

10 Jan Koller; Milan Baros

11 Leonardo; Branco

12 Switzerland

13 Vieri's career split the Finals of 1994 and 2006, while Nesta was unluckily injured in a group match in 2006. Baggio, Baresi & Maldini all played in the 1994 team that lost to Brazil

14 Asamoah Gyan, their lone forward, who had a splendid tournament. To his enormous credit he stepped forward and took the first penalty in the shoot-out and scored. The handball was by Luis Suárez (of course it was)

15 Brazil (in Sweden in 1958 and Japan/South Korea in 2002); Spain (in South Africa in 2010); Germany (in Brazil in 2014)

Answers 131

1 Colin Viljoen

2 Alf Ramsey; Tottenham Hotspur

3 Joe Mercer

4 In order of first cap: Mick Mills, Kevin Beattie, Colin Viljoen, David Johnson, Paul Mariner, Brian Talbot, Trevor Whymark, Terry Butcher, Russell Osman, Eric Gates; Butcher (45 to Mills' 42); goalkeeper Richard Wright

5 Luther Blissett

6 Michael Owen

7 Saudi Arabia

8 Mark Wright

9 Switzerland beat England twice, in 1938 and 1981

10 Jonjo Shelvey

11 Sixty-five

12 Geoff Hurst

13 Three

14 Gary Cahill; Bolton Wanderers

15 Frank Lampard jnr (29), David Platt (27), Bryan Robson (26)

Answers 132

1 Billy Bingham, who played in the 1958 finals and was manager in both 1982 and 1986

2 Derek Spence. He only managed three goals in 29 games for Northern Ireland, and in the main had a lower division career, although he was enterprising enough to try spells at Olympiakos and Sparta Rotterdam

3 Michael Hughes; Crystal Palace

4 None of them scored a goal – Chris Baird, with 77 caps and now thirty-three years old, may be joining this shot-shy elite

5 Danny Blanchflower

6 Noel Brotherston; Terry Cochrane

7 Rangers

8 Arsenal & Hull City; Tottenham Hotspur

9 Jimmy Nicholl; Gerry Armstrong – Northern Ireland scored only six goals in eight games but their defence was solid, letting in only three; Scotland

10 Billy Hamilton

11 Pat Rice & Sammy Nelson; Nelson won 51 (Rice was the better player but the competition at left back was less stiff; Rice and Jimmy Nicholl overlapped, whereas Mal Donaghy was a direct replacement for Nelson)

12 Willoughby beat William Renshaw to win the Wimbledon Men's Singles title in 1890

13 Daniel Lafferty, both he and Kyle have played for Burnley

14 Jimmy Nicholl, Chris Nicholl, Mal Donaghy, Martin O'Neill, Sammy McIlroy, Norman Whiteside, Billy Hamilton

15 Olphert Stanfield, the first great of Northern Ireland football – he scored ten goals in 30 games and was a legend at the Distillery club in County Down

Answers 133

1 Spain

2 Johnstone's Paint, it is the knock-out trophy for teams from the two lower divisions of the Football League

3 Switzerland; Trello gained 52 caps before dying in a train accident in 1944; Max (68 caps) was Switzerland's top scorer (34) until Alexander Frei broke the record in the twenty-first century. A third brother, Jean, also gained three caps for his country

4 The Lightning Seeds

5 Charlie Nicholas, five

6 Andoni Zubizarreta

7 Thiago Motta

8 Nigeria; Kanu

9 Oxford United; they were in the First Division (top tier) having won promotion at the end of the previous season; Ray Houghton & John Aldridge

10 They were a student team from Bath University, the first to appear in the competition proper for 122 years

11 Brad Friedel, Henning Berg, Keith Gillespie, Mark Hughes, Damien Duff, Andrew Cole. Graeme Souness.

12 He is Maradona's son-in-law

13 Aston Villa

14 Billy Bremner & Norman Hunter

15 Mick Channon; horse racing, he is a trainer of some note

Answers 134

1 Blackburn Rovers & Liverpool; Henrik Larsson, Chris Sutton, John Hartson & Alan Thompson

2 The top division in Polish club football

3 Udinese. He was top scorer in Serie A in 2009–10 and 2010–11 – a good effort in a team that finished fifteenth in that first season. Even more impressive for a guy standing at 5'7" in an era of strapping giants.

4 Real Madrid

5 Stan Bowles

6 Gianfranco Zola; Dennis Wise; Gianluca Vialli; Joachim Löw

7 Dino & Roberto Baggio

8 Jim Leighton

9 Dnipro Dnipropetrovsk; Sevilla

10 Wigan Athletic; Tottenham Hotspur – it went downhill thereafter: Pascal, alas, was never quite as good as he thought he was

11 PSV Eindhoven

12 Ferenc Puskás

13 Borussia Dortmund

14 Ian Culverhouse, Ian Butterworth, Jeremy Goss, Mark Bowen, Chris Sutton

15 Spain, they have a better win-loss ratio against teams of any other nationality

Answers 135

1 Aston Villa
2 It was the first pay-per-view game on TV
3 Liverpool, Chelsea, Southampton, Liverpool (again), Aston Villa, Newcastle United (he did play in almost every game that season but he was awful), Portsmouth (a Harry special), Charlton Athletic
4 Southampton
5 Marc-Vivien Foe; Paolo Di Canio
6 Wimbledon; Selhurst Park, the home of Crystal Palace, with whom the Dons were groundsharing
7 Sheffield Wednesday; Alan Shearer put five past Kevin Pressman; Pavel Srnicek
8 John Jensen
9 Carl Cort
10 Thierry Henry
11 CSKA Moscow; he scored one (and another five during a loan spell at Everton)
12 Jonathan Walters
13 Carlos Tevez
14 Seven; Ricardo Gardner (92); Jason Euell, Gardner again & Robbie Earle
15 Mark Bosnich, Paul McGrath, Steve Staunton, Ian Taylor, Tommy Johnson, Dean Saunders; Warren Barton

Answers 136

1 Paddy Mulligan
2 Blackburn Rovers, Chelsea, Newcastle United, Fulham
3 Manchester City; he played more than 300 games for Barnsley before joining City and was twenty-five before winning the first of 57 caps
4 Richard Dunne (one of the most underrated players of the Premier League era)
5 Belgium
6 Tehran, Iran

7   Robbie Keane – his goals for Ireland are equal to all those other players' goals added together. Not bad considering the first three are second, third and fourth in the Irish all-time scoring list. Sure, he has played a lot of games (143 to date) but those three have played 231 between them and still fall short

8   Shane Long; Reading

9   Kenny Cunningham

10 Tony Dunne (1968) & Dennis Irwin (1999); John O'Shea

11 Ian Harte; 12; Levante

12 Liam Brady, David O'Leary & Frank Stapleton

13 Alan Kelly senior & Alan Kelly junior

14 Brighton & Hove Albion; Spain – he ended his playing career at Osasuna

15 Jonathan Walters, Glenn Whelan, Marc Wilson

Answers 137

1   Kolo Touré & Emmanuel Eboué

2   David Mills

3   Nigel Clough

4   Peter Shilton

5   Ian Woosnam; Phil Woosnam ended his career playing for Atlanta Chiefs in the US; he later became a prominent administrator in the game and took up US citizenship

6   Jeff Astle

7   Gerry Hitchens – he moved in 1961 and played for various Italian clubs during a nine-year stay

8   Bert Millichip – Wiseman was his successor

9   Stuart McCall, Robert Page & Phil Jagielka; Neil Warnock; they were beaten in the play-off Final after finishing third; Sheffield Wednesday were relegated to Division 2

10 Strasbourg

11 Billy Bonds, Frank Lampard snr, Trevor Brooking, Alan Devonshire, Paul Goddard (who scored the West Ham goal); Alan Hansen

12 Cafu

13 Sam Allardyce; the England manager's job when Roy Hodgson resigned after the European Championships

14   Malcolm Macdonald; Newcastle United & Arsenal
15   Danny Ings & Sam Vokes

Answers 138

1   Barclays (who then transferred sponsorship to the Premier League), Nationwide & nPower
2   Herbert Chapman
3   Jimmy Dickinson; only nine (and he failed to score in 48 England games). Tactical systems were slowly shifting to four at the back, and Dickinson was a very defensive wing half, a breaker of play rather than a playmaker
4   Bill Nicholson; also Tottenham – he was a one-club one man for 36 years as player and manager
5   Plymouth Argyle
6   Tottenham Hotspur
7   Wolverhampton Wanderers won the league with West Bromwich Albion second
8   Pat was the goalkeeper, Tony played left back – Alex Stepney was the new 'keeper for the 1966–67 season. Pat Dunne was only twenty-two when he got his League winner's medal, but he didn't stay the course and was shipped off to Plymouth Argyle a couple of years later
9   Four (1973, 1976, 1977, 1979)
10 All won the title on goal average or difference after finishing on the same points as the runners-up (in order: Cardiff City, Wolverhampton Wanderers, Preston North End, Leeds United, Liverpool, Manchester United)
11 Paul Walsh, Liverpool – he was bought as a potential replacement for Kenny Dalglish, but it never really worked out
12 John Docherty; two; Teddy Sheringham & Tony Cascarino
13 Notts County
14 Ian Botham
15 Jim Smith, Ron Saunders, Barry Fry, Steve Bruce, Alex McLeish, Lee Clark

Answers 139

1 Johnny Hansen; Karl-Heinz Rummenigge
2 Malmö FF (Sweden), who were runners-up to Nottingham Forest in 1979
3 AC Milan; Paolo Maldini
4 Paulo Sousa
5 Bayern Munich beat Real twice in the second group phase, but lost 2-0 in Madrid in the SF and could only win 2-1 at home
6 AC Milan; they drew 0-0 and 1-1 with Inter – the clubs share the San Siro stadium
7 Koke
8 Leeds United & Arsenal (who have made it to the Final), and Derby County (1973) & Tottenham Hotspur (1962), who have made a single semi-final appearance
9 Inter Milan
10 Yossi Benayoun
11 Borussia Mönchengladbach; Allan Simonsen
12 Karl-Heinz Riedle
13 Rafa Benítez & Roberto Di Matteo
14 Dida (Brazil, goalkeeper), Alessandro Nesta (defender), Paolo Maldini (defender), Gennaro Gattuso (midfield), Andrea Pirlo (midfield), Clarence Seedorf (Netherlands, midfield)
15 They are the five Finals that have been decided in extra time without going to penalties

Answers 140

1 Ricardo Zamora
2 Ademir; Alcides Ghiggia
3 He was the second linesman alongside Tofik Bakhramov. Galba was the one who played no part in the controversial decision surrounding Geoff Hurst's second goal
4 Gerd Müller; England
5 Bryan Robson; Robson scored again in a 3-1 win for England
6 Eric Gerets

7   Colombia; Australia

8   North Korea; Eusébio; Goodison Park, Liverpool; England; Bobby Charlton

9   Jairzinho; Pelé & Bobby Moore

10 Mo Johnston; Yugoslavia

11 Roy Hodgson

12 Bulgaria beat Germany 2-1 and Romania knocked out Argentina 3-2

13 Mauricio Pochettino; David Beckham

14 Thomas Müller

15 James Rodríguez; Real Madrid (inevitably) paid a small ransom to Monaco for his services

Answers 141

1   South Korea

2   Barcelona

3   Dynamo Kiev & Dinamo Tbilisi

4   Nick Hancock

5   Eamon Dunphy; U2

6   Leicester City (Foxes); Wolverhampton Wanderers (Wolves); Huddersfield Town (Terriers)

7   Angel Di María

8   David Beckham, Arsenal

9   Branislav Ivanović, Gary Cahill, César Azpilicueta, Kurt Zouma, Willian, Eden Hazard

10 Robbie Savage – Savage only ever received two red cards despite eighty-nine yellows; he was cute enough to know when he could get away with the heavy stuff

11 Carlos Tevez

12 Michael Ballack

13 Dean Sturridge, father of Daniel; Steve McLaren

14 Queens Park Rangers

15 David Pleat, manager of Luton Town; Manchester City

Answers 142

1   Oldham Athletic; Chris Armstrong
2   West Ham United and Everton – it was the acceptable and honourable side of the puzzling Di Canio
3   Jens Lehmann
4   Manchester United (9-0 v Ipswich Town, 1995); United again, 8-1 v Nottingham Forest, 1998
5   Rory Delap; Virgil van Dijk
6   Cristiano Ronaldo; a rather tubby Mário Jardel – compare and contrast
7   In descending order: Gianfranco Zola (229), Paolo Di Canio, Benito Carbone, Carlo Cuducini, Alessandro Pistone, Gianluca Festa & Roberto Di Matteo
8   Andrew Cole; Peter Beardsley
9   Alan Ball; Uwe Rösler; Georgi Kinkladze
10 Sunderland
11 Arsenal; their opponents, Manchester City
12 Emmanuel Adebayor & Roque Santa Cruz
13 Middlesbrough
14 Liverpool striker Robbie Fowler protested that he had not been fouled by Arsenal goalkeeper David Seaman – the referee was accused of arrogance in insisting his decision stand. Seaman saved Fowler's penalty; Jason McAteer scored from the rebound to give Liverpool a 2-1 win
15 Artur Boruc, Tommy Elphick, Matt Ritchie, Josh King, Max Gradel, Callum Wilson

Answers 143

1   Six places. Although Liverpool won the League fairly easily, Wimbledon finished seventh, having been sixth the previous season. They only lost 2-1 at Anfield and drew their home game with the champions elect 1-1. The previous year they had actually won at Anfield, so they clearly were a force to be reckoned with, and were not intimidated by Liverpool in the slightest
2   Nottingham Forest. Newcastle won the tie 1-0 after another replay – they went on to reach the Final. Today they would have forfeited the game

3 Blackburn Rovers (1884)

4 Ted MacDougall

5 Oxford University

6 Tottenham Hotspur

7 Kevin Davies

8 George Burley, Kevin Beattie, Mick Mills, John Wark, Clive Woods & Paul Mariner

9 Chelsea; Millennium Stadium, Cardiff

10 Barnsley, twice

11 Willie Young; Kevin Moran

12 Howard Kendall; Everton

13 Peter Schmeichel, Roy Keane & Ryan Giggs

14 Wayne Bridge; he was selected ahead of Ashley Cole, and very briefly took Cole's England place that season

15 Kanu, Papa Bouba Diop and John Utaka although only James appeared in both starting line-ups; Harry Redknapp in 2008, in 2010 it was Avram Grant, left to pick up the pieces after Harry jumped ship with the club penniless

Answers 144

1 Theo Zagorakis; Stelios Giannakopoulos of Bolton Wanderers

2 Francisco Gento

3 West Germany

4 Antonín Panenka; Sepp Maier

5 Belgium & Yugoslavia

6 Lothar Matthäus gave West Germany the lead and Ronald Koeman equalised

7 Republic of Ireland; Patrick Kluivert

8 France, who knocked out the Netherlands and then lost to the Czech Republic: Gareth Southgate

9 Andreas Charisteas; Czech Republic; Otto Rehhagel; if a goal is scored in the first period of extra time, the opposition only have until half time in extra time to level or the game is over. Utter nonsense, only FIFA or UEFA could have come up with such twaddle

10 Miguel Ángel Nadal; Andoni Zubizarreta

11 Cyprus; Raúl; Fernando Hierro
12 Jan Koller
13 Andorra, who scored 1 and let in 25, and San Marino, whose goals
    columns read for 0, against 53
14 Faroe Islands
15 England; Austria

Answers 145

1 They were the four players sent off during a spiteful match between the
   Netherlands and Portugal. Suggestions from both sides (and pundits)
   that the referee lost control are way off – both teams were a disgrace.
2 1910s – 1916 to be precise
3 Zurich
4 The scorer of the goal that enabled the United States to pull off a remarkable 1-0 win over England at the 1950 World Cup finals
5 The Olympic Association Football competition; Upton Park were an
   amateur team chosen to represent GB at the Paris Olympics. They were
   also one of the fifteen teams to enter the first FA Cup – they have no
   connection to West Ham other than proximity
6 Sunderland (Black Cats); Millwall (Lions); Hull City (Tigers)
7 Walsall
8 Alan Pardew
9 The 1970s, Tony Book was in charge from 1974–1979
10 Farnborough United
11 Brad Friedel, Carlos Cuéllar, James Collins, James Milner, Stiliyan
    Petrov, Emile Heskey – the manager was Martin O'Neill, whose depar-
    ture because he was fed up with the owners' lack of ambition signalled
    the end of Villa as a force in the Premier League
12 Fabio Cannavaro
13 Phil Thompson
14 Two, one with Derby and one with Nottingham Forest
15 Bristol Rovers; Queens Park Rangers; Blackpool & Crystal Palace

Answers 146

1 Ron Springett & Peter Bonetti
2 Gary Stevens, Terry Butcher, Trevor Steven and reserve goalkeeper Chris Woods were all at Rangers, Chris Waddle was playing for Olympique de Marseille
3 Sansom
4 Joe Hart, by a distance and still adding
5 Bohemia
6 Teddy Sheringham
7 Tony Adams
8 None
9 Jimmy Greaves (Lineker managed five)
10 Walter Winterbottom: the team continued to be chosen by a selection panel (when Alf Ramsey replaced Winterbottom he insisted on full control over team selection)
11 Kevin Keegan
12 Ray Clemence, Phil Neal, Terry McDermott, Emlyn Hughes, Kevin Keegan, Ray Kennedy and Ian Callaghan. Callaghan was recalled at thirty-five, having previously played for England in the 1966 World Cup
13 Arsenal
14 George Cohen & Jack Charlton had been naturally supplanted, but Hunter for Hurst was a selection borne of fear
15 Michael Carrick, who won his first cap in 2001

Answers 147

1 Manchester City
2 Adam Johnson
3 Mark Viduka
4 Liverpool
5 Everton
6 Benito Carbone; Southampton
7 Jens Lehmann (38), Thierry Henry (37), Kolo Touré (36), Sol Campbell (35), Robert Pires (33), Ashley Cole (32), Lauren (30), Gilberto Silva (29), Patrick Vieira (29) & Freddie Ljungberg (27). Denis Bergkamp

and Edu played in more than 25 games but their totals included lots of substitute appearances

8 Vedran Ćorluka, Niko Kranjčar & Luka Modrić

9 Chelsea

10 Jermain Defoe; Peter Crouch; Nico Kranjčar

11 Barcelona & Wolfsburg

12 Robert Earnshaw

13 Eighteen points

14 Lucas Radebe (Leeds United) & Mark Fish (Bolton Wanderers)

15 Wes Morgan, Christian Fuchs, Marc Albrighton, Danny Drinkwater, Leonardo Ulloa, Jamie Vardy; centre back Robert Huth scored twice

Answers 148

1 The restrictions on foreign players (three per team), which applied to Welsh, Scottish and Irish players, who had long been a mainstay of English clubs

2 Careca

3 IFK Göteborg (Gothenburg); Roger Gustafsson – his five wins makes him the most successful manager in Swedish football; Thomas Ravelli

4 Lyon; Pauleta (at Bordeaux & PSG); Karim Benzema; Lens, Monaco, Paris Saint Germain, Lille, Bordeaux & Marseille; Bordeaux were runners up in 2006 and 2008 and won in 2009

5 Germany didn't lose any of those twenty-five matches – it is the most caps won by a player who has never been on the losing side

6 Jari Litmanen

7 Poland

8 Copenhagen

9 Because he was the goalkeeper – all the goals were penalties

10 Atlético Madrid

11 Glasgow Rangers

12 Besiktas

13 Newcastle United; Joe Harvey

14 Birmingham City

15 Sporting Lisbon, FC Porto & Barcelona

Answers 149

1 Dimitar Berbatov

2 Referee the match

3 East Germany (Germany is wrong)

4 Paul Elliott

5 AC Milan, Portsmouth

6 George Eastham; Newcastle United

7 Zinedine Zidane against Saudi Arabia (violent conduct, deserved, utterly stupid in an easy match); Laurent Blanc (violent conduct, undeserved, the result of shameful play-acting by Slaven Bilić); Marcel Desailly (two yellows in the Final, a bit tame)

8 Trevor Brooking

9 Gary Breen

10 It was the Final of the LDV Vans Trophy (for lower division clubs only) at Wembley

11 Paul Robinson, Ledley King, Jermaine Jenas, Steed Malbranque, Teemu Tainio, Robbie Keane: Woodgate scored the goal, Malbranque was the only uncapped starter (he was better at Fulham, but surely one of the best uncapped players to have played in the Premier League – Kaboul & Huddlestone, the subs, were uncapped at the time although both got call-ups later); the manager was Juande Ramos

12 Didier Deschamps

13 Richard Wright

14 Colin Lee

15 Carlisle United, Luton Town, Oxford United

Answers 150

1 Czechoslovakia; Bologna (this is not a Serie A record, as that competition only started midway through Schiavio's career)

2 Norman Hunter – he got his chance in 1970

3 Just Fontaine; 13

4 Chile in 1962 – and Chile is mostly seaboard!

5 Once, against Brazil in 1982

6 Poland

7 England drew 0-0 in 1958, little good though it did them, and Czechoslovakia drew 0-0 in '62, in an odd sort of gentlemanly stalemate; after Pelé was injured early in the game both teams seemed to hold off their tackles and the game was played out more like a training match

8 Italy, who beat them 1-0 in a group fixture

9 Paul Bodin

10 Rigobert Song; Zinedine Zidane

11 Florin Raducioiu

12 Cagliari, they had six players in the 1970 squad as a consequence – Riva scored 7 of Italy's 10 goals in qualifying (in four games) including a hattrick against Wales

13 Rivaldo

14 Denmark: a poor second half led to a slating from the English press, some of whom claimed England were lucky. 3-0 is never lucky

15 Júlio César, David Luiz, Marcelo, Hulk, Fred (MISSING is appropriate for all of them; they all performed spectacularly badly). Hummels, Howedes, Schweinsteiger, Kroos, Ozil, Schurrle. Germany won 7-1, arguably the most extraordinary result in World Cup history

Answers 151

1 Japan

2 Mia Hamm; Birgit Prinz

3 Germany

4 Sweden (2-1 after extra time) and Brazil (2-0)

5 Charlton Athletic Ladies; Eniola Aluko

6 Lucy Bronze; hosts Canada, Japan; Laura Bassett; Fara Williams

7 Hope Powell

8 All the matches were played on an artificial surface; Hawk-Eye goal-line technology was used for the first time

9 Gemma Fay; Julie Fleeting (accept Julie Stewart, her married name)

10 Manchester City; Portland Thorns; Arsenal

11 Germany (nine out of 14 times)

12 Carli Lloyd; Japan

13 It is 1. FFC Turbine Postdam, who won six titles including four consecutively from 2008–09 to 2011–12

14 Marta; Birgit Prinz & Abby Wambach

15 Atlanta & Miami

Answers 152

1 Preston North End: they won the League and Cup Double and remained unbeaten

2 Huddersfield Town

3 Bryan 'Pop' Robson

4 Crystal Palace; one

5 John Bond, Norwich City

6 Arfon Griffiths; Wrexham clinched promotion in style, thrashing Rotherham 7-1 and going on to win the divisional title

7 Peterborough United; Terry Bly

8 Wolverhampton Wanderers; Birmingham City

9 Leeds United

10 Paul Cooper

11 Aston Villa; the previous incumbent Graham Taylor was appointed England manager; Ron Atkinson

12 Stoke City (Stein) & Bolton Wanderers (Walker); Bob Taylor

13 Kevin Phillips (23) & Niall Quinn (18)

14 Rushden & Diamonds; they aren't – the club suffered relegation in 2004 and 2006 and went into liquidation in 2011 while in the Conference

15 Jimmy Armfield, Alan Ball, Peter Doherty, Stanley Matthews, Stan Mortensen

Answers 153

1 John Sivebaek & Jesper Olsen were at Manchester United, Jan Molby with Liverpool

2 Fritz and Ottmar Walter with West Germany in 1954

3 West Ham United

4 Bruce Grobbelaar; Southampton

5 Toulouse

6   Andy Townsend

7   John Harkes, reserve goalkeeper Jürgen Sommer and Roy Wegerle

8   Andriy Shevchenko; Chelsea; Dynamo Kiev

9   Huddersfield Town, his previous club

10 He was banned for life by both FIFA and UEFA for taking and offering bribes

11 David Moyes; Preston North End

12 Maradona (91), Batistuta (78), Kempes only 43

13 Rio Ferdinand

14 Frank Worthington in 1978–79

15 Graham Taylor, Dave Jones, Glenn Hoddle, Mick McCarthy, Stale Solbakken, Kenny Jackett

Answers 154

1   Roque Santa Cruz of Blackburn Rovers and (briefly) Manchester City

2   Roger Milla

3   Ronaldo won 98 to Ronaldinho's 97; Pele won 91 and Romario 70. Ronaldinho scored 33 goals, the others all scored more than fifty

4   Palacios, Honduras

5   Aaron Mokoena

6   South Korea. The Elephants are now known as Yukong United and play out of Jeju; the Hyundai side play out of Ulsan, POSCO Atoms are now the successful Pohang Steelers. Lucky-Goldstar are now known simply as FC Seoul, and are the answer to part two

7   Jason Roberts

8   Brazil, who won the 1994 World Cup and the Copa América in 1997 – they repeated the feat in 2004 after winning the 2002 World Cup

9   Colombia

10 Paraguay, Chile

11 Nigeria

12 Zambia

13 Togo; Angola

14 Japan: Saudi Arabia & Iran

15 Costa Rica (4), Honduras (3), Cuba, Canada, El Salvador, Haiti, Jamaica, Trinidad and Tobago (1)

Answers 155

1 Alex Manninger

2 Newcastle United; Kevin Keegan & Dennis Wise. Keegan resigned and sued for constructive dismissal, claiming the signing, orchestrated without his consent by Wise and club owner Mike Ashley, was in breach of his contract: Keegan won the case

3 Dean Richards; Southampton; Bradford City

4 Sunderland; Mick McCarthy

5 Pierluigi Casiraghi

6 Sol Campbell, Tony Adams, Martin Keown, Oleg Luzhny, Matthew Upson & (huge brownie points for the last one) Igor Stepanovs. Gilles Grimandi played a couple of games in central defence but he was not a centre half by trade

7 Nikos Dabizas (130 for Newcastle United, 51 for Leicester City) & Stelios Giannakopoulos (137 for Bolton Wanderers, 2 for Hull City)

8 Michael Bridges

9 Tottenham Hotspur; Laurent Blanc

10 Test cricket – the nation became absorbed in the climax to the fantastic 2005 Ashes series

11 Leighton Baines (Everton) & Martin Škrtel (Liverpool)

12 West Bromwich Albion

13 They all failed to win a game away from home – an especially startling statistic for Leeds considering they were the reigning League champions

14 Des Lynam; Andy Townsend; twenty-eight (thirteen mins of ads, twenty-seven mins of yak); only three, mercifully; *Beautiful Day*; Gabby Logan & Ally McCoist

15 Heurelho Gomes, Craig Cathcart, Valon Behrami, Étienne Capoue, Odion Ighalo, Troy Deeney

Answers 156

1 Ruud van Nistelrooy

2 Feyenoord; full back Tommy Gemmell; Leeds United

3 Ajax, Real Madrid & AC Milan

4 Dida

5 Peter Schmeichel

6 Panathinaikos

7 Hamburg SV; Ernst Happel

8 Ajax & PSV Eindhoven

9 Raphael Varane & Karim Benzema; Sergio Ramos

10 Eidur Gudjohnsen & Deco

11 Graeme Souness

12 Juventus, when they lost to Borussia Dortmund in 1997

13 London – five at the old Wembley and two at the new stadium

14 Victor Valdés, Carles Puyol, Gerard Piqué, Sergio Busquets, Xavi and Pedro played in three Finals, while Andrès Iniesta played in all four (Xavi was an unused sub in 2006)

15 Nottingham Forest, who won the League, then the European Cup, and then retained the latter having entered as holders – they haven't qualified since

Answers 157

1 Aston Villa

2 Stuart Pearce

3 Mick Quinn

4 Jim Magilton

5 Heart of Midlothian

6 South Africa, following the dismantling of the apartheid system

7 Preston North End

8 Sapporo

9 C. B. Fry

10 The Leatherhead Lip

11 Leyton Orient

12 Cliff Jones

13 Melchester Rovers

14 Simple Minds

15 James Beattie, Darren Bent, Stan Collymore, Les Ferdinand, Robbie Fowler, Andy Johnson, Harry Kane, Frank Lampard, Matthew Le Tissier, Kevin Phillips, Wayne Rooney, Alan Shearer, Teddy Sheringham, Daniel Sturridge, Chris Sutton, Ian Wright

Answers 158

1 Kingsley Black
2 Cesc Fàbregas
3 Liverpool won the trophy from 1981 to 1984
4 Aston Villa; Joe Mercer
5 Ron Saunders, Aston Villa
6 Tottenham Hotspur; John McGinlay
7 Wycombe Wanderers; Chelsea; Paul Lambert
8 Huddersfield Town; Fulham
9 Wolverhampton Wanderers; John Richards; Alan Sunderland
10 Allan Nielsen; Leicester City
11 Terry Cooper
12 Stoke City; Robbie Fowler
13 Cardiff City: Steven Gerrard and his cousin, Anthony, who came on as a substitute for Cardiff
14 Wayne Rooney; Manchester City, Carlos Tevez; Rooney again
15 Don Rogers

Answers 159

1 Oldrich Nejedly
2 Peter McParland
3 Bonetti; Newton, Labone, Moore, Cooper; Ball, Mullery, Charlton, Peters; Lee, Hurst
4 Sweden & France
5 Gottfried Dienst
6 *Back Home*
7 Hansi & Dieter; both scored in a 6-0 thrashing of Mexico in the group and then did little else
8 David Narey, with his only goal for Scotland in thirty-five games
9 Northern Ireland
10 Alan Shearer, Michael Owen & Paul Merson: Hernán Crespo
11 Denmark; Alan McLoughlin
12 David O'Leary
13 Goalkeeper José Luis Chilavert

14 Algeria

15 David Luiz. His rise to national hero status was short lived as he had a horror show in the semi-final

Answers 160

1 Carl Cort & Ben Thatcher

2 Manchester United & Portsmouth

3 Everton

4 Abel Xavier

5 Jamie Carragher; Martin Keown & Dennis Bergkamp

6 Peter Schmeichel, Thierry Henry & Cristiano Ronaldo

7 Eric Cantona

8 Sheffield United; Graham Stuart; Hans Segers

9 Leeds United; Youri Djorkaeff, Mark Viduka

10 Joe Cole, Frank Lampard and John Terry – the award was given to Steven Gerrard

11 It was the only home game in that season's Premier League that United failed to win; Roberto Di Matteo was the WBA manager but he failed to last the season

12 Paul Kitson (six of his 18 West Ham goals were in hat-tricks), Marlon Harewood & Kevin Nolan

13 Blackpool scored 55 in 2010–11 and had a great first half of the season, but they were naïve and let in too many

14 Jürgen Klinsmann, Eric Cantona, Gianfranco Zola, Dennis Bergkamp, David Ginola

15 Scott Dann, Damien Delaney, Yohann Cabaye, Joe Ledley, Bakary Sako, Yannick Bolasie

Answers 161

1 Gary Stevens – one was known as Gary A. Stevens to make a distinction; Gary played for Everton, Gary A. for Tottenham; Gary was the first-choice right back, Gary A. made only a couple of substitute appearances. Gary A. scored for Brighton in 1983, but they lost in a replay, Gary won the Cup with Everton in 1984 but didn't score – hope that's clear!

2 Dave Sexton

3 Both have top-flight football clubs called Everton

4 Riyad Mahrez (who joined Leicester City from Le Havre in January 2014)

5 Luis García

6 Aitor Karanka

7 Nigel Clough

8 Wenger won his sixth in 2015 to overtake his rival, who won five

9 Chris Woods, Viv Anderson, Carlton Palmer, Chris Waddle & David Hirst (of Sheffield Wednesday)

10 David Lloyd; a chain of health and fitness clubs

11 Twenty-three

12 Jussi Jaaskelainen, Bruno N'Gotty, Emerson Thome, Kevin Nolan, Iván Campo, Kevin Davies. The key was Okocha, who delayed his departure for the African Cup of Nations and produced an inspired performance

13 Alex Ferguson

14 Bristol Rovers

15 Benin; Stéphane Sessègnon

Answers 162

1 Newcastle United; Hughie Gallacher

2 John Charles

3 Blackburn Rovers: Rovers finished tenth in McEvoy's purple season but were relegated in 1965–66, following neighbours Bolton into the second tier; Blackpool would follow a year later

4 Malcolm Macdonald

5 Keith Curle

6 Jim Montgomery

7 Aston Villa

8 It was Alan Mullery (Melia came later, the other two never managed Brighton)

9 Luton Town

10 Barnet: Barnet were relegated back to the Conference while Blackpool won promotion via the play-offs

11 Tony & Mark Hateley, Coventry City

12 Swansea City & Cardiff City

13 Brighton & Hove Albion & Crystal Palace

14 Alvin Martin; Newcastle 'keeper Martin Thomas went off at half-time and two outfield players kept goal in the second half (it was Peter Beardsley who faced Martin's penalty)

15 Billy Meredith, Peter Doherty, Frank Swift, Bert Trautmann, Denis Law, Colin Bell, Trevor Francis, Peter Schmeichel

Answers 163

1   Sporting of Lisbon; Aston Villa

2   Peter Enckelmann (Aston Villa); Jussi Jaaskelainen (Bolton Wanderers): Antte Niemi (Southampton)

3   Peter Ndlovu; Zimbabwe

4   Bolton Wanderers; Kevin Nolan

5   He was sent off for the first time in his career

6   Frank Lampard (13), Eidur Gudjohnsen (12) & Didier Drogba (10): Claude Makélélé (36), John Terry (36), Petr Cech (35), Eidur Gudjohnsen (30)

7   Jared Borgetti – a prolific scorer in Mexico and at international level (46 goals in 89 games), he struggled with the pace of the Premier League and moved on after a year

8   Les Ferdinand

9   Matthew Le Tissier, the greatest Saint

10 Paul Robinson & Ben Foster

11 Feyenoord; 144 – it stacks up to 13 per season which isn't that many, but van Persie was somewhat injury prone. His strike rate is still better than a goal every two games, which is very healthy

12 Dean Holdsworth

13 Craig Gardner; back near home at West Bromwich Albion

14 They all came from 3-0 down to win the match; United won 5-3, the others all won 4-3

15 Asmir Begović, Ryan Shawcross, Glenn Whelan, Charlie Adam, Peter Odemwingie, Marko Arnautović, Peter Crouch; the game was Steven Gerrard's last for the club

Answers 164

1 George Wood
2 Ally McCoist (twice) & Henrik Larsson
3 John Robertson
4 Martin O'Neill & Neil Lennon
5 Queen's Park
6 Chris Woods
7 It was 1994–95 when Rangers, Motherwell and Hibernian filled the top three spaces
8 Martin Buchan, Joe Jordan, Lou Macari, Gordon McQueen – McQueen was injured at the start of the tournament and played no part
9 One
10 Edinburgh; Livingston
11 Anton Rogan; Theo Snelders
12 Collins won 58, Bremner & Souness 54 each, Hartford 50 – probably the major factor was Collins played in more recent times and had more opportunities; they were all good players
13 Jock Stein
14 Fletcher, who, remarkably, has two where none of those other, more celebrated players could manage one. In fairness, they never played Gibraltar, against whom Fletcher scored both his threesomes
15 Craig Gordon, Graham Alexander, David Weir, Celtic, Rangers, Barry Ferguson, Celtic, James McFadden

Answers 165

1 Sweden
2 Brighton & Hove Albion and Southampton
3 They lost the FA Cup Final and were relegated in the same season
4 Both played for Dunfermline – Ferguson had a spell with Rangers, Moyes a good spell at Preston, Houston Dynamo I plucked from nowhere
5 Jan Molby
6 Guus Hiddink & Dick Advocaat
7 Gérard Houllier

8 Kanu

9 Ray Wilkins; Wilkins was officially team manager, with Keegan as 'chief operating officer', but by the end of the season Wilkins ceded place to Keegan, who was never likely to be happy with anything other than full control

10 They signed Saadi al Gadaffi, son of the Libyan leader, who later tested positive for recreational drugs

11 They are the names of the official match ball

12 Roland Nilsson, Nigel Pearson, Danny Wilson, John Harkes, David Hirst. Sheridan scored the goal; Ron Atkinson was manager and Trevor Francis sat on the bench all game. Wednesday were promoted from third place in the Second Division – they proved it was no fluke by finishing third in the First Division the following season

13 Jean Tigana, who managed Fulham from 2000–2003 (he took them into the Premier League in his first season)

14 Kevin Keegan & Ray Clemence

15 Kolo came from Arsenal, Yaya from Barcelona

Answers 166

1 Egypt

2 Juan Schiaffino; Milan

3 Bobby Charlton & Jimmy Greaves

4 Craig Burley

5 Overath & Weber

6 Hungary; Laszlo Kiss

7 Alan Mullery

8 Zbigniew Boniek; Juventus

9 Italy; Lucas Neill; Francesco Totti

10 Argentina; Diego Maradona

11 France; Eric Cantona; Emil Kostadinov; Gérard Houllier; David Ginola

12 England, Russia. Italy drew three games, which let in England, who lost one but won six matches to Italy's five

13 Francesco Totti – it was a harsh decision; Paolo Maldini

14 Serbia; Lionel Messi

15 Switzerland (against Ukraine)

Answers 167

1 Luis Arconada
2 Luxembourg
3 Gerd Müller
4 Marco Tardelli
5 Nenê, Jean-François Domergue; Michel Hidalgo
6 Score for the Soviet Union
7 Hristo Stoichkov
8 Oliver Bierhoff; Jürgen Klinsmann
9 Hal Robson-Kanu; Portugal
10 Zinedine Zidane; Nuno Gomes
11 Paul Jones, Danny Gabbidon, Gary Speed (and yes, he did play at left back), Simon Davies, Robbie Savage, John Hartson
12 Milan Baros
13 Sweden; Zlatan Ibrahimović & Olof Mellberg
14 Andrei Arshavin
15 Zlatan Ibrahimović; Albania; Serbia, whose fans ran on after a drone flew overhead trailing an Albanian flag – for the record, even had Serbia won this game and not had points deducted they would still have been a point behind Albania

Answers 168

1 Sunderland
2 Dixie Dean
3 Jimmy Greaves
4 Northampton Town; Dave Bowen
5 Bruce Rioch
6 Gary Lineker in 1984–85 (jointly) & 1985–86
7 Terry Venables
8 Crystal Palace: Kenny Dalglish & Steve Coppell
9 Nottingham Forest
10 Derby County
11 Carlisle United; Barrow; Workington Town
12 John Aldridge (21) & Pat Nevin (13)

13 Andy Payton

14 Paul Furlong & Kevin Gallen; Ian Holloway – since Holloway left in 2006, QPR have managed a farcical twelve managers in ten years, not counting caretakers, and two years of that was Neil Warnock's tenure

15 Blackpool, Queens Park Rangers, Watford & Southampton have never won the League, Preston North End, West Bromwich Albion, Sheffield Wednesday & Newcastle United haven't won it since the war

Answers 169

1 Central Hall in Westminster

2 Cafu

3 All started in non-League football

4 Blackpool; Bolton Wanderers

5 Charlie George

6 England & Wales; Ryan Giggs; South Korea; Daniel Sturridge

7 Tino Asprilla

8 Paul Goddard – he played in a friendly against Iceland, scored England's only goal in a 1-1 draw and was then ignored by Ron Greenwood

9 Glenn Hoddle

10 Score a penalty for the away side at Old Trafford

11 Bradford City of League Two (fourth tier); Nathan Dyer; Michael Laudrup; Ashley Williams & Ben Davies

12 Eric Cantona, George Best, Ryan Giggs & Bobby Charlton; more hindsight would suggest the brevity of Cantona's time puts him behind the other three, not at the top

13 Darren Peacock

14 Sheffield United; Keith Edwards

15 Ken Bates & Matthew Harding

Answers 170

1 Crystal Palace, Wimbledon, Ipswich Town, Charlton Athletic and Portsmouth

2 Patrick Vieira & Emmanuel Petit at Arsenal and Frank Leboeuf at Chelsea

3 Sunderland (last in 2007), West Bromwich Albion (2010), Crystal Palace (2014) & Leicester City (2015)

4 Mario Stanić – the two included a stunning 35-yard strike, but it was the high point of Stanić's time at the club

5 Rory Delap

6 Liverpool, Middlesbrough & Queens Park Rangers

7 Mikel Arteta

8 Teenager Wayne Rooney

9 Swindon Town; Glenn Hoddle, John Gorman

10 Alan Shearer

11 Jeff Astle. The former Baggies centre forward had recently collapsed and died, aged 59, at his daughter's home

12 West Ham United; West Bromwich Albion

13 Peter Swales; Francis Lee; Thailand; Abu-Dhabi, UAE

14 Nigel Worthington, Paul Lambert & Alex Neil

15 Tom Heaton, Michael Duff, George Boyd, Sam Vokes, Danny Ings

Answers 171

1 Porto & AS Monaco: it will never happen again until the financial stranglehold of the big clubs is broken or challenged

2 England

3 Fernando Morientes; Chelsea

4 Real Madrid

5 AC Milan; Marcel Desailly; Fabio Capello

6 Chris Waddle

7 Kim Milton Nielsen, Villareal

8 Belgium

9 Spain (31) & England (30)

10 Parc des Princes & Stade de France

11 Teddy Sheringham & Ole Gunnar Solsjkaer; Sheringham came on for Jesper Blomqvist after sixty-seven minutes and Solsjaker replaced Andy Cole with ten minutes to go; Peter Schmeichel

12 Gianluca Vialli, Fabrizio Ravanelli & Didier Deschamps

13   Stuttgart
14   Argentina (four) & Brazil (three); Marco Materazzi
15   Newcastle United

Answers 172

1   John Connelly, Terry Paine & Ian Callaghan; The Wingless Wonders
2   Jack Charlton (31) and Alan Ball (21)
3   Marco van Basten at the 1988 European Championships
4   Peter Beardsley, David Batty, Kieron Dyer, Alan Shearer
5   Steve Bloomer
6   He scored a hat-trick (v Turkey in an 8-0 win)
7   England! He was sportingly 'loaned' to Wales as a sub
8   Alan Smith
9   Peter Crouch (11 goals)
10 Ian Wright; San Marino – it was a pointless game as England had already failed to qualify for the 1994 World Cup
11 Phil Parkes, Jimmy Rimmer, Nigel Spink
12 Dietmar Hamann; a typically emotional resignation from England manager Kevin Keegan
13 Zlatan Ibrahimović for Sweden, who won the friendly match 4-2
14 Russia & Croatia; Roman Pavlyuchenko
15 David Seaman (75), Gordon Banks (73), Ray Clemence (61), David James (53)

Answers 173

1   Paris, Stockholm, Munich, Mexico City, Pasadena. They are the cities that hosted the World Cup Finals in the twentieth century
2   Arjen Robben
3   José Altafini
4   Religion (Saints, Quakers and Pilgrims respectively)
5   Gretna
6   Queens Park
7   Rudi Völler & Jürgen Klinsmann
8   Adrian Mutu; Juventus, Romania

9   Mark Viduka; Melbourne, Australia

10 Paul Gascoigne; Alan Stubbs

11 Nigel Quashie; Chris Hughton

12 Ivan Zamorano

13 Stephen Hunt

14 Coventry City

15 Arsène Wenger, José Mourinho, David Moyes and Harry Redknapp –
    although what Harry is doing in there is anyone's guess

Answers 174

1   Costa Rica

2   Uruguay in 1950

3   Argentina

4   Antonio Rattín of Argentina in 1966 and Ronaldinho of Brazil in
    2002

5   Carlos Alberto, the right back and captain

6   Ally MacLeod; Ayr United; Peru; Iran; *Ally's Tartan Army*

7   Diego Maradona; Athletic Bilbao

8   Saudi Arabia; Carlos Alberto Parreira, who would coach Brazil to
    victory four years later

9   Roger Milla; Russia won 6-1, with Oleg Salenko scoring five of the most
    meaningless World Cup goals as the Russians were already out

10 Gianfranco Zola

11 Dennis Bergkamp

12 Lúcio, Roberto Carlos, Juninho, Gilberto Silva, Rivaldo

13 Tomas Rosicky

14 Roberto Carlos

15 Goalkeeper Júlio César, right back Maicon and centre half Lúcio

Answers 175

1   Toni Polster

2   Wolverhampton Wanderers

3   FC Porto; Henrik Larsson

4   Andrea Brehme, Jürgen Klinsmann & Lothar Matthäus

5 AZ Alkmaar have won twice, Twente Enschede won for the first time in 2009–10; Louis van Gaal & Steve McLaren were the two managers

6 Athens

7 Sevilla, 4-0

8 Marc Wilmots; Paul Ince

9 Bernard Tapie

10 Liechtenstein

11 Ivan Zamorano; Youri Djorkaeff & Ronaldo

12 Pamplona, home of the bull run

13 Valencia

14 Corsica; French

15 Leeds (1968, 1971), Newcastle (1969), Arsenal (1970), Tottenham (1972, 1984), Liverpool (1973, 1976, 1001), Ipswich (1981), Chelsea (2013)

Answers 176

1 Colchester United (3-2); Ray Crawford; Ipswich Town

2 Harlow Town

3 Newcastle United

4 Stuart McCall (Everton); Ian Rush (Liverpool)

5 Arsenal and Liverpool; it was boring and played havoc with the fixture list

6 Steve McManaman; 4-2 to United

7 Freddie Ljungberg

8 Gianfranco Zola

9 Nicolas Anelka & Marc Overmars

10 Gary McAllister (sub for Liverpool in 2001), Darren Fletcher (Manchester United, 2004), Shaun Maloney & James McArthur (Wigan Athletic, 2013)

11 Ronnie Rosenthal

12 Ryan Giggs; Peter Schmeichel

13 Wimbledon, Chelsea, Millwall

14 Arsenal (1993), Liverpool (2001) & Chelsea (2007)

15 Juninho & Emerson

Answers 177

1 Watford
2 They had built stadia for the 1968 Olympic Games in Mexico City
3 Qualification for the World Cup finals; they gained entry as the hosts in 1966 and holders in 1970, and failed to qualify in 1974 and 1978
4 Bill 'Fatty' Foulke
5 Alexei Lalas; he was soon back in the US, Italy didn't suit his all-in style. Lalas went on to win 96 caps for the US and he is a popular pundit on US TV
6 Roberto Baggio & Franco Baresi; Cláudio Taffarel – not that he saved either penalty, both were blazed over the bar
7 Kenneth Wolstenholme
8 Clive Allen
9 Pelé, who was here in his capacity as Brazilian sports minister
10 Patrick Kluivert
11 Armenia, Azerbaijan, Belarus, Estonia, Georgia, Kazakhstan, Latvia, Lithuania, Moldova, Russia, Ukraine
12 Abedi Pele
13 Lee Bowyer (*quelle surprise!*) & Kieron Dyer
14 Brian & Jimmy Greenhoff
15 It was (c) – a cheeky tease by a member of United's travel team (or maybe a bit of wishful thinking)

Answers 178

1 Racecourse Ground, Wrexham
2 Barry Town; Aberdeen
3 Juventus; Swansea Town
4 Ashley Williams
5 Fred Keenor
6 Dennis Bergkamp; Hakan Sukur
7 Faroe Islands
8 Temuri Ketsbaia
9 Alf Sherwood

10 Swansea City; Cardiff City (brief loan); Brighton & Hove Albion; Oxford United; Derby County; Liverpool; Aston Villa; Galatasaray; Nottingham Forest; Sheffield United; Benfica; Bradford City

11 Grimsby Town

12 The team contained two pairs of brothers, Ivor and Len Allchurch plus John and Mel Charles

13 Fulham

14 Kenny Jackett

15 Melville, with 65 (Phillips 62, Ratcliffe 59 and Symons 36)

Answers 179

1 Manchester United

2 Cliff Bastin; Herbert Chapman died of pneumonia in January that year

3 Dennis Viollet

4 Manchester United

5 Middlesbrough

6 Just Villa in 1992–93 (they finished runners up, Birmingham and Wolves were in the second tier, West Brom winning promotion from the third). In 2010–11 all four were back in the top flight, although Birmingham were relegated that season

7 Swindon Town beat them in the Final but were demoted for financial misdemeanours; Eric Gates and Marco Gabbiadini

8 A paltry 29 – go figure

9 Jimmy Armfield

10 Middlesbrough

11 Tommy Lawton; Chelsea; Notts County

12 Tony Capaldi

13 As a mark of respect for Bobby Moore, who had just died, the no.6 shirt wasn't used

14 Ipswich Town; Preston North End; Bobby Zamora

15 Burton Albion, Chesterfield, Crewe Alexandra, Derby County, Mansfield Town, Nottingham Forest, Notts County, Port Vale, Shrewsbury Town, Stoke City

Answers 180

1 Tottenham Hotspur & Leicester City
2 Steve Coppell
3 Bolton Wanderers (who were a division below, albeit top) & Newcastle United
4 Luděk Mikloško, Pavel Srníček, who sadly died in 2015 aged forty-seven; Baník Ostrava
5 Henning Berg (Blackburn Rovers)
6 Ledley King; Alan Shearer
7 Kevin Davies; Southampton, Egil Ostenstad (worth about £2.5M?);
8 Juninho
9 Stuart Ripley, Jason Wilcox (the SAS in question were, of course, Alan Shearer and Chris Sutton)
10 Sam Allardyce (Bolton Wanderers) & Alan Curbishley (Charlton Athletic)
11 'DJ' Campbell; Charlie Adam, Liverpool; Richard Kingson; Liverpool
12 Steven Caulker, Mile Jedinak, Ahmed Elmohamady & Mark Noble
13 Wayne Rooney, for Manchester United
14 Sheffield Wednesday, West Ham United & Charlton Athletic; Swindon Town & Sunderland
15 Michel Vorm, Ashley Williams, Ben Davies, Jonathan de Guzmán, Wayne Routledge, Wilfred Bony

Answers 181

1 Cardiff City
2 They were all born in what was East Germany, and would have played in much weaker teams than the unified Germany
3 Score their penalty kicks in a shoot-out (against Argentina) – both missed in the Final shoot-out against Brazil in 1994
4 Bristol City
5 Graham Taylor
6 Pep Guardiola and Luis Enrique
7 Matthew Harding
8 Cliff Bastin; Thierry Henry

9 Stevenage Borough – they did give Newcastle a tough tie, drawing 1-1 at home and only going down 2-1 in the replay

10 Fabrizio Ravanelli, Gianluca Festa, Marco Branca (tricky one, Branca only played a few games for the club)

11 Rio Ferdinand, Ashley Cole, Owen Hargreaves (the sub, playing on his home ground), Paul Scholes, Nicky Barmby, Emile Heskey

12 Augustine 'Jay-Jay' Okocha

13 Andy Johnson, Clinton Morrison

14 It was Stoke, and the record stood for twenty-one years. It took them a while to get back.

15 Sunderland; Clive Mendonca, Michael Gray; Saša Ilić; Alan Curbishley (Charlton) & Peter Reid (Sunderland)

Answers 182

1 Mick McCarthy, Paul McGrath & Kevin Moran

2 Steve Staunton

3 Cantwell was a left back. He later managed Peterborough in two spells as well as coaching in the US. He also played cricket for Ireland

4 Giovanni Trappatoni; Martin O'Neill, who is Irish, but from the North rather than the Republic

5 Manager Mick McCarthy; Keane's outburst was way out of order and also wrong – McCarthy's lineage was through his father, not a stray grandparent as was the case with one or two others picked up by Jack Charlton

6 Tony Cascarino, one of those late developers who was better in his thirties (which he attributed to the discipline of playing in France)

7 Wolverhampton Wanderers, Coventry City, Inter Milan, Leeds United, Tottenham Hotspur, Liverpool, Celtic, West Ham United, LA Galaxy: He has played more than 100 games for Tottenham & LA Galaxy

8 Johnny Carey

9 Kevin Doyle

10 Steve Finnan

11 None

12 Mark Kinsella, Matt Holland

13 Clinton Morrison

14 Frank Stapleton

15 Ronnie Whelan snr

Answers 183

1 Alan Kennedy; Kennedy again

2 Atlético Madrid & Valencia

3 Liverpool & Aberdeen

4 Jerzy Dudek

5 Benfica. These were the four teams United beat on the way to the 1968 European Cup Final – even older fans like myself have to admit it's a little tougher today

6 There's a clue in the way the question is phrased: Jens Lehmann was sent off, and Robert Pirès was sacrificed for the sub goalkeeper, Manuel Almunia

7 Ferenc Puskas – for the losers!

8 Transylvania

9 They scored the goals that helped Celtic to a 2-1 win against Barcelona in the Champions League group stage, probably their best result in the competition since they won it

10 Michael Essien

11 Jari Litmanen (Ajax, 1995) & Sami Hyypia (Liverpool, 2001)

12 Kevin De Bruyne

13 Rotterdam in the Netherlands

14 Steve Finnan, Jamie Carragher, Xabi Alonso, Steven Gerrard & John Arne Riise

15 London (Arsenal, Chelsea); Madrid (Real, Atlético); Belgrade (Red Star, Partizan)

Answers 184

1 Gonzalo Higuaín

2 Uruguay; he was in goal when they won the World Cup in 1950

3 Raymond Kopa – he was born Kopaszewski but dropped the ending

4 Alfredo Di Stéfano: it was the closest he got to appearing in the finals

5 Haiti, Zaire (now Democratic Republic of Congo) & Australia

6 Willie Johnston

7 0-0, so West Germany went through the mini group because they beat Spain

8 Morten Olsen

9 Mexico, it was the last time they failed to make the finals; United States, who finished second to Costa Rica in the final qualifying group

10 Mark Wright

11 Rough; Kennedy, Forsyth, Buchan, Donachie; Gemmill, Souness, Hartford, Rioch; Dalglish, Jordan. Bruce Rioch was the captain

12 Lilian Thuram

13 Estonia. It's a long story . . .

14 Michael Ballack; sadly for Germany he was suspended for the Final, leaving them a little toothless

15 Paulo Ferreira, Ricardo Carvalho & Deco

Answers 185

1 Los Angeles Aztecs, Fort Lauderdale Strikers and San José Earthquakes

2 He admitted to an affair with the wife of the club's physiotherapist

3 Stanley Matthews; Blackpool & Stoke City

4 Peter Beagrie

5 Both scored own goals

6 Ivory Coast

7 Bobby Charlton – a scandalous piece of mismanagement, far more contentious than Alf Ramsey's substitution of a tiring Charlton in 1970

8 Eric Young & Vinnie Jones

9 Aki Rihilati

10 Alex Ferguson

11 Emile Heskey, James Milner, Stewart Downing & Ashley Young; Downing didn't score in the second match, but Stephen Warnock (yes, he did, two caps) & Gabriel Agbonlahor (three caps) did

12 Uruguay (in the 1980s and early '90s)

13 David Pleat

14 Derek Mountfield; Dave Watson

15 Paolo Ferreira, Ricardo Carvalho, Deco, Maniche (8 games on loan) & José Bosingwa

Answers 186

1 Newcastle United; Sir John Hall, Doug's father – how proud he must have felt . . .

2 Eric Cantona, Dennis Bergkamp, David Ginola, Ruud van Nistelrooy, Thierry Henry (twice), Cristiano Ronaldo (twice), Robin van Persie, Luis Suárez, Eden Hazard

3 Don Revie & David O'Leary

4 Mali; Sevilla

5 Steve Bruce: cue rant from Sheffield Wednesday boss Trevor Francis – he had a point about the amount of injury time, but his players should have born the brunt of his anger, conceding two similar goals in quick succession

6 Gustavo Poyet

7 Middlesbrough, Derby County

8 Eyal Berkovic

9 Tottenham Hotspur; Robbie Keane; Jermain Defoe

10 Derby County; -69; they scored 20 goals

11 Jay Bothroyd; Queens Park Rangers. Bothroyd was never quite good enough for the Premier League, never mind England, and his career stalled

12 Denis Irwin & Steve Bruce (twice)

13 Sadio Mané

14 Arsenal & Everton

15 Dwight Yorke, Ruud van Nistelrooy, Cristiano Ronaldo, Wayne Rooney, Dimitar Berbatov, Robin van Persie

Answers 187

1 Jock Stein, the Scotland manager, died of a heart attack shortly after the final whistle

2 Scott Gemmill

3 Ally McCoist

4 Henrik Larsson & Brian Laudrup

5 Rangers

6 Neil Sullivan

7   Third Lanark

8   John Greig, Ally McCoist & Jim Baxter

9   Twenty-three. You can't beat continuity . . . (but you might well beat Livingston . . .)

10 They were managed by brothers – on the day, Tommy McLean's Motherwell beat brother Jim's Dundee United 4-3

11 Dave Narey, Maurice Malpas & Paul Hegarty. Malpas (the most accomplished of the three) won 55 caps, Narey 35 and Hegarty just 8

12 George Young; The Iron Curtain

13 Tosh McKinlay. Fans of most Scottish clubs outside Glasgow will tell you it's doubly hard to win a cap if you're not part of the Old Firm

14 Cooke won 16, mainly during his time at Chelsea

15 Johan Mjällby, Bobo Baldé, Paul lambert, Neil Lennon, Stiliyan Petrov, Alan Thompson, Henrik Larsson, John Hartson

Answers 188

1   Rob Rensenbrink; West Ham United

2   Philip Cocu

3   CSKA Moscow; Sporting Lisbon

4   Ray Parlour

5   Warsaw, Poland & Donetsk, Ukraine

6   Andreas (Andi) Herzog

7   Roberto Baggio, a former hero at Fiorentina

8   Atlético Madrid

9   Michel Platini & David Trezuguet

10 Cardiff City

11 Villa Park; Lazio

12 Ipswich Town beat AZ Alkmaar; Frans Thijssen for Ipswich; Johnny Metgod

13 Juan Sebastián Verón & Hernán Crespo

14 Leicester City; Fiorentina; Inter Milan (x3) & Manchester City; José Mourinho & Manuel Pellegrino

15 Fiorentina

Answers 189

1 Manuel Neuer, Bayer Leverkusen (to Bayern Munich) & David De Gea, Atlético Madrid (to Manchester United)

2 Ireland. Mike England played for Wales, Scotland played for Trinidad and Tobago, and Don Welsh won three caps for England just prior to the Second World War

3 Score a hat-trick; he was the co-founder, with his brother Tom, of the chain of newsagents that bear his name, RS McColl

4 Kevin Sheedy

5 Stewart Imlach of Nottingham Forest; the book, a winner of the William Hill Sports Book of the Year prize in 2005, was written by his son, Gary

6 Bastian Schweinsteiger

7 El Salvador & Honduras; El Salvador won with two extra-time goals. A full-scale war erupted soon after – the football was one of a number of triggers, not the sole reason as some reports suggest

8 Stefan Effenberg; he was a huge talent but a divisive figure

9 Tom Finney & Danny Blanchflower; Thierry Henry

10 Ruud Gullit, Ronald Koeman, Michael Laudrup, Roberto Mancini, Luca Vialli

11 Ray Harford; Arsenal (although Arsenal only finished three places above Luton that year, so the result wasn't a seismic shock); this was during the ban on English clubs after the Heysel disaster

12 Yaya Touré

13 James Rodríguez of Real Madrid

14 Garth Crooks

15 There were no arrests – perhaps the shock of the events of 9/11 four days previously was a calming factor

Answers 190

1 Middlesbrough (Middlesbrough Ironopolis were disbanded in 1894)

2 David Jack; Bolton Wanderers

3 Colin Boulton

4 Ray Wilkins; Eddie McCreadie

5 Tony Cottee

6 Bristol City; Bob Taylor

7 Terry Paine

8 Swindon Town

9 Leyton Orient (as they were at the time) – for one year they were a division ahead of Sunderland, Middlesbrough, Newcastle, Derby, Stoke, Southampton & Chelsea

10 Wimbledon & Norwich City respectively

11 Arthur Milton

12 Ipswich Town

13 Colchester United; acrobatic goal celebrations

14 Grant Holt

15 Barnsley, Bradford City, Doncaster Rovers, Huddersfield Town, Hull City, Leeds United, Middlesbrough, Rotherham United, Sheffield United, Sheffield Wednesday & York City

Answers 191

1 Miroslav Klose

2 Hungary & Czechoslovakia; Brazil (1-0, a valiant rearguard from Wales), France 4-1 (Northern Ireland were simply too tired)

3 Lev Yashin

4 Portugal, who reached the semi-finals

5 Helmut Haller

6 Diego Maradona

7 Uruguay

8 Fabio Grosso & Alessandro Del Piero

9 Roger Milla; René Higuita

10 Gabriel Batistuta

11 Mijatović, who played for Real Madrid. If these games were played now both Mijatović and Savićević would play for Montenegro. Bokšić wasn't available for Yugoslavia, he was Croatian, and they had already broken away; Milošević, who was at Aston Villa, was the only Serb

12 Joaquin; South Korea

13 Paul Robinson

14 Italy: Materazzi, Pirlo, Del Piero, Totti, Toni. France: Barthez, Gallas, Ribéry, Makélélé, Henry

15 New Zealand

Answers 192

1 Johnny Haynes

2 Ron Greenwood

3 They won 185 caps (Ashley 107, Joe 56, Andrew 15 & Carlton 7). Joe scored 10 of those eleven goals, neither Ashley nor Carlton found the net

4 Chris Woods, Rob Green & John Ruddy

5 Australia, a free England cap with every air fare

6 Brian Labone

7 They were in England's 1966 World Cup squad but never took the field

8 Alan Thompson

9 Thierry Henry; Kenny Sansom

10 Sweden, Swedes 2 Turnips 1; David Platt, Tomas Brolin

11 David Platt, Des Walker, Trevor Francis

12 The Olympic Stadium in Munich, where Germany were unbeaten since 1973

13 Gary Mabbutt; he is diabetic; Tony Adams

14 Danny Welbeck; Steven Gerrard

15 Nobby Stiles (28)

Answers 193

1 Liverpool

2 Nayim

3 They are all English referees who have taken charge of a World Cup Final; 1950, 1954, 1974 and 2010 respectively.

4 Joe Ledley, who plays for Crystal Palace via Cardiff and Celtic

5 Atlético Madrid; Burton Albion

6 Carlo Ancelotti

7 Roger Hunt & Michael Owen. Ian Rush has been top scorer most times for Liverpool (nine times to Hunt's eight), but never more than three times consecutively

8 Avi Cohen; Bolton Wanderers

9 For his absurd over-reaction in pretending he was hurt after chasing a fan who had invaded the pitch

10 Crystal Palace; Terry Venables

11 Roland Nilsson (Sheffield Wednesday) & Anders Limpar (Arsenal); Eric Cantona (Leeds United), Peter Schmeichel, Andrei Kanchelskis (both Manchester United)

12 Ronaldo

13 Graham Taylor

14 Coventry City: Coventry still had three games left when Norwich completed their campaign and needed to win all three. Norwich went down with 49 points and could consider themselves hard-done-by

15 Everton

Answers 194

1 Nottingham Forest

2 Phil Neal

3 Brussels

4 Dundee United; Phil Neal; Joe Fagan

5 Paolo Maldini; his father Cesare Maldini also captained Milan to victory

6 Ronaldinho; John Terry

7 Viktoria Plzen

8 Pavel Nedved; David Trezeguet

9 Juventus & Barcelona; Arjen Robben

10 United won 7-1

11 Deportivo de La Coruña

12 Daniel Agger; Kaká

13 Lúcio; Zinedine Zidane, Real Madrid; Iker Casillas

14 Philipp Lahm, Bastien Schweinsteiger, Arjen Robben, Thomas Müller & Mario Gómez (the first four started all three games, Gómez was a sub in 2010 and 2013)

15 Athens (AEK, Olympiacos & Panathinaikos) & London (Arsenal, Chelsea & Tottenham Hotspur)

Answers 195

1 Newcastle United, Bournemouth; Manchester City & Everton; none

2 Mark Schwarzer (Australia), Brad Friedel (United States) & Jussi Jaaskelainen (Finland). Tim Howard fell agonisingly short of joining his countryman Friedel this group – Howard was left on 399 appearances when he was released by Everton at the end of 2015–16

3 They were all at Highbury – Arsenal remained unbeaten away from home

4 Mark Robins (with 15 goals); Chris Sutton; Mike Walker

5 Jonás Gutiérrez; he won a battle against testicular cancer

6 Patrick Vieira & Remi Garde; Niall Quinn

7 Arsenal; Matt Le Tissier

8 Dwight Yorke; Alan Wright

9 Charlton Athletic; Clive Mendonca

10 Wes Brown, Jonny Evans (loan only) & John O'Shea

11 Max Gradel – he was unlucky, he tore a cruciate ligament and missed most of the club's first season in the Premier League

12 Petr Cech

13 Duncan Ferguson (serial offender), Patrick Vieira (team enforcer) and Richard Dunne

14 Bruce Rioch & Colin Todd

15 Emmanuel Adebayor (Togo), Gareth Bale (Wales), Dimitar Berbatov (Bulgaria), Thierry Henry (France), Jürgen Klinsmann (Germany), Cristiano Ronaldo (Portugal), Luis Suárez (Uruguay), Mark Viduka (Australia)

Answers 196

1 Linfield (51) & Glentoran (23)

2 Maik Taylor; Fulham & Birmingham City

3 Billy Bingham; Sunderland (he left later that summer for Luton Town, who had just finished eighth)

4 Kyle Lafferty; Craig Cathcart

5 Lawrie McMenemy

6 John McClelland

7 Tommy Wright, Gerry Taggart, Alan McDonald, Jim Magilton, Michael Hughes, Colin Clarke; the sub was current manager Michael O'Neill

8 Aston Villa & Southampton

9 Peacock was a defensive half back who played well over 300 games as a defender for Celtic

10 Wales

11 Jonny Evans with Manchester United in 2012–13

12 Alex Bruce, son of Steve. He was allowed to switch because his RoI appearances were only in friendlies and he was eligible for both sides. One wonders how many caps his dad might have won for either had he made himself available

13 Neil Lennon; Crewe Alexandra, Leicester City & Celtic; Bolton Wanderers

14 They all played for their country, but Murdock was a centre half

15 Norman Whiteside

Answers 197

1 Chelsea & Nottingham Forest

2 Kenneth Wolstenholme; David Coleman; Jimmy Hill; Des Lynam; Gary Lineker

3 All three moved from Leeds to Manchester United

4 Morten Olsen

5 Eduardo; Arsenal

6 Kevin Keegan & Billy Bremner

7 Georgiou Kinkladze

8 It was a header, and Brooking was known as a conspicuously reluctant header of the ball

9 Stan Collymore

10 Laurent Blanc (for Franck Lebouef), Patrick Vieira (for Christian Karembeu), Thierry Henry (for Emmanuel Petit) & Christoph Dugarry (for Stephane Guivarc'h)

11 Verona

12 Garrincha

13 Les Ferdinand

14   Swindon Town
15   West Bromwich Albion; Gary Megson; Lee Hughes; Jason Koumas

Answers 198

Squad:

Goalkeepers: Gordon Banks (England), Gianluigi Buffon (Italy), Lev Yashin (USSR/Russia). Full backs: Cafu (Brazil), Philipp Lahm (Germany), Paolo Maldini (Italy), Daniel Passarella (Argentina) & Carles Puyol (Spain). Centre backs: Franco Baresi (Italy), Franz Beckenbauer (West Germany), Fabio Cannavaro (Italy), Bobby Moore (England), Marcel Desailly (France).

Deep Midfield: Ruud Gullit (Netherlands), Andrea Pirlo (Italy), Xavi (Spain). Midfield: Bobby Charlton (England), Diego Maradona (Argentina), Pelé (Brazil), Zinedine Zidane (France). Wide players: George Best (Northern Ireland), Garrincha (Brazil), Cristiano Ronaldo (Portugal): Johan Cruyff (Netherlands), Alfredo Di Stéfano (Argentina), Lionel Messi (Argentina), Gerd Müller (West Germany), Ferenc Puskás (Hungary), Ronaldo (Brazil).

If pressed, the eleven I would pick, in a modern 4-3-3, would be Yashin; Lahm, Cannavaro, Moore, Maldini; Beckenbauer, Pelé, Maradona; Messi, Müller, Cruyff. The question marks for me would be Cannavaro (or Desailly?) and Messi (or Best?). Beckenbauer, in the modern game, would be the perfect holding midfield player.

Answers 199

Squad:

Goalkeepers: Gordon Banks (England), Peter Shilton (England), Neville Southall (Wales). Full backs: Jimmy Armfield (England), Ashley Cole (England), Danny McGrain (Scotland), Stuart Pearce (England). Centre backs: Tony Adams (England), Rio Ferdinand (England), Richard Gough (Scotland), Paul McGrath (Republic of Ireland), Bobby Moore (England). Defensive midfield: Billy Bremner (Scotland), Roy Keane (Republic of Ireland), Dave Mackay (Scotland). Midfield players: Alan Ball (England),

Jim Baxter (Scotland), Danny Blanchflower (Northern Ireland), Paul Gascoigne (England), Bryan Robson (England), Paul Scholes (England).

Wide players: Gareth Bale (Wales), George Best (Northern Ireland), Tom Finney (England), Ryan Giggs (Wales), Stanley Matthews (England). Forwards: Bobby Charlton (England), Jimmy Greaves (England), Denis Law (Scotland), Gary Lineker (England).

Probable starting XI (4-3-3): Banks; McGrain, McGrath, Moore, Cole; Keane, Robson, Gascoigne; Matthews, Charlton, Best. (I was very tempted to go with Bale instead of Matthews, he is a bona fide superstar.)

Answers 200

Squad (principal club and nationality listed):

Goalkeepers: Petr Cech (Chelsea, Czech Republic), Jussi Jaaskelainen (Bolton Wanderers, Finland), Peter Schmeichel (Manchester United, Denmark). Full backs: Ashley Cole (Arsenal, Chelsea, England), Patrice Evra (Manchester United, France), Branislav Ivanović (Chelsea, Serbia), Gary Neville (Manchester United, England), Pablo Zabaleta (Manchester City, Argentina): Centre backs: Tony Adams (Arsenal, England), Rio Ferdinand (Manchester United, England), Sami Hyypia (Liverpool), John Terry (Chelsea, England).

Defensive midfield: Roy Keane (Manchester United, Republic of Ireland), Claude Makélélé (Chelsea, France), Patrick Vieira (Arsenal, France). Midfield: Cesc Fàbregas (Arsenal, Spain), Steven Gerrard (Liverpool, England), Juninho (Middlesbrough, Brazil), Frank Lampard (Chelsea, England), Paul Scholes (Manchester United, England).

Wide players: David Beckham (Manchester United, England), Ryan Giggs (Manchester United, Wales), Freddie Ljungberg (Arsenal, Sweden), Cristiano Ronaldo (Manchester United, Portugal). Attackers: Dennis Bergkamp (Arsenal, Netherlands), Eric Cantona (Manchester United, France), Didier Drogba (Chelsea, Côte d'Ivoire), Thierry Henry (Arsenal, France), Alan Shearer (Blackburn Rovers, Newcastle United, England), Gianfranco Zola (Chelsea, Italy).

And the best XI? This would be mine: Cech: Neville, Terry (in this context, even though I selected Adams ahead of him for the England squad), Ferdinand, Cole: Gerrard, Vieira, Lampard (ditto, ahead of Scholes): Ronaldo, Shearer, Henry.